POSTCOLONIAL POPULAR CULTURE IN INDIA

POSTCOLONIAL POPULAR CULTURE IN INDIA

Edited by

ABIN CHAKRABORTY
RAMANUJ KONAR
SAYAN AICH BHOWMIK

Orient BlackSwan

POSTCOLONIAL POPULAR CULTURE IN INDIA

ORIENT BLACKSWAN PRIVATE LIMITED

Registered Office
3-6-752 Himayatnagar, Hyderabad 500 029, Telangana, India
E-mail: centraloffice@orientblackswan.com

Other Offices
Bengaluru, Chennai, Guwahati, Hyderabad,
Kolkata, Mumbai, New Delhi, Noida, Patna

First published 2025

ISBN 978 93 5442 441 0

Typeset in Minion Pro 11/13.5 *by*
Shine Graphics, Delhi 110 094

Cover design elements from Freepik

Printed at
Avantika Printers Private Limited, New Delhi 110 020

Published by
Orient Blackswan Private Limited
3-6-752, Himayatnagar, Hyderabad 500 029, Telangana, India
E-mail: info@orientblackswan.com

This volume is dedicated to the memory of
our fellow contributor Puja Sen Majumdar
who sadly passed away in December 2023.

Contents

Introduction

Abin Chakraborty

The domain of popular culture has always been a fraught one. Raymond Williams's detailed discussion of the ambiguities and polyvalences embedded in terms like 'culture' (87–98) or 'popular' (236–38) had, a long time ago, offered enough evidence of various problems associated with such a term as 'popular culture'. Since then, other theorists have also explored the theoretical complexities associated with popular culture. John Storey, for example, offers six possible definitions in his *Cultural Theory and Popular Culture* (5–13) while Dominic Strinati categorically confesses that 'the possibility of a theoretically informed definition receiving widespread agreement is a long way off', particularly because the study of popular culture involves 'competing conceptions of the nature of the social relationships' (xv). In the case of postcolonial nations such as India, the complexities are even more intricate and multidimensional. On the one hand is the baggage of colonial stereotypes which continue to circulate through the films and shows churned out by Hollywood and often repeated in cultural artefacts produced by Indians themselves, while on the other hand are the pressures exerted by a nationalist discourse which remains contoured by considerations of class, caste, gender, sexuality, religion and so on. The space of popular culture remains replete with cultural representations across multiple media. These either consolidate derogatory, exclusionary stereotypes which a majoritarian, heteronormative, elitist, brahminical discourse sanctions and proliferates, or create room for counter-discursive representations that problematise or subvert the dominant ones in various dialogic manoeuvres of diverse intensities. So, films like *Padmavat*, *Tanhaji* and *Kesari* delve into the Indian past only to highlight different episodes of apparent heroic prowess by

Hindu or Sikh individuals against Muslim armies and leaders of different eras that are portrayed as bestial, ruthless and immoral. At the same time, films and web shows like *Sacred Games*, *Article 15*, *Lipstick Under My Burkha*, *Patal Lok* and *Newton* serve to highlight the cracks and fissures that exist within the nation space of India and the unmitigated horrors and suffering the nation-state often generates due to the pressures of dominant discourses. Similarly, there are innumerable cases of yellow journalism—for instance, the sensationalism of the probe into the suicide of Sushant Singh Rajput and the supposed drug use by certain film stars—that amplify age-old stereotypes of women as femmes fatales. This was evident from the vilification of Rhea Chakraborty, which even led to a spurt in online abuse against Bengali women. In parallel are investigative reports examining mob lynching by cow vigilantes, rampant casteism in various walks of life, the nexus between governmental agencies and corporates, and other such pressing concerns. On the one hand, troll armies spew venom at all individuals who dare to dissent and criticise governmental regimes, while on the other hand, meme makers and stand-up comics mock and expose the contradictions within the peddlers of power, divisiveness and repression. Similarly, myriad popular representations mimic the logic of global capital and the consumerist need it generates, teaching us that 'all izz well' though 'dil maange more', even as there are shows, films and advertisements which keep critiquing the same discourse from within the networks of popular media. A case in point would be the organisation Games for Change which hosts online games on diverse topics, including challenges faced by LGBTQ youth and autistic children, refugee lives, histories of racist violence and resistance, ecological sustainability, and so on. Such games create a digital counter-narrative to the toxic combination of hypermasculinity, xenophobia and racism that often contaminates the online gaming world. The BARC *Student Journey* game or the UNHCR-produced game *Against All Odds*, which are based on refugee experiences, are further examples of counter-discourses of amity and empathy that dominant discourses too often destroy.

Such a convergence of contraries testifies to the opposites that jostle within the rubric of 'common sense' ('senso commune') as explored by Antonio Gramsci. Speaking of the consciousness of subalterns and industrial workers, Gramsci states:

> His theoretical consciousness can indeed be historically in opposition to his activity. One might almost say that he has two theoretical consciousnesses (or one contradictory consciousness); one which is implicit in his activity and which in reality unites him with all his fellow-workers in the practical transformation of the real world; and one, superficially explicit or verbal, which he has inherited from the past and uncritically absorbed. (333)

The consciousness which is 'inherited from the past and uncritically absorbed' is generally in conformity with dominant ideology, which expresses itself through both religion and secular maxims. At the same time, however, Gramsci contends that embedded within common sense is a 'healthy nucleus', which may be interpreted as those strands of thought and values that promote ideals of equality and justice that anti-colonial movements repeatedly highlighted. However, these strands also failed to materialise in most postcolonial nation-states across the world as the nation-states attempt to confront the triple threat posed by the logic of global capitalism, colonially engendered discourses of domination and division, and the continuity of precolonial modes of systemic exclusion and violence. What becomes unavoidable, therefore, as Gramsci himself admits, is:

> the necessity for new popular beliefs, that is to say a new common sense and with it a new culture and a new philosophy which will be rooted in the popular consciousness with the same solidity and imperative quality as traditional beliefs. (424)

This is precisely why common sense becomes a key battleground in any attempt to radically challenge the status quo, and popular culture becomes integral to this process because such cultural representations not only cater to but also emerge from the evolving matrix of common sense. Popular culture thus becomes that contact zone where uncritically accepted values of the past—laden as they are with the burden of caste, class, gender, ethnicity, creed and sexuality—inevitably encounter those evolving sensibilities of the present which often challenge inherited beliefs in the hopes of forging, as Gramsci states, a new common sense and a new culture. As Stuart Hall reminds us, 'cultural meanings are not only "in the head". They organize and regulate social practices, influence our conduct and consequently have real, practical effects' (3). The study of popular culture is essential precisely because we need to map the connections between popularly produced and assimilated cultural meanings and the real and practical effects they generate so that visions of an as-yet-unborn, just future society may be cultivated while contesting the cultural practices and significations that resist any such future and consolidate the status quo.

Yet, it is curious that postcolonial studies, as a discipline, has not systematically sought to engage with popular culture with the same enthusiasm and rigour it traditionally invested in the analysis of literary and cinematic texts, even though cinema indeed constitutes one of the key components of popular culture. As Simon Featherstone, a key theorist focusing on postcolonialism and popular cultures, explains:

> None of the major anthologies and course readers which mapped the theoretical and pedagogic priorities of postcolonial studies in the 1990s devote much attention to the study of popular culture, and more recent reassessments have generally maintained this inattention even as they have established a case for the significant revision and redevelopment of politics and purpose in the field. (381)

This is precisely why elements such as reality shows, memes, selfies, digital games and such other manifestations of contemporary culture often remain outside the purview of postcolonial studies even as cultural studies itself often remains indifferent to the insights which postcolonial studies might offer in the analysis of various aspects of contemporary culture, from real estate to campus activism. This is evident from the recurrence of allusions and references to Harry Potter and *Game of Thrones* in the recent anti-CAA and anti-NRC protests in India. Posters comparing the prime minister or the home minister with Cersei Lannister or Voldemort, or warning such leaders that 'Winter Is Coming' operate as typical examples of postcolonial transformation which select specific aspects of major Western cultural phenomena—which are implicated in varying degrees of colonial discourses—in order to generate an entirely new vocabulary of dissent aimed at contemporaries with similar inclinations which target the ironically colonial strategies adopted by postcolonial nation-states. As Featherstone points out:

> The inclusion of sport, music, dance and other performance cultures as central concerns, and the recognition of such vernacular materials' capacity to generate theory as well as to be objects of theorizing, present abundant possibilities for a postcolonial studies that is open to dialogue across disciplines and across the varieties of cultural production. (393)

This anthology dedicates itself to precisely such an objective, within the Indian context, as it critically examines texts, films, digital media, cyberspace, reality shows and sports, while being mindful of the intersections that exist between multiple representational modes. The journey begins with an instructive exploration, by E. Dawson Varughese, of the evolving terrain of Indian graphic novels which have been gaining in popularity over the last two decades. Her analysis employs the theoretical frameworks of Gilles Deleuze and Félix Guattari to situate graphic novels or, as she calls them, 'graphic narratives', and goes on to examine the ways in which such narratives foreground critical ideas of Indianness, post-millennial Indian modernity and, specifically, Indian ways of visual decoding. While Varughese's explorations follow a more generalised arc, the other papers focusing on graphic novels and texts are more specific in nature. This is evident from Rishi Ghosh and Oindrila Mitra's analysis of the popular Bengali comics series *Bantul the Great* by Narayan Debnath. Seen through a lens that utilises postcolonial theory as much as Gramsci and Michel

Foucault, Ghosh and Mitra emphasise the ways in which Debnath attempted to craft a Bengali superhero with specifically Indian and Bengali sensibilities and contexts, which subtly interrogated the hegemonic assumptions that went into the making of American superhero comics. They also focus on the humorous aspect of Bantul's apparently heroic acts, which adds a new dimension to the genre of superhero comics. Furthermore, they locate Bantul within discussions of power, agency and the authority of the state, which reveal the complex strains that went into the making of this popular but underrated comic series. The focus on graphic narratives continues with Puja Sen Majumdar and Rini P. Kujur's 'Terrorism, Graphic Novels and the Making of a Cosmopolitan Hero', which focuses on the character of the superhero Nagaraj, particularly in relation to the World Terrorism series brought out by Raj Comics, one of the biggest comic-book publishers in India. While this paper also discusses how the paradigm of superhero comics is Indianised, the focus is more on ideas of nation, internal security and the ethos of cosmopolitanism. The paper goes on to explore how, quite unlike Bantul, Nagaraj intervenes in various international events to save humanity from terrorism and dedicates himself to the service of humanity at large, as opposed to only national interests. In the process, however, it also explores various absences and the tensions that underlie the overall representational paradigm.

The next essay in the series focuses on another interesting recent development within the Indian cultural world, and that is the emergence and development of chick lit. Puja Chakraborty's 'Tales from Shining and Sinking India: Configuring the Postcolonial Identities in Indian Chick Lit' explores the themes and characters of several recent examples of Indian chick lit and the plethora of manoeuvres around gender identity, tradition and nation that are instrumental in the process of shaping the lives of individuals. Particularly interesting is the way in which such an essay looks at the heterogeneity of the genre itself as various novels offer different answers to similar questions, thereby reflecting the jostling of multiple discourses within the site of popular culture. This multiplicity is also evident in the subsequent paper by Suchetana Banerjee which looks at the varied invocations of Shakespearean rhetoric in different aspects of Indian public life—from judicial proceedings to budget speeches. While the introduction of Shakespeare within the Indian context was obviously freighted with colonial authority and led to a considerable amount of mimicry which continues to this day, the paper also highlights other kinds of usage which tend towards mockery and generates various degrees of ambivalence. Another kind of ambivalence is explored in Medha Bhadra Chowdhury's study of various female poets publishing their poems on Instagram which has given rise to a new genre called 'Instapoetry', even though some of the poets themselves refuse to accept such a label for their work. Chowdhury uses several examples to illustrate how these poets' explorations of questions related to the body, self, and sexual and gendered abuse serve to create 'subaltern counterpublics' which critique dominant patriarchal discourses. However, Chowdhury also addresses the hegemonic tendencies within such poetic discourses which tend to assume a universalised female reader/viewership and thereby ignore the contextual specificities associated with individual identities, especially the hierarchies of class and caste that often limit access to platforms such as Instagram.

There is no denying, however, the significance of digital platforms in the shaping of popular cultural spheres. It is this recognition that fuels Siddhartha Chakraborti's study of digital gaming, with special reference to a game called *Missing*, which addresses the issue of female trafficking and the attendant socio-cultural predicaments. His analysis situates *Missing* as a radically unique gaming experience which not only defies the paradigm of national allegory which so many other games utilise but also foregrounds the need for action and thus creates a possible praxis for desired social change. The digital platform also takes centre stage in Ananya Chatterjee and Nisarga Bhattacharjee's paper on memes, which not only emphasises the 'glocal' nature of most digital cultural representations but also underscores the carnivalesque energy which characterises the generation and circulation of such memes for varied desires and viewers. The significance of digital technology is also the theme of Mita Bandyopadhyay and Arindam Modak's essay on the use of VFX technology in Indian films, especially in the wake of such astounding commercial successes as *Baahubali*. Their essay suggests that the cultural supremacy of Hollywood has largely depended on the use of enhanced digital technology and the use of such technology by Indian films creates the possibility of a more level playing field.

An important consequence of the growth and growing viability of digital technologies across the world is the emergence and popularity of OTT platforms like Netflix, Disney+ Hotstar, Prime Video and so on, which allow viewers access to a plethora of online content that remains free from those constraints which often impinge upon films made for auditoria and shows aired by television networks. These films and shows therefore make room for such expressions of dissent or nonconformist cultural negotiations which might prove to be commercially challenging for traditional films and television shows. It is in this context that Jayati Ganguly's analysis of three web shows explores an interesting terrain where notions of 'westernisation' and consumerist capitalism jostle with Indian sensibilities to create hybridised identities and aesthetics that refuse conventional binaries and stereotypes.

Interrogation of traditional stereotypes is also the focus of Shyaonti Talwar's analysis of recent Hindi films, which shows how the hegemonic nationalist discourse continues to recycle older stereotypes to create desirable femininities for the present. Her analysis of three separate films showcases that even when the female protagonist is ostensibly assertive and endowed with agency, the characterisation appeals to repressed cultural and nationalist fantasies latent in the patriarchal unconscious, thus cementing traditional binaries. However, that is certainly not true for several other representations such as those discussed by Somrita Misra in her analysis of four recent films focusing on Kashmir and Kashmiris, which brings the idea of the Indian nation-state under a critical gaze. Away from the representation of Kashmir either as a paradisal backdrop or as a violent terrain where the Indian army proves its heroism, such films as *Harud*, *Hamid*, *Shikara* and *Haider* explore varied degrees of trauma, antagonistic memories and abiding ambivalences at the heart of the nation-state.

Such ambivalences are also critically explored by Anindya Sekhar Purakayastha in an incisive analysis of the tele-publics created by 24×7 news channels and the shrill, authoritarian nationalism often sensationally espoused by them as well as the counter-narrative and counterpublics generated by digital news networks of varied modalities. These create different avenues for public participation in the circulation of facts and their interpretation. His analysis shows how the existing public arena, dominated as it is by prejudicial corporate media, is gradually also moving towards a mediatised public sphere based on the micro-politics of everyday struggle and public negotiations, which may have significant consequences for democracy, liberty and decoloniality. Television shows of a different kind are explored in Sarbani Banerjee's subsequent paper, which focuses on the performance of Indian beauty-pageant winners and actors in American talk shows and the discursive contexts within which such performance is embedded. Banerjee deftly illustrates, after examining the origin and role of talk shows and beauty pageants, that American talk shows often position Indian female superstars within a discourse that is both consumerist and orientalist at the same time, even though the icons themselves may either operate as re-orientalising agents within a global cultural framework or subtly undercut the discursive limits within which their hosts try to confine them.

The final paper leaves these spaces of texts, screens and virtual reality to literally land on the grounds and fields on which popular ludic energy finds recurrent manifestation. It examines the affects and associations associated with the East Bengal Football Club and the history of Partition and refugee identity with which it remains inextricably linked. The paper not only explores the history of the club, the evolution of its community of supporters and the affects it generated, but also ties the event of the game to recent anti-NRC, anti-CAA movements through the documentation of fans' banners, placards and slogans. In the process, popular culture, political dissent and the sporting arena converge to generate a fascinating site through which popular articulation of collective ideals, outside the confines of political parties, becomes possible.

This anthology, through all these papers, thus explores all the myriad sites and spaces through which different forms of popular cultural activities take shape and the diverse significations they articulate. These multi-accented articulations testify to the heterogeneous nature of the fluid realm of popular culture where plural, often contradictory, ideologies and discourses jostle and collide. The anthology aims to showcase to readers various glimpses of such fractious interplay of concurrent forces while enabling future exploration in other directions. In that sense, it serves as an invitation to critical dialogue regarding the realm of popular culture, which will foster regular multidimensional engagement.

Works Cited

Featherstone, Simon. 'Postcolonialism and Popular Cultures'. *The Oxford Handbook of Postcolonial Studies*, edited by Graham Huggan, Oxford UP, 2016, pp. 380–395.

Gramsci, A. *Selections from the Prison Notebooks*. Translated by Quintin Hoare and Goeffrey Nowell-Smith, Orient BlackSwan, 2007.

Hall, Stuart. 'Introduction'. *Representation*, edited by Stuart Hall, SAGE Publications, 2003, pp. 1–11.

Storey, John. *Cultural Theory and Popular Culture*. 7th ed., Routledge, 2015.

Strinati, Dominic. *An Introduction to the Theories of Popular Culture*. Routledge, 2004.

Williams, Raymond. *Keywords: A Vocabulary of Culture and Society*. Oxford UP, 1983.

Rhizomatic Readings

Insights into the Post-millennial Indian Graphic Narrative Scene

E. Dawson Varughese

Post-millennial Indian Graphic Narratives: Doubly Marginal

Graphic narratives have systematically critiqued ideas of 'India' and 'Indianness' since their debut in the Indian market. Orijit Sen's *River of Stories* (1994) is often hailed as India's first graphic novel and gained notoriety through its engagement with the environmental, social and political issues of the controversial Narmada dam project. Following Sen's work, throughout the post-millennial years to date, Indian graphic narratives have embarked upon problematising erstwhile safe, settled ideas and projections of Indian society, histories and identities. Such problematic and unfavourable depictions of Indianness, both textual and visual, have been crafted through Sarnath Banerjee's critique of urban, 'modern' society (*The Harappa Files*, 2011; *All Quiet in Vikaspuri*, 2015), Amruta Patil's portrayal of sexuality in *Kari* (2008), Appupen's critique of celebrity culture in *Legends of Halahala* (2013), Prateek Thomas and Rajiv Eipe's portrayal of sexual abuse in the 'silent' graphic short story *Hush* (2010), Vishwajyoti Ghosh's re-imagining of the Emergency in *Delhi Calm* (2010), Navayana's[1] retelling of the life of B.R. Ambedkar in *Bhimayana* (2011) or that of Jotiba Phule in *A Gardener in the Wasteland* (2011), portrayals of the conflict in Kashmir in Naseer Ahmed and Saurabh Singh's *Kashmir Pending* (2007), and representations of gender violence in Zubaan's edited collection *Drawing the Line: Indian Women Fight Back* (2015). All these works engage variously in the narration of problematic, difficult and yet timely issues which communicate their immediacy and impact via both form and content.[2] Although much of post-millennial Indian graphic narrative production has appeared as the Indian graphic novel, I employ the phrase 'Indian graphic narratives' here as an umbrella term for the Indian graphic novel, 'graphic commentaries' (following Banerjee, *Harappa Files*), graphic short stories, the graphic novella, and creative, graphic non-fiction (an example of which is Navayana's *Bhimayana*).

In appearance and content, Indian graphic narratives of the post-millennial years have little in common with the famed Amar Chitra Katha series of comics, a popular Indian staple of the mid- to late-twentieth century, in which life stories were celebrated not only through narrative content but also through visual language such as a bold colour palette and clear, clean-lined, realistic images or iconography (see Chandra for more on the Amar Chitra Katha aesthetic). I have written in detail elsewhere (Dawson Varughese, *Visuality and Identity*) about the aesthetic shift from the Amar Chitra Katha series to the graphic narratives of the post-millennial Indian moment wherein the deployment of sketch-like images, stark line drawings, muted colours, blurred and indistinct characters, monochrome colourways, multimedia, and collage-like approaches to storying the narrative and characters invoke a 'visual' inauspiciousness. Common to both, that is, the Amar Chitra Katha series and the body of Indian post-millennial graphic narratives to date, is the invitation or, indeed, the call to 'see' ideas of Indianness. The works of Banerjee, Ghosh and others summon the reader–gazer to engage with a decoding of Indianness, a call to unpick and, in turn, delve into ideas of Indianness that lie in the dark, shadowy washes of Banerjee's watercolours and in Appupen's grotesque 'white space', and hide in the sepia tones of Ghosh's *Delhi Calm*. In other graphic narrative production circles, such as those of the USA and Europe, the anchoring of graphic narrative in dark and challenging aesthetic is widely recognised as often being *of the graphic narrative mode* (although not wholly representative of it). Indeed, some of the most famed graphic novels of the twentieth century are indicative of this aesthetic: *Watchmen* and *V for Vendetta* by Alan Moore, *Fun Home* by Alison Bechdel, *Persepolis* by Marjane Satrapi, and *The Sandman* volumes by Neil Gaiman are examples. For India, however, where the visual especially has traditionally depicted and represented Indianness in positive and 'proper' ways, the advent of the post-millennial Indian graphic novel (and graphic narratives, more broadly) has proved challenging to (domestic) Indian readerships as ideas of Indianness have been portrayed in less favourable ways. The work of Kajri Jain on calendar art in public spaces explores the need to depict India in 'a proper light', as any other manner of depiction would be regarded 'inauspicious'. Jain talks of the 'proper light syndrome' (165) specifically as: '[T]he value (or potential devaluation) of an image is evidently linked to the extent to which its investment or disinvestment is performed within the public gaze' (166). Her work underscores the established, presumed practice of portrayals of Indianness to be celebratory, 'proper' and befitting.

Deleuze and Guattari

Previously, the graphic novel has typically occupied a 'minor' position in US and European cultures when compared to the ubiquitous novel; the post-millennial years, however, are seeing a (global) rise in the graphic novel's (and graphic non-fiction's) production and consumption (see Weiner 59–64). Moreover, in Western academies (and reading cultures), as the now widely cited Hillary Chute article 'Comics as Literature? Reading Graphic Narrative' of 2008 has come to testify, graphic narratives are no longer seen as the 'marginal' literary products that they once were established as being. The situation in India, however, writes Suhaan Mehta, is otherwise: 'the idea of reading graphic novels as an intellectual activity is even more alien in India than in North America and Europe' (185). If, then, the graphic novel as a material product is a 'minor' form within India in relation to the pervasive Indian English-medium novel (or, in more recent years, the pervasive genre fiction novel—see Dawson Varughese,

Reading New India, *Genre Fiction*), then the Indian graphic novel is doubly 'minor' since the mode of graphic narrative marginalises itself through the visual and textual depictions of India, Indian practices, beliefs and, in general, ideas of 'Indianness'. To be clear, I posit that this 'double marginality' is borne out of: (a) a tradition of the 'graphic novel' originating in American and European literary–visual cultures in which the graphic novel/narrative began as 'minor' within the larger 'literary' scene (where the novel is the dominant literary mode), and (b) the depiction and communication of the *inauspicious* within Indian context(s) specifically—a shift in narrative form and content which, in turn, problematises erstwhile safe, settled ideas and projections of Indian society, histories and identities.

Given the established socio-cultural tradition of 'seeing' Indianness through (and of) a particular aesthetic within public cultures, the publishing of graphic narratives within India must have proven to be a bold business decision. The leading publisher of Indian graphic narratives to date has been HarperCollins Publishers India. Notably, the publishing interest in graphic narrative was driven by HarperCollins India's chief editor V.K. Karthika during her tenure in the company from 2006 to 2016. The company published some of the most reputed Indian graphic novelists to date, namely Amruta Patil, Sarnath Banerjee, Vishwajyoti Ghosh, Vikram Balagopal and Appupen. As a branch of HarperCollins Publishers LLC, one of the largest English-language publishing houses globally, with its headquarters in New York City and publishing groups in Canada, the United Kingdom, Australia and New Zealand, the Indian branch is one of only a few other branches worldwide that are regarded as 'non-Western'. On this positioning, Pavithra Narayanan warns: '[I]f the global visuality of Indian writers is a significant consequence of de/reterritorialized corporations, its most adverse effect is the hegemony of these corporations as the prime global producers of Indian writing' (107).[3] Subsequently, I posit that it is a curious time, post-millennium, wherein Indian authors (based in India)[4] interact and negotiate with Indian publishers who are usually part of global publishing houses; such is the case of HarperCollins or Penguin Random House (and Zubaan Books, which distributes through Penguin Random House India).

This negotiation of the local within the global is of particular interest here as I explore the 'major-favourable' and the 'minor-inauspicious' for it seems (at least, to date) that graphic novelists are anchored in the major (and, by extension, the favourable) in terms of the production of their works whilst simultaneously being anchored in the minor (and, by extension, the inauspicious) through the content and visual aesthetic of their works. Indeed, this is a curious and ever-layered existence; Indian graphic novels are published by way of a global publisher in the case of HarperCollins (or Penguin Random House or Hachette) yet the 'Delhi office' might be regarded as something of an outpost in relation to the global (Western) network of the other HarperCollins offices; furthermore, 'graphic narratives' are perceived to be 'minor' when compared to the mainstream (major) publishing trends; finally, but crucial for the subsequent analysis of the graphic narrative as *rhizome* here, the Indian graphic novel (and graphic narratives more broadly) is an Anglophone-centric product within the Indian linguistic context (Appupen's 'wordless' visual narratives aside)[5] and a *luxury* purchase given its retail price at typically 500 rupees and above. These factors anchor the Indian graphic narrative in a middle-class, Anglophone milieu which extends to both the producers as well as the consumers of the texts.

Although I posit that Indian graphic narratives, being anchored in an Indian inauspicious, beget Indian ways of seeing and thus knowing, I support A. Raghuramaraju in his desire to 'bend Deleuze and Guattari and transport them to India' (486). Raghuramaraju's position 'rejects those who are against borrowing from the outside [of India]'. But crucially, he goes on to say that:

> ... while borrowing, the borrower should know what to borrow, how much to borrow, from whom to borrow, her or his capacity to use what is borrowed, and the capability to repay. (486)

It is in this spirit that I 'borrow' from Deleuze and Guattari. I maintain that chiefly Indian graphic narratives beget Indian ways of seeing and thus knowing, but I find that I am able to extend this notion much further by invoking Deleuze and Guattari's notion of 'minor literature' and the visual metaphor of the rhizome (see the discussion below). I suggest that Deleuze and Guattari's focus on (a) the interface of the minority and the 'major language', (b) the political, and (c) collective value, all speak to and of the post-millennial Indian scene of graphic narratives. I elucidate on these ideas below as well as present my thoughts on the visual trope of the rhizome.

The Rhizome

That a minor literature is not the literature of a minor language but the literature a minority makes in a major language connects in interesting ways, I suggest, with the phenomenon of the Indian graphic narrative. For the most part, Indian graphic narratives are in the English medium, with the exception of Appupen's wordless graphic narratives and with some Hindi (or other Indian languages) appearing infrequently in speech balloons in their respective script or in transliterated English. In this manner, Indian graphic narratives employ a major language for a minor mode of expression. Being English-medium, written and created by author–artists who work in the English medium, the Indian graphic narrative interlocks with major global publishing houses such as HarperCollins, while it, as a cultural product, narrates the 'minor-inauspicious'. The author–artist who publishes with such a corporate publishing house inhabits a space both of the major (as middle-class, as English-speaking, as a professional) and the minor (the graphic narrative as a marginal form, the narration and depiction of the inauspicious or challenging). Furthermore, as Deleuze and Guattari state in their essay, a characteristic of minor literature is the connection of the individual to the political, an obvious feature of Banerjee's *The Harappa Files* and *All Quiet in Vikaspuri*, of Ghosh's *Delhi Calm* and Navayana's *Bhimayana*, all of which foreground individual and collective memory, politically oriented in nature and expression.

I suggest that the visual trope of the rhizome invoked through Deleuze and Guattari's essay 'What Is a Minor Literature?' offers a valuable entry point into thinking about the context(s), cultural products and movement that Indian graphic narratives are engaged in before we get to thinking about the minor-inauspicious in content and form. I see the rhizome root system weaving and creeping around panels, in and out of its assemblage, interlacing with illustration, sliding itself around speech balloons and wrapping itself around penned characters. I visualise the rhizome as the body of the root system, hence one that *embodies* ideas and contestations of Indianness. Thus the root system as an offshoot of the rhizome inherently carries with it exploratory ideas and sentiments of contemporary, post-millennial Indianness.

The analogy of the rhizome might be extended further when we consider the manner in which graphic narratives often take root as an underground literary and artistic medium, buried within the layers of subculture; although present (they may be published in some form and thus in circulation), they are often initially unseen. Typically, a graphic narrative scene develops in unconventional and organic ways often through a network of artists and writers, sometimes resulting in the creation of 'collectives' (such as the Pao Collective or the Kadak Collective). Typically, graphic narratives story challenging subject matter, often pushing socio-cultural boundaries. With the growth system of the rhizome, graphic narratives often develop perpendicular to the force of gravity or orthodoxy. Moreover, as part of the rhizome's own ecosystem, rhizobacteria are essential for growth; they are nitrogen-rich, promoting the development and sustaining the evolution of the rhizome. This semiotic of bacteria promoting growth and development is also useful for thinking through how the Indian graphic-narrative scene has proven to be rhizobacteria-like in its being, particularly since the early 2000s wherein it has spawned new roots, grown in size and scale and, consequently, pushed up shoots into the full light of the local literary (and visual) cultural scenes. The 'product' that is the Indian graphic novel (or graphic novella or graphic short story) belies its narrative content somewhat as does a rhizome whose shoots, leaves and flowers display a conventional, expected beauty somewhat at odds with the unseen, dirty, convoluted and complex rhizome and root system from which it emanates. The Indian graphic novel presents itself in a similar fashion—a recognisable, conventional and predictable 'global' product communicated by its publishing-house provenance and its material manifestation (it is recognisable as 'a graphic novel'), all made the more accessible by its English-language medium and subsequent global circulation patterns. But its textual and visual narratives story a different kind of existence; they depict issues of caste, class, rape, and bound and restricted choice; they contest erstwhile received ideas of historical 'truth'; and they usurp notions of Indianness as revered and celebratory. The 'inside' of the material product that is the post-millennial Indian graphic narrative, just as the rhizome's root system, is complex, murky and non-linear; it demands a different way of seeing, a different way of knowing.

Some Insights into the Themes and Aesthetic of a Selection of Post-millennial Indian Graphic Narratives

Bhatti and Pinney remind us that 'vision in South Asia, it seems, has never been concerned with just looking: it has always sought in many arenas to incorporate other senses and emotions, uniting vision with the somatic while concurrently diminishing the distance between subject and object' (227). If we think of 'seeing' in this multisensory manner, seeing then is a kind of 'knowing'; in the case of post-millennial Indian graphic narratives, we are being invited to 'know' through the textual and visual language of the mode itself. Depictions of Indianness in Indian graphic narratives challenge erstwhile favourable ideas of Indianness. Through a curious lineage of the Amar Chitra Katha series and the invitation 'to see' (and 'to know'), I suggest that Indian graphic narratives, being anchored in an Indian inauspicious, beget Indian ways of seeing and thus knowing. By the very nature of its medium, the question of 'reading' Indian graphic narrative necessitates *visual* decoding as much (if not more) as it does textual decoding from which *seeing–reading* is enacted. As a 'minor' literary (visual) product (as discussed above), Indian graphic narratives usurp ideas of linearity and sequential processing and this troubles the notion of 'modernity' (when such narratives are conceptualised only through Western paradigms). Turning now to a selection of post-millennial Indian graphic narratives, I aim to explicate the idea of 'double marginality' that I have raised here and thus this section offers instances of seeing–reading the inauspicious.

Sarnath Banerjee's graphic narratives foreground issues of class, caste and urban living. In *The Harappa Files* (2011), Banerjee interrogates a present-day 'New India', often by revisiting an India of the past. This graphic novel described as 'loosely bound graphic commentaries' (3) by Banerjee himself is a direct critique of Indian society as he unearths questions of corruption, hierarchy, casteism and the 'working classes' against the decisions made to liberalise the Indian economy. Whilst Banerjee writes as a 'major' author, his carefully crafted characters are 'minor' in the sense that they are of the working or labour classes, often peripheral in their inhabitation of the urban societal space—the watchman, the slum dweller, the repair man, the beggar are examples. *All Quiet in Vikaspuri* (2015) is equally direct in its critique of politics and society as it centres on the water wars of a drought-stricken New Delhi. Banerjee's epic tale narrates the plight of Girish, a plumber who has come to Delhi looking for work; he is tasked with drilling down into the earth to reach the Saraswati river (a river referenced in the Vedas but one that has not been located in the modern day). The obvious 'underground' trope of Banerjee's story feeds into the idea of the rhizome as water-searching, tendril-like roots and non-linear searching.

As part of the story arc of *All Quiet in Vikaspuri*, Banerjee weaves into the narrative a creative interlude of graphic observations entitled 'short-termism', which raise questions about popular politics, consumerism, waste, the Commonwealth Games and the safety of women on Delhi's streets, amongst other topics. One page of this 'short-termism' interlude (Figure 1) is divided into two slim, vertical panels which depict a politician addressing the masses, shouting 'Janta maaf nehi karegi' (The people will not forgive). Above the image, the text describes such 'popular

Figure 1 *All Quiet in Vikaspuri* (2015)[6]

politics' as full of 'bombast, grandstanding and chamchagiri' (54) ('chamchagiri' might be translated as flattery and veneration of those in power). Here we apprehend a sea of people looking up at the politician, some raising their fist like the man before them in support of his politics and the call that 'the people will not forgive', while in the adjoining, yet separate panel a female body is foregrounded, identified through the skirt (or dress) she is wearing. Men turn to look at her and we imagine an uncomfortable, intimidating moment. The text connects the spatially separate panels by the words: 'When, by decree, the streets and markets of Delhi are emptied of women, to prevent their getting raped' (54). The literally drawn connection as well as the implied one here is a critique of society's veneration of those in power who, despite their position, remain powerless in the fight against sexual violence towards women when the politician's only idea is to ban women from Delhi's streets in order to keep them 'safe'. The panels publicly 'display' the troubling, offensive and completely misplaced attitudes of men towards women in society and thus uncover murky and inherent patriarchal attitudes for all to see.

Whereas Banerjee's works engage with urban ideas of citizenship, some post-millennial Indian graphic narratives engage with ideas of citizenship in terms of national allegiance. *Kashmir Pending* (2007) by Naseer Ahmed and Saurabh Singh is unlike the majority of post-millennial Indian graphic narratives to date in that it employs clean and technically smooth artwork, evoking a feeling of the 'comic form' through its homogeneous and uniform presentation. Julia Round writes that such stylised artwork is engaged in 'blurring the lines between the signifier and signified—to create a comic is not a way of telling a story with illustrations replicating the world it is set in, but a creation of that fantastic world from scratch' (318). The consistent use of a highly pigmented orange for skin tone—faces, limbs, etc.—is often placed in contrast to much of the darkness created by black, grey and muted greens in *Kashmir Pending*. Thus, in turn, this colourway choice reimagines the narrative, recreating it within its own world despite the story being based on real-life events. The darkness and weight of the pages that constitute *Kashmir Pending* echo the darkness and the weight of the narrative—a story set in the valley of Kashmir amidst violence, imprisonment and death. The rhizome is invoked here through the motif of darkness, of non-linear movement as resistance as the Kashmir Valley is contested and fought over.

In another example of military violence, Pratheek Thomas and Aindri Chakraborty's *Twelve: How It Ends* (2013), a graphic short story, begins with an army officer's pledge of faith and allegiance to India. It unravels across five pages and is set against dark yet textured panels and full-page illustrations which depict the foliage of a forest in which the Indian soldiers are supposedly fighting. The dominance of the natural world, the dark and shadowy depths created on the page as well as the soldiers hunting (and being hunted) in the dark all lend themselves to a rhizomatic reading wherein struggle and the need for 'light' take precedence. On the first page of the oath, sensory diegetic images are central to the image: the surfaces of the tree trunks and the patterns on the leaves are created through the play of light and dark, irregular patterns and organic patterning taken from the natural world (specifically photomicrographs) coalescing and morphing into potential 'eyes'. This use of patterning creates a sense of being watched, a leitmotif which carries throughout *Twelve: How It Ends*. The story is as shadowy as the visual forms it is told through; the ethical position of the soldier and his reluctance to give his life for his county plays out across the pages. The story usurps the revered 'Indian jawan' (soldier) by revealing textually and visually his incapacity to face death for his country, an act that, by extension, dismantles the idea of allegiance for the motherland.

Other post-millennial graphic narratives take their starting point from recent social or historical events. The collection of graphic short stories titled *Drawing the Line: Indian Women Fight Back* (2015), edited by Priya Kuriyan, Larrisa Bertonasco and Ludmilla Bartscht, is one such example as it was conceived and curated as an artistic and socio-cultural response to the Delhi gangrape case of Jyoti Singh in December 2012. Reshu Singh's graphic story 'The Photo', which features in the anthology, narrates and visualises the story of a young woman who is being pushed to get married. She is taken to the local photo studio in order to have her photo taken as part of the process; this image will be the one that suitors will view (and judge her by). The graphic short story visualises the female-centric space of the home and the contested identities of two female subjects as mother and daughter. 'The Photo' usurps traditional positive and celebrated visualisations of the 'mother', the home and desired female (social) behaviour. Specifically, I suggest that we are invited to see the embodiment of this opposition in the absence of bright colourways, the depiction of a physically worn-down mother, the presence of confrontational dialogue, and the juxtaposition of generational, personal artefacts. Both the visual and textual portrayal of the female subjects put forward a difficult depiction of the post-millennial experiences of women, both young and old(er), and in so doing foreground some of the urgent generational differences and opinions—the daughter as a rhizomatic offshoot, representing exploratory ideas and sentiments of contemporary, post-millennial Indianness.

Another mother–daughter story appears in *Drawing the Line*, although in this narrative the women are more united by their gender than divided. Entitled 'The Prey' by Neelima P. Aryan, the short graphic story is dark in both form and content as it narrates one young woman's attempts at reordering a violent world where women are regarded as (sexual) 'prey'. Replete with dark, gothic semiotics, this graphic short story depicts a young woman watched over by her mother as she lays a trap in their backyard. Having bought the bait from a butcher, the young woman carefully places the meat in the trap, setting it in the yard, and watches from the kitchen doorway. We see an eagle observe the area outside the house for some time before swooping down to take the meat, only to get caught and killed in the trap. The image of the eagle morphs into a male figure who is seen leaning against a fence, scratching the inside of his leg, picking at his teeth as he looks at a girl walking home from school. The space in which this graphic story takes place is female-centric and domestic but the story itself usurps established, safe ideas of womanhood in such a context; moreover, it assumes a complicity of sorts as the girl's mother looks on, simply exclaiming at the close of the story, 'Oh, girls these days!' (See also Dawson Varughese, 'Neelima P. Aryan's "The Prey"'.)

In *Mixtape 3* (2016), Studio Kokaachi's curated collection of graphic short stories, a story entitled 'The Wind Blows White' by Nimisha T. Jose and Vishnu Madhav explores the right to choose when to die in old age and thus, by extension, the ethical difficulties around euthanasia and assisted suicide. The wordless story opens with an old woman in a white saree collecting items in a bag and leaving a box, tied neatly with string, in a house in which a couple is sleeping. We see the old woman apprehend a male figure who joins her and leads her by the hand; they walk out of the house into the night. As they leave the house, the old woman notices a bright, white seedhead from a plant floating on the nighttime breeze. She acknowledges it with a smile. The image of the seedhead acts as a leitmotif, appearing also as the closing image on the final page. A series of panels show how the couple walks together in the night and one full-page illustration (Figure 2) depicts the old woman looking up as if she is reminiscing—a scene plays out behind them, drawn using hatching, showing images of the couple in their younger days, their marriage and the old man taking part in a protest or political rally. We turn the page to see the couple approaching the sea. Through a series of five slim, horizontal panels, the two figures are subsumed by the black sea, visible only through the white waves and eventually they appear only as white seedheads floating in the wind (Figure 3). The play of black and white, the thin guttering separating the panels, and the line of sight as we view the couple from behind allow for a smooth transition of human form through to organic, plant form as the couple takes flight, freely floating in the night

Figure 2 'The Wind Blows White', *Mixtape 3* (2015)[7]

air. This scene is challenging in that it suggests the right to take your life at your wish but this is somewhat complicated by the fact that the woman is elderly and, as is revealed on the following page, a widow. The family is shown mourning her death as they sit next to her body on the floor, incense burning; on the wall hangs a garlanded picture of her husband. It is at this point that

Figure 3 'The Wind Blows White', *Mixtape 3* (2016)

we realise the old woman had decided to end her life and that she had imagined her husband coming to take her to be with him; he was never alive in this story as the widow had imagined him. An image of the beach reveals the bag the old woman had carried with her; her glasses, a bottle of some unknown liquid and a book lie strewn on the beach. The closing aerial image looks down on the mourners; in the foreground at the top of the panel are two white seedheads floating in the sky above it all.

Given the Indian context of this story, we cannot ignore the intertextual and social-cultural references to sati, the ancient practice of a widow burning on the husband's funeral pyre. In this sense, the graphic narrative explores murky and problematic ground as it oscillates between the ethics of the right to die when suffering (physical or mental suffering at the loss of her husband) through (assisted) suicide and a prescriptive religious–cultural directive that widows should die at the time of their husband's cremation. The use of a monochrome palette in this story further underscores this dialectic while simultaneously invoking the traditional funeral colour of white—'The Wind Blows White'. Foregrounding the natural force of nature, the wind, also suggests an organic and natural turn of events, signalling perhaps that one knows when one's own time has come.

Concluding Thoughts

In offering some examples of both narrative content and aesthetic form in recently published Indian graphic narratives, I have aimed to explicate the 'double marginality' that I suggest marks out Indian graphic narratives from other post-millennial cultures of graphic narrative such as those in Europe or the US due to their anchoring of 'seeing inauspicious Indianness'. Closer examination of the broader body of post-millennial Indian graphic narratives reveals how both content and form are engaged in depicting India in a less than favourable light. Unfortunately, a more extended exposition of this theory is outside of the limits of this essay.[8] Crucially, though, the challenging aesthetic and narrative content of the Indian graphic narrative are a response to, and therefore a product of, the post-millennial period. The vast changes that have occurred at pace across Indian society have not simply translated into a celebration of Indian post-liberalisation modernity; rather, many of these aspects of such a changed society have equally allowed for various artistic and literary responses to such vicissitudes. Indian graphic narratives in the post-millennial period help explore this new terrain. Integral to this journey, to the very navigation of this new landscape, is an evolving sense of questioning and critique. I posit that post-millennial Indian graphic narratives, by way of the text–image interface and their identity as 'marginal' (perceived 'marginal'), inhabit a particular position that fosters the development of a visual and textual vocabulary of the inauspicious which, in turn, creates a space for a critique of society and culture(s).

This essay has considered post-millennial Indian graphic narratives as sites of major and minor literary production. Specifically, it has focused on how Indian graphic narratives are a site of double marginality given the context specifics of 'seeing' (and reading) Indianness in terms of the inauspicious. I have suggested that the positioning of post-millennial Indian graphic narratives in a to-and-fro negotiation of the major-favourable and the minor-inauspicious gestures towards a reception anchored in evolving ideas of Indianness, Indian post-millennial modernity and Indian ways of 'seeing'. On the one hand, the role of the international publishing house is a significant one in terms of making the literary–artistic material visible and facilitating its entry into, and circulation within, global markets; on the other hand, Indian graphic narratives speak to, and of, local concerns. Importantly, through a certain aesthetic, they usurp established modes of 'seeing' Indianness, at least in popular culture. The argument of the major–minor here relies on more than 'readings' (postcolonial or otherwise); indeed, the crux of the argument lies in the Indian graphic novel as a material and cultural product—thus its circulation and reception both domestically and globally.

Notes

1. Here, I use Navayana, the publishing house, as shorthand for the creators of both books: Durgabai Vyam, Subhash Vyam, Srividya Natarajan and S. Anand (*Bhimayana*), and Srividya Natarajan and Aparajita Ninan (*A Gardener in the Wasteland*).

2. See Nayar for a 'history–human rights–literary studies' approach to the same.
3. It should be noted that the literary scene in India is not, for the time being at least, completely beholden to global publishing houses such as HarperCollins and Penguin Random House, although they have an increasing presence within the Indian publishing scene. The continued rise of independent presses, online communities, and writing (and artist) collectives is encouraging in the wake of the global corporate publishing house trend.
4. Although Banerjee divides his time between India and Europe.
5. Although I readily acknowledge the production of Indian graphic narratives in other languages across India (in Malayalam—see DC Books' recent publications—and in Bengali, for example).
6. Figure 1: Image from *All Quiet in Vikaspuri* by Sarnath Banerjee (2015), first published by HarperCollins India © Sarnath Banerjee. Reproduced here with permission from HarperCollins Publishers India Private Limited.
7. Figures 2 and 3: Images from 'The Wind Blows White' by Nimisha T. Jose and Vishnu Madhav (2016) in *Mixtape 3* © Kokaachi. Reproduced here with permission from Kokaachi.
8. See, instead, Dawson Varughese, *Visuality and Identity in Post-millennial Indian Graphic Narratives.*

Works Cited

Ahmed, Naseer, and Saurabh Singh. *Kashmir Pending*. Phantomville, 2007.

Appupen. *Legends of Halahala*. HarperCollins Publishers India, 2013.

Banerjee, Sarnath. *All Quiet in Vikaspuri*. HarperCollins Publishers India, 2015.

———. *The Harappa Files*. HarperCollins Publishers India, 2011.

Bhatti, Shaila, and Christopher Pinney. 'Optic-Clash: Modes of Visuality in India'. *A Companion to the Anthropology of India*, edited by Isabelle Clark-Decès, Wiley-Blackwell, 2011, pp. 225–240.

Chandra, Nandini. *The Classic Popular: Amar Chitra Katha 1967–2007*. Yoda Press, 2008.

Chute, Hillary. 'Comics as Literature? Reading Graphic Narrative'. *PMLA*, vol. 123, no. 2, Mar. 2008, pp. 452–465.

Dawson Varughese, E. *Genre Fiction of New India: Post-millennial Receptions of 'Weird' Narratives*. Routledge, 2016.

———. 'Neelima P. Aryan's "The Prey" from *Drawing the Line*: A Graphic Narrative Response to the Delhi Gang Rape'. *Journal of Graphic Novels and Comics*, vol. 9, no. 3, 2018, pp. 251–263.

———. *Reading New India: Post-millennial Indian Fiction in English*. Bloomsbury, 2013.

———. *Visuality and Identity in Post-millennial Indian Graphic Narratives*. Palgrave Macmillan, 2017.

Deleuze, Gilles, and Félix Guattari. 'What Is a Minor Literature?' Translated by Robert Brinkley. *Mississippi Review*, vol. 11, no. 3, 1983, pp. 13–33.

Jain, Kajri. 'The Efficacious Image: Pictures and Power in Indian Mass Culture'. *Polygraph*, vol. 12, 2000, pp. 159–185.

Kuriyan, Priya, et al., editors. *Drawing the Line: Indian Women Fight Back*. Zubaan Books, 2015.

Mehta, Suhaan. 'Wondrous Capers: The Graphic Novel in India'. *Multicultural Comics: From 'Zap' to 'Blue Beetle'*, edited by Frederick Luis Aldama, University of Texas Press, 2010, pp. 173–188.

Mixtape 3. Studio Kokaachi, 2016.

Narayanan, Pavithra. *What Are You Reading? The World Market and Indian Literary Production*. Routledge, 2012.

Nayar, Pramod K. *The Indian Graphic Novel: Nation, History and Critique*. Routledge, 2016.

Patil, Amruta. *Kari*. HarperCollins Publishers India, 2008.

Raghuramaraju, A. 'Bending Deleuze and Guattari for India: Re-examining the Relation between Art and Politics in Europe and India'. *Sophia*, vol. 57, 2018, pp. 475–487.

Round, Julia. 'Visual Perspective and Narrative Voice in Comics: Redefining Literary Terminology'. *International Journal of Comic Art*, vol. 9, no. 2, 2007, pp. 316–329.

Sen, Orijit. *River of Stories*. 1994. Blaft Publications, 2022.

Thomas, Pratheek and Aindri Chakraborty. *Twelve: How It Ends*. Manta Ray, 2013.

Weiner, Stephen. *Faster than a Speeding Bullet: The Rise of the Graphic Novel*. 2nd edn., Nantier Beall Minoustchine, 2012.

The 'Indian' Superhero and the Discourse of Power

A Study of Narayan Debnath's *Bantul the Great*

Rishi Ghosh and Oindrila Mitra

Comics have always been a powerful medium of popular culture for cultural and ideological dissemination; the Indian context is no exception. Postcolonial popular culture has utilised comics as a sound tool for communication with a wide and varied reading public. Narratives in the form of drawings have been in existence since the inception of human civilisation, but as a genre, comics developed during the 1940s in America. Superhero comics have been a thriving and admired sub-genre. According to Matthew J. Smith in 'Superhero Comics' in *The Routledge Companion to Comics*:

> Although the superhuman has been a part of storytelling throughout recorded history, the distinctive brand of superhero adventure codified in the superhero bloomed in the twentieth century and continues to captivate the imaginations of audiences in comics and other storytelling mediums well into the twenty-first century. (128)

Superhero comics witnessed a surge in publication in India during the 1960s. There were several regional manifestations of superheroes and Narayan Debnath's *Bantul the Great*, which used Bengali as its medium, was one of the foremost Indian superheroes to appear in print. Indian superhero comics were influenced by and drew heavily on American superhero comics, but at the same time, they were marked by a postcolonial tendency to register their 'Indianness', posing a discourse of countering white supremacy. As a superhero, Bantul the Great possesses many of the basic traits of a superhero, but he defies certain stereotypical features associated with the figure as well. He asserts his individuality and his 'Indianness' through his characteristics and habits, but at the same time he can easily emerge as an international figure crossing regional and linguistic boundaries. While keeping an unflagging mass appeal, as a postcolonial narrative, *Bantul the Great* adapted the American superhero comics and superheroes to an Indian, specifically Bengali, context, introducing various alterations and deviations. The narratives of *Bantul the Great* can be seen in dialogue with the discourses of power on more than one level as they engage extensively with ideas of decolonisation, cultural appropriation, identity formation and discourses of coercion, consent and co-option.

Superhero comics have always addressed the discourse of power and the question of violence, both unleashed upon and by the state. They have depicted the role of the superhero who is caught amidst the web of power and violence. As they have a widespread mass appeal, superhero comics bear a capacity to influence young readers, but as a genre they possess a marginal status and thereby hold a conflicted place in power relations. Comics as a part of popular culture can be used as a potent tool for disseminating particular sociocultural ideologies in order to mould young minds in a manner validated and enforced by the state, but their marginal status enables them to question the same ideological standpoints sanctioned and promoted by the state and, along with it, dismantle the sociocultural hierarchy. Therefore, comics have the power to question and challenge the very sociocultural forces which produce it. The intricate relationship between comics and the discourse of power is subtly captured in Debnath's *Bantul the Great*. In these comics, Bantul, the superhero, assists in maintaining law and order in his locality, which in its turn brings out the lacunae within the system and serves as a commentary on how power operates and individuals are used as tools in this operational machinery with their consent.

Bantul the Great was immensely popular when it was first serialised and continues to have an extensive mass appeal both amongst children and adults. It has been a huge success since its early days because of its contemporaneity, novelty, innocent approach and ability to create a superhero figure who is very relatable. It captures the themes of robbery, terrorist activities, bombings, attacks by goons and dacoits, use of weaponry and the functioning of various institutions of the state in a manner that does not appal its young readers. *Bantul the Great*, therefore, engages with the themes of violence, domination, oppression and exertion of power like most successful superhero comics do. But its relationship with the idea of power is far more layered than any American superhero comics. It presents, of course, the discourse of power struggle between good and evil and the extraordinary individual's victory over evil. It also serves as an engaging but implicit commentary on the power relationship between the state and the individual, and the individual either in conflict with the state or being co-opted into the state machinery. Apart from these power struggles, it addresses and counters the marginal position assigned to comics in the oeuvre of art and literature. But it also explores the discourse of power, marginality and conflict to another extent, when it is caught in the power struggle between the overarching influence of the coloniser and the making of a postcolonial identity. *Bantul the Great* questions the parameters of superhero comics set by American superhero comic books from a postcolonial position.

The figure of the superhero has been associated with power from the early years of the genre of such comics because on the one hand superheroes are extraordinary beings who yield enormous power and on the other hand that power is almost always focused on sustaining the institutions and the state, thereby aiding proper governance of the city/nation by the state. But it is interesting to observe that the state obtains authority over its subjects by exercising power not always through violence, which results in the subjugation of the subjects. This makes the position of the superhero quite problematic and it often happens in superhero comics that due to the adventurous and heroic feats of superheroes, the system is exposed with its operational network of power, violence, domination and subjugation which challenges the entire system of governance altogether. Superheroes stand as symbols for the salvation and freedom of mankind from the clutches of evils of all kinds. But superhero comics often put forward the question whether superheroes fight independently against all evils, even if that evil is state-sponsored, or if they sacrifice their free will under government supervision, becoming state-employed agents for fostering peace worldwide. In *Bantul the Great*, Bantul can be seen fighting the forces of evil just as a quintessential superhero is expected to, and his activities, knowingly or unknowingly, always somehow end up in assisting the machinery of the state, ensuring smooth governance.

All superheroes are extraordinary beings who possess tremendous physical strength and, sometimes, certain other kinds of special powers as well. They are distinct from an average human being. Many superheroes have mythical origins, such as Thor; many are results of scientific experiments or certain fateful accidents, such as Captain America, the Hulk and Iron Man; some owe their origin to genetic mutations like the X-Men; and some are simply extra-terrestrial creatures such as Superman. In his book *Superhero: The Secret Origin of a Genre*, Peter Coogan provides a definition of superhero characters:

> A heroic character with a selfless, pro-social mission; with superpowers—extraordinary abilities, advanced technology, or highly developed physical, mental, or mystical skills; who has a superhero identity embodied in a codename and iconic costume, which typically express his biography, character, powers, or origin (transformation from ordinary person to superhero); and who is generically distinct, i.e. can be distinguished from characters of related genres (fantasy, science fiction, detective, etc.) by a preponderance of generic conventions. Often superheroes have dual identities, the ordinary one of which is usually a closely guarded secret. (30)

This definition characterises almost every American comic-book superhero, but the first Bengali superhero, Bantul the Great, does not share all these conventional features of a superhero. Coogan emphasises four aspects of a superhero—mission, powers, identity and costume. As Bantul does not completely fit into this kind of character sketch, it becomes necessary to redefine superheroes from a postcolonial perspective.

Bantul is, undoubtedly, an extraordinary being whose physical prowess is well acknowledged in his locality. But information about him comprises only a handful of facts: he lives with his *pishima* (paternal aunt); his sidekick is Lambakarna, whose special power is that he can hear sounds from a long distance; and his constant opponents are two mischievous boys named Bachchu and Bichchhu. Bantul also defies the generic convention about superheroes having a certain selfless, pro-social mission as his adventures are simply to wipe out any evil that he comes across and thereby to inculcate good values amongst his juvenile readers. Bantul is also not on a quest to hunt down his enemies to avenge the death of a loved one, which is again a feature that distinguishes him from stereotypical superheroes. Such deviations foreground the resistance of postcolonial Indian comics against their Western counterparts that is built into Bantul's very characterisation.

The generic definition of superheroes often maintains that a dual identity is necessary for superheroes. But Chris Gavaler observes in his *Superhero Comics* that the idea of dual identity has been found in many earlier definitions but the characters have gradually evolved from that. There have been certain popular Western superhero characters as well who do not hide their identity from the public, such as Iron Man. Debnath's Bantul has never been obligated to conjure up any secret identity; rather, everyone in the town is aware of his physical superiority and he enjoys their admiration. Bantul neither wears a cape nor a mask as well, which is very unlikely of a superhero, and he does not have any costume as such.

In twentieth-century Western superhero comics, Asian or African countries (former colonies of Western imperial powers) had little to no representation. When the import of American superheroes was dominating the imagination of the children, it was necessary to create an indigenous superhero and *Bantul the Great* was conceptualised to cater to that need. Circulation of American superhero comics was widespread and children everywhere idolised and became obsessed with figures like Superman, Batman or Captain America who were symbols of justice, righteousness and superiority. This can be interpreted as one of the strategies of neo-colonialism. These narratives inject into young minds the idea that the West is superior, advanced, progressive and the possible saviour of the entire human race, and that their own country is the complete opposite. The West glorifies 'the self' at the expense of 'the Other'. In his book *Orientalism*, Edward W. Said discusses the West's invention of the Orient as a savage, barbaric, uncivilised, exotic, mystical, mysterious and degenerated place in order to establish their own cultural, moral, social, political and civilisational superiority. The West developed a gamut of academic and scholarly texts (geographical, historical, political and literary) targeted toward constructing the Orient, which Said identifies as the discourse of orientalism. He defines 'Orientalism as a Western style for dominating, restructuring, and having authority over the Orient'. According to him, 'European culture gained in strength and identity by setting itself off against the Orient as a sort of surrogate and even underground self' (3). To a certain extent, American superheroes thrived and grew in popularity worldwide due to the absence of their Asian or African counterparts. This necessitated representation from the formerly colonised countries to counter the Western discourse of domination and supremacy. Just as Indian English literature sought to adapt English language to suit Indian sensibilities, Indian vernacular comics sought to counter the supremacy of Western superheroes by creating regional counterparts of those figures as the Indian superhero. *Bantul the Great* appeared at this juncture and addressed the issue of Indianising the genre of superhero comics. It created a niche for its own type of comics, which were not necessarily required to be measured according to international standards; rather, they were capable of finding their readership and appreciation without sacrificing their indigenous elements.

Narayan Debnath successfully accomplished this mighty task of Indianising the superhero in his *Bantul the Great* by sketching an alternative superhero to the dominant discourse of Western superheroes and creating a narrative oeuvre, profoundly rooted in contemporary sociocultural context of Bengal, operating in Bengali itself. The society that *Bantul the Great* portrays is undoubtedly a Bengali society invested with Bengali sensibilities and sentiments. Within his circle of family and friends, Bantul appears to be a very commonplace man who engages in mischievous activities like stealthily entering pishima's kitchen to devour the Bengali sweet delicacy payesh and then trying to place the blame on others; when he is caught, he is rebuked by pishima, of whom he is quite afraid. Bantul being a grown man living with his pishima is an Indian custom that has never been a part of Western culture, where moving out is the norm. Bantul engages in playing friendly neighbourhood cricket with the boys and also becomes a partner in their mischief such as stealing mangoes, an activity that most Bengali children have indulged in during their childhood. It can be assumed that Debnath found inspiration for Bantul's character and sketch from the bodybuilders and gymnasts of his neighbourhood. In India, since colonial times, bodybuilding had been associated with the rebuilding of the nation and resisting the coloniser's domination. Apart from the use of Bengali as its linguistic medium, such social and cultural nuances scattered into the narrative establish Bantul the Great as a Bengali superhero. Further, his regional context and sensibilities mould him as an Indian superhero because India embraces and celebrates its regional, linguistic and cultural diversity.

To determine whether Bantul is an 'Indian' superhero or an international one, it is important to consider his clothes as well. Clothes are an important marker of one's culture and identity. Being a superhero, Bantul is supposed to have a costume, but it is interesting that he does not. All he wears is a sleeveless t-shirt and a pair of black tights which do not denote traditional Indian attire. Bantul's attire shows the influence of the Western style of dressing and is a comment on the cultural hybridity caused by the colonial experience. The superiority of the West and the myth of its progressive and advanced culture had been sustained through borrowing the coloniser's attire as well. Bantul's westernised costume is significant as it differentiates him from other inhabitants of the town, thereby somewhat pointing out his superiority over other commoners of that locality. Lambakarna and Bachchu and Bichchhu also wear westernised clothes as do those representing institutional authority such as the policemen or the municipal chairman, whereas most of the common people in the comics are seen donning mostly traditional clothes. The entire visual universe of *Bantul the Great* presents a hybrid postcolonial culture which is still suffering from colonial hangover and desperately attempting to break away from colonial stereotypes.

Bantul was meant to be a Bengali and an Indian superhero, but he was sketched in such a manner that even if he was put into any other cultural scenario, he would fit right in. Narayan Debnath provides sketchy outlines regarding his biography, and his locality bears no particular name. Bantul is embedded in a Bengali social, cultural, political context but at the same time he is situated at no particular time and place. He lives somewhere which can be a village, town, city or metropolis, but exists nowhere. It is somewhere very near, not 'far far away' like fairy tales, but still cannot be found. The patterns and sketches give it a resemblance to a Western landscape, but its cultural nuances and language negate the possibility of the place being somewhere in the West. Being a teenager during the Second World War, Debnath must have been influenced by the Western troops marching during the war and the comics they left behind might have influenced Bantul's character sketch. The narrative does not follow any chronological sequence; rather, it is quite random. Thus, it can be read as a whole and also as separate sequences. Due to this liberty, Bantul exists in no specific time and place and at the same time he can exist in every time and place. This gives *Bantul the Great* a quality of timelessness and enables it to transcend regional borders and become appealing to children of other countries as well (if linguistic barriers are overcome through translation). Bantul is thus very close to Bengali sensibility and culture and at the same time far enough to become almost timeless and universal.

Bantul the Great deftly incorporates the struggle of a budding genre being adapted from the West and appropriated to the culture of the East by way of introducing various alterations and deviations and thereby challenging the authority of the West over the genre of superhero comics. It challenges, questions and alters the generic conventions of the superhero, ultimately carving its own niche within the universe of superheroes. This power struggle is, thus, not about toppling the order; instead, it is about conflict, coercion and ultimate co-option. This ideology is apparent in the storyline of *Bantul the Great* as well where Bantul's engagement with the state and its institutions occupy the central position.

The narratives of *Bantul the Great* portray the power relations between the state and an individual of superhuman abilities. The relationship between the state and its individual subjects has different layers and the state wields its power over the individuals in varied forms, that is, through institutions like family, school, municipality, hospitals, police, the army and so on; and the individual also plays a certain role in shaping this power relation. Louis Althusser discusses two types of state apparatuses, respectively Repressive State Apparatus (RSA) and Ideological State Apparatus (ISA), in his essay 'Ideology and Ideological State Apparatuses'. He defines these apparatuses as the following:

> The (Repressive) State Apparatus functions massively and predominantly *by repression* (including physical repression), while functioning secondarily by ideology. (There is no such thing as a purely repressive apparatus.) ... For their part, the Ideological State Apparatuses function massively and predominantly *by ideology*, but they also function secondarily by repression ... (There is no such thing as a purely ideological apparatus.) (138)

RSAs control, subdue and dominate the individual by the use of force, whereas ISA operates through ideology conditioning and habituating the individual to a particular way of living which ensures that law and order are intact. In *Bantul the Great* Bantul is not apparently oppressed by RSA; ISA does not condition him completely as he is free to exercise his superhuman strength and there is no conflict as such between Bantul and the state apparatuses because his power and strength is always beneficial for the state. Thus, Bantul seems to have developed a relationship of consent, not coercion, with the state. The consent shared between the individual and the state machinery takes place in what Antonio Gramsci calls a civil society. He distinguishes between political society and civil society operating respectively by exercising force and consent. According to Gramsci, the individual must give consent to being governed. He writes in his *Prison Notebooks*:

> ... the more an individual is compelled to defend his own immediate physical existence, the more he will uphold and identify with the highest values of civilization and humanity, in all their complexity. (170)

According to his argument, any civil society operates through 'hegemony' that denotes governance through consent with almost no possibility of conflict or dissent. In Gramsci's words, this can be acquired when:

> The assertion that the State can be identified with individuals (the individuals of a social group), as an element of active culture (i.e. as a movement to create a new civilisation, a new type of man and of citizen), must serve to determine the will to construct within the husk of political society a complex and well-articulated civil society, in which the individual can govern himself without his self-government thereby entering into conflict with political society—but rather becoming its normal continuation, its organic complement. (268)

In *Bantul the Great* Bantul as an individual has the right to exercise his power, but he never exercises it to counter or challenge the state. But the discourse of power embedded in *Bantul the Great* is not as simple as the state conditioning the individual; rather, it sheds light on the role of the individual in this power structure as well. But when Bantul catches thieves and criminals, putting an end to robberies and other crimes, handing them over to the police or the guardians of the town, it exposes the lacuna in the machinery of the state and criticises the state itself as it requires the intervention of a superhuman creature to maintain law and justice.

Bantul possesses enormous physical strength which needs to be controlled and mastered, and not by himself only, but also by the state. With his physical power and valour, Bantul protects his locality and the town against external attacks, and sometimes national threats and internal sabotage as well. He unleashes his might upon the forces of evil and this act is almost always either previously sanctioned or later appreciated and acknowledged by the authorities of the state. But there are hazards of possessing such immense strength as well, as Bantul himself is often unaware that his small action can cause troubles in the lives of other people. For example, when he plays ball with Bachchu and Bichchhu, two mischievous boys of the neighbourhood, he unintentionally kicks the ball so hard that it cuts all the trees in one stroke and apparently also breaks all the windowpanes of the neighbourhood in another. Finally, the police arrive to inform Bantul that the windowpanes were broken by the mischief of the boys and also to congratulate Bantul as his ball has broken only the window of the shop that sells such balls and punctured all the balls, thus bringing an end to the menace. In another incident, Bantul accidentally breaks into the prison and releases Bachchu and Bichchhu who have been held captive there; the police initially rebuke Bantul but he puts his strength to use to catch the two runaways, doing so by catching them on the rail line by simply lifting up the tracks. He is applauded by the police for his heroic act. In another strip, Bantul helps a man to fix a lamppost but pushes it down so hard that it goes into the ground entirely; then, to salvage the situation, he uproots it and, in the process, it falls on a robber's head. In another strip, the police dismiss Bantul's services to maintain order in the town as they have a robot for that; however, the robot turns evil and loots the bank. The situation is controlled by Bantul and the police accepts his invincibility. Bantul is not once charged for damaging roads, houses, bridges, railway tracks and so on because the notorious troublemakers of society are caught through these acts. On many occasions he unknowingly catches criminals and goons and benefits everyone in the town by his deeds. On one occasion, Bantul is playing a friendly sport of throwing bowling balls which he throws very far; when he goes to fetch the ball, he mistakes a runaway prisoner's ball-and-chain shackle for the ball and throws it along with the prisoner—who ultimately lands in jail. Bantul's minor physical problems like sneezing, burping and so on can cause great inconvenience for others, but all inconveniences are justified when his physical perils are used for the protection and benefit of the state. For example, when Bantul sneezes ceaselessly the entire township suffers as it is like a storm, but because of his sneezes the bank robbers are caught which brings out the humorous aspect as well.

This structure of Bantul's hazardous activities being turned into benefits for the public and helpful in maintaining law and order in society is prevalent in *Bantul the Great* and occurs frequently. This pattern/structure seeks to normalise everything that is unusual about Bantul and turns him into an instrument for preserving stability, law, order and morality in society. The outline of the narrative shows the pattern that brings out the essence of *Bantul the Great*. Following this pattern, Bantul shows enthusiasm and courage and takes various tasks upon himself, then his acts cause inconveniences for others. However, his acts are seen as beneficial, assisting the state in a very creative manner, which results in his appropriation and acceptance into the social structure. Thus, Bantul's adventures resolve into the normalisation of abnormal or enhanced abilities. His great adventures add a new dimension to the discourse of power, such that power is not absolutely about oppression and domination but also about adaptation and appropriation, not in a forceful manner but in a creative way.

Bantul the Great serves as commentary on the operation of power within society and its relations with individual subjects living within that society. This structure and operation of power brings the comics in line with Foucauldian discourse of power. In his books *The Birth of the Clinic* (1973), *Discipline and Punish* (1977), *The History of Sexuality* (1978) and *Power/Knowledge* (1980) Foucault discusses the operation of power within society and its relationship with the individual; he does not always view power as oppressing and dominating the subjects, controlling them through force. According to Sara Mills:

> Rather than simply viewing power in a negative way, as constraining and repressing, he argues, particularly in *The History of Sexuality, Vol. I* (1978), that even at their most constraining, oppressive measures are in fact productive, giving rise to new forms of behaviour rather than simply closing down or censoring certain forms of behaviour.
>
> Foucault, unlike many earlier Marxist theorists, is less concerned with focusing on oppression, but rather in foregrounding resistance to power ...
>
> Foucault's bottom-up model of power, that is his focus on the way power relations permeate all relations within a society, enables an account of the mundane and daily ways in which power is enacted and contested, and allows an analysis which focuses on individuals as active subjects, as agents rather than as passive dupes. (33–34)

Foucault's analysis of power explores its multidimensional operation, which does not perceive the individual as a passive subject dominated and controlled against will by power; rather, the individual emerges as an active participant in the operation of power networks and Bantul the Great is one such individual. He is not one of the subjects of Louis Althusser who are recipients of ideological discourses and governed by the state apparatus. On the contrary, Bantul's actions are actually incorporated in ensuring the smooth operation of power in society. He is not in conflict with power and does not pose a threat to existing power networks; on the other hand, the possibility of any kind of conflict or coercion is averted by co-opting him inside the running system itself.

Illustrating this idea about relations between the individual and networks of power in *Power/Knowledge*, Foucault writes:

> Power is employed and exercised through a net-like organisation. And not only do individuals circulate between its threads; they are always in the position of simultaneously undergoing and exercising this power. They are not only its inert or consenting target; they are always also the elements of its articulation. In other words, individuals are the vehicles of power, not its points of application.
>
> ... The individual is an effect of power, and at the same time, or precisely to the extent to which it is that effect, it is the element of its articulation. The individual which power has constituted is at the same time its vehicle. (98)

Bantul the Great deals with the discourse of power in this manner, where Bantul is made a superhero by the networks of power and its institutions. At the same time, Bantul has the agency of articulating or exercising that power. In an interview, 'Truth and Power' given to Alessandro Fontana and Pasquale Pasquino, Foucault states:

> If power were never anything but repressive, if it never did anything but to say no, do you really think one would be brought to obey it? What makes power hold good, what makes it accepted, is simply the fact that it doesn't only weigh on us as a force that says no, but that it traverses and produces things, it induces pleasure, forms knowledge, produces discourse. It needs to be considered as a productive network which runs through the whole social body, much more than as a negative instance whose function is repression. (119)

The strength of the superhero is to be co-opted and not to be in conflict with. Bantul would not become a saviour and benefactor of society unless his relations with the networks of power allowed that to happen. His strength cannot be contained, but the networks of power direct it towards maintaining law and order in society, abandoning any possible conflict between the super-subject and the state.

To conclude, *Bantul the Great*, which is apparently a very simplistic narrative of a superhero's adventures, engages with the discourse of power in an intense manner, capturing its multidimensional nature and identifying the several levels of its operation. Through *Bantul the Great*, Narayan Debnath successfully established comics as a powerful genre which will continue to flourish and shape the popular imagination for generations to come. It foregrounds Bantul as the Indian superhero to pose a challenge to the American superhero in terms of representation. And lastly, it explores the power relations between the governing body and the individual, thereby making a strong statement about the functioning of society at large. Bantul the Great has dominated popular culture for many decades and its timelessness ensures it will continue that legacy.

Works Cited

Althusser, Louis. *Lenin and Philosophy, and Other Essays*. Translated by B. Brewster, New Left Books and Monthly Review Press, 1971.

Coogan, Peter. *Superhero: The Secret Origin of a Genre*. MonkeyBrain Books, 2006.

Debnath, Narayan. *Narayan Debnath Comics Samagra 1*. Edited by Debasis Deb and Santanu Ghosh, Lalmati, 2011.

———. *Narayan Debnath Comics Samagra 2*. Edited by Chandi Lahiri and Santanu Ghosh, Lalmati, 2011.

———. *Narayan Debnath Comics Samagra 3*. Edited by Pradip Gorai and Santanu Ghosh, Lalmati, 2011.

Foucault, Michel. *Power/Knowledge: Selected Interviews and Other Writings 1972–1977*. Edited by Colin Gordon, translated by Colin Gordon et al., Pantheon Books, 1980.

Gavaler, Chris. *Superhero Comics*. Bloomsbury Academic, 2018.

Gramsci, Antonio. *Selections from the Prison Notebooks*. Edited and translated by Quintin Hoare and Geoffrey Nowell Smith, International Publishers, 1971.

Mills, Sara. *Michel Foucault*. Routledge, 2003.

Said, Edward W. *Orientalism*. Penguin Books India, 2001.

Smith, Matthew J. 'Superhero Comics'. *The Routledge Companion to Comics*, edited by Frank Bramlett et al., Routledge, 2017.

Terrorism, Graphic Novels and the Making of a Cosmopolitan Hero

Puja Sen Majumdar and Rini P. Kujur

Introduction

The first recorded visual text in India was the *Delhi Sketch Book*, which ran from 1850 to 1857. *Awadh Punch*, an Urdu satirical weekly, followed soon after, running from 1877 to 1936. In the early 1900s, Tamil-language cartoons by Chinnaswami Subramania Bharathi appeared in the journal *India* till 1910 and, in 1947, *Chandamama*, a children's storybook with illustrations, was started. However, comic books finally made a marked entry in the Indian market in the 1960s.

It is difficult to trace a comprehensive history of comic books before the 1960s, due to reasons which include but are not limited to, regional languages which limited their reach, short publishing runs and unpredictable market conditions.

A smattering of comic strips emerged in newspapers and magazines such as *Dabbuji* in 1956. A monthly magazine called *Khilauna*, launched in 1947, carried Urdu translations of American comics such as *Tom & Jerry* and *Richie Rich*. *Khilauna* also ran a comic strip called *Hilal*, which featured the adventures of a character named Miyan Faulad. Raminder Kaur and Saif Eqbal write that the character Miyan Faulad, first introduced in the 1950s, may have arguably been one of the first Indian comic-book heroes. The 1950s also saw a steady stream of publications of translations of American superhero comic books. Soon after, the Bengali Indian comic series *Batul the Great* and *Handa Bhonda* were created by Narayan Debnath in 1965 and 1962, respectively.

In 1964, Indrajal Comics published its first issue titled *Vetal Ki Mekhla*. The first issues that were run by Indrajal Comics carried translations of *Phantom* created by Lee Falk. Consecutively, they started publishing translations of other foreign superhero comic books created by American cartoonists, such as Falk's *Mandrake*, Alex Raymond's *Flash Gordon*, *Rip Kirby* and *Phil Corrigan*, Roy Crane's *Buz Sawyer*, Allen Saunders's *Mike Nomad*, *Kerry Drake* and Steve Dowling's *Garth*. The regional translations that were run by Indrajal made these comics accessible to a large section of young Indian readers.

Amar Chitra Katha was first published in 1965 in Kannada and then in English from the eleventh issue onwards. Drawing its stories from Hindu mythologies, it soon became a forerunner in the comic-book industry in India. Thereafter, Raj Comics, founded by Rajkumar Gupta, arrived on the scene in 1984. Despite arriving after its Indian comic-book counterparts, it went on to become a major player in the comic-book scene alongside Amar Chitra Katha, Indrajal Comics, Diamond Comics, Manoj Comics and so on, partaking in popular visual culture addressing themes around modernity, nationalism and globalisation. Mostly published in Hindi barring some special editions which are in English, it found its niche in the Hindi comic-book market and went on to develop its own aesthetic and discursive space. Although many other comic-book publishers had to close their business for several reasons, Raj Comics continues publishing new issues to this day, which effectively positions it as one of the largest comic-book publishing houses in India. Ushering in the Indian superhero genre, it has published close to 5000 titles and written numerous characters. It continues to publish four genres of comics. However, for the purposes of this essay we focus only on the genre of superhero comics, specifically on the World Terrorism series which was written around the character of Nagraj and the creation of what can be termed as a 'cosmopolitan hero'.

The discourse around the nation and the project of nationalism has relied a great deal on popular culture and its proliferation.

Visual texts at once represent the historical, social and cultural specificities of their time while also becoming signifiers of the nation's vision of its future and its burgeoning possibilities. These themes have been broached in diverse ways: starting from calendar art which showcased religio-political iconography on gods/goddesses, religious/historical figures and events, popular leaders of the nationalist struggle and the figures of the kisan/jawan to popular art prints such as *Karni Bharni* and *Adarsh Balak*, both of which carried messages on good behaviour and moral decorum although *Karni Bharni* (as you reap you will sow) was more precautionary in nature. It showcased individuals suffering in hell due to morally transgressive acts that they had engaged in while alive. Christopher Pinney locates the 1970s as the point when the *Karni Bharni* template gets appropriated into *Adarsh Balak* posters carrying messages on moral standards, being a good citizen and one's duties towards the government. Aside from these popular prints, Indian history and mythology has also provided rich source material to Amar Chitra Katha, *Tinkle* and other visual texts.

The themes in Raj Comics have also cultivated, to an extent, this project of cultural nationalism. The superheroes in the Raj Comics universe are a curious amalgamation and, at times, an uneasy negotiation of the categories of mythology and the modern, the national and the global, which this essay touches upon subsequently. In Raj Comics the superhero's quest for 'justice' and 'truth' conceals complex questions around the nation and internal security, what being an ideal citizen entails, the nation's reliance on science and technology, and anxieties with respect to nuclear power. As a result, despite the presence of some broad-ranging similarities that can lead to equating this comic-book universe with Western comic-book universes, doing so would be ill-wrought because the factors of historical specificities, sociopolitical and cultural particularities that have contributed to the making of the Indian superhero, whose trajectories are then imagined against these very factors, would be diminished. This would also serve to create an immediate methodological foreclosure of the study of Indian comic books in their own right.

This essay attempts to understand these concerns in view of the sociopolitical backdrops against which the World Terrorism series is set, the historical events that find artistic representation in the events that unfold, and the superhero's interaction and negotiation with the same. It seeks to unpack the trajectories through which the Indian superhero is constructed both locally and globally, his confrontation of historical events and the subsequent interventions he makes to that end. Divided into three sections, the first section dwells briefly on the origin stories of these superheroes, the accompanying implications and their 'Indianness'. The second section focuses on the portrayal of the superhero Nagraj and his tense placement at the crux of the local and global, and identifies the strains that contribute to his characterisation as a 'cosmopolitan' hero. The third section is a detailed analysis of the category of 'cosmopolitanism' and its negotiation with the local and the global.

From National Hero to Global Hero

One of the driving motivations which led to the inception of Amar Chitra Katha was when Anant Pai, while watching a quiz show, realised that although the children showed great familiarity with Greek myths, they were unable to name Rama's mother. To that effect, Amar Chitra Katha started publishing stories drawn from Indian history and mythology. One subsequently sees the continuation of this legacy of writing stories borrowed heavily from Hindu mythology and fashioned according to the tenets of popular culture in comic books.

In the Raj Comics universe, the origin stories of most of the superheroes and superheroines who band together under the organisation known as Brahmand Rakshak or Protectors of the Universe, are drawn from a diverse blend of popular Indian mythology, Western folklore and technology. Frequently, they are not just humans with superpowers but also hybrids, cyborgs and manifestations of gods, goddesses and mythical creatures. While some boast an impressive repertoire of supernatural abilities, others rely on external elements such as their weapons and costumes that arm their wearer with special powers. Raminder Kaur writes to that end:

> These Hindi-language comics have evolved their own aesthetic, combining contemporary superheroes in modernized mythologies where a conflation of ideas from the scriptures (shastra) or 'ancient spiritual science' (paravigyan) and developments in modern science and technology (vigyan) battle it out in dynamic graphics. (330)

This tense negotiation is evident when, quite often, despite locating the superheroes' origin stories in medical science and technology, the figure of the mystical guru is a ubiquitous presence. Bearers of great wisdom in matters related to fighting and governance, gurus exercise no small degree of influence on the lives of these superheroes. Their roles in the lives of these superheroes are manifold: ranging from acting as confidantes, functioning as sounding boards for them to figure out questions around morality and ethics to intervening when the superhero's moral compass has gone awry, in which case it becomes their duty to ensure, either through force or counsel, that the superhero realises the error of his ways as is seen in the origin stories of Nagraj, Kobi/Bheriya, Super Indian and Bhokal.

Roma Chatterji suggests that part of the reason for the varied origin stories is because Raj Comics was produced from 'a vantage point of a globalizing India where comics seem to reflect trans-cultural rather than purely local or national concerns' (12). The international and national contours that inform some of the themes in these comics are India's foreign relations and its portrayal as a nation poised as an emerging superpower with a burgeoning nuclear future. The superhero Parmanu is engendered against this backdrop. The source of his powers is his superhero costume created by his uncle, Professor K. K. Verma. His powers allow him to split atoms, shoot atomic bolts, fly at the speed of sound and teleport. Concerns around energy are addressed in his storyline and directly linked to the utilisation of his powers. The comic books assert that his atomic energy is advantageous to society's betterment (Kaur 335). With the emphasis placed on science and technology, these origin stories concurrently signal to a mythical past which root the characters. The dialogue between the categories of the 'mythical' and the 'modern' provides the mise-en-scène for the writers and artists to create templates based on which newer arcs specific to certain characters are constructed and the ensuing drama unfolds against this backdrop. An appropriate example of this would be the character of Nagraj. In Hindu and Buddhist mythology, Nagraj is considered to be the king of snakes: known as Vasuki in Hindu myths, he is a companion of Vishnu whereas in Buddhist myths, he is at once Buddha's worshipper and protector, appearing at his sermons with his snakes. The creators decided that snakes were not just ubiquitous in the Indian popular imagination but were also seen as an important icon of India by foreigners. The juxtaposition of national and foreign icons thus creates an aesthetic space which is at once familiar and adventurous. Symbols which are seen as inherently Indian are also situated across various foreign spaces such as an arena for gladiator fights or a Spanish festival, portraying spaces which are multiracial and global. Kaur and Eqbal locate the emergence of snake stories to late nineteenth-century Hindi and Urdu literature on snake spies and Hindi films. The figure of the ichhadhhari nagin or shapeshifting snake was also taken into account alongside these myths by the creators. In the Raj Comics universe, mythical and geographical constraints are not placed on Nagraj: he features in three parallel timelines as Nagraj, Aatankharta Nagraj and Narak Nashak Nagraj. The timeline this essay explores is that of Aatankharta Nagraj. In this timeline, Nagraj is portrayed as a strapping, global jet-setting, cosmopolitan hero with seemingly zero regard for legal hindrances, appearing in other countries to tackle international crime rings and 'terrorists'.

One of the concerns that have been repeatedly raised in the extensive scholarship on Indian comics is if there is an 'Indian' way of writing stories. It is quite often the case that Indian superhero comics are treated as derivatives of Western superhero comics, a concern which Sanjay Gupta, one of the co-founders of Raj Comics, addresses:

> We had to devise a character from our own imagination that didn't have anything to do with them (Superman and Batman). Because if we had kept in mind how powerful Superman and Batman are, we would've reacted to it and somehow allowed that to play a part in our creative process. Our first goal was to make a total Indian character. We didn't want to copy. That wasn't going on in our heads. But we were definitely inspired by them. We are still inspired by them. Even today we don't copy . . . we are inspired by them. After all, everything has an origin. (qtd. in 'Raj Comics: A Brief Overview', para. 19)

He further states that they wanted a pure Indian superhero who would be based on a purely Indian understanding of the world. In the World Terrorism series, in spite of Nagraj travelling regularly to different continents, these foreign places are made familiar through strategic measures such as the starkly obvious presence of Indian restaurants, and Nagraj's encounters with individuals of Indian origin such as Jhappi Singh and Rhea who go on to assist him on his missions. Throughout the series Nagraj is compared to Abhimanyu, a character from the Mahabharata who keeps getting caught in the famous 'chakravyuh'. References to religious and cultural aspects of India keep cropping up in odd places, with foreigners invoking cross-cultural references with remarkable ease. In one of the issues, British citizens remark that when Nagraj is present, people do not require 'nimbu mirchi'. Sex offenders in Italy, when beaten up by a woman, allude to her as a manifestation of 'Chandi'. Nagraj is also referred to as an 'avatar', thereby recalling his connection with the Hindu god Vishnu. However, the fact that almost all of these references are to Hindu myths and traditions cannot be overlooked. The clear absence of Muslim superheroes from Raj Comics and the continuous slippage of the categories of Indian and Hindu is something that remains yet unaddressed.

From National Security to Saving the World

The World Terrorism series, launched in 2007, published twenty-three issues. A significant portion of this series unfolds in different parts of the world such as Italy, USA, Mexico, Spain and Japan; two of these deal with the 26/11 terror attack in Mumbai, locating the attacks in a global network. A continuation of Anupam Sinha's muscular super-heroic avatar, Nagraj travels from one country to another, fighting terrorists and negotiating, albeit in an uneasy and often fantastical manner, issues concerning terrorism.

In 1998, readers had encountered Nagraj and other Raj Comics heroes grappling with the spirit of Hitler transposed on a South Asian landscape. In *Tanashah* (The Dictator), Hitler's discontented and wandering soul shows up a long way off from his homeland and possesses the body of a young boy in an Indian church. However, in the World Terrorism series, the treatment of Hitler is markedly different; he is shown to be connected to a larger terrorist organisation known as the Order of Babel, with an extensive network across the world. The questions the portrayal of this worldwide network give rise to are: What makes a national hero? And how is a national hero different from a cosmopolitan hero?

The issue that closely touches on this is *Shikata Ga Nai*. A rough translation of 'shikataganai' from Japanese means 'nothing can be done anymore' or 'it cannot be helped'. In his first-ever press conference in 1975, Emperor Shōwa used the phrase when asked to comment on the bombing of Hiroshima. In the comic, Japanese characters, with great patriotic fervour, make use of Mount Fuji to create the ultimate weapon or a brahmastra to visit retribution on America for the wanton destruction it rained down on Japan during the Second World War. The weapon is built to protect the honour or maryada of the nation, to which end one of the villains ominously points out: 'Aaj America Banega Nagasaki' or 'Today America will Become Nagasaki'.

Personal history joins forces with the political history of the nation, thereby producing characters portrayed as terrorists working in tandem with state machinery. For example, Mr Jetlee, who is initially seen as a respected war hero, is later revealed as a terrorist. Anyone opposing them and their endeavours is either labelled a deshdrohi or American stooge. Nagraj, along with the people who aid him on his missions while going up against these patriot/terrorist figures, tries to explain how these extreme measures will not abate violence in any way, also pointing out that the 'patriot's' actions only end up furthering America's cause. The comic arrives at the claim that an authentic patriot is someone who, while loving and pledging allegiance to their own country, can also rise above national history. The binary of the terrorist and the patriot is collapsed in an interesting way which resonates across a number of instances in the series. Nagraj is shown to be capable of rising above national history and participating in world history, which distinguishes him from other superheroes of his time. Another aspect that separates Nagraj from the rest of the superheroes in the Raj Comics universe is his portrayal as protector of the world. In *Teen Sikke* (The Three Coins) when Nagraj accomplishes certain impossible feats, he is asked by an Italian crowd: 'Are you Russian? Are you Chinese?' Nagraj's ally Jhappi Singh responds that Nagraj is 'pure Indian' but Nagraj cuts across and says that he belongs to all of humanity.

This brings us to exploring the shifting portrayal of Nagraj from the local to the global, especially in this series. The question it raises is: What implications does this hold for the Indian superhero and for the readers of these comic books? To quote Kaur and Eqbal, who elaborate on the possible implications of Nagraj's portrayal:

> Those that bought vernacular adventure comics would be largely from mofussil middle classes—those who live in small towns and semi-urban areas where vernacular is preferred over English. While

> they range from the lower middle to relatively more comfortable classes, they are distinct from the jet-setting cosmopolitan lives of social elites or metropolitan middle classes who, as Leela Fernandes states, play the most 'national visible role as the agents of globalization in India'... the readers might also extend to children from lower working class and rural families when considering rental outlets for adventure comics. (10)

Thus, Nagraj can be said to be a cosmopolitan hero to most of his young readers who are not travellers of the world. As a superhero, he takes them around the world on adventures while remaining rooted to his Indian identity. Foreign lands and foreign affairs are made familiar to the readers who might otherwise be unable to access them. One also needs to consider the international events informing this time. Gerald Delanty grounds cosmopolitanism and its various strands in the 1990s and 2000s. He locates the sense of epochal change in the 1990s with the approach of the new millennium and writes to that effect:

> From 11 September 2001 with the emergence of the 'war on terror' to the global crisis of capitalism that began on 14 September 2008 with the collapse of the Lehmann Brothers, anti-cosmopolitan tendencies emerged to reshape the world according to new doctrines of security and capitalist crisis. (4)

The 1990s also brought major changes to India's digital history. There were new entertainment options available as a result of market policies, which also enabled trans- and multi-national collaboration. As a direct outcome of this, there were proliferations of experimental graphic narratives but at the same time many Indian companies could not keep up with these drastic changes (Kaur and Eqbal ch. 2). Raj Comics was one of the few publishing houses which managed to seize these opportunities. There is a notable change in the superhero comics from those produced in the early 1990s to the early twenty-first-century ones. Principally, stories have become more global, graphics more adventurous and bodies more muscular, aided by newer technologies in three-dimensional rendering and digitisation. The polished, well-built and spectacular Nagraj, whom we see travelling around the world, intervening in global historical events, is also a result of these innovative graphic and digital formats.

While it would be methodologically inaccurate to draw direct historical parallels with the development of the character of Nagraj and the World Terrorism series as it would overlook the creative license of representation and storytelling, one cannot shy away from these historical events providing the backdrop for the exploration of Nagraj's role as a cosmopolitan hero and the problems embedded in the narrative.

Nagraj: The Making of a Cosmopolitan Hero

Commenting on Nagraj as a global crime-fighting phenomenon in this series, Sanjay Gupta states:

> We wanted that international image. We didn't want to show him tied down to one place. He could go anywhere; any crime happening anywhere in the world would be stopped by Nagraj. His crusade was against crime in general and not against crime in a particular area or territory. (qtd. in 'Raj Comics: A Brief Overview', para. 10)

Often working individually and setting off on trips across the world to investigate global networks of terrorism, he also acts on the behest of foreign governments who ask him for his assistance to deal with organised crime. Criminals, crime and evil, despite having their political and cultural specificities, are represented as a universal problem; over each incident, Nagraj asserts that he belongs to and owes allegiance to the universal category of humanity and good. Despite the criticism launched against cosmopolitanism for its 'rootlessness' and diminishing feelings of national allegiance and solidarity, one sees Nagraj attempting to overcome these boundaries by at once being a citizen of the global community and a national hero. In some of the issues he also specifically engages with the cultures that he encounters. For example, in *Shikata Ga Nai*, as Nagraj battles fighters skilled in jujutsu and kudo, he tries to think of the weapon in the same way that the fighters do. He attempts to clear his mind of all thoughts and to concentrate on the weapons of each of his adversaries. This brings into the text notions of openness as opposed to closure, which can be treated as one of the characteristics of cosmopolitanism.

There are, however, a few concerns which this essay addresses regarding Nagraj as a cosmopolitan superhero. One of the political projects of cosmopolitanism is the understanding that all people have universal rights and the project of strengthening political rights for the same. However, we see Nagraj only engaging with one aspect of this, which is working from the understanding that everyone has inalienable universal rights. But, at the same time as an extrajudicial agent, due process is not a process one sees Nagraj placing much significance in. He takes lives at will and the category of the terrorist remains elusive and unexplored. The figure of the 'terrorist', as seen through Nagraj's perspective across this series, is someone who poses an immediate threat to ordinary citizens and communities. The approach Nagraj takes to terrorists effectively treats them in a vacuum, as individuals bereft of any sympathetic markings. Their life boils down to the crimes they have perpetrated and the retribution that immediately follows is swift and unforgiving. However, the treatment of figures from history who have posed a similar threat in the past is approached slightly differently. The figures are dealt with as abstractions. They show up carrying the weight of all the historical wrongs they have committed. They move across different timelines, inextricably linked with contemporary events of terrorism. However, there is no hope for transformation as their past only becomes indicative of the obvious choices they will continue making. Their actions only further drive home the point that they are and will continue to commit evil as always. In that sense, Nagraj is often not interested in the structural aspects of what creates a terrorist in a certain country even though the history of the country, especially as an aftermath of the Second World War, is looked into. Particularity is overlooked in order to find the universal terrorist, who is seen as a homogenous category everywhere in the world. Thus, one notes a discrepancy between the political project(s) of cosmopolitanism(s) and Nagraj as a cosmopolitan hero.

Nagraj's crime-fighting skills border on the spectacular, his methods of justice often swiftly retributive. Nagraj kills with impunity, in some series going as far as publicly executing his enemies at the Oblique Tower in Delp Apollo which is then broadcast on television. In the same comic earlier on, the justice system catches up with Nagraj and he has to answer in court for his alleged murder of a don, but later in the series he escapes jail to fight organised crime which cannot be tackled by institutional forms of justice. Nagraj enjoys extrajudicial powers and does not hesitate to take lives; neither does he show any external signs of dilemma in doing that.

The judgement that Nagraj exercises to this effect is absolute, as portrayed in one of the comics when a certain character, Rhea, whom he had rescued from goons, discovers that Nagraj was responsible for the death of her brother who was a terrorist. When she exclaims that he was her brother, Nagraj responds that a terrorist is nobody's brother, son or father, they are just a terrorist. At the same time, he claims that the terrorist has no religion, no country and no nation. As a result, terror becomes a homogeneous force that has to be relentlessly fought without paying much attention to the complexities associated with it.

Conclusion

One has to note that there are various ways in which cosmopolitanism can be understood. A number of pitfalls such as relativism and forced universalism have to be taken into account. In the series, at times these pitfalls become very evident. Nagraj constantly refuses to elaborate on or engage with the loaded political comments that he makes. In *Mission Critical*, he obliquely connects the 2005 London attacks to the Iraq War and then returns to his assertions about the ubiquity of evil.

Despite Nagraj's comments which touch upon the specificities of the historical, political and sociocultural factors of crime and 'evil', there is a distinct absence of any further engagement with it. The figure of the 'criminal' and the 'terrorist' is universalised as they are treated as relentlessly moving towards causing irreparable damage, pain, chaos and confusion to the global community.

However, one of the significant aspects of this series is that it challenges, even if in a light-hearted way, the idea that cosmopolitanism is a Eurocentric notion. Humeira Iqtidar talks about how cosmopolitanism can be understood 'as a distancing of the self, the ability to re-evaluate one's own norms and practices' (qtd. in Delanty 6). This is something that Nagraj takes part in, especially when he is confronting enemies from a different culture. Therefore, when fighting in an arena full of gladiators, he has to constantly change his tactics, take into account the history of gladiator fights and reflect on it in order to survive. Delanty explains:

> Cultures do not collide, but borrow from each other and adapt in different ways without an overall convergence being the result. This is often taken to be a case for cosmopolitanism. However, cosmopolitanism properly defined is not a condition of hybridization, but one of the creative interaction of cultures and the exploration of shared worlds. As such it suggests heightened reflexivity. (6)

This is something that the character of Nagraj seems to portray, even though the persistent tension between the historical and the ahistorical, the national and the cosmopolitan remains.

Works Cited

Chatterji, Roma. *Graphic Narratives and the Mythological Imagination in India*. Routledge, 2019.

Delanty, Gerard. 'Introduction'. *Routledge Handbook of Cosmopolitanism Studies*, edited by Gerard Delanty, Routledge, 2012.

Kaur, Raminder, and Saif Eqbal. *Adventure Comics and Youth Cultures in India*. Routledge, 2018.

Kaur, Raminder. 'Atomic Comics: Parabolic Mimesis and the Graphic Fictions of Science'. *International Journal of Cultural Studies*, vol. 15, no. 4, 2011, pp. 329–347.

'Mission Critical'. *YouTube*, uploaded by Comic World, 22 May 2020, www.youtube.com/watch?v=5h8KWcjbTos. Accessed 27 Oct. 2024.

Pinney, Christopher. 'Interview with Christopher Pinney'. Interviewed by Zoe Headley, *CEIAS Newsletter*, no. 17, summer 2019.

'Raj Comics: A Brief Overview'. *The Pao Collective*, 2007, paocollective.wordpress.com/2010/03/11/raj-comics-a-brief-overview. Accessed 27 Oct. 2024.

'Shikata Ga Nai'. *YouTube*, uploaded by Comic World, 17 June 2020, www.youtube.com/watch?v=MbDhChoeUEI. Accessed 27 Oct. 2024.

'Tanashah'. *YouTube*, uploaded by Comic World, 2 Sept. 2019, www.youtube.com/watch?v=dPPEA_bG3xw. Accessed 27 Oct. 2024.

'Teen Sikke'. *YouTube*, uploaded by Comic World, 23 May 2020, www.youtube.com/watch?v=PYZQEYbiF7M. Accessed 27 Oct. 2024.

Tales from Shining and Sinking India

Configuring the Postcolonial Identities in Indian Chick Lit

Puja Chakraborty

Indian chick lit is a comparatively new genre that has gained popularity in the last few decades due to the newly emergent publishing houses in India which cater to the urban aesthetics of reading Indian fiction in English. A remarkable proliferation of such commercial fiction has paved its way as one of the major diversifications of mainstream Indian literature in English. In fact, according to Suman Gupta, this new Indian 'commercial fiction' is specified by a domestic flavour as it is produced and consumed primarily in India unlike the more 'literary' Indian writing in English that finds acclamation in the West. He further categorises the two: 'Literary fiction is the respectable public face of Indian literature in English abroad and home, while commercial fiction is the gossipy café of Indian writing in English at home' (47). In a similar vein, Salman Rushdie has worshipped the elite position of the Indo-Anglian literature, making it out to be the sole representative of the Indian contribution to world literature and dismissing the role of any 'vernacular languages' with literary value. He asserts:

> This is it: the prose writing—both fiction and non-fiction—created in this period by Indian writers working in English, is proving to be a stronger and more important body of work than most of what has been produced in the 16 'official languages' of India, the so-called 'vernacular languages', during the same time.... (Rushdie and West viii)

His statement has been vehemently criticised by Pankaj Mishra, Radhakrishnan Nayar and Amit Chaudhuri, who have not only questioned the periphery of world literature but also defended the claim of the much-ignored position of vernacular literatures, pivotal to much congruous presentation, as a nexus of diversified India. However, the reason behind the sudden bloom of commercial fiction has been pointed out by Arjun Appadurai and Carol Breckenridge in their writing in the late 1990s, in which they envisioned a change in literature consumption in post-millennium India. They claim:

> Even at the most conservative estimates, there are at least a million Indians who already have disposable incomes that make them the economic support of new forms of cultural consumption. (7)

Therefore, the socioeconomic infrastructure of this New India has prepared the bedrock of a variety of generic forms of market-based fiction, which includes Indian chick lit, crime fiction, fantasy fiction and the graphic novel, to mention only a few. Although a trendy import from the West, Indian chick lit, more commonly termed 'desi chick lit', has demonstrably marked its position as a post-millennial Indian literary counterpart, foregrounding the diverse contours of postcolonial female subjectivity. While adapting to the Western style, these novels simultaneously project how difficult it can be for female protagonists to assimilate their cultural background with their modern worldview. Many of the novels deal with diasporic subjects where cross-cultural experiences create different shades of identity, contouring some of the major postcolonial issues. In fact, a dialectic reading of some of these novels entices a series of compelling queries. For instance, how does the hyphenated identity of the protagonists affect their lived experiences? Or what are the ways in which the act of immigration overlaps with gender inequality and its ramifications? What kind of role does globalisation or, more specifically, economic liberalisation, play in the grand narrative of postcolonial positioning of third-world women? In the quest for answers to these questions, this essay examines two novels:

The Village Bride of Beverly Hills by Kavita Daswani and *The Mango Season* by Amulya Malladi; while the former delineates a picture of going away from home, the latter problematises the concept of home by coming home from abroad. Furthermore, the essay seeks to decode the representational resonance of transcultural female subjectivities through a discursive dialogue with postcolonial concerns of acculturation and hybridisation, along with the conflict between the home and host cultures and the contestation vis-à-vis negotiation of diverse ethnic identities. The aim is also to map the cultural *dispositif*, that is, 'the system of relations' which can be established between institutions, discourses, ethical decisions and imperative intentions (Foucault 194), by unfolding the complex matrix of identity formation through an intimate involvement of the neoliberal tropes of consumerism and the politics of populism within the much-contested urban space of contemporary India.

New India and Popular Fiction

The construction of New India after independence in 1947 was a project that Nehru took up enthusiastically. His unique contribution to the architecture of a secular state-image through economic prosperity impacted and shaped the more radical ideas of *Indianness* (Khilnani 50). Nehru pursued a model that was 'committed to protecting cultural and religious difference rather than imposing a uniform "Indianness"' (Khilnani 167). Nehru's economic policies were built around state-sponsored investment, which was committed to providing importance to state identity. However, with the changing time it became difficult to maintain Nehru's vision of a diverse yet unified India, and finding an analogous rhetorical threshold moment associated with India's economic liberalisation became more challenging. According to Waquar Ahmed et al., it was the introduction of the New Economic Policy (1991) by Manmohan Singh, the then finance minister, that actualised the India Shining metaphor through a globalised India. With this new move, the nation witnessed many more opportunities to make money and more avenues to spend it.

This liberalisation eventually fostered new middle-class alignments across a spectrum of professional, educated, white-collar workers in India (Tickell 41). Alex Tickell underscores the effect of post-liberalisation:

> The emergence of a dynamic private sector in India, employing skilled white-collar professionals, has added new strata to India's middle class. Alongside an 'old middle class' of secular professionals who dominate administration and education, and tend to see themselves as the keepers and arbiters of Indian cultural values against public, globalized culture, a 'new middle class' that is likely to work in emergent sectors such as the media, technology and commerce. (42)

Such enhanced fiscal activities established India as a new global player in the world's economy. Consequently, a growing body of new writing found its voice in these new lives of India—of IT professionals and corporate living, of call centres and film industries. Indeed, the literary taste of these urban socialites shifted from canonical writers, for instance, Salman Rushdie, Amitav Ghosh and Vikram Seth, to the post-millennial popular fiction of Shobhaa De, Manju Kapur, Chetan Bhagat, Githa Hariharan, Amitabha Bagchi and Amish Tripathi, to mention a few. The reception of these canonical works and their non-canonical counterparts unfolded several contentious contours of critical enquiry, entailing the politics of canon formation, the taxonomical categorisation of literary aesthetics and the tacitly framed binaries between literary and commercial bestsellers. Although this distinction can never demean the international literary fame of the former, the oft-mooted argument on the appeal of commercial fiction is geared expressively for its potential *Indianness*, that is, exceptionally made for the Indian audience. This is how Claudia Kramatschek has described it: 'easily-digestible novels of the exotic variety, or else elucidations of "Indianness" as such' or, in Suman Gupta's words:

> [Literary fictions] are descriptions of a defamiliarised relationship between the English language (for literature) and the Indian context. Underlying commercial fiction's claim of a familiarised relationship

> between language and context, we may detect insecurities related to some essentialist notion of Indian identity or nationalistic protectiveness about India's 'image' abroad .... (50)

Regarding this statement, if we focus on Indian chick lit, a rhizomatic stem of Indian commercial fiction, we find a variety of subjects, though dealt in an 'easily-digestible' manner that can recalibrate a host of critical discourses, for example, female sexuality, post-feminist concerns regarding the idea of agency, transnational identity, female empowerment, cultural hybridity, and so on and so forth. Such a diversified position of this genre promises to open up the liminality of popular fiction for further critical enquiry through its 'familiarised relationship' with the context. Put more succinctly, the relatable appeal of this homegrown variety not only exoticises the native culture but simultaneously uncovers its political–discursive potential. In order to consider these possible alternatives, it is important first to present a brief review of the history of this genre in the light of its relevance to popular culture, considering its critical entwinement with postcolonial ideas.

Defining the Genre

Despite receiving much scathing criticism, chick lit has successfully carved a niche for itself in the history of world literature. Roughly defined as fiction written by women for women, this genre has been generally discussed in reference to post-feminism and consumerism. Critics are contemptuous of such writing, considering it 'fluffy', 'frilly', 'formulaic vapid prose' (Ponzanesi 157) or 'snack-food literature' (Oberoi 127). Yet the genre remains immensely popular despite all this backlash. In fact, when the term was coined by Cris Mazza and Jeffrey DeShell in their polemical 1995 volume *Chick Lit: Postfeminist Fiction*, little did they anticipate that their mocking use of the term would come to name a leading phenomenon in the publishing industry, stretching its reach to films and television shows and creating a culture of its own. From the formal literary perspective, chick lit does, indeed, constitute formula stories about women. As Suzanne Ferriss and Mallory Young have defined it, 'simply put, chick-lit features single women in their twenties and thirties "navigating their generation's challenges of balancing demanding careers with personal relationships"' (3). The stories are about well-educated, professional women living in urban centres, who are constantly worried about their challenging careers and complicated relationships. The women are more sympathetic and fallible in their demeanour and easily identifiable, like the girl-next-door. In the words of Sandra Ponzanesi:

> [T]hough the genre reveals common patterns of denomination, linked to consumerism, female upward mobility and rapid urbanization, it presents inherent features linked to the country-specific economic development, particular histories of feminism and locally inflected responses to commoditized patterns of behaviour. (176)

On the other hand, the stylistic contributions of these writings are limited to their use of humour, satire and witty colloquial humdrum, engaging mostly in an autobiographical or confessional tone. However, from the perspective of the 'culture industry', much emphasis has been given to the packaging style of the books. The covers have vibrant colours, along with depictions of various feminine fashionista items such as lipsticks, handbags, stilettos, sunglasses and others. This packaging not only makes the genre easy to identify for potential readers but also gives a visual representation of hip culture.

As a desi counterpart of Western chick lit, Indian chick lit has successfully created ripples in post-millennial English fiction. This ethnic version has its own desi flavour, with all the spices and ingredients added to the plot and narrative. Sunaina Kumar, a leading columnist of the *Indian Express*, addresses this homegrown variety as 'ladki-lit' and remarks:

> Ten years after the publication of *Bridget Jones's Diary*, the genre of fiction most recognisable for its pink cover art of stilettos, martini glasses and lipsticks, is now being colourfully infused with bindis, sarees and bangles.

Apart from overlapping themes with chick lit in general, this sub-genre deals with many cross-fertilising issues and aesthetic traditions in the Indian context, whose structural simplicity is at times misleading for the nuanced texture of cultural references. The simple framework of romance and resolution is often embedded into multiple layers of critical discussion, including neoliberalism, postcolonial identity politics, diasporic experiences, heteronormativity, racism, magic realism, myth, history and diversity. A few relevant examples would enhance the understanding of the epistemologies mentioned above. Jhumpa Lahiri's *Interpreter of Maladies* (1999) clearly reflects the trauma of self-transformation through immigration; Chitra Banerjee Divakaruni's *The Mistress of Spices* (1997) creates an exotic world of magic and myths; *Battle for Bittora: The Story of India's Most Passionate Lok Sabha Contest* (2010) by Anuja Chauhan is a retelling of history and romance; and Amulya Malladi's *The Mango Season* (2003) questions the in-between space of tradition and modernity. However, within its limited space, this essay will essentially focus on the two aforementioned novels with reference to the 'postcolonial' connotations of identity, nationality and neoliberal structures.

Neoliberalism and Cosmopolitan Identity

Pamela Butler and Jigna Desai, in a 2008 article on South Asian American chick lit, offer an important reinterpretation of Indian chick lit. They argue that the typical post-feminist criticism on this sub-genre, focusing only on its consumerist functions and tagging it simply as 'apolitical', has a tendency to overlook the diverse political structures embedded within it. They make a convincing argument that these functional works need to be read with a broader perspective as they produce 'a (trans)national racialized feminine subject embedded within neoliberalism, heteronormativity and racism' (2). Neoliberalism may be defined broadly as a state policy of economic practices that aim to expand the market through the context of globalisation. Butler and

Desai comment, 'As a political ideology, neoliberalism involves a reformulation of liberal individualism through the notion of "choice" and "consumer sovereignty"' (7). Foregrounding the central position of 'choice' in the framework of subject formation, they emphasise that new-gen women's fiction unwittingly promotes individual female subjectivity along with cultural, economic and political baggage. According to them, much of this genre imagines its heroine's agency through their desires and actions as part of a globalised culture, that is, a cosmopolitan way of life that enables the liberation of this new woman, simultaneously mediating the local–national–global matrix (8). Thus, within the much conflicting and ever-shifting paradigms of neoliberalism, these fictional works, despite arguably endorsing some of the laden tropes of ever-evolving patriarchy, bear the potential of resisting vis-à-vis distancing from such stereotypes by placing women's subjectivity as a palimpsest response to male chauvinism.

Priya, the protagonist in Kavita Daswani's *The Village Bride of Beverly Hills*, appears to be a diasporic subject. She moves to California after marriage, where she is continuously coaxed to naturalise Western paradigms of modernisation or, to be more specific, 'neomodernism', culminating in her forced decision of opting for a job. Her mother-in-law asserts: 'This is not India. In the US everybody works' (1). Rajeswari Sunder Rajan has astutely noted the arrival of the 'new Indian Woman', synonymous with the idea of the modern woman, as an ideal model for the capitalist agenda of the state. She identifies the essential characteristics of this class of women as '"new" in the senses both of having evolved and arrived to the response of the times, as well as of being intrinsically "modern" and "liberated"' (124). However, as Ipshita Chanda has succinctly pointed out, the process of this 'modernisation' and 'liberalisation' has been valorised by the state as harmonious and non-conflictual against the contradictions produced by political feminism (67) so that voices of dissent can be suppressed. Priya, being a prototype of this 'new woman', has no option but to take up the job of a receptionist at an entertainment magazine. For the sake of her job, she has to reconsider her sartorial choices with erotic Western attire, though cheap and non-designer, thus taking part in consumerism and the consumption culture. But unlike most chick lit novels, this novel exhibits the desire for beauty culture through economic and ethnic lenses. Priya retains her subjective position through her constant resistance to the homogenous structure of a Western working woman. She cannot afford expensive designer clothes nor does she prefer to evade her ethnic identity; to prove that she attends film premieres in traditional Indian sarees. Her initial inability to consume Western culture makes her ignored and unrecognised; it is only when she successfully consumes and creates her ethnicised feminine identity that she is acknowledged as an equal participant of the ever-dynamic composition of cultural identity. Her hybridity is, therefore, what Homi K. Bhabha identifies as 'a problematic of colonial disavowal, so that other "denied" knowledges enter upon the dominant discourse and estrange the basis of its authority—its rules of recognition' (114). Priya's experience in the diaspora community changes her views of the deep-rooted, prejudiced native discourses regarding the role of working women. As she admits, 'no one in [her] family ... ever worked' (251). Her accidental career makes her realise the basic difference between a working woman, a producer and consumer of the capitalist market, and a homemaker as only a reproductive labourer. Butler and Desai sum this up admirably:

> Here clothing represents a certain form of social capital that reflects the status of the immigrant woman located in the economy of marriage as she moves from her natal home to her marital home; control over consumption is a maker of social hierarchy and status within the immigrant heterosexual household economy. (13)

However, Priya's decision to return to India from the oppressive clutches of her mother-in-law exhibits her choice as a liberated woman who can stand up for herself. Her neoliberal subjectivity enables her to seek a new job in India; at the same time, she realises that she can never fully embrace an American identity. She resides in a hybrid space that marks the complexity of transnational identity. Priya's experience also underlines discursive traces of plurality, pivotal to her sense of identity and notion of existence. Her resistance to falling into the stereotypical categories of chick lit where beauty, consumerism and marriage hold the narrative, makes all the diversions that Indian chick lit can offer.

On a diasporic note, Amulya Malladi's *The Mango Season* presents the other side of transnationalism. Priya Rao, a successful professional living in California, decides to return to India after seven years, but immediately after doing so, she finds her perceptions of India rapidly changing. Whatever as a child was normal to her is now strange: the smells, cows in the streets, the hot and humid weather, all the things she had not noticed before, come to life with different realisations. She wonders, 'Everything that had seemed natural just seven years ago seemed *unnatural* and *chaotic* compared to what I had been living in and within the United States' (14, emphasis mine). The effect of oppositional biculturalism, the anxiety of non-belonging, creates a chasm between her cognitive acculturation of home and host cultures. As a diasporic subject she is both 'rooted and routed' (Gilroy 175), hence a myriad process of 'syncretisation' vis-à-vis contestation must be situated and embodied in the framework of her identity formation. The sense of alienation she experiences in her (imagined) homeland indicates the complex matrix of cross-culturalism. Thus, India seems to be the locus of nostalgia and exoticism to her and the West is the land of freedom and choice, where consumption of both is equivalent to feminist subjectivity. Therefore, the idea of home is transformed from communal, historical and geographical affinity to the culture of cosmopolitanism, consumption and free will:

> Home was in San Francisco with Nick. Home was Whole Foods grocery store and fast food at KFC. Home was Pier 1 and Wal-Mart. Home was 7-Eleven and Starbucks. Hyderabad was a stranger; India was as alien, exasperating, and sometimes exotic to me as it would be to a foreigner. (134)

Although Malladi has demarcated a clear line between the West and the East, where Western culture is exemplary of an unwavering signifier of all possible modalities of emancipation, whether it is economic, social or personal, the novel contains a form of internal incoherence when it comes to neoliberal feminist discourse (Ponzanesi 216). Priya may be categorised as India's new class of capitalist elite brought about by India's economic boom. This emerging class of capitalist elitists is the harbinger of a New India in terms of its international representation. Priya's NRI image reinforces her different status as a new middle class, demographically young, urban and self-consciously cosmopolitan in orientation (Ponzanesi 216). The novel explicitly shows how Priya's 'westernised' interventions change the oppressed ways of life of other female characters. Her aunt keeps the child even though it might be the third girl in a row; the niece becomes vocal of her terms before marriage, emphasising her desire to have a professional life. Therefore, Priya's critique of the orientalist ideologies through the 'Western gaze',[1] in a way, questions the efficacy of the neoliberal ethics in the discursive postcolonial contexts. Such values and politics can be exemplified in Saadia Toor's insightful assertion, 'the way in which the New Orientalism is articulated and used within the global cultural industry, and most importantly, how Indians are turning the Orientalist gaze back upon themselves' (13). This self (oriental) criticism is acknowledged by Malladi with ample sarcasm, 'The American-returned daughter brings in some fancy ideas' (117), yet a great deal of generalisation is applied while analysing the struggle of the 'Third World women' (Mohanty 341) and that of the westernised individual.

Arranged Love Marriage: Conflict or Conciliation?

The claim that chick lit stories are 'formulaic' in structure can be ideally justified by the recurrent themes of marriage and romance. Marriage, whether arranged by the family or a 'love marriage', may appear as a performative trope in most popular fiction, especially in Indian chick lit, where tradition and culture often converge. However, the cultural revival of the post-millennial era has changed the pretext of arranged marriage in India. The new surge of neoliberal feminist subjectivity not only dismantles heteronormative marital prospects but also debunks the social stigma of caste, race and other cultural hegemonies. Marian Aguiar traces the twofold critique of arranged marriage, pointing out that new-age women denounce the functions of an arranged marriage which reflect and support the 'patriarchal, religious, economic, and/or heteronormative power structure' (181). They, rather encouragingly, participate in 'a liberal discourse of freedom' that can be identified with a culture driven by 'Western modernity', a culture that offers Match.com, Tinder, OkCupid and similar dating sites and apps. Put simply, the discourse of romance or love becomes the idealised repository for subjective assertion. The love quest of the young urbanised protagonists thus dominates the main plot of the novels, which eventually leads to a confluence of love and arranged marriage.

The narrative of *The Village Bride of Beverly Hills* opens with the ceremonial marriage of Priya and Sanjay, following the proper traditional customs of arranged marriage. Priya is expected to play the traditional role of a daughter-in-law by cooking, cleaning and reproducing, and yet she has to do a job to maintain her cosmopolitan identity. She takes the abusive remarks of her mother-in-law as a mark of traditional Indian culture, which is intensified by Sanjay's apathy. Furthermore, her assimilation with US culture creates a chasm in her relationship with her husband. It is through this conflict and contradiction between conventional values and modern sensibilities that she finally discovers her true potential. While confessing the truth about her profession, she realises, 'I am not who you think I am, but have become who I always wanted to be' (240). Marriage, in her case, serves as a desirable tool through which she can refurbish her newly discovered self as well as her conjugal life. She had no power over her selection of life partner but, in the end, she rightfully earns her equal place in the marriage. It is only when Sanjay promises to break out from the strings of parental surveillance and abuse that Priya accepts her arranged love marriage.

The Mango Season, on the other hand, focuses more on the aspect of choice than to be chosen in terms of marriage. Priya, as an independent being, takes full charge of her life and refuses to fall into the trap of conventional marriage, even if that jeopardises her relationship with her family. Her transnational feminist vision on the consumption of marriage solely relies upon the 'culture of choice'.[2] That is why, instead of meditating on her family's tradition of finding a proper Indian groom, Priya decides to marry her live-in boyfriend Nick, an African-American, which also foregrounds the interracial conflict, wittily hinted at in the last part of the novel:

> 'And at least', *Ammamma* said with a broad shrug, 'he is white, not some *kallu*.'
> I froze.
> Damn it!
> Had I forgotten to mention Nick was black? (224)

The revelation of Nick's racial identity comes only in the final resolution when Priya's family, after much contestation, agrees to accept an American (but not an African-American) son-in-law. This narrative ploy leaves much space for speculation on the intersectionality of ethnic identities which, in a way, lies at the heart of postcolonial critique. Colourism in South Asian countries, unlike European ones, especially in India, is dialectically interrelated more with casteism than racism. Historically, it goes back to the Aryan invasion in 2000 BCE when caste discrimination was materialised, based mainly on skin colour distinction, which gradually culminated in brahminic supremacy (almost like White 'supremacy') in sociocultural structures, gaining permanent acceptance during British colonial period.[3] Nonetheless, with cultural evolution over time, light skin colour is inextricably associated with economic superiority, success and betterment in life, whereas blackness is perpetually stigmatised as a social signifier of impurity, inferior standard and disgrace. Such dualism of power structure finds its resonance in Frantz Fanon's theorisation of the Manichean worldview of the colonisers, where 'lightness' bears the ascription of goodness and superiority, representing the coloniser, and 'blackness' corroborates uncivilised nature and ignorance, hence associated with indigenous peoples. Bernor Hesse has postulated the continuation of oppression through colourism in contemporary social settings of non-West, non-White countries like India and Sri Lanka through the concept of 'onto-coloniality'. He elaborates on it as:

> the modernity of social realities historically brought into racialized being by colonial regimes of demarcations, designations and deployments, that is to say, as the effects of onto-colonial taxonomies. (658–659)

In Indian matrimonial culture, fairness of skin plays a pivotal role in being socially acceptable for a successful life.[4] Although the novel leaves the conflict unresolved—whether Priya's family ever comes to know about Nick's racial identity, whether she finally marries him or not—the subtle corporeality of 'racialized casteism' (Jayawardene 327) in *The Mango Season* brings forth the conundrum of imperialism, capitalism and neocolonialism, all of which function, quite ironically, under the rubric of postcolonialism.

Conclusion

Given its analytical endeavour, this essay, therefore, has been an attempt to divulge the untapped regions of Indian chick lit with reference to select novels. Although often disregarded as a genre without literary aspiration and excellence, this commercial phenomenon remarkably plays a vital part in upholding the domesticised version of sociopolitical movements in India in a light and humorous manner. The rendition of urban life and customs is exceptionally colourful, with deep insight into the zeitgeist of the nation that is undergoing a rapid transformation under the pressure of globalisation. With the shifting notions of medium specificity and the rapid change in the forms of communication and travel, the co-temporality of commerce and political contestation is presented in the sub-genre with new ideological connotations and peculiarities. The theme of transnationalism is often central, as are the dilemmas that the protagonists face between conforming to homogenised epistemologies, visceral opportunities and the uncertainties of a free will. The two novels discussed above bear testimony to this genre's value as a cultural artefact; more precisely, in Terry Eagleton's view:

> The fact that we always interpret literary works to some extent in the light of our concerns ... might be one reason why certain works of literature seem to retain their value across the centuries. (10)

Indian chick lit's importance lies in its presentation of the heroines' cultural struggles in a neoliberal world that challenge the societal operation of religion, economy and community. In a digitally advanced era, the success of chick lit commendably encourages the enduring force of women telling their stories and forging their identities across generation and cultures.

Notes

1. *Re-Orientalism and Indian Writing in English* by Lisa Lau and Om Prakash Dwivedi offers an insightful discussion of how Indian authors are re-projecting the orientalist gaze back to themselves through the lens of Western epistemological structure. Lau distinguishes the difference between Edward Said's *Orientalism* and *Re-Orientalism,* as the latter is primarily based on a nuanced reading of both Orientalism and Indian writing in English, rather than focusing on a singular idea, functioning as a subversive strategy to question the West/East dichotomy.
2. The idea of 'choice feminism' as an explicit mode of power feminism has been thoroughly elaborated on by Shelley Budgeon in her essay 'The Contradictions of Successful Femininities'.
3. Indrani Chatterjee's 'Abolition by Denial' provides a fascinating study of Indo-Aryanism and its role in establishing the brahminical superstructure and caste discrimination during the colonial period.

4. N. Hussein's 'Colour of Life Achievements' highlights that skin-colour preference alongside caste consciousness are the two major decisive points to judge the parameters of success and failure. With the advent of print media, lighter skin tone has become the signifier of better possibilities in life achievements, hence a highly demanding prospect in matrimonial culture.

Works Cited

Aguiar, Marian. 'Regenerating Tradition through Transnational Popular Culture'. *Arranging Marriage: Conjugal Agency in the South Asian Diaspora*, by Marian Aguiar, University of Minnesota Press, 2018, pp. 181–213.

Ahmed, Waquar, et al., editors. *India's New Economic Policy: A Critical Analysis*. Routledge, 2011.

Appadurai, Arjun, and Carol Breckenridge. 'Public Modernity in India'. *Consuming Modernity: Public Culture in a South Asian World*, edited by Carol Breckenridge, University of Minnesota Press, 1998, pp. 1–20.

Banerjee Divakaruni. *The Mistress of Spices*. Anchor, 1998.

Bhabha, Homi K. *The Location of Culture*. Routledge, 1994.

Budgeon, Shelley. 'The Contradictions of Successful Femininities: Third-Wave Feminism, Postfeminism and New Femininities'. *New Femininities, Postfeminism, Neoliberalism and Subjectivity*, edited by Rosalind Gill and Christina Scharff, Springer, 2011.

Butler, Pamela, and Jigna Desai. 'Manolos, Marriage, and Mantras: Criticism and Transnational Feminism'. *Meridians: Feminism, Race, Transnationalism*, vol. 8, no. 2, 2008.

Chanda, Ipsita. 'Birthing Terrible Beauties: Feminisms and Women's Magazines'. *Economic and Political Weekly*, vol. 26, no. 43, 1991, pp. 67–70.

Chatterjee, Indrani. 'Abolition by Denial: The South Asian Example'. *Abolition and Its Aftermath in Indian Ocean Africa and Asia*, edited by Gwyn Campbell. Routledge, 2005, pp. 137–153.

Chaudhuri, Amit, editor. *The Picador Book of Modern Indian Literature*. Picador, 2001.

Chauhan, Anuja. *Battle for Bittora: The Story of India's Most Passionate Lok Sabha Contest*. HarperCollins Publishers, 2010.

Daswani, Kavita. *The Village Bride of Beverly Hills.* Penguin Plume, 2005.

Eagleton, Terry, editor. *Literary Theory: An Introduction.* University of Minnesota Press, 2003.

Fanon, Frantz. *Black Skin, White Masks: The Experiences of a Black Man in a White World.* Grove, 1967.

Ferriss, Suzanne, and Mallory Young, editors. *Chick Lit: The New Woman's Fiction.* Routledge, 2006.

Foucault, Michel. 'The Confession of the Flesh'. *Power/Knowledge: Selected Interviews and Other Writings, 1972–1977*, edited by C. Gordon, Pantheon, 1980, pp. 194–228.

Gilroy, Paul. *The Black Atlantic: Modernity and Double Consciousness.* Verso, 1993.

Gupta, Suman. 'Indian "Commercial Fiction" in English, the Publishing Industry and Youth Culture'. *Economic and Political Weekly*, vol. 47, no. 5, 2012, pp. 46–53.

Hesse, Bernor. 'Racialized Modernity: An Analytics of White Mythologies'. *Ethnic and Racial Studies*, vol. 30, no. 4, 2007, pp. 643–663.

Hussein, N. 'Colour of Life Achievements: Historical and Media Influences of Identity Formation Based on Skin Colour in South Asia'. *Journal of Intercultural Studies*, vol. 31, no. 4, 2010, pp. 403–424.

Jayawardene, Sureshi M. 'Racialized Casteism: Exposing the Relationship between Race, Caste, and Colorism through the Experiences of Africana People in India and Sri Lanka'. *Journal of African American Studies*, vol. 20, no. 3/4, 2016, pp. 323–345.

Khilnani, Sunil. *The Idea of India.* Penguin India, 1999.

Kramatschek, Claudia. 'Farewell to Spice and Curry'. Translated by Ian Pepper, *Signandsight*, 3 Jan. 2007, www.signandsight.com/features/1117.html. Accessed 7 Nov. 2024.

Kumar, Sunaina. 'The Rise of Ladki-Lit'. *The Indian Express*, 7 Oct. 2006.

Lahiri, Jhumpa. *The Interpreter of Maladies.* Houghton Mifflin, 1999.

Lau, Lisa, and Om Prakash Dwivedi. *Re-Orientalism and Indian Writing in English.* Palgrave Pivot London, 2014.

Malladi, Amulya. *The Mango Season.* University of Ballantine Books, 2003.

Mazza, Cris, and Jeffrey DeShell. *Chick Lit: Postfeminist Fiction.* University of Alabama Press, 2000.

Mishra, Pankaj. 'Midnight's Grandchildren'. *Prospect*, 19 Apr. 1997, www.prospectmagazine.co.uk/culture/55266/midnights-grandchildren. Accessed 7 Nov. 2024.

Mohanty, Chandra T. 'Under Western Eyes: Feminist Scholarship and Colonial Discourses'. *Boundary 2*, vol. 12, no. 3, spring–autumn 1984, pp. 333–358.

Nayar, Radhakrishnan. 'Tryst with Westerny'. *Times Higher Education Supplement*, 27 June 1997.

Oberoi, V.S. 'Indian Chick-lit: A Genre for Desi Girls'. *Transteller: International Journal for English and Literature*, vol. 7, no. 2, Apr. 2017, pp. 127–132.

Ponzanesi, Sandra. 'Postcolonial Chick Lit: Postfeminism or Consumerism?' *The Postcolonial Cultural Industry*, by Sandra Ponzanesi, Palgrave Macmillan, 2014.

Rushdie, Salman, and Elizabeth West, editors. *The Vintage Book of Indian Writing: 1947–1997*. Vintage Books, 1997.

Sunder Rajan, Rajeswari. 'Real and Imagined Women: Politics and/ of Representation'. *Real and Imagined Women: Gender, Culture and Postcolonialism*, by Rajeswari Sunder Rajan. Routledge, 1993, pp. 123–139.

Tickell, Alex, editor. *South Asian Fiction in English: Contemporary Transformations*. Palgrave Macmillan, 2016.

Toor, Saadia. 'Indo-Chic: The Cultural Politics of Consumption in Post-Liberalization India'. *SOAS Literary Review*, vol. 2, July 2000.

Shakespeare in Indian Political Rhetoric

Suchetana Banerjee

> [Shakespeare] is the grandest thing we have yet done. For our honour among foreign nations, as an ornament to our English Household, what item is there that we would not surrender rather than him? Consider now if they asked us, will you give up your Indian Empire or your Shakespeare, you English; never have had any Indian Empire or never have had any Shakespeare? Really, it were a grave question. Official persons would answer doubtless in official language; but we, for our part too, should not we be forced to answer: Indian Empire or no Indian Empire; we cannot do without Shakespeare! Indian Empire will go, at any rate, some day; but this Shakespeare does not go, he lasts forever with us; we cannot give up our Shakespeare!
>
> —Thomas Carlyle, 'Lecture III'
> *On Heroes, Hero-Worship, and the Heroic in History*

Introduction

The importance of Shakespeare in India was first defined in educational institutes and legitimised by courses in British universities, by Anglicised India's reverence for the vast expanse of scholarship on him, and by the political power associated with the English language which worked hard to propagate the image of Shakespeare as Carlyle describes him. But the reception of Shakespeare in India is vast and varied, and narrates a complex story of Western influence on Indian literature. It is essential to note that Shakespeare is the most prestigious cultural symbol for the educated middle class which, according to Sisir Kumar Das, no serious reception study can ignore. Das, in his essay 'Shakespeare in Indian Languages', stresses that the 'Indian encounter with Shakespeare is an essential part of the history of

Indian literary transformation in the last century' (112). Apart from his academic reception, Shakespeare first spoke to Indians from a Calcutta stage in 1756, and since then there have been interpretations and reinterpretations of his works. Shakespeare is still relevant in contemporary culture and is not restricted to only schools, universities and stages, but pervades popular culture and media like cinema, popular music, animation and advertisements. Many of Shakespeare's characters have become standalone cultural stereotypes of romance (Romeo), indecisiveness (Hamlet), jealousy (Othello) or ambition (Lady Macbeth). Shakespeare is an important part of the Indian socio-cultural and political-legal consciousness. His words have often been quoted and misquoted for the purposes of persuasion or argumentation. This essay focuses on instances of quotations from Shakespeare in political and judicial opinion in India. The enquiry leads to larger issues related to the intentionality of text, ambivalence, polyphony and aspects of literary reception of Shakespeare in postcolonial India. This study analyses how the literary is performed in the extra-literary domain of Indian political/legal rhetoric, and how formulations and interpretations of popular stereotypes are made out of his texts to comment on the influence, reception and appropriation of Shakespeare in popular culture. But why quote from Shakespeare in public speeches, statements and judicial opinions? That, as Shakespeare would have said, is the question. Does it signify only a rhetorical need or is it a need to recall a memory of imperial power? Or is it a source of challenge to the Indian literary community outside the scholarly world? The primary intent of this essay is to establish how the appropriation of Shakespeare and his representation helps postcolonial societies intervene in dominant discourses in order to interpolate their cultural realities and utilise the dominant language to explain those realities to a larger audience.

To Be or Not to Be Popular

Is Shakespeare part of popular culture in India? There are various ways to define popular culture because it brings into play a complex combination of meanings of the term 'popular' and 'culture'. An obvious starting point is to say that popular culture is by the people, for the people and of the people. Raymond Williams, while examining notions of 'high culture' and 'popular culture', talks about two kinds of 'popular culture':

> There is a kind of culture that has been developed *by* a people or by the majority of a people to express their own meanings and values, over a range from customs to works. There is also a different kind of culture that has been developed *for* a people by an internal or external social group, and embedded in them by a range of processes from repressive imposition to commercial saturation.

If we agree with the first part of the statement then the utterances of Shakespeare in shared public spaces, social media and judicial institutions are an expression of Shakespeare which holds the intended meaning, albeit Shakespeare is an external import. This was a seminal part of the linguistic imposition but was naturalised into the cultural code of India through various measures. Contemporary research on Shakespeare and popular culture is concerned with Shakespearean productions and reproductions in material culture apart from the usual theatrical and film adaptations. It is also interested in the reinvention, translation, adaptation, citation and appropriation of the plays across a wide range of media. Robert Shaughnessy observes:

> Throughout history, Shakespeare's enduring high-cultural status has coexisted with a multiplicity of other Shakespeares, recycled in stage performance and cinematic adaptation, political discourse, literary and theatrical burlesque, parody, musical quotation, visual iconography, popular romance, tourist itineraries, national myth, and everyday speech. (1)

As noted earlier, the 'popular' is not a singular uncontested term or frame of reference. 'Popular', as well as 'culture', is adaptive as well as imitative. When analysed through variable historical and social conditions, it represents shared values, democratic participation and accessibility. Does the Indian reception of Shakespeare lie only in the literary canon? Is the translation and appropriation of Shakespeare in India vexed only with questions of cultural ownership? Citing examples from social media, newspapers and court judgements, this essay analyses Shakespeare in Indian political rhetoric and thereby questions the cultural ownership of Shakespeare in a postcolonial society.

From Colonial Heritage to Present Reality

In his essay 'Shakespeare in India', Das emphasises that the case of the reception of Shakespeare in India is a unique phenomenon because it does not follow a familiar framework of translation studies or reception studies. The translation of Shakespeare began in India when English education was more or less established and a sizeable population had emerged for whom Shakespeare had become a cultural icon. This elite, English-educated class in India was critical of its literary heritage and wanted to replace the old canon with a new one. The translation of Shakespeare was undertaken by this class which did not require translations but acted as passionate guardians, keeping an eye on all attempts to translate Shakespeare. They were aimed at readers who did not have knowledge of English. These translations were never treated with respect and were looked at only as a useful aid towards the introduction of the bard to the Indian public, the goal being to read Shakespeare in the original language. As mentioned earlier, it was the classroom where Shakespeare was first introduced. The tradition of teaching Shakespeare began with Henry Louis Vivian Derozio, who was also the first Indian to write a poem in English admiring Shakespeare.

Beyond the classroom, Shakespeare has dominated the Indian stage and has heavily influenced the formal structure of dramatic literature in India. Michael Madhusudan Dutt was one of the first modern playwrights to have adopted Shakespeare as his model in judging the newly emerging dramatic literature. Venugopala Charyarr translated *The Merchant of Venice* into Tamil as *Venice Vyapari* in 1874 and claimed that one of his aims was 'to help the Hindu pundit in seeing the great difference between the verisimilitude of the English drama as represented by Shakespeare and the unreality of Hindu drama as a whole' (qtd. in Das, 'Shakespeare in Indian Languages' 116). In the preface of *Vikara Vilasit* (1883), a translation of *Hamlet*, Ganesh Agarkar, a renowned social reformer and close associate of Lokmanya Tilak, writes that one of the main objectives of reading plays of different cultures is to realise the limitations of one's own society (Das, 'Shakespeare in Indian Languages' 120). Girish Chandra Ghosh, Jyotirindranath Tagore, Bharatendu Harish Chandra, Gopal Ganesh Agarkar, Govind Ballal Deval, Mahadev Kolhatkar, Mirza Beg and Aga Hashr, to mention the most distinguished playwrights of the nineteenth and early twentieth centuries representing various Indian languages, were all translators of Shakespeare. Parsi theatre used Shakespeare as the most profitable commodity of entertainment and created a space for successful appropriation. Narratives of appropriation of Shakespeare include translations and adaptations of various kinds, which present a stratified structure, each representing a different Shakespeare formulated and sustained by different cultural groups often working at cross purposes.

The existence of this ambivalence is further observed in the history of the Indian stage, as the Indianisation of Shakespeare followed different strategies. The first was to recast dramatic form into the narrative and assign it to a new and pseudo-Sanskritic sub-genre. The second was to retain the dramatic forms—where all external features of Shakespearean plays were retained but their moral and philosophical aspects discarded. Therefore, a new drama of entertainment was formed, a drama of spectacle and grandeur which culminated in Parsi theatre. Parsi theatre is one of the earliest examples which played an important role in the formation of Indian popular culture. The main objection against Parsi theatre was its total Indianisation of the plays of Shakespeare. Early translations and adaptations reflected the Indian ambivalence to Shakespeare very explicitly, not by altering and restructuring of the texts but at times transforming the tragedies into happy-ending plays. Shankar Ranade's Marathi adaptation of *King Lear* as *Atipid Charit Natak* (1881), a play with a happy ending and no deaths, strongly justified in its preface, was not the Indian inability to grasp the grimness of the great play but an exercise in interpreting one complex cultural text to an equally complex cultural community.

The more serious theatre concerned with strategies of appropriation of Western dramatic traditions responded to Shakespeare with a greater anxiety, towards a synthesis between traditions of music, stage and styles of acting in two different cultures. After independence, Indian theatre directors and playwrights were situating political readings of Shakespearean texts from their historical positions. Names like Ebrahim Alkazi, Utpal Dutt, K.N. Panikkar, Habib Tanvir, Ratan Thiyam and Rajat Kapoor need mention, as all of them came up with different theatrical methodologies of appropriating Shakespeare to create an authentic Indian Shakespeare commensurate to the English bard. Tanvir advocated changes to invest Shakespearean text with new meanings; his play *Kamdev Ka Apna Vasant Ritu Ka Sapna*, an adaptation of *A Midsummer Night's Dream*, utilises non-literate peasant actors and the folk form of Chhattisgarh—nacha.[1] Dutt insisted on interpretations in accordance with what he calls 'the need of the people'. He declares emphatically that 'we are committed to an interpretation of Shakespeare in accordance with the need of our epoch' (qtd. in Majumder 97). Kapoor's productions of Shakespeare are in the format of clown theatre and are in gibberish. In *Hamlet: The Clown Prince*, clowns relate to Hamlet's existential crises, while *I Don't Like It, As You Like It* deals with gender. *Nothing Like Lear* is the journey of an authoritative king and his three daughters. *What's Done Is Done* (an adaptation of *Macbeth*) has a political undercurrent as the play shows what ambition does to a human being, with two clowns coming in and commenting on the scenes. The process of reception of Shakespeare in India is problematised by this plurality of attitudes and experiences, as well as the diversity of interpretations and strategies of appropriation.

This plurality of attitudes and experiences can be analysed through Hans Robert Jauss's argument that the indeterminacy of the text requires a reader to realise its meaning and that readers and readings are always historically situated within specific conditions of reading. This is a rejection of the belief in the timelessness of a literary work. Jauss states, 'A literary work ... is much more like an orchestration that strikes ever new resonances among its readers and that frees the text from the material of the words and brings it to a contemporary existence' (44). Therefore, he establishes that the literary canon contains texts that are able to challenge and extend their readers' expectations and cause the generation of new texts with new meanings.

Uttering Shakespeare

Shakespeare is certainly the most venerable figure in the history of Indian response to Western literature. There have been other writers who have had a recognisable impact on the Indian literary community across time—John Milton, Percy Bysshe Shelley, Lord Byron, Charles Baudelaire, George Eliot, as well as Molière, Bertolt Brecht and Henrik Ibsen. But the Indian response to Shakespeare is not only widespread across languages and cultures but has also persisted the longest. This engagement with Shakespeare began from the early phase of British colonisation in India and continues to thrive. It is not limited only to a literary history of contact, influence, reception and survival, but raises larger questions of politics and culture. In India, an elected representative or bureaucrat or judge addressing a citizen takes a decision about the language they speak in. It may not be a consequential decision, but the language they choose reflects their social and political position in terms of many complex relationships, and implies some cultural burdens. It can be argued that it is the fact of this choice (this self-consciousness about language) that lends to the political rhetoric of India its habitual relationship with the literary. This relationship can be explored through an illustration.

In 2019, Member of Parliament Shashi Tharoor shared a photo on his official Twitter account in which somebody had morphed his face to resemble that of Shakespeare. While sharing the post, the MP responded, 'The most flattering image going around on WhatsApp today—amazed that someone thought of making me into Shakespeare and then actually took the trouble to create this! Thanks to whoever did so (though I am completely unworthy of the honour!)' (qtd. in 'To Be, or Not to Be'). The question is, why was this 'honour' bestowed on him? Tharoor is known for his wordplay and is infamous for baffling the media and the public with recondite words from the English lexicon. He claims that he chooses his words because they are the best ones for the idea he wants to convey. The identification of Tharoor with Shakespeare is possible because the receptive reader in India is cultured in Shakespeare and has a notional idea about his literary language. It needs to be noted that when Tharoor's rhetoric reminds readers of Shakespeare's old English, it is only then the aesthetics of reception bears fruit. The aestheticisation of politics (Benjamin 241) is a synthesis of ideologically opposing categories wherein art is ultimately subordinated to political life and is attempted to be incorporated for political use. The aestheticisation of politics begins by identifying the normative notion of the aesthetic it presupposes—in this case, Shakespeare, set up as an imperial enterprise to educate Indians, is appropriated in Indian literary, performative and cultural representation. Even a quick glance at the history of Shakespeare reception in India confirms the intimate relationship between the process of 'apotheosization of the bard' (Das, 'Shakespeare in India' 45) and the growth of the English-educated community that accepted and appropriated the Western literary canon without much resistance and also defended it with zeal.

The need of the Indian state to enchant India's intellectual life has always been a priority. During his 2012 budget speech, Finance Minister Pranab Mukherjee quoted from *Hamlet* while commenting on tough policy decisions he had to take for the welfare of the economy. Mukherjee quoted, 'I must be cruel only to be kind', to justify the 'cruel' budget and 'kind' intentions of the government ('From Kautilya to Shakespeare'). This quote from Shakespeare is intended to contribute to the positive juxtaposition of the words 'cruel' and 'kind' in the same sentence. This, according to Paul Ricoeur, can be best explained through the idea of 'live metaphors' from his forms of extended discourses. Live metaphor is a kind of discourse, a product of sentences; it presupposes a 'metaphorical twist' (105). It is different from logical propositions which state something is and something is not the case; a live metaphor says 'is' and 'is not' at the same time, resulting in a re-description of reality (Scott-Baumann 598). Shakespeare's poetic language certainly re-describes the reality of the government's 'kind' intentions and 'cruel' budget and Mukherjee's utterance points at the performativity of the live metaphor.

Aristotle defines 'rhetoric' as the ability to see what is possibly persuasive in every given case and the rhetorician as someone who is always able to see what is persuasive. Shakespeare was obsessed with rhetoric (the art of persuasion through language), continually representing not only acts of persuasion, but also the discussion of such acts. Shakespeare is occasionally quoted with the intention of persuasion and to contribute directly to the argument. In 2018, the Supreme Court quoted from *Romeo and Juliet*, 'What's in a name? That which we call a rose / By any other name would smell as sweet', while passing its historic verdict on Section 377 of the Indian Penal Code. Section 377 was introduced in 1861 and made sexual activities 'against the order of nature' illegal. The SC decriminalised the section and legalised gay sex among consenting adults. According to the court, Shakespeare's phrase 'in its basic sense, conveys that what really matters is the essential qualities of the substance and the fundamental characteristics of an entity but not the name by which it or a person is called' (Ray). According to the verdict:

> [T]he name may be a convenient concept for identification but the essence behind the same is the core of identity. Sans identity, the name

> only remains a denotative term. Therefore, the identity is pivotal to one's being.... Identity is equivalent to divinity. (Thakur)

'A rose by any other name would smell as sweet' is a famous saying taken from Juliet's speech where she claims that Romeo's name is her enemy. The name 'Montague' is not really any part of Romeo's physical body; so, what is in the name? Romeo, even if not called 'Romeo', would still retain perfection. Robert Skilton claims that 'such citations share with the traditional citations a utilitarian purpose' (5). The purpose, in this case, would be the recognition of gay sex and perhaps love beyond the heterosexual construct in Indian society. In Shakespeare's Elizabethan England, homosexuality in principle was a crime akin to murder or blasphemy (Bray 2). Therefore, invoking him to decriminalise homosexuality in India might not have been prudent. However, this quotation, as far as the essence of the verdict is concerned, is intended to contribute to the argument. For the purpose of popular persuasion, in order to appeal to the emotional state of the audience, the judge included Shakespeare in his rhetoric.

Another example is the Pebam Ningol Mikoi Devi case of 2010, where Supreme Court quoted Shakespeare to make a point about liberty:

> Individual liberty is a cherished right, one of the most valuable Fundamental Rights guaranteed by the Constitution to the citizens of this Country, wrote Justice H.L. Dattu and proceeded to quote Shakespeare: 'On "liberty", William Shakespeare, the great play writer, has observed that "a man is master of his liberty".' (Varier)

Varier reports that the courts have relied on the bard to deliver insightful judgement on members of the legal community. In 2003, in a case before the Bombay High Court, where the petitioner was a legal practitioner impugned for professional misconduct, the judgement quoted Shakespeare's satirical advice about lawyers: 'We are reminded by what the great English author William

Shakespeare had said about lawyers: "The first thing we should do is let us kill all the lawyers."' (sic).

Romeo, as a literary character, does not anymore concern himself with textual contextualisation. The reason why Shakespeare's characters can survive as freestanding cultural stereotypes is because his heroes can lend dignity to the 'Stoff' (subject matter). According to Raymond Trousson, the heroes of Heroic Themes outgrow their original frame of reference and their memory is kept alive by a body of text (Bandyopadhyay 13). 'The hero of Heroic Themes establishes a system of resonance and coherence—and "resonance" here includes displacement to the extremity of distortion, along with clone-like duplication' (Bandyopadhyay 14). There are generally two possibilities—'difference-in-identity' and 'identity-in-difference'. Romeo fits the first category, 'difference-in-identity', in which the same figure in his revisiting may display a different and even opposite character, whereas in 'identity-in-difference', although bearing different names, each character may be like an emanation of some self-same hero. Romeo, in one such revisit to India, does take on a complex role. The most controversial appropriation of Shakespeare in recent years in the political circles of India was the formation of 'anti-Romeo squads' in Uttar Pradesh to safeguard women. To label the squad after the Shakespearean hero invites a curious reading and is a deliberate political act.[2] The origins of the character of Romeo can be traced back to Pyramus in Ovid's *Metamorphoses*. Pyramus and Thisbe are two ill-fated lovers in Ovid's narrative poem. Romeo's role as an idealistic lover has made the name synonymous with a passionate male lover across languages and cultures. However, in Uttar Pradesh, the idealistic lover who kills himself for his love has turned out be no less than a molester and a criminal. Juliet, while waiting for Romeo, says:

> Come, gentle night, come, loving, black-brow'd night,
> Give me my Romeo; and when he shall die,
> Take him and cut him out in little stars,

> And he will make the face of heaven so fine
> That all the world will be in love with night
> And pay no worship to the garish sun.
> ('Tragedy of Romeo and Juliet')

But to quote the Uttar Pradesh police, a 'Romeo' is an 'asamajik (anti-social), mawaali (ruffian), chichore-type ladke (young man of a frivolous kind)' (Thakur). This ambivalence is interesting to note: it disrupts the authenticity of the text and instead of 'mimicry' leads to 'mockery'. When lines from one of Shakespeare's plays are quoted, should it matter which character, play, act and scene the words are set in? Quoting some fine-sounding words from Shakespeare to embellish a point is a common trend towards mimicry. Mimicry is a kind of performance and every performance intends to reach an audience. The following analysis of a quotation by the prime minister of India highlights the performativity of these quotations in the public sphere popularised by the mainstream media. Narendra Modi, in his radio show *Mann Ki Baat*, displayed his knowledge of Shakespeare while addressing his 'countrymen' about diversity and festivals in India. While making a case for forgiveness, non-violence and brotherhood, he quoted Portia begging Shylock for mercy:

> Shakespeare in his play, *The Merchant of Venice*, while explaining the importance of forgiveness, has written, 'Mercy is twice blest: It blesseth him that gives and him that takes', meaning, the forgiver and the forgiven both stand to receive divine blessing. (qtd. in Thakur)

The ambivalence is very well utilised by these quotations, as it is open to interpretation and justifies the arguments.

This propensity to include Shakespeare's words in political rhetoric is not a recent phenomenon in India. Das, in 'Shakespeare in India', writes:

> In February this year an Indian politician while being hustled off to the prison on a criminal charge, declared his determination to

> fight for justice with a quotation from Shakespeare, 'Fight for the last straw when honour is at stake.' ... [O]ne of the newspapers suggested that a more relevant quotation in the context of financial bungling in the country would have been Iago's words 'put money in thy purse' ... Only within a week the same newspaper ridiculed another political figure for misquoting the last lines of Macbeth, that his speech was indeed 'signifying nothing'. (44)

Ricoeur states that there is an autonomy of text: each time a text is made there is an intentional meaning[3] which is carried out through 'internal dynamic' and 'external projection' (127). The internal dynamic relates to 'the force of belief' that texts carry 'in what is being said' and the external projection relates to saying something '*to somebody*, with the intention of affecting the reader' (Simms 34). The mode of intentionality accompanies the text; it motivates the meaning of a text regardless of the author, so long as the author and the recipient are part of a same culture. In the case of Romeo, for example, the situations of desire, love, passion, hate, violence and death (each leading to the other) are a 'universal constant so long as human nature is a universal constant' (Ricoeur 132). Ricoeur finds this 'autonomy' of the text liberating; the text creates its own world. Then it is the reader's choice to inhabit that world, finding in it situations which explain their own situation:

> What must be interpreted in a text is a proposed world that I could inhabit and wherein I could project one of my ownmost possibilities. That is what I call the world of the text, the world proper to this unique text. (173)

Ricoeur's thinking coincides with that of Roland Barthes, who claims that:

> [A] text is made of multiple writings, drawn from many cultures and entering into mutual relations of dialogue, parody, contestation, but there is one place where this multiplicity is focused and that place is the reader, not, as was hitherto said, the author. (148)

Conclusion

These quotations are points of literary transaction and manifestation of cultural interactions with the colonial heritage. Although they are symptomatic of an attitude of the English-educated Indians for whom Shakespeare is a cultural icon, they expose a range of ambivalent cultural moods and formations which accompany periods of transition and translation. The introduction of Shakespeare in India was a colonial process and it continues as a dominant structure of feeling in Indian literary culture. Carlyle's choice between the Empire and Shakespeare was guided by his vision of unity of the English-speaking people—'virtually one nation'—and the domination of the British bard over a much larger empire than India. Any such vision is irrelevant for India but the legacy of the Empire still persists in the Indian psyche, albeit in a hybridised form. According to Jauss:

> A literary event can continue to have an effect only if those who come after it still or once again respond to it—if there are readers who again appropriate the past work or authors who want to imitate, outdo, or refute it. (23)

A literary work does not offer the same idea or view to each reader in each period. It does not have the timeless essence of a monument. Each time a literary work is read, it strikes new resonances that frees the text/work from the physical world of words and brings it to a contemporary existence. The philological understanding always remains related to interpretation, which focuses on the completion of knowledge (that is, the act of interpreting) via reflection and description as a moment of new understanding. This presupposes a dialogic relationship of present to past, when the work located in the past is drawn back from seclusion and can respond to us when the present reader/listener has posed the question. Alluding to something beyond its realm, the performativity of these quotations from Shakespeare in the public sphere—whether in parliament, courtroom or any form of media—is, in a Bakhtinian sense, a case of hybrid utterance.

It employs only a single speaker but makes use of different kinds of speech; the juxtaposition of different speeches brings with it contradiction and conflict. According to Martina Björklund, every utterance is dialogic—everyday speech as well as written text. This is so because real understanding is responsive and every speaker is a respondent presupposing the existence of preceding utterances, which they may 'build on, polemicize with, or presume as known to the reader'. Hence a special case of links 'in the chain of utterances is formed by the dialogical relations into which utterances on the same theme enter, even if they belong to different people who know nothing about one another' (Björklund 43).

The process of Shakespeare reception in India is problematised by the plurality of attitudes and experiences, and by the diversity of interpretation and strategies of appropriation. Studies on the reception of Shakespeare in Indian popular culture are limited only to theatre and cinema (inevitably Bollywood), and has not been expanded to the arena of the public sphere or rhetoric. The Indian ambivalence to Shakespeare as manifested in political and official rhetoric through diverse modes of appropriation and negotiation reinforces the truth that the political independence of India did not bring any significant change in its relationship with Shakespeare. The relationship is ambivalent because the postcolonial subject is never simply or completely opposed to the colonial literary heritage (Shakespeare) and, as explained above, demonstrates an ambivalent or fluctuating relationship. Therefore, what gets created through this popular (not academic or theatrical but literary) reception of Shakespeare are transcultural forms in India—the Indian reception of the bard decentres him from the canon of English literature and theatre and creates multiple 'hybridised' texts inflected by various cultures.

Notes

1. It is important to note that Tanvir does not feel the need to change the names of either the characters or the locations of the play.

2. Utpal Dutt, in his adaptation of *Romeo and Juliet*, in the form of jatra, changes Verona into Murshidabad and Mantua into Calcutta. By relocating Shakespeare, he transforms Escalus, Prince of Verona, into Nawab Sirajuddaula. Dutt uses a legendary historical figure whose struggle with the British and pathetic defeat was etched in public memory. What was most important in this radical transformation was the postcolonial twist given to the Montague–Capulet strife. By making the two families Hindu and Muslim, the historical and post-partition significance was enhanced.
3. 'For Ricoeur, something only means if it is imbued with what Husserl called *Bedeutungsintention*, "meaning-intention"—in other words, if someone intended the discourse he is examining to be meaningful to someone perceiving it.... [T]he intentional meaning is *not* the same as "what the author intended"' (Simms 34).

Works Cited

Bandyopadhyay, Sibaji. 'Introduction'. *Thematology: Literary Studies in India*, edited by Sibaji Bandyopadhyay, Jadavpur University, 2004, pp. 1–29.

Barthes, Roland. *Image, Music, Text.* Translated by Stephen Heath, Hill and Wang, 1977.

Benjamin, Walter. 'The Work of Art in the Age of Mechanical Reproduction'. *Illuminations*, translated by Harry Zohn, edited by Hannah Arendt, Schocken Books, 1969, pp. 217–251.

Björklund, Martina, 'Mikhail Bakhtin'. *Philosophical Perspectives for Pragmatics*, edited by Marina Sbisà, et al., John Benjamins, 2011, pp. 38–52.

Bray, Alan. 'Homosexuality and the Signs of Male Friendship in Elizabethan England'. *History Workshop Journal*, vol. 29, no. 1, spring 1990, pp. 1–19.

Carlyle, Thomas. *On Heroes, Hero-Worship, and the Heroic in History.* James Fraser, 1841.

Das, Sisir Kumar. 'Shakespeare in India'. *Jadavpur Journal of Comparative Literature*, vol. 35, 1997–98, pp. 40–53.

———. 'Shakespeare in Indian Languages'. *Jadavpur Journal of Comparative Literature*, vol. 36, 1998–99, pp. 111–136.

Dutt, Utpal. 'Taking Shakespeare to the Common Man'. *Utpal Dutt: Godyo Sangraha*, edited by Samik Bandyopadhyay, Dey's, 2011, pp. 7–9.

'From Kautilya to Shakespeare: Budget Gets Modern on Quotes'. *The Hindu*, 16 Mar. 2012, www.thehindu.com/news/national/from-kautilya-to-shakespeare-budget-gets-modern-on-quotes/article3002355.ece. Accessed 20 May 2024.

Jauss, Hans Robert. *Toward an Aesthetic of Reception*. Translated by Timothy Bahti, Harvester, 1982.

Majumder, Swapan. 'Bidyaayotanik Shakespeare'. *Jadavpur Journal of Comparative Literature*, vol. 20–21, 1982–83, pp. 94–117.

Ray, Kalyan. 'Sec 377: Judges Delve into World History, Philosophy'. *Deccan Herald*, 6 Sept. 2018, www.deccanherald.com/india/sec-377-judgment-judges-delve-691382.html. Accessed 20 May 2024.

Ricoeur, Paul. *From Text to Action: Essays in Hermeneutics, II* Translated by Kathleen Blamey and John B. Thompson, Northwestern University Press, 1991.

Scott-Baumann, Alison. 'Text as Action, Action as Text? Ricoeur, λογοσ and the Affirmative Search for Meaning in the "Universe of Discourse"'. *Discourse Studies*, vol. 13, no. 5, Oct. 2011, pp. 593–600.

Shaughnessy, Robert. 'Introduction'. *The Cambridge Companion to Shakespeare and Popular Culture*, edited by Robert Shaughnessy, Cambridge University Press, 2007.

Simms, Karl. *Paul Ricoeur*. Routledge, 2003.

Skilton, Robert. 'Shakespeare and the Supreme Court'. *Gargoyle*, vol. XXI, no. 4, spring 1991, pp. 4–8.

Thakur, Vikram Singh. 'Where Art Thou, Shakespeare?' *The Hindu*, 2 June 2019, www.thehindu.com/opinion/open-page/where-art-thou shakespeare/article27401088.ece. Accessed 20 May 2024.

'"To Be, or Not to Be": Tharoor Says He's Unworthy of Shakespeare Comparison'. *DNA*, 11 Aug. 2019, www.dnaindia.com/india/report-to-be-or-not-to-be-tharoor-says-he-s-unworthy-of-shakespeare-comparison-2780911. Accessed 20 May 2024.

'The Tragedy of Romeo and Juliet, Act III, Scene 2'. *Open Source Shakespeare*, George Mason University, 2003–2024, www.opensource shakespeare.org/views/plays/play_view.php?WorkID=romeojuliet&Act=3&Scene=2&Scope=scene. Accessed 20 May 2024.

Varier, Megha. 'From Dylan to Shakespeare'. *The News Minute*, 22 Jan. 2017, www.thenewsminute.com/article/dylan-shakespeare-literature-often-finds-its-way-indian-courtroom-56122. Accessed 20 May 2024.

Williams, Raymond. 'On High and Popular Culture'. *The New Republic*, 22 Nov. 1974, newrepublic.com/article/79269/high-and-popular-culture. Accessed 20 May 2024.

Millennial Women 'Instapoets'

Online Communities and Subaltern Counter Discourse

Medha Bhadra Chowdhury

The colonial/postcolonial dichotomy that introduced a new geographical configuration of the world as a consequence of European imperialism created its own kind of homogenisation. However, current processes of global and local cultural circulation have produced a sum of various cultural systems and meanings, a sum going far beyond the simple addition of its components. Since the emergence of social media and popular platforms such as Facebook, Twitter, Tumblr and Instagram, a gamut of social experiences and everyday processes of people and communities have entered into the domain of public discourse, creating a new global space. The conditions in Marshall McLuhan's 'Global Village' stressed that the multi-sensuous and multimedia quality of an oral society is, in a new way, restituted in electronic culture.

Social media has transformed the nature of human culture by enabling a conglomeration of voices, identities and purposes. An inter-culturally oriented view of this phenomenon reveals how mass culture has been transformed by social networking services. The cultural landscape has altered substantially in the last few years and the culture industry, which involves the production of works for reproduction and mass culture, has more vigorously adopted a digital character. Here, the term 'culture industry' is used to denote the idea of an affirmative postmodernist culture promoted by mechanisms of the internet and the World Wide Web. From revolutionising fashion, food and travel through trends and hashtags, to creating awareness for social and political issues through cultures of protest, these online applications have challenged the conventional methodological and epistemological limits set upon them.

In light of migration and the globalisation of economic, political and cultural processes, and the transnational character of media representation, no community can now effectively protect itself from coming into contact with other alien or non-native influences. Any culture that mediates itself and communicates itself through media to a public has also inevitably become intercultural, to the extent that the possibility of an ostensible cultural confrontation is largely mitigated in favour of a common discourse which absorbs a variety of influence.

It is easily understood that the overall presence of media in contemporary societies change and shape individual experiences in a number of ways in terms of cognitive processes of perception, aesthetic representations, narrative strategies, institutional and social networks, and collective or private memory. Social media accommodates divergent perspectives focusing on different geographical areas, cultural locations and generations, in order to reveal, as a whole, the complexity and connectedness of a larger virtual society.

Cultures and communities on Instagram and Facebook are bound by common interests and may often reveal underlying ideological inclinations. Through the process of interpellation, they also have a profound impact on self-perception and the construction of identity. This essay focuses on the reconceptualisation and problematisation of the woman subject through online communities on social media. The aim of the study is to explore the specific forms of identity politics and the negotiation of gender relations through this new public sphere.

Taking into consideration the importance of processes of globalisation for the production and transformation of knowledge and cultural norms, the essay will discuss the poetry of Rupi Kaur, Nayyirah Waheed and Nikita Gill on Instagram, and the complexities of interpretation which emerge in their approach towards the identity of 'postcolonial' women in popular culture. The broad context within which these writings are located may be identified as postcoloniality, a condition that describes a specific historical identity, politics and method, and therefore relevant to the present body of research.

Interestingly, two of these writers are a part of the Indian diasporic community and their works are characterised by a hybridity which provokes the articulation of sameness and difference to Western culture. In this discussion, the biological conceptions of race are elided and cultural issues and identity politics are given primacy. The hybridity emerges in a semiotic, discursive and cultural realm, and is further enhanced by the cross-cultural readership it caters to.

Introduced in *The Location of Culture* (1994), Bhabha's theory of hybridity and the third space has dominated postcolonial and cultural studies. Bhabha redefines culture, discourse and identity as fluid and ambivalent, rather than fixed and one-dimensional. As theorised by Bhabha, the third space is interchangeable with hybridity, or more precisely, hybridity is the third space:

> All forms of culture are continually in a process of hybridity. But for me the importance of hybridity is not to be able to trace two original moments from which the third emerges, rather hybridity to me is the 'third space' which enables other positions to emerge.... [T]he process of cultural hybridity gives rise to something different, something new and unrecognisable, a new area of negotiation of meaning and representation. (211)

In its actual formulation, the third space, like hybridity, is posited as a site of subversion, displacement, newness, renegotiation of cultures and identities, and multiple positionality. Bhabha emphasises the creative and radical potential of the third space in terms of a site where new discourses emerge.

The works of these young women poets suggest a wide range of cultural references and appeal to a mass culture, displacing the traditional canon of English poetry for its modern readers who are more familiar with an Instagram culture than the discipline of literature. They exist in a hybrid digital universe with a plethora of communities mimicking the structures of collective society and developing through interpersonal interaction. To use Bhabha's terminology in the present context, this re-imagined third space may be interpreted in terms of a positive, emancipating arena where aesthetic and generic boundaries collapse and sub-cultural identities assume a fluid nature based upon the specifics of interaction. The multiple, open-ended intellectual and interpretative paradigm present here enables the emergence of new meaning and representation.

These new 'hybrid' poets, who have acquired celebrity status, function as both influencers and creative producers, and through their poetry they present vastly multiplying opportunities for exchange and reproduction. Through their work they attempt to construct belonging and identity, albeit through a virtual society. They have changed the character of leisure to a neo-liberal notion that the leisure space on Instagram or Facebook can serve as an identity-making space with serious implications.

The hybridity of form and language in this poetry is also an important consideration. Firstly, the aesthetic of Instagram and Facebook enables the creation of thematic collages from multiple media and represents a form of visual art. Secondly, the minimalist expression, the colloquialism and neologism challenge the discourse of poetic language and the creations are thus opened up to young readers from diverse cultural backgrounds.

Their poetry further establishes an intersectionality of social and ideological positions and cross-cultural identities within a new space. Within the shared media culture where this poetry has grown, these poets allow for new and wider modes of personal and collective cultural identification. The politics of identity which is played out is in this sense intrinsically connected to a particular understanding of agency, apprehended as the faculty that enables autonomous subjects to transform certain practices or norms or to act self-consciously for their emancipation.

The polarities of cultural location are often diminished as this poetic movement engages in a shared critique of the troubled and fixed boundaries of patriarchal thought and of the 'constituted female subject' which is produced through mechanisms of male power. Of equal significance is the fact that this poetry contests institutional structures and transforms political issues. It has a galvanising political effect on women of the poets' generation. These poets not only express ideas, but in their recent support of the Me Too and Time's Up campaigns, they have shifted emphasis and created young active political communities. Rupi Kaur, for instance, discusses the trauma of sexual abuse in her poem '#metoo' by relating the patterns of exploitation to close family members or acquaintances, who often exhibit the same male predatory tendencies which women survivors have recently drawn public attention to as a part of the Me Too movement. Nikita Gill, in her poems 'Me Too (Trigger Warning)' and 'When They Catch the Abuser', also addresses the issues of sexual abuse and exploitation of women, emphasising the need for public redressal of 'monstrous actions' and crimes against women.

In many ways, through their poetry, the conceptualisation of a collective international youth culture is actually made possible. The effect of this feminist rethinking of politics is to shift the terrain of what could be counted as 'political' and introduce the issue of gender into mainstream politics.

These women poets critically engage with structures of domination—patriarchy's forms of sexual essentialism, belittlement and contempt—and resistance through writing. Examining issues of gender inequality and empowerment, their resonance is far-reaching and has resulted in a new kind of feminist activism. Rupi Kaur and Nikita Gill have gone on to publish anthologies of poems in print and have avoided classification as 'Instapoets'. Rupi Kaur, for example, who has 4.5 million followers on Instagram (as of February 2024), published her first anthology *milk and honey* (2015) combining poetry with hand-drawn illustrations. The publication of Kaur's book witnessed unprecedented sales which were encouraged no doubt by online marketing. Other Instagram writers such as Amanda Lovelace, r.h. Sin and Atticus have also made a foray into the dominant print culture capitalism and successfully transitioned from social media to print publishing. However, the publication of their poetry does not undermine their radical identities as 'Instapoets', since the young readers they cater to not only subscribe to their pages online but actively purchase physical copies, making these writers international bestsellers. The cultural trends spawned on social media are enthusiastically absorbed by the print industry and the publication of Instapoetry has proved profitable for publishing houses by reviving the fledgling popularity of printed volumes of poetry among youngsters.

While it is easy to dismiss this as writing that relies on flashy visual triggers and homespun language rather than a critical engagement with rhythm and words, Instapoetry is distinct in terms of promoting self-help and self-improvement among women of the younger generation. It relates to millennial 'coming of age' experiences and creates a strong sense of collaborative ethos by inviting engagement from the wider audience who can post responses or share their own experiences via comments.

Through their poetry, these poets have openly or implicitly spelled out, in a terminology of empowerment and disempowerment, issues related to women's experiences. They reflect on typically feminist issues such as emancipation from patriarchal control and oppressive standards of femininity. Through their very position as women subjects, they trace the subjective patterns of women's experiences determined by power, prejudice and discrimination, and indicate the need to reclaim agency.

The construction of women in terms of their body and sexuality is an important aspect of Instapoetry and the visceral quality of description makes these poems appealing to a generation struggling with issues of identity. Many of these poems deal with mental health, depression, anxiety and body image issues. Nikita Gill writes about the need for women to overcome their dissatisfaction with their bodies and distorted perceptions of beauty in her poems 'If All Girls' and 'Don't Be Beautiful'.

Addressing a young audience on a digital platform, where the flow of information has gained such speed and dynamic that it often becomes difficult to relate to available content in a meaningful way, these poems are expressions of desire and intimate feeling. Nikita Gill, in an interview with *Culture Trip* published on 25 April 2016, spoke about the subjective quality of her poetry:

> My greatest influence is empathy and my greatest teacher is experience. And for a sensitive person who wears her heart on her sleeve, empathy for other people's suffering has always made me want to help them in any way I can. And experience from my own suffering as well as theirs has taught me how to write about it. (Millar)

Though reclusive in person, Nayyirah Waheed does not shy away from critiquing the notions of desirability and consequently its distortions which accompany the popular representation of women in the public domain. The relationship of the self with one's body and the need for bodily autonomy is at the centre of Waheed's poetry. These issues are further extended to puberty, menstruation, reproduction, motherhood, queer love, and other experiences, in order to associate with a wider spectrum of readers of different ages and social groups, who often seek a form of emotional well-being through reading.

In this respect, Rupi Kaur's controversial post on Instagram with an image of her posing in a pair of period-stained track pants and bed sheet is worth mentioning, since it recorded an outpouring of public support when the post was removed by the social media site. In an interview with CBS News published on 26 February 2018, she mentioned how it 'just turned [from] being a small project to my form of protest' ('Rupi Kaur'). While the poetry of women poets on Instagram is generally supportive of feminism, the status of social media sites as capitalist products makes it difficult to regard them as unproblematically feminist. The tension between maintaining a sustainable position in the market and practising feminist principles was articulated by Rupi Kaur in her interview with CBS News where she discussed how the image was censored for 'violating community guidelines'. However, it is important to consider the fact that the images and poems are also designed to cultivate certain responses and generate followers. The free access and democratised content of their poetry arguably encourage a mass consciousness by downplaying the hierarchies between reader and writer and shifting towards the idea of a progressive feminist media, but the liberal feminist consciousness is often complicated by commercial interests and publicity strategies.

The response of audiences has also been sufficiently conflicted and range from sincere appreciation to scathing attacks. Instapoetry does not elicit scholarly interest in the same way as more traditional 'literary' texts. Jed Rasula argues: 'In a curious way, Internet poetry can be compared to the American colonies circa 1760: full of enterprise and ingenuity, but a world apart, a realm of negligible consequence to an unheeding mother country and its culture' (183). Rasula observes in the chaotic and complex structure of digital poetry a schism or separation from norm. Instapoetry moves away from conventional style and diction, presenting perceptual challenges and testing the boundaries of the 'literary'. Audience feedback is therefore pivotal in confirming the aesthetic dimensions of Instapoetry.

Jay Sizemore, writing for the *Medium*, an online publishing platform, remarks that 'Rupi Kaur is not a poet. It's a disgrace to the art to pretend this is the case.... [H]er work consists of short, truncated maxims, easy to digest cliches, pandering sentimental tropes, and pretentious plays on words presented as photographic memes intended to go viral online'. The article further attributes the popularity of Kaur's poetry among young women to her 'contrived' posture as 'an oppressed feminist'.

Contrarily, Priya Khaira Hanks, writing in the *Guardian* (4 October 2017) asserts that 'to read Kaur's success as an omen of the death of poetry would be to unfairly dismiss writing that contains bravery, beauty and wisdom'. Pooja Sivaraman writes in *Homegrown* (8 June 2021): 'Her descriptions of the South Asian experience, diluted as they may be, were a beacon to readers feeling poetically abandoned.' Furthermore, Ephrat Livni, in *Quartz* (31 January 2018), associates Kaur and other Instagram poets with rebellious artists across generations who have interrogated norms and introduced innovations by defying conventional wisdom, a modern digital version of the nineteenth-century Parisian 'show of rejects':

> The poets are innovating by using social media to popularize a form of writing, a tradition, that seemed not long ago like it was about to be irrelevant—poetry. They're igniting intellectual debates. And they're calling into question the authority of their elders, as well as stuffy old rules about what an artist must know before she can create. They're doing exactly what rebellious artists have always done.

Kaur's poetry has even been the subject of academic dissertations, such as Valerio Guido Masini's 'Rupi Kaur's Poetry: Trauma and Healing' in which the author claims that

> Rupi Kaur's works are representatives of a traumatic post-memorial type of literature, which enables its author, and its readers, to reflect on one's own traumatic memories, as well as on others' trauma-related memories, in order to give a meaning to one's trauma and reclaim one's active life back. (3)

Rupi Kaur has written on rape, domestic violence and alcoholism, which she admitted, in an interview with the *Guardian*, was 'scary' considering the discomfort it may have caused, but she mentions that her followers 'stayed for the poetry and that was such a beautiful gift in disguise' (Kassam). The issue of sexual abuse among children and adolescents is explicitly evoked through Kaur's poem 'midweek sessions' and is one of the many complex subjects discussed through her Instagram posts. The public sphere, characterised by a cultural hybridity, exists in a de-territorialised cyberspace and builds communities which are based on a strong sense of general interest. Women find themselves actively involved in this virtual public space expressing the need for self-interpretation within a male-centric society and indicating a movement towards a far-reaching social transformation. This discursive intervention is accompanied by feminist efforts to provide for some of the needs that are politicised and reinterpreted.

Nancy Fraser conceptualises the emerging public sphere in an age of global media as transforming the normative legitimacy and political efficacy of public opinion. According to Fraser, the public opinion expressed within a public sphere is traditionally considered legitimate if all who are potentially affected are able to participate as peers in deliberations considering their common affairs. Inclusiveness and consequently participatory parity are key features of this public domain and implies that all interlocutors must, in principle, enjoy roughly equal chances to state their views, discuss relevant issues, question the tacit and explicit assumptions of others, switch levels as needed, and generally receive a fair hearing.

Rebutting the liberal view that it was possible for interlocutors in a public sphere to bracket status and class differentials and to deliberate 'as if' they were peers, Fraser discusses the massive inequalities which exist within this broad field. Complicating the standard liberal picture of a single comprehensive public sphere, Fraser claims that the proliferation of 'subaltern counterpublics' could enhance the participation of subordinate strata in stratified societies. The public sphere is dominated by a 'universal class' or a stratum of bourgeois men who control the basis of power.

In this context, these online communities on Instagram and Facebook may be regarded as 'subaltern counterpublics', consisting predominantly of women who contest the bourgeois masculinist bias in the public domain through their writing. This involves building a counter civil society of alternative women-only voluntary associations on digital platforms. According to Fraser, the public sphere of discourse is intimately associated with the state apparatus and an overarching patriarchal vision, which assumes an authoritarian absolute form instead of a participatory democratic form. Women often find themselves excluded from the public sphere and faced with established forms of male, epistemic superiority even within a virtual world, which claims to be objectively democratic.

The approximate ideals of democracy, equality and fairness which are projected by social media create an impression that it promotes egalitarian relations between different sections of society. However, women are systematically exposed to misogyny, discrimination, and patterns of dominance within the virtual public space. The poetry of women writers on Instagram critiques the structures of power and masculine privilege and initiates a counter discourse which seeks to reveal the hostility and gender inequality perpetuated through social tradition.

Nayyirah Waheed writes about the systems of patriarchal oppression which operate on the individual from a young age. She presents the image of a male child who grows in the mother's womb but learns the practices and codes of masculinity which undermine the presence of the feminine (8). Waheed's poems not only react to male authority but also recognise the intersecting oppressions and the entwinement of women-specific struggles with other hierarchies of power. She investigates the traditional notions of subjectivity, agency and autonomy that have been created for women and addresses broader issues of responsibility and emancipation. The poetry of Waheed and her contemporaries indicate an adaptive, responsive online movement encompassing both social and cultural symbolic concerns. They are in some ways interconnected, informing, stimulating and shaping each other.

The new generation of women poets who have emerged onto the scene suggest alternative norms of public speech and modes of participation. They negotiate their position within the official public sphere by forming subaltern online groups of women, who coalesce in order to voice their private needs and interests. Challenging the nexus of patriarchy, globalisation and neo-liberalism, the online communities compete with the exclusionary norms and ideological values which determine what is fit to be a part of the mainstream 'public' discourse.

Nancy Fraser, in her essay 'Rethinking the Public Sphere: A Contribution to the Critique of Actually Existing Democracy', records the discrepancies between the masculinist public discourse and the counter discourse which originates from subordinated positions:

> Feminist research has documented a syndrome that many of us have observed … men tend to interrupt women more than women interrupt men; men also tend to speak more than women, taking more turns and longer turns; and women's interventions are more often ignored or not responded to than men's. (63–64)

Informal societal pressures persist on social media and everyday life contexts are often replicated in terms of marginalised positions which women assume even in the virtual world. Women are often subject to trolls and vicious memes online, and they continue to be victims of cyber-bullying and a shame culture on public platforms, which suppress their agency and uphold structural gender inequalities.

Within the 'democracy' of social media, women's voices are often interrupted and therefore these parallel discursive arenas 'where members of subordinated social groups invent and circulate counter discourses … in turn permit them to formulate oppositional interpretations of their identities, interests, and needs' (67). Fraser finds the most striking example of an effective feminist subaltern counterpublic in the United States, where feminist women in the public sphere 'invented new terms for describing social reality, including "sexism", "the double shift", "sexual harassment", and "marital, date, and acquaintance rape"' (67). These are terms which have gained further currency through social media and these are precisely the kind of issues which millennial poets on Instagram write about.

But while the proliferation of 'subaltern counterpublics' implies a widening of discursive contestation and may largely be considered positive, this digital space occupied by Instagram poets is not a neutral cultural domain. The poetry constitutes a culturally and ideologically charged medium with significant epistemological implications. It is conditioned by cultural, ideological and political cartographies in which power operates in the guise of an ethics of cultural exchange and solidarity.

While this kind of poetry may be understood as creating new spaces and structures, influencing new cultural trends and thought, it is also hegemonising in terms of the elite privileged class it caters to. It may be erroneous to categorise bourgeois or educated middle class women as 'subaltern', since they often wield a hegemonic power over those excluded from this category and replicate patterns of subordination. In promoting a universal mode of being and meaning for women, this new discourse tends to flatten out the very multiplicity it celebrates. Despite their diasporic backgrounds, these poets write for a predominantly Western or westernised audience even though Rupi Kaur, an Indian-born Canadian, has claimed that she writes about the experiences of South Asian women.

The reality of multiple divisions within contemporary Indian society complicates the analysis and reception of this form of poetry, and it cannot be given equal epistemological, ideological and ethical value as in the Western context. The issue of class hierarchy and a homogenised female subjectivity occur profoundly since they often collude with or reinforce dominant structures of privilege related to cultural identity and class, despite the gestures of defiance or subversion implicit in them. Therefore, the sign of global feminism in these works may in fact appear to be simplistic upon a context-based examination. These counterpublics often fail to accommodate a wide cross-section of women who remain on the margins.

Developing countries are characterised by severe inequities in class, caste, community and gender relations, which profoundly weaken the analytical, ethical and epistemological potential of this kind of writing. Social media may be regarded as capitalism's promotion of new patterns of consumption in the interests of profit. Within third-world capitalist societies, inequalities are even more pronounced. While this poetry contains an emancipatory potential for women as undervalued subjects, it is a privileged means of expression and resistance. The discursive conditions of dominance exist within a rhetoric which appropriates a foreign language and is a reified presentation of deep, high-thinking ideas already ingrained within a privileged set of individuals. It uses a vocabulary to write for and appeal to a mind that is comfortable thinking and presenting their thoughts in English.

The medium of circulation is also an important subsidiary concern since Instagram is fundamentally a tool which is popular with a privileged, predominantly young, and urban population in the country. While it may appear to be a truism that the internet has become a product of mass consumption, proliferating interior districts and villages, there are still many sections of society who are deprived of this privilege and cannot be stakeholders in this enterprise. Undoubtedly, Instagram is a multi-layered system of cultural transaction and representation which excludes as much as it includes even within subaltern counter cultures. It is distinctly urban and commercial although it assumes a world where we are all classless consumers, picking and choosing our identities.

Instagram poetry discusses subjects which are largely restricted to an urban culture with a degree of political autonomy and economic development. Social pathologies like adultery, alcoholism, loneliness and depression have a distinct class consciousness and cultural echo in these works and appeal to the sensibilities of a young, Western-educated, urban demographic that is closely involved in a process of cultural westernisation in terms of adapting to the persistent intellectual, creative and habit-forming effect of Western societies. Further, urban cultural roles necessitate certain lifestyles and youngsters are drawn into online communities in order to be integrated within a popular culture.

The category of experience must therefore be re-evaluated since it requires the investment of our desires and the acknowledgement of our politics as women. Formative and professional experiences often play a critical function in terms of shaping identity and accessing these online communities on social media. The general applicability of concepts and cultural translatability is complicated because experiences are curtailed to particular locations, identities and class affiliations. These assimilative attempts based on the politics of inclusion reinforce the elements shared but they also tend to perpetuate the difference in power that social hierarchies within counter cultures produce. Therefore, focusing on class distinctions and identity-based politics is important in the context of reading this poetry within multicultural, socially diverse postcolonial countries, where subalternity may assume a variety of definitions.

Works Cited

Bhabha, Homi K. *The Location of Culture*. New York, Routledge, 2012.

Fraser, Nancy. 'Rethinking the Public Sphere: A Contribution to the Critique of Actually Existing Democracy'. *Social Text*, 25.26, 1990, pp. 56–80.

Gill, Nikita. 'Don't Be Beautiful'. Screenshot of poem posted by Jennifer Gray. *Facebook*, 31 Jan. 2017, www.facebook.com/photo.php?fbid=10212389369559199. Accessed 17 Apr. 2024.

Gill, Nikita [@nikita_gill]. 'If All Girls'. *Instagram*, 12 Jan. 2018, www.instagram.com/p/Bd04fyBnUPg. Accessed 17 Apr. 2024.

———. 'Me Too (Trigger Warning)'. *Instagram*, 19 Oct. 2017, www.instagram.com/p/Bab4x9Qgd9P. Accessed 17 Apr. 2024.

———. 'When They Catch the Abuser'. *Instagram*, 16 Dec. 2021, www.instagram.com/p/CXjCVWuo3wT. Accessed 17 Apr. 2024.

Kassam, Ashifa. 'Rupi Kaur: "There was no market for poetry about trauma, abuse and healing"'. *The Guardian*, 26 Aug. 2016, www.theguardian.com/books/2016/aug/26/rupi-kaur-poetry-canada-instagram-banned-photo. Accessed 17 Apr. 2024.

Kaur, Rupi. '#metoo'. *Facebook*, 16 Oct. 2017, www.facebook.com/rupikaurpoetry/photos/a.697466973680915/1563054113788859. Accessed 17 Apr. 2024.

Kaur, Rupi [@rupikaur_]. 'midweek sessions'. *Instagram*, 7 Sept. 2015, www.instagram.com/p/7T-7wsnA_o. Accessed 17 Apr. 2024.

Khaira-Hanks, Priya. 'Rupi Kaur: the inevitable backlash against Instagram's favourite poet'. *The Guardian*, 4 Oct. 2017, www.theguardian.com/books/booksblog/2017/oct/04/rupi-kaur-instapoets-the-sun-and-her-flowers. Accessed 17 Apr. 2024.

Livni, Ephrat. 'In defense of Rupi Kaur and Instagram's "pop poets"'. *Quartz*, 31 Jan. 2018, qz.com/quartzy/1192915/in-defense-of-rupi-kaur-and-instagrams-pop-poets. Accessed 17 Apr. 2024.

Masini, Valerio Guido. *Rupi Kaur's Poetry: Trauma and Healing*. 2019. Università degli Studi di Padova, Master's degree dissertation.

McLuhan, Marshall. *Understanding Media: The Extensions of Man*. McGraw-Hill, 2003.

Millar, Remy. 'Poetry in the Social Media Age: Interview with Nikita Gill'. *Culture Trip*, 25 Apr. 2016, theculturetrip.com/europe/united-kingdom/england/london/articles/poetry-in-the-social-media-age-interview-with-nikita-gill. Accessed 17 Apr. 2024.

Rasula, Jed. *Syncopations: The Stress of Innovation in Contemporary American Poetry*. University of Alabama Press, 2004.

'Rupi Kaur on the simplicity of her poetry and the rise of "Instapoets"'. *CBS News*, 26 Feb. 2018. www.cbsnews.com/news/rupi-kaur-on-instapoets-the-sun-and-her-flowers. Accessed 17 Apr. 2024.

Sivaraman, Pooja. 'In Defence of Rupi Kaur'. *Homegrown*, 8 June 2021, homegrown.co.in/homegrown-explore/in-defense-of-rupi-kaur. Accessed 17 Apr. 2024.

Sizemore, Jay. 'Rupi Kaur Is Not a Poet'. *Medium*, 20 Nov. 2020, medium.com/the-pom/rupi-kaur-is-not-a-poet-4994829f18f9. Accessed 17 Apr. 2024.

Waheed, Nayyirah. *salt*. 2013.

Missing Girls Trafficked and Saved

Meaningful Social Change through Digital Gaming in Postcolonial South Asia

Siddhartha Chakraborti

Digital gaming in South Asia started out with popular titles from the first world finding appreciation amongst the budding console-gaming, and later personal-gaming, aficionados of the region. The earliest memories of digital gaming in the subcontinent would be of console games like *Super Mario Bros.* (Nintendo, 1985) and *Contra* (Konami, 1988) which retained their popularity well into the 2000s. With the advent of personal computers and MS-DOS–based games like *Prince of Persia* (Broderbund, 1990) and *Wolfenstein 3D* (id Software, 1992), gaming shifted from controllers and joysticks to keyboards and mice. Later, with the return to consoles with Xbox and PlayStation, mainstream gaming in South Asia continued to be dominated by titles designed and created outside the region, particularly in the advanced first world.

At this juncture, it is important to highlight that I am situating the first world in its traditional sense of constituting advanced Western capitalist nations. Strikingly, the second world, that is the communist bloc, did not significantly influence narrative-based gaming in the subcontinent, although the megahit popularity of the game *Tetris* (1985) by Alexey Pajitnov is proof that there was interest in games being produced there. In the third world—united in its shared history of being postcolonial, besides its telling feature of mixed economies with strong regulations—the gaming industry took some time to take off.

As such, the sensibilities and concerns of the games, and by extension the concerns regarding gaming in South Asia, continued to mimic the concerns of the first world. Without going into specifics, the concerns can be divided into two axes. The first was the impact of the depiction of violence, in particular after the popularity of the first-person shooter *Counter-Strike* (Valve, 2000) and its sequels. The second, arguably milder concern, was the place of women in gaming, both as characters in game worlds and their participation as gamers. Recently, there has been a shift to include concerns regarding the representation of persons with disabilities, dalits, Muslims and tribals in digital media. Indeed, even a cursory search online brings up many popular narratives, news pieces and 'scholarly' articles that argue whether violent video games cause real-life violence or psychological disorders (with a growing consensus that they do not), and debate how women and other marginalised groups are depicted, or discuss how they do not find space and acceptance—either as playable characters or as gamers—within largely male, upper-caste, upper-class, ableist, gaming communities. Again, both these concerns mirror existing concerns within the wider community of gamers and gaming scholars globally. Such scholars are particularly rooted in discourses of and from technologically advanced nations, and carry the mantle of the first world into our unipolar present.

Today, we must also place digital gaming in South Asia in the context of the fledgling gaming industries of the region. While Pakistan has yet to develop any role-playing games apart from *GTA* mods[1] (Attarwala), Bhutan has not yet made any games or gaming mods at all (Fujiwara). The gaming industry is comparatively more developed in Nepal, but there too the focus is mostly on single-player mobile games owing to problems related to financial viability (Rana). More interestingly, in 2019, a playable demo of the game *Chronicles of the Himalayas* (Sroth Code Games) was released with the storyline of a young Sherpa boy in search of his father. The game proceeds through exploration and interaction in a semi–open-world game map, and works hard to establish a unique Nepali voice through set design and architecture, background music, character features, costumes and so on.

The game also makes use of the Nepali exotic—yetis and other mythical Himalayan monsters appear as antagonists who must be overcome. Unfortunately, the game was never commercially released. Bangladeshi coders, on the other hand, have produced role-playing games based on the Liberation War. Two games—*Arunodoyer Agnishikha* (Trimatrik Interactive, 2004) and *Heroes of 71: Shamsu Bahini* (Mindfisher Games Inc, 2015)—exemplify the general concerns that can be found across various spinoffs and sequels that are designed to relive the events leading up to the independence of Bangladesh, including the rounding up of Bengalis in camps, armed uprisings and guerrilla action. The games almost identically present uniformed Pakistani soldiers or Urdu-speaking characters as villains who must be killed in order to liberate Bengali-speaking, lungi-clad Mukti Bahini guerrillas or saree-clad Bengali women. Sri Lankan games have a wider range, with games like *Koombiyo* (KodeX, 2019) taking off from the popular television series of the same name; *Operation Wanni* and *Operation Wanni 2* (DragonD soft, 2010) based on the war against the LTTE; and the epic open-world RPG *Kanchayudha* (Arimac Games, 2017) set in ancient Sri Lanka. As such, in Sri Lanka too the dominant gaming voice is an assertion of the nation, whether it be in opposition to Tamil aspirations of armed self-determination in the northern province of the island, or in the evocation of a rich, glorious, mythical past.

In India, which is disproportionately larger in terms of resources, the gaming industry is nonetheless at a nascent stage. With an inglorious beginning, in an attempt to cash in on the wave of patriotism generated by the Kargil War, India's first game was *Yoddha: The Warrior* (Indiagames, 2000), followed by low-quality games to popularise Bollywood movies like *Bhagat Singh* (2002), a trend that continued with *Ghajini* (2008) and *Ra.One* (2011). Most efforts of the Indian gaming industry in the early 2000s were eminently forgettable in terms of narrative, plot or gameplay. However, at least two game developments must find mention in creating an effective gaming experience.

The first, *Unrest* (Pyrodactyl Games, 2014), employing choice-based gameplay involving voluminous text, bravely foraged into unknown territory, bringing a range of social issues from gender to caste into its story, set in a fictional ancient Indian city. The second, *Asura* (Ogre Head Studio, 2017), while employing hack-and-slash gameplay, draws from Indian mythology and takes up the issue of caste in its intricate cinematic backstory. Both games use words from Sanskrit and employ background scores that are distinctively based on Indian classical music, besides character and set designs that take into account influences from the Vedic to the Indo-Saracenic in order to clearly place themselves as assertions of the Indian nation.

After this short survey, what is clear is that gaming in the subcontinent must be placed largely in a postcolonial context, that is to say, they are determined by the overarching historical fact of colonialism and the struggle for national identity. This is particularly highlighted in mature role-playing games from Bangladesh, Nepal and Sri Lanka that go back, respectively, to the independence struggle, to a search for identity, and to the horrors of the Tamil uprising or to an ancient past. The games from India too, all go back to the same seminal issues of asserting a 'post-' identity, with gaming literally beginning with the assertion of the Indian nation during the Kargil War, perhaps somewhat problematised later along the lines of gender and caste. However, in all these games the protagonist is in search of asserting a subsumed identity—whether it be of class, race, caste or nation. In some ways, the majority of the gaming experiences being offered would tie in neatly with Fredric Jameson's observations in his seminal 1986 essay 'Third-World Literature in the Era of Multinational Capitalism', where he notes that:

> All third-world texts are necessarily, I want to argue, allegorical, and in a very specific way: they are to be read as what I will call national allegories, even when, or perhaps I should say, particularly when their forms develop out of predominantly western machineries of representation.... (69)

These include, I argue, digital gaming. Of course, we must keep in mind that the allegory of the nation may be different for various groups within the boundaries of a country, especially in large countries with significant diversity. Nonetheless, the dominant expression of an imagination—that is, the social imaginaries—articulated through these games is that of a form of cultural identity assertion which is rooted either in a moment of crisis for the nation in the recent present or drawn from some ahistorical, but mythically real, past designed to relive some golden age.

At the same time, we must take note that all the games surveyed also seek to be representational voices. In this context we must keep in mind Nancy Fraser's observations, first articulated in her 1996 Tanner Lecture on Human Values, 'Social Justice in the Age of Identity Politics: Redistribution, Recognition, and Participation', where she observes:

> The discourse of social justice, once centred on distribution, is now increasingly divided between claims for redistribution, on the one hand, and claims for recognition, on the other. Increasingly, too, recognition claims tend to predominate. The demise of communism, the surge of free-market ideology, the rise of 'identity politics' in both its fundamentalist and progressive forms—all these developments have conspired to decentre, if not to extinguish, claims for egalitarian redistribution. (3–4)

In this context, it becomes important to highlight that the survey of games that I have gone through points to an emphasis on representing identities—whether it be of a nation, of a caste or a people in the context of that nation's particular postcolonial history. Further, since all of the games produced in the subcontinent were developed after the demise of the Soviet Union, and arguably the demise of the second world, the concerns of redistribution and resistance have given way to concerns either of representation (for example, in games like *Chronicles of the Himalayas*, *Koombiyo*, *Kanchayudha*, *Unrest* and *Asura*), or of a jingoistic, uncritical nationalism instead of meaningful social change (exemplified in *Yoddha: The Warrior*, *Arunodoyer Agnishikha*, *Heroes of 71: Shamsu Bahini*, *Operation Wanni* and *Operation Wanni 2*).

While taking into account the two theoretical propositions mentioned above, it must be emphasised that all discussions are limited to solely role-playing games that allow for a plot-and-game narrative. Casual games do not, naturally, feature in this study. However, the existing situation and discourses of gaming within South Asia seem to be overwhelmingly driven and derived from the first world, and that too in the representational and not in the redistributive or resistive sense of a national allegory.

In contrast to all of the above, I would like to present the game *Missing* (Flying Robot Studios, 2016) as a text that breaks out of the usual paradigm by introducing a completely different motive—gaming for social change, that steers clear either of a specific location in a nation space or of concerns of representation. Taking up the fight against the rampant trafficking of girl children prevalent in many parts of the subcontinent, the game was developed for the Missing Link Trust, an NGO created by Leena Kejriwal, a street artist based out of Kolkata, in 2015. The trust has been working to help track down and return trafficked girls across India, Bangladesh and Nepal. The game was released as a 2D narrative-driven puzzle, which shows players the horrors and reality of the flesh trade. The game won the NGDC Indie Game of the Year Award in 2016 and is available in eleven South Asian languages, besides German ('Missing: Game for a Cause'). At the time of writing, it has been downloaded from Google Play Store over 500,000 times (Missing Link Trust). The game has been successfully utilised not only to raise awareness regarding sex trafficking and how to help trafficked girls, but also to raise money for the other programmes of the Missing Link Trust ('About Us'). Moreover, its popularity has led to the development of a sequel for PC which is currently in production.

It would not be out of place to describe for the non-ludic the nature of gameplay and the plot of *Missing*. The game begins in medias res with the character of a girl already kidnapped and locked away in a dark room. The game involves textual interface, with players being told: 'Hi! I hope you are safe at your home because right at this moment a girl is being abducted and nobody will ever know how and why she has gone missing!' The title of the game's first chapter, 'Death of Innocence', primes the player for things to come. It is soon revealed that the player is playing as the missing girl. What is worse, she has been drugged and does not remember either her name or where she is from. The real horror of being missing lies not in the acknowledgement of the missing status of the girls, but rather the impossibility of registering that missing status. There is no memory of what was before—and it is this missing from the self that perhaps accentuates the growing uneasiness of the player as they realise that they will be renamed and recast into their new role as a prostitute, through forced starvation, thirst, and finally, violence and rape, while being slowly cajoled and persuaded by the manipulative female brothel keeper, who is called 'Masi'. Masi refuses to tell the girl how she got there, apart from indicating that she may have been heavily drugged, and sells off her virginity to a customer for good money. She is also responsible for giving the character the name 'Ruby'. The interactions between the other women of the brothel accurately depict the mix of limited help, manipulation, false promises and outright violence that make up the reality of forced prostitution. In particular, the character Meena becomes a sort of ally who not only helps 'Ruby' settle in to the new settings, but also fills in the backstory that people from her village have sold her to Masi as a sex slave. Further, it is she who tells the protagonist to escape, though, of course, the gameplay does not allow that. After the first rape, it is again Meena who convinces the character to go on living. The gameplay of the first chapter is limited to a tiny square room where the player has very little mobility or options. The entire screen is left black with only a small, semi-lit space that accentuates the feeling of being slowly suffocated. We are also introduced to Masi's pimp Shontu, who acts as a sort of enforcer, making sure the girls are kept in line. It is only by navigating through this quagmire, gaining money through prostitution, and finding time to explore the locality after fulfilling the goals set by the female brothel keeper that the player proceeds to the second chapter titled 'Life of a Whore'. There is a depiction of alcohol and its role in facilitating the sex trade. Despite its depiction of prostitution, the game refuses to sexualise the female figures. The gameplay proceeds by making the player character aware of the national helpline for children in distress and the street art installations of the Missing Link NGO as ways for abducted children to reach out for help. The rest of the gameplay revolves around how the player character manages to escape back to their village. The plot is realistic and, through its sound and game design, evokes strong responses ranging from claustrophobia and suffocation to terror and hope. While the game's story is located in Bengal, with the setting of Kolkata forming the backdrop of the narratives of the brothel and explorations that lead to freedom, the narrative is open enough to appeal to a wide range of lived experiences across regions that are reflected in the languages that the game is available in, apart from English and German: Bengali, Hindi, Maithili, Gujarati, Kannada, Tamil, Nepali, Marathi, Malayalam and Punjabi. In scope and spread, the game is perhaps unique in being truly South Asian in its linguistic range, covering most of India, besides Bangladesh and Nepal, and crossing national boundaries following the routes of missing trafficked children.

To create again an argument for essential difference between 'the West' and 'the East' based on meta factors—location, history, technical and economic development, religion and ethics—must be a project fraught with caveats. For who can deny that computer games, even those being created and disseminated in South Asia, largely follow the same formulaic expressions that are so native to the genre in general? Nonetheless, to deny the pressures of immediacy on individual cultural artefacts, like the game *Missing*, would be equally misplaced. It is perhaps through the process of resolving this binary between the particular and the general that this paper must proceed in its attempt to theorise the nature of digital gaming in South Asia today, albeit in a limited fashion. It is necessary to keep in mind the limited scope of this work which examines only a few digital games, and only one in any detail.

It is in this context that I place the game *Missing* in order to appreciate how it forms a radically differing voice amidst the dualities of mimic gaming and the assertions of national imaginaries that form and inform the binary of choices available to subcontinental gamers. The imaginations of the post-colony, complete with the nation and its fragments, combine with the continued concerns of the absent-but-virtually-dominant advanced first world to provide a matrix—a mesh for discourses—creating the postcolonial paradigm that determines the dominant binaries of discourses regarding cultural production today, especially in South Asia, and even more so in the field of digital gaming. After all, the purpose of this essay is not merely to uncover the underlying differences between digital gaming cultures, but rather to propose that attitudes towards digital gaming cultures must be based on their immediate materiality as much as they must be placed in any tradition of dialectics between binaries of the postcolonial West and postcolonial East.

Contrary to popular notions that pit the dialectics of violence or participatory/representational biases as being the true grounds of contention for digital games—perhaps in order to escape from the continued shadows of the postcolonial—it becomes more important to forge ahead in a radically new way. We must be clear as to how this development is truly radical, truly an intrusion into the roots of existing world imaginaries propped up by the dominant powers. First, the game *Missing* is novel in that it breaks out of the paradigm of nationalist representation—similar to the issue of girl trafficking which it is trying to address—and moves freely across limitations, indeed despite the boundaries of lands and laws. While it is expected that postcolonial spaces centre their cultural production and identities on the postcolonial fact of the nation, the gaming imaginaries of *Missing* stand in steadfast refusal to be branded into a national imagination. Second, *Missing* stays away from issues of depiction or representation, and instead focuses on addressing issues of oppression. This makes for a movement away from purely ludic concerns, which naturally raises questions of participation/representation as in children's games where someone gets to play a certain role and someone does not. It is no longer important to worry about who is being represented and who is not—the point is the underlying resistive concern. This requires a sort of 'strategic use of positivist essentialism' (Spivak 342) since it would be missing the point to ask why a particular caste, identity or group is being represented and another is not. As such, it is this refusal to engage with the games of the (neo) empire which demands that we look upon *Missing* as radical, going to the root of the issue regarding the nature of representation in cultural texts in the post-colony today.

To conclude, while most of the games of the South Asian subcontinent either seek to represent constituents of the postcolonial nation or become allegories of the postcolonial nation, the game *Missing* breaks away in order to provide a unique transnational redistributive and resistive praxis for social change. In doing so, it makes for an original voice that goes beyond the nation-bound modalities of representation which one generally encounters in the gaming world.

Note

1. A 'mod' is a modification, often cosmetic, made to the original version of a game.

Works Cited

'About Us'. *Save Missing Girls*, Missing Link Trust, 2024, www.savemissinggirls.com/about-us. Accessed 26 Apr. 2024.

Arunodoyer Agnishikha. Designed by Razib Ahmed, Microsoft Windows, Trimatrik Interactive/SHOM Computers Ltd., 2004.

Asura. Designed by Zainuddeen Fahadh, Microsoft Windows, Ogre Head Studio, 2017.

Attarwala, Fatima S. 'Can Pakistan's Gaming Industry Move On from "Copy-Paste"?' *Dawn*, 6 Nov. 2022, www.dawn.com/news/1719246. Accessed 26 Apr. 2024.

Chronicles of the Himalayas. Designed by Uttam Adhikari, alpha demo, Microsoft Windows, Sroth Code Games, 2019.

Contra. Designed by Koji Hiroshita, Shigeharu Umezaki and Shinji Kitamoto, NES, Konami, 1988.

Counter-Strike. Designed by Minh Le and Jess Cliffe, Microsoft Windows, Valve/Sierra Studios, 2000.

Fraser, Nancy. 'Social Justice in the Age of Identity Politics: Redistribution, Recognition, and Participation'. The Tanner Lectures on Human Values, delivered 30 Apr.–2 May 1996 at Stanford University, Tanner Foundation for Human Values, 1996.

Fujiwara, Hitoshi. 'What Does It Mean to Play a Video Game in Bhutan?' Twelfth International Convention of Asia Scholars, doi.org/10.5117/9789048557820/ICAS.2022.020. Accessed 26 Apr. 2024.

Heroes of 71: Shamsu Bahini. Android, Mindfisher Games Inc, 2015.

Jameson, Fredric.'Third-World Literature in the Era of Multinational Capitalism'. *Social Text*, no. 15, autumn 1986, pp. 65–88.

Kanchayudha. Designed by Chamira Prasad Jayasinghe, Microsoft Windows, Arimac Games, 2016.

Koombiyo. Microsoft Windows, KodeX, 2019.

Missing Link Trust. *Missing*, Google Play, version 21, 29 Jan. 2024, mobile app, play.google.com/store/apps/details?id=com.MissingLinkTrust.Missing. Accessed 26 Apr. 2024.

Missing. Version 21, Android, Flying Robot Studios/Missing Link Trust, 2016.

'Missing: Game for a Cause'. *Save Missing Girls*, Missing Link Trust, 2024, www.savemissinggirls.com/innovate/#game-for-cause. Accessed 26 Apr. 2024.

Operation Wanni 2. Designed by Dilshan Abeygunawardana, Microsoft Windows, DragonD soft, 2010.

Operation Wanni. Designed by Dilshan Abeygunawardana, Microsoft Windows, DragonD soft, 2010.

Prince of Persia. Designed by Jordan Mechner, MS-DOS, Broderbund, 1990.

Rana, Prajesh S.J.B. 'Starting Small, Aiming Big: Game Development in Nepal'. *The Kathmandu Post*, 6 Oct. 2020, tkpo.st/3jFM8c4. Accessed 26 Apr. 2024.

Spivak, Gayatri Chakravorty. 'Subaltern Studies: Deconstructing Historiography'. *Subaltern Studies IV*, edited by Ranajit Guha, Oxford UP, 1985, pp. 330–363.

Super Mario Bros. Directed by Shigeru Miyamoto, NES, Nintendo, 1985.

Tetris. Designed by Alexey Pajitnov, Electronica 60, Alexey Pajitnov, 1985.

Unrest. Designed by Arvind Raja Yadav, Microsoft Windows, Pyrodactyl Games, 2014.

Wolfenstein 3D. Designed by John Romero and Tom Hall, MS-DOS, id Software/Apogee Software, 1992.

Yoddha: The Warrior. Designed by Vishal Gondal and Ninad Chhaya, Microsoft Windows, Indiagames, 2000.

Hybrid Locality and the Glocal Nature of Memes

Ananya Chatterjee and Nisarga Bhattacharjee

In the twenty-first century, the very light through which postcolonial developments are viewed tends to gain an anti-colonial tint. The local gains its significance only discursively in the context of postcolonial globality, and a conservative attitude that intends to extract a purely local meaning loses sight of the already existing discursivity within itself. As noted by Roland Robertson, in the glocal paradigm, the expected contradiction between the local and the global becomes invalid. A purist attitude seeking a clear demarcation between the two tends to overlook

> the extent to which what is called local is in large degree constructed on a trans- or super-local basis. In other words, much of the promotion of locality is in fact done from above or outside. Much of what is often declared to be local is in fact the local expressed in terms of generalized recipes of locality. (26)

This means that the postcolonial subject is always already interpreting his or her respective standpoint within the global scenario whenever he or she interacts with any particularised cultural artefact. So, whether they recognise it or not, this inevitable reciprocity between the general and the particular cripples the subject's aspirations for independent identity. This incessant interpretive function is especially evident when one looks at the memes generated and circulated by postcolonial millennial culture. In other words, meme culture tells us that the local is always already glocal.

Traditional and indigenous artworks are generally considered singular and with a sanctity that defies replication. Pristine, traditional artworks are, in particular, supposed to resist the drive towards commodification that the Western market introduces globally. In contrast, image macros are easily replicable and freely modifiable. Memes actively participate in the currents of circulation, rather than obediently conveying the existence of some unalterable origin. This relaxed and protean nature of memes means that they are less bound by spoken or unspoken rules of behaviour. The rapid and random cultural appropriation practised in the case of memes working across cultural boundaries is quite antithetical to the diplomatic culture of political correctness that prevails in academic circles internationally. Hence, the millennial culture of free associations that memes thrive in allows bold expressions of hybrid identity by those who create, modify, or circulate internet memes. While it would be an error to regard cyberspace as boundlessly amoral, the relative relaxation of morality and the near impossibility of policing allows netizens to engage in irresponsible free play. As a result, internet memes represent a confluence of interests, perspectives and opinions with almost infinite inclusivity. Thus, the glocal nature of memes makes them a prominent platform for political representation, although the general flippancy of the medium disallows solid argumentation. The valorisation of the local nature of memes as counter-cultural would be a fallacy since such an attitude presumes an outmoded confrontational worldview:

> a world of local assertions *against* globalizing trends, a world in which the very idea of locality is sometimes cast as a form of opposition or resistance to the hegemonically global. (Robertson 29)

Instead, memes with local colour point out that in the twenty-first century, 'there can be no cosmopolitans without locals' (Hannerz 250). This means that the local attains its image on not a confrontational finality but on a comparative and competitive basis. Both the local and the global, both the postcolonial cultures and their erstwhile colonisers, inevitably seek each other's recognition. This often manifests in a competitive parochial culture in which memes seek to prove the superiority of one culture above another. In one of the memes that became popular on the internet following the popularity of the Marvel movie *Avengers: Infinity War*, we see Ranjit Mallick, an actor performing predominantly in Bengali commercial movies, overcome Thanos, the main antagonist of *Infinity War*, with the mere power of his reputed belt—his signature weapon, that has successfully subdued the villains in his movies (Lyadh kheteo). However, even such a confrontational meme has to recognise and, in turn, seek the recognition of the global in order to justify its postcolonial aspirations—Ranjit Mallick's prowess cannot be established without the widely recognised yardstick set by Thanos.

Further, the very comparative approach to culture that intends to highlight the local in superlative terms is itself a global tendency. Postcolonial cultures participate in the same race, and in their intention of winning this race, they further prove their colonial bearings rather than their freedom from the global paradigm. Paul Virilio notes that, like extreme sports, we currently have a practice of 'extreme science' (3)—'a race to achieve limit performances in the fields of robotics or genetic engineering' (2). This scientific practice in turn installs a competitive spirit in 'mass techno-culture' (3). Through this competitive approach, meme culture often tends to bring into prominence the undermined half of established hierarchical binaries, thus expressing concern for and interest in the people living in the periphery. For example, there exists the convention of transcriptions presented along with image macros for visually impaired social media users, as provided on specific Facebook pages like 'Writing About Writing'. These cases of transcription in particular show a plurality of discourses when it comes to the modes of cognition. The present digital culture inevitably assumes the predominance of ocular communication, which makes the visually impaired feel out of place. But the transcript meme suspends the majoritarian ocular dimension to allow audible renditions of image macros for the differently abled. This is just one example of the multiple angles through which meme culture enables the representation of minorities and prepares content for them.

Such a decentralisation of discourse indicates the mainstreaming of the subaltern as a reaction to the normative effect of marginalising discourses. But the general levity and relativity of the medium keep these counter-reactionary discourses from attaining any substantial justification. There is hardly ever a final point made since the meme remains open to further modifications. For instance, the practice of transcription has also further enabled parodic transcripts as the writer might give a comically misguiding account of the image macro. Thus, the 'Batman Slaps Robin' meme has resulted in transcripts that speak of a man in a yellow cape being slapped by a man in black, without revealing the identity of the two characters.

The inability to take matters seriously can indeed be counted as a weakness in the meme medium of didactic art. Factors such as the unascertainable nature of credibility, the openness to manipulated representations, the uncertainty of popularity, and the interpretive freedom offered by memes make memes a heavily unreliable medium for serious discourse. Generally, memes bring about developments and changes in the political imagination more effectively through performance rather than narrative discourse. In this case, neither the ideological pertinence nor the aesthetic quality ensures the popularity and effectiveness of a particular meme. Rather, the effectiveness of a meme heavily depends upon its incessant repetition and circulation to the effect that, as Theodor Adorno puts it, 'The familiarity of the piece is a surrogate for the quality ascribed to it' (30). Repetition and modification are intrinsic to the performative essence of memes.

The advantage of this fact is that memes become a locale of the carnivalesque as they act like the fools in Shakespearean drama; that is, they possess the license to question what thinkers and intellectuals hesitate to pose. The fact that memes engage popular taste, rather than operating upon standards of quality and appropriateness, does not mean that they attain popularity and propagate ideas indiscriminately. Rather, their 'successes' are attained as per standards that are set more involuntarily and on a situational basis. The elements of partial anonymity and cost-effective circulation are two factors among many that make these glocal memes more accessible to the masses. But if the 'successes' of memes were solely dependent upon these external factors, then every meme would have attained equal prominence.

Institutional interests certainly play a part in promoting certain memes online. However, analysts like Limor Shifman have identified some structural features that make a meme 'popular', 'a focus on ordinary people, flawed masculinity, humor, simplicity, repetitiveness, and whimsical content' (74) being along those elements. Apart from these apolitical features, political associations have begun to consciously promote and monitor memes in order to further their political agenda as well as to catch the attention of Generations Y and Z. However, memes become problematic locations that do not abide by any particular political interest, as they are able to contain multiple layers of meaning through the combination of images and text. The exclusivity of parochial locality is impossible in the glocal age because neoliberalism encourages permissible boundaries and unlimited exchange on economic and cultural terms. Cultural hybridity is defined by William Rowe and Vivian Schelling as 'the ways in which forms become separated from existing practices and recombine with new forms in new practices' (231). Hence, owing to their discursive nature and multi-layered metaleptic structures, memes are particularly attuned to the glocal paradigm and its hybrid expressions.

The meme demonstrates how, in an age where cinematic crossovers abound, postcolonial memes come to express hybridised localities or 'hybrid localities' by crossing cultural boundaries or drawing attention to those boundaries that are already bridged. The term 'hybrid locality' needs to be coined for the purpose of expressing the offshoots of the cultural locale that stretch the boundaries of the products born within popular culture. Hybrid localities characterise those products of popular culture that intend to express local flavour by both exerting and disclaiming the parochial boundaries of the cultural locality. The glocal context of memes invests them with a hybrid identity because of which they are able to shape public opinion in a very subtle but effective manner in postcolonial urban societies. Upon further consideration of the critical utility of the carnivalesque, we shall be able to read a substantial social commentary in memes. Memes designed by millennials critically examine the prevalent social system, starting with its basic unit—the family. The image of the typical Indian family is adequately captured in the series of memes which, at the cost of being slightly distorted and exaggerated, act as a protest against the dated traditions and practices of Indian families. At the cost of stereotyping their feudal norms, economic, cultural and social aspirations, and the political orientations of traditional fathers, these memes replicate the colonial power relations that organise the average Indian family. Parental expectations commingled with an authoritative dominance towards their children find expression as the 'Typical Indian Father' in image macros.

Memes often become expressions of popular resentment against Eurocentric cultures. The interpretive task, in either case, happens on a collective or community level because memes work with reference to particular cultural aspects or events. The community engaged in that act of interpretation is not any fixed entity but one discursively constituted along the lines drawn in the opening of this essay. The metaleptic protean nature of memes hence corresponds with the fluidity of the community that invests meaning in memes and is responsible for the circulation of those memes. The mobilisation and circulation of memes, especially in postcolonial cultures, can therefore be traced effectively with reference to the idea of 'interpretive communities' in reader-response theory. Stanley Fish notes that:

> Interpretive communities are made up of those who share interpretive strategies not for reading (in the conventional sense) but for writing texts, constituting their properties, and assigning their intentions.

> In other words, these strategies exist prior to the act of reading and therefore determine the shape of what is read rather than, as is usually assumed, the other way around. (483)

In the same way, postcolonial memers create content that appeals to their specific audience who may or may not have gone through the original image which has been converted into an image macro by the content creators. This inability to relate to the original context of the image in the meme may arise from the postcolonial subject's unfamiliarity with the Western culture from which the images are very often borrowed. Despite the cultural difference, the audience as well as the memer may engage in a radical acquisition of the image in order to read into that image meanings that hardly exist in the original.

The interpretive process is not likely to come to a close here. Down the communication chain, the meme gets passed on to smaller groups and pockets of the audience who once again assign their own meanings to the image macros, overwriting the meanings assigned to them by the memer. This act of assignment happens not because that meme itself has constituted meanings in that audience's mind with relation to the intentions of the original memer, but because the audience itself has already authored certain meanings which the meme attracts and attaches to itself in their perception. The qualities of a popular meme identified by Shifman are exactly fitting for this phenomenon because all of them together indicate the meme's ability to be an incomplete vessel that can be receptive in this manner. This small group once again may or may not be familiar with the original source of the image, a clause that significantly affects their way of understanding the memes.

This phenomenon does not occur when the circulation is wider because the images tend to go viral in that case and, as a result, the meanings of the meme tend to get more established and therefore less likely to be discursively interpreted. For instance, the disappointed Pakistani fan meme, which became popular after the Pakistan versus Australia match during the 2019 ICC

Cricket World Cup, is far too familiar a face to be interpreted as an expression of anything other than exasperation and confounded disappointment, whatever impact may be applied to it.

The memer's and his or her audience's regular disregard for the cultural specificity of the original image or quote is indicative that, even within popular culture, meme culture is capable of subverting mainstream taste. It might be pointed out that this apparent disregard and subversion springs from complacency with half-knowledge, and therefore memes are a particularly potent mode of communication in the post-truth era. The significance that memes hold in the day-to-day existence of the millennial generation is unprecedented in this culture that is not afraid to cross the boundaries of the validity of facts and ideas. Memes should not be regarded as a fad or a passing trend. Their reiterative quality has made memes the dominant model of communication in popular international and local societies.

Works Cited

Adorno, Theodor. *The Culture Industry: Selected Essays on Mass Culture.* Routledge, 2004.

Fish, Stanley E. 'Interpreting the "Variorum"'. *Critical Inquiry*, vol. 2, no. 3, 1976, pp. 465–485.

Hannerz, Ulf. 'Cosmopolitans and Locals in World Culture'. *Global Culture*, edited by Mike Featherstone, SAGE Publications, 1990, pp. 237–252.

Lyadh kheteo aj kal lyadh lage *yawn*. 'belt > infinity stones'. *Facebook*, 21 May 2018, www.facebook.com/LyadhPage/photos/2018297141523202. Accessed 17 Apr. 2024.

Robertson, Roland. 'Glocalization: Time-Space and Homogeneity-Heterogeneity'. *Global Modernities*, edited by Mike Featherstone, Scott Lash and Roland Robertson, SAGE Publications, 1995, pp. 25–44.

Rowe, William, and Vivian Schelling. *Memory and Modernity: Popular Culture in Latin America*. Verso, 1991.

Shifman, Limor. *Memes in Digital Culture.* The MIT Press, 2014.

Virilio, Paul. *The Information Bomb*. Translated by Chris Turner, Verso, 2005.

Writing About Writing. Meme and accompanying transcription. *Facebook*, 18 May 2020, www.facebook.com/100077736131324/posts/2790617594380858. Accessed 17 Apr. 2024.

Digital Effects in Indian Cinema

A Technological Jujitsu

Mita Bandyopadhyay and Arindam Modak

Indian cinema has come a long way since the days of *Raja Harishchandra*. At present, the industry has numerous releases around the year, the estimated number being around 1,700 feature films across the country, compared to the United States which released just over 500 films in 2018 (Basuroy). The film industry of multilingual India is not confined to Bollywood, but extends beyond it. Besides Hindi, regional films produced in Kannada, Marathi, Malayalam, Tamil, Telugu and Bengali make up nearly 30 per cent of all box-office content (Basuroy). Cinema that entertained merely a small group of viewers has now turned into a massive industry: a 2017 report expected the Indian film industry to reach a gross turnover of Rs 23,800 crores ($3.7 billion) by 2020 (ET Bureau).

Though this has been the broad scenario, over the years the industry has been facing steep competition from the international market. It has been observed that the lure of Hollywood movies with visual effects (VFX) has become more tempting to the Indian audience than indigenous movies. Films like *Avengers: Infinity War* (2018) and *Avengers: Endgame* (2019) have broken their earlier records, setting a new trend among the audience in India and, at the same time, posing a threat to the Indian film industry (Raghavendra). In recent years, Hollywood movies have started playing a prominent role in the Indian film market to an extent that their share in the Indian box office escalated from 8.4 per cent in 2015 to 20.8 per cent in 2019, whereas the share of Hindi films dropped from 60–65 per cent in 2015 to 45 per cent in 2019 (Laghate and Naidu).

According to experts, 'the share of Hollywood films in total box-office collection is expected to go up to 25–30% in the next two to three years' (Laghate and Naidu). This substantial growth of Hollywood film viewers in the Indian market can be traced to two causes: first, the extensive use of digital VFX in cinematography, making it an entirely different experience for young viewers who were used to watching traditional indigenous movies, and second, the use of digital marketing tools for the advertisement of these films, creating a fan base before their actual release. The Indian film industry counters this form of imperialism through a viable option which can be viewed as 'If you can't beat them, join them', in which digital VFX technology is incorporated into films as well as their marketing strategies. The last decade has seen the release of several films like *Krrish 3* (2013), *Eega* (2012), *Baahubali* (2015 and 2017), *Enthiran 2* (2018) and *Tanaji* (2020) which have composited digital VFX with Bollywood narrative style. For the sake of convenience, we have considered the films *Krrish 3* and *Baahubali 1* and *2* as cases of 'technological jujitsu'.

Digital VFX and the Marketing of Hollywood Movies

Digital visual effects or digital VFX is a digital imaging technique used in visual media in which live action scenes are composited with computer-generated imagery (CGI) at different stages of production. The technique of visual effects is especially used in creating scenes that cannot be shot in a live-action setting. In other words, digital VFX is a technical tool like the previous techniques of sound and colour effects, which is now used by film producers across the globe. George Lucas' film (*Star Wars*, 1977) can be listed as an early example of the implementation of digital VFX. This new technique slowly turned to be a game changer because it could now show audience what earlier was an impossibility. Since then, the technique has been used by producers and filmmakers mostly in America to create films which have been huge successes worldwide. The economic boom enjoyed by VFX movies had production houses in America invest more into the development and usage of the new technology, leading to blockbuster VFX films like *Terminator 2: Judgement Day* (1991), *Jurassic Park* (1993), *Independence Day* (1996), *Titanic* (1997) and *The Matrix* (1999), all of which did big business around the globe. China became the biggest importer of Hollywood films, while India ranked fourth (Follows).

In addition to the technological upgradation, globalisation has made the distribution of these movies simple and easy. By 1997, the international box-office revenues for American movies surpassed domestic earnings. 'But it wasn't until 2003 when international revenue dominated the domestic market for good' (Follows). With *Avengers: Endgame*, the earnings shot to Rs 244 crores within the first six days of its release in India. The film was way ahead of its predecessor, which had ended with a grand total of Rs 222.69 crores (Farooqui). This boom in the revenue can be attributed to the digital marketing strategies. The release of scenes and trailers from the *Avengers* movies on social media, the interaction of the actors and directors with their audience, the sale of merchandise, the release of comic books and video games prior to the release of the film are all marketing tools set into trend by the filmmakers of Hollywood. Films belonging to the Marvel series steadily built a huge fan base through the successive twenty-one films that propelled the sale of tickets for *Avengers: Endgame*, the twenty-second film in the series. With the release of trailers and posters on social media, brands in India hosted contests on Twitter and Facebook to leverage their entities. Cinepolis, a multiplex chain, screened a marathon of nine MCU films for the price of a single expensive ticket. Oppo launched an Avengers-themed phone on the very day the film released in India.

> Even digital wallets were in on the trend. PayTM, a homegrown payments app backed by Alibaba, ran a 'First Day, First Show' contest where paying for tickets using the platform could

> win users two free passes to the first show of *Avengers: Endgame* on the first day of its release. (Gill)

The net outcome of this marketing was:

> When bookings opened on April 20, PayTM received over 250,000 requests per minute and sold over 1.5 million tickets making *Avengers: Endgame* the highest advance-grossing movie till date for the platform. (Gill)

The Cultural Impact of Hollywood Movies

The expansion of Hollywood films into the Indian film industry and its growing share in the market is an indicator of cultural imperialism in the age of digitalisation and globalisation. Hollywood cinema, which targets a global audience, is a synthesis of the following traits: an easy-to-understand narrative in combination with a spectacular setting, adventure- and action-filled sequences that mostly gain prominence through the science-fiction genre and the creation of such movies that are divided episodically through successive movies, creating a fan base for the forthcoming movie.

Besides post-production marketing, Hollywood movies from the very onset target a global audience, so the movies generally tend to have a universal style of narrative—a narrative in which action and spectacular scenes prevail over the drama that explicitly depicts American culture. Critics like Frederick Wasser and Charles R. Acland consider the reason for global success of Hollywood films to be their universality of themes as well as the form of language, which is not culture-specific. But according to certain critics, beneath this visible theme of 'universality' is sown the seed of the latest form of cultural imperialism. 'Deculturalization, acculturalization, and reculturalization' is the latest form of 'transparization' of the global Hollywood movies as propounded by critics Georgette Wang and Emilie Y. Yeh.

Critics like Wang and Yeh assert the reality underneath the universal narrative style of Hollywood.

> Although deculturalization may be the key to entering the global market, its 'acultural' outlook may in fact be deceptive, as storytelling cannot be accomplished without touching on beliefs, attitudes, values and behavioral patterns. When characters are pushed into action and decisions are made, the underlying beliefs and values emerge.... Reculturalization, therefore, is often as symbiotic with deculturalization as it is with acculturalization. (178)

According to Wang and Yeh, though Hollywood stresses its universality of narrative style and theme, deep within it actually propagates a deculturalised product that finds expression through the characters' action, belief and values that lurk within the story. As an effect of the deculturalised products featured through the Hollywood VFX movies, Thanksgiving Day and Halloween have become a part of the celebrations by Indians.

In contrast to Wang and Yeh, Wasser cites an interesting conversation between himself and an American film executive on the aspect of the globalisation of the Hollywood narrative:

> In my conversations with American film executives, it was obvious that they perceive the world-wide market as desiring a certain image of America to be featured in the movies. Each executive may have differing and changing notions of the desired image—one season it may be hedonist consumers on the open road with fast cars—the next season it may be the American ethic of an individual hero struggling against all corrupt collectives. The point is not whether international viewers are actually seduced by such images but that film producers set for themselves the task of portraying an "America" that is a dreamscape for "universal" desires rather than a historical reality. (435)

Wasser argues that Hollywood films are already globalised because they do not project anything on screen that bears any connection to the historical past of the US. Hollywood movies are imperial, but only economically, not culturally. Judging from the cultural aspect, according to Wasser, these films are global because they target a global audience. Going by Wasser's logic, even if the Hollywood style is considered to be global, it cannot be similar to the nationalised style of any country. Hollywood VFX films follow a style that is easy to understand, which is what makes these movies desirable and easy to be marketed, but for the local film industry, Hollywood films are just another form of economic and cultural imperialism threatening the growth of the national film industry.

Indian Film Industry in the Age of Digitalisation

To counter the effects of this form of imperialism by Hollywood VFX films, the Indian film industry too started making use of the latest technique of digital VFX into the indigenous themes and also changed its marketing strategies. Very soon, several films in Hindi and south Indian languages became the products of such an endeavour. This essay studies digital VFX techniques used both as cinematographic and marketing strategies, as well as tools of counter resistance offered by domestic films like *Krrish 3* and *Baahubali 1* and *2*, as an alternative to Hollywood VFX films.

In the films *Krrish 3* and *Baahubali*, the Indian film industry takes up the grand style of showcasing the superhero through spectacular and adventurous scenes, making use of special effects and digital effects and blending the narrative of these films with song-and-dance sequences, resulting in the same 'masala mix', but with a different flavour added to it. This combination of the Indian film narrative to the Hollywood style has been well appreciated in the global market and films like *Krrish 3*, *Baahubali 1: The Beginning* and *Baahubali 2: The Conclusion* have proven to be a grand success not only in India but across the globe. The success of these films cannot be attributed solely to the use of digital VFX used in the cinematography; much of it has also to do with the marketing strategies of these films, which operate through the fan base built before the release of the film.

Digital VFX is a comparatively new entrant in the Indian film industry, though American studios have been using this tool since 1977. *Love Story 2050* (2008), with 1,200 VFX shots, was the first Bollywood production to have made extensive use of digital VFX, but ended up becoming a box-office flop. Among contemporary movies, *Krrish 3* used the maximum number of VFX shots, creating a stunning action hero that left an indelible mark in the minds of the audience. During its early period, the film became a new trendsetter for the Indian film industry. The trailer for *Krrish 3* became the most watched online Bollywood trailer on YouTube, crossing the mark of 12 million views within two weeks (Gupta), surpassing that of the superheroes *Thor* (2011) and *The Avengers* (2012) ('Krrish 3 Trailer'). The grand success of *Krrish 3* was due to the use of digital VFX capable of featuring a masked fantasy along with some astounding stunts performed by a native superhero. The idea of a native superhero, Krrish, resembling the deeds and achievements of the mythological Krishna, who despite having spent his childhood in the plains and mountains of rural parts of northern India, becomes capable of performing stunts and life-saving tricks to save the world from the clutches of Kaal, the Indian version of villain whose wrath and vengeance is supposed to take over every worldly possession from human beings in due course of time, was received exuberantly by the national audience. The film used VFX techniques to rejuvenate the nationalist sentiments of the audience in a techno-centric digital world. Besides the narrative, the background setting, the music and dance along with the sweet and bitter taste of romance, brought into effect by the female characters, turned the film into a typical Bollywood movie that merged the Hollywood technique within the act of Indian storytelling. Keeping within the frame of a typical Bollywood movie, the film features a futuristic vision, when Kaal devours everything and only Krrish, who possesses superhuman qualities, saves humanity from disaster. While *Krrish* resonates with the heroic achievements of the mythological character of Krishna in a contemporary setting, to an extent futuristic too, the film *Baahubali* reproduces the heroic achievements of a mighty superhero who bears affinity with the mythological character functioning at the heart of the ancient country dating back to the historical period; a time when kings and ministers were the rulers and administrators of the empires.

Baahubali 1: The Beginning (2015) and *Baahubali 2: The Conclusion* (2017) were first released in Tamil and Telugu and later in Hindi. These were the first digital VFX films to have transgressed regional borders and become pan-Indian films, later achieving international acclaim. '*Baahubali 2: The Conclusion* shattered all major records at the box office since the day of its release, to become the highest grossing movie at the ticket window' (Narasimhan and Malvania). Digital VFX used in the film played a pivotal role in the narrative of the film. The story of *Baahubali*, though set against the backdrop of sibling rivalry of the Mahishmati Kingdom, crystallises the mythological story of the Mahabharata and plays a crucial role in shaping the national identity. Audiences say that the film displays the rich cultural heritage of the country, while the spectacular scenes and stunning action sequence of the Indian superhero and the villain became a feast for the eye and the heart. The narrative revolves around a simple story which bears similarities with the great epic, in the end becoming an all-time favourite with audiences not only in India but across the world. The spirit of nationalism and Indian cultural heritage reveals itself within the sets created, the outfits worn by the actors, the communities featured in the movie, the music played and the background carefully knitted into the aesthetics of Hollywood style. *Baahubali* represents the cultural emblem of the nation, successfully projected through visual means. The film imbibes within itself the true spirit of ancient Indian culture, minutely detailed with the use of digital VFX.

Technological Jujitsu and the Politics of Resistance

During the past decade the Indian film industry has made a considerable advancement by adopting the Hollywood style of filmmaking. The existing pattern of filmmaking was incompatible with the latest style brought into the market by Hollywood films. As a result, the new form developed by using Hollywood stylistic expressions to serve as an anti-Hollywood strategy to defend the national film industry from the clutches of Hollywood dominance.

The merging of the American style of filmmaking and its marketing strategies with that of the Indian context of the movies is to be considered 'technological jujitsu', a term borrowed from Ella Shohat and Robert Stam's 'media jujitsu', used in their book, *Unthinking Eurocentrism*. The term reiterates the use of the forces of the dominant culture in an advantageous way by the dominated cultures in order to resist and subvert it (328).

Unthinking Eurocentrism is a critical study of Eurocentrism as 'unacknowledged' and 'bad epistemic habit' brought into effect by the use of mass media. Shohat and Stam's analysis of Eurocentric criticism is not only confined to the political oppression but expands to 'esthetic banality and futility' (10). Accordingly, Eurocentrism is not limited to colonialism by Europe but it extends throughout the entire Western world, 'from classical Greece to imperial Rome and then to the metropolitan capitals of Europe and the US' that have constantly marched ahead with their oppressive acts of 'colonialism, slave-trading, and imperialism since 1492' (2–3).

Shohat and Stam use the term 'media jujitsu' with regard to anthropophagy, a Brazilian art movement of the 1960s. The term 'media jujitsu' is used to display a strategy of resistance put up by the supposedly inferior local culture against the superior, dominant Eurocentric culture. According to Shohat and Stam, it is a process through which the colonised people take advantage of the powers of the dominant class so as to resist them and thereafter gain supremacy over them. Although the term 'anthropophagy' means cannibalism, according to the dictionary, in this context it is used as a term that signifies the appropriation of products which have cultural significance. In the particular case of cultural studies, anthropophagy has been considered as an appropriation of cultural elements by the subjugated class which then are further rearranged to be used against the dominant class as a form of resistance, that is, a process whereby Western techniques are accepted first by local cultures and then shaped accordingly for their indigenous development, which later turns into a cultural resistance against the prevailing Western domination. Shohat and Stam consider anthropophagy and media jujitsu as 'excorporation' that challenges 'elements of the dominant culture and redeploys them in the interests of oppositional praxis' (328). Here, I have made a shift from the original term and used it as 'technological jujitsu' because ever since the 1990s, an upsurge in the technological change has become a predominant force in shaping culture in almost all the nations across the globe. Technological changes have given rise to an entirely new form of culture called visual digital culture, a culture that prioritises digital images created through computer graphics over the analogue images used earlier for visual display.

Here, it must be mentioned that the use of the term 'technological jujitsu' is similar to the postcolonial term 'catachresis'. In the edited volume *Post-Colonial Studies*, 'Catachresis is the process by which the colonised takes and re-inscribes something that exists traditionally as a feature of Imperial culture' (Ashcroft et al. 43). The term has been used repeatedly by postcolonial critics like Gayatri Chakravorty Spivak and Homi K. Bhabha. Spivak considers catachresis as a form of expression that begins to take shape when the exchange of ideas takes place between the colonisers (the West) and the colonised (the East), and in the process the word acquires a new meaning. It is a pattern without any referent. By employing catachrestical means of 'reversing, displacing, and seizing the apparatus of value-coding', postcolonial critique should criticise and develop resistance against the colonialist power (Chakravorty Spivak 228). It is due to the misapplication of the assertions of the colonial made by the postcolonial or the decolonised people that these claims 'are tacitly recognized as coded within the legacy of imperialism' (225). However, such claims are considered to be a 'concept-metaphor', lacking a necessary referent in the postcolonial space and hence a catachresis (225).

Spivak explains that the adaptation of First-World strategies by the Third World is not only for the purpose of survival but is also a form of self-defence against the rule of the oppressor. In other words, catachresis has become an instrument for resistance. The discourse of domination produced under the influence of postcolonial criticism locates 'neither inside nor outside the history of Western domination but is in a tangential relation to it', insists Gyan Prakash (8). In other words, viewed from a different angle, the whole idea of postcolonialism is very similar to catachresis itself. The application of the concept of catachresis to Indian VFX films has led to a new form of cultural theorisation produced under the effect of the Hollywood VFX films. The new form of Indian films thus created fights back the growing influence of Hollywood films, while making use of their stylistic devices to blend with the national cultural context. In the discourse of postcolonialism, the concept of catachresis becomes parallel to 'technological jujitsu', borrowed from 'media jujitsu', because active resistance is an integral part of the art of jujitsu and the same is applied to evaluate Indian films against their Hollywood counterparts.

'Jujitsu' is originally a term borrowed from the traditional unarmed Japanese martial arts in which the defender uses the enemy's tricks and skills to defend themselves against the enemy. In the traditional art form the defender does not stop the attacker, but initially accepts it and then reverts the same by throwing the attacker to the ground (Wikipedia). Such a strategy that first accepts the strike of the opponent and then boomerangs it back to the enemy to overpower them is applied in the context of the films *Krrish 3* and *Baahubali* for the purpose of analysis in this essay. The film industry both in Mumbai and south India uses digital effects both in cinematography and marketing, leading to commendable success worldwide.

Indian cinema has been making use of digital VFX for a decade, but the technology was applied to only a few shots compared to Hollywood films where almost an entire film is made using digital effects. For the first time, digital VFX scenes shown in *Krrish 3* and *Baahubali 1: The Beginning* and *Baahubali 2: The Conclusion* made use of thousands of digital VFX shots to produce the image of a native superhero who saves the people from the clutches of the overpowering evil forces similar to that of the *Avengers* series, but in a different context and setting. Both the films received overwhelming response from the Indian audience, nurturing a feeling of confidence regarding the creativity of films using the VFX technique. Reports published by CNBC reveal a substantial growth in the Indian VFX market globally.

> In 2017, box office collections for Indian films overseas took $367 million—up almost three times from $125 million the year before, the report said. Earnings this year are expected to do just as well and may rise to $411 million in 2020—up by 12 percent from 2017, according to the report. (Vohra)

While much of the success of these VFX films is attributed to the use of the technology within the context of the Indian narratives, a major part of the credit also lies with the change in marketing strategies now followed by these Indian films. As noted in the case of the *Marvel* series, wherein the marketing tools were efficient in attracting a greater number of audiences, the Indian movies, especially *Baahubali*, left no stone unturned to enhance the customer experience through digital marketing techniques. It formed a partnership with the top brands for creating online games, TV shows and an animated series on Amazon Prime; in fact, the digital marketing team worked hard assiduously for two years at a stretch to reach out to the audience. Besides this, the first part withheld the answer to the question 'Why did Kattappa kill Baahubali?' which led to a huge sale of tickets days before the release of the second part of the film. The posting of the spectacular scenes in combination with hashtags on Twitter was also effective in drawing in audiences. *Krrish 3* also carried out a good promotion for the film prior to its launch, using the platform of social media; it released comic books, merchandise and masks to reach out to the audience.

The discussion above shows the relevance of the term 'technological jujitsu' used in the context of the films *Krrish 3* and *Baahubali.* In both the films not only were digital tools introduced within the cinematography; they were also used as marketing tools. Thus, the use of digital technology, both for cinematography and marketing, has led to an increase in the viewership of these Indian movies, nationally as well as globally, making the term 'technological jujitsu' relevant.

Works Cited

Acland, Charles R. *Screen Traffic: Movies, Multiplexes, and Global Culture.* Duke University Press, 2003.

Ashcroft, Bill, et al., editors. *Post-Colonial Studies: The Key Concepts.* Routledge, 2013.

'"Baahubali 2: The Conclusion" Box Office Collections: Box-Office Records Shattered by the Film'. *Times of India*, 1 Dec. 2018, timesofindia.indiatimes.com/entertainment/hindi/bollywood/photo-features/box-office-records-shattered-by-baahubali-2-theconclusion/photostory/58527385.cms. Accessed 8 Nov. 2024.

Baahubali: *The Beginning*. Directed by S.S. Rajamouli. Dharma Productions, 2015.

Baahubali: *The Conclusion*. Directed by S.S. Rajamouli. Dharma Productions, 2017.

Basuroy, Tanushree. 'New Film Releases in India 2017–2023'. 8 Apr. 2024, *Statista*, www.statista.com/statistics/1346845/india-number-of-film-releases. Accessed 07 Oct. 2024.

'Brazilian jiu-jitsu'. *Wikipedia*, Wikimedia Foundation, en.wikipedia.org/wiki/Brazilian_jiu-jitsu. Accessed 8 Nov. 2024.

Chakravorty Spivak, Gayatri. 'Poststructuralism, Marginality, Postcoloniality and Value'. *Literary Theory Today*, edited by Peter Collier and H. Geyer-Ryan, Cornell University Press, 1990, pp. 219–244.

Farooqui, Maryam. 'Avengers: Endgame Becomes India's Highest Earning Hollywood Venture, Eyes Rs 400 Crore'. *Money Control*, 2 May 2019, www.moneycontrol.com/news/trends/entertainment/avengers-endgame-becomes-indias-highest-earning-hollywoodventure-eyes-rs-400-crore-3923021.html. Accessed 8 Nov. 2024.

'Film Industry in India to Hit $3.7 Billion by 2020, Says Report'. *Economic Times*, 9 Oct. 2017, economictimes.indiatimes.com/industry/media/entertainment/media/film-industry-in-india-to-hit-3-7-billion-by-2020-says-report/articleshow/60998458.cms. Accessed 8 Nov. 2024.

Follows, Stephen. 'How Important Is International Box Office to Hollywood?' *StephenFollows.com*, 15 May 2017, stephenfollows.com/p/important-international-box-office-hollywood. Accessed 8 Nov. 2024.

Gill, Prabhjote. 'Brands in India Are Cashing In on the Hype around Avengers Endgame'. *Business Insider*, 26 Apr. 2019, www.businessinsider.in/avengers-endgame-marketing-boosts-sales-forbrands-in-india/articleshow/69051707.cms. Accessed 8 Nov. 2024.

Gupta, Priya. '"Krrish 3" Is the Most Watched Bollywood Trailer Online'. *Times of India*, 24 Sept. 2013, timesofindia.indiatimes.com/entertainment/hindi/bollywood/news/krrish-3bollywoodchennai express/articleshow/22938348.cms. Accessed 8 Nov. 2024.

Krrish 3. Directed by Rakesh Roshan. Filmkraft Productions, 2013.

'"Krrish 3" Trailer Gets More Views than "Thor" & "Avenger"'. *Times of India*, 18 Aug. 2013. timesofindia.indiatimes.com/entertainment/hindi/bollywood/news/krrish-3-trailer-gets-more-views-than-thor-and-avengers/articleshow/21893098.cms. Accessed 8 Nov. 2024.

Laghate, Gaurav, and Rajesh Naidu. 'Indians Can't Get Enough of Hollywood'. *The Economic Times*, 28 Jan. 2020, economictimes.indiatimes.com/industry/media/entertainment/indians-cant-getenough-of-hollywood/articleshow/73683006.cms. Accessed 8 Nov. 2024.

Narasimhan, T.E., and Urvi Malvania. 'Baahubali 2 Beats PK's Lifetime Collection, Becomes India's Top-Earner'. *Business Standard*, 6 May 2017. http://mybs.in/2UVetXs. Accessed 8 Nov. 2024.

Prakash, Gyan. 'Postcolonial Criticism and Indian Historiography'. *Social Text*, vol. 31/32, 1992, pp. 8–19.

Raghavendra, Nandini. 'Hollywood Blockbusters Make Big Money in Indian Movie Market'. *Economic Times*, 29 May 2012, economictimes.indiatimes.com/industry/media/entertainment/hollywood-blockbusters-make-big-money-in-indian-movie-market/articleshow/13614239.cms. Accessed 8 Nov. 2024.

Shohat, Ella, and Robert Stam. *Unthinking Eurocentrism: Multiculturalism and the Media*. Routledge, 1994.

Vohra, Partha. 'Indian Movies Attract Millions Around the World—and That Number Looks Set to Grow'. *CNBC*, 2 Aug. 2018, www.cnbc.com/2018/08/03/indian-films-attract-millions-globally-and-it-appears-to-be-growing.html. Accessed 8 Nov. 2024.

Wang, Georgette, and Emilie, Y. Yeh. 'Globalization and Hybridization in Cultural Products: The Cases of Mulan and Crouching Tiger, Hidden Dragon'. *International Journal of Cultural Studies*, vol. 8, no. 2, 2005, pp. 175–193.

Wasser, Frederick. 'Is Hollywood America? The Transnationalization of the American Film Industry'. *Critical Studies in Mass Communication*, vol. 12, no. 4, 1995, pp. 423–437.

Representation of 'Westernisation' in India in Three Web Series

Permanent Roommates, Little Things and *Adulting*

Jayati Ganguly

Films and television are the most popular media of cultural representation and the sphere of academic enquiry into them has been expanding. But a very recent shift in viewership patterns is being perceived with the arrival of the genre of 'web series' and a variety of fresh online content, most of which try to capture many relatable aspects of contemporary life. Thus, the reading of web shows as postcolonial cultural texts within the paradigm of 'globalisation' can provide fresh perspectives on contemporary sociocultural dimensions in India and the media discourses around them. This essay studies the representation of 'westernisation' in India in three web series: *Permanent Roommates* (two seasons, one audio season), *Little Things* (four seasons) and *Adulting* (two seasons). The essay questions the emergence of a dominant Western hegemony in contemporary Indian society that may be perceived in these portrayals. Analysing some patterns of ideological framework, lifestyle, food culture and the capitalist market, the essay argues that a dominant Western (European and American) hegemony persists, whether consciously or unconsciously, overtly or covertly—but that this domain of influence/hegemony is fissured by sensibilities and tastes that are considered uniquely/traditionally 'Indian' or those associated with traditional Indian society. The paper seeks to locate how far the representations reflect an evolving, hybridised Indian culture and at what juncture westernisation tends towards a 'neo-colonial' and 'neo-orientalist' discourse. The paper also discusses the radical shift in dominant media discourses that these web series have ushered in the domain of popular culture.

The genre of web series emerged in the West. As it began to be considered a profitable medium, with increasing digitisation in India, Indian producers began to patronise the web platform. It is a relatively recent phenomenon in India that took place as the popularity of YouTube and other over-the-top (OTT) platforms like Netflix, Amazon Prime and Disney Hotstar shot up. The majority of the Indian population is young and active online. Wearied of repetitive and melodramatic saas–bahu sagas, this young audience seems to have turned towards web-based content. The reason for choosing to analyse the three web series is that they are youth-based shows which do not have a 'plot' per se but represent the 'everyday' lives of the urban youth, their aspirations, emotions, complexities and ideologies in contemporary India. Such shows are, thus, appropriate texts for studying the representation of a changing Indian society and its evolving popular culture in the contexts of postcoloniality and globalisation. As Leela Gandhi reminds us, 'Postcoloniality ... is just another name for the globalisation of cultures and histories' (126).

The SAGE Glossary of the Social and Behavioural Sciences defines 'westernization' precisely as:

> The influencing of the customs and practices of westernized societies on non-Western civilizations.... Westernization emerged in the mid-19th century with the colonization of India.... At this time, other western European nations ... and later the United States, were also seeking dominion over foreign nations.... Today, Westernization still exists through globalization, which entails the loosening of trade barriers, through capitalistic ventures, and the promotion of democratization, both of which are values established by the Western world. (Sullivan 542)

Globalisation has gradually made the ideas/constructs of 'westernisation', 'Indianness', etc., quite problematic due to their fluidity. Yet, going by the concept of 'westernisation' mentioned above, the construction of a contemporary social discourse and its media representations may be examined.

The first issue in reading the representation of 'westernisation' in India in these web shows is that of unmarried, live-in relationships between young urban couples. It is argued that this 'Western' model has been portrayed as a dominant ideology and practice in the marriage-phobic, rather, 'commitment phobic generation' (Titzmann 2) in contemporary urban India. This has significantly altered the already-evolving idea of the 'family' in India. How this representation shows the rise of a new 'metropolitan' middle class with changing 'value systems' is part of the argument. Live-in relationship couples live together under the same roof as they have 'marriage like relations in which there has been no marriage ceremony' (Kok and Leinarte 491). Also, there is no guarantee of marriage as a culmination of the relationship. This concept is largely Western as it originated in the West and gradually became a popular practice there. Jan Kok and Dalia Leinarte state that unmarried cohabitation may have quite a long history but 'from the late 1960s onwards, cohabitation began to spread rapidly in Western countries, and is still on the increase' (505). As the youth (of the urban middle/upper class in India) is becoming increasingly aware of Western/global trends (whether through media, or due to rationalisation of popular discourses of 'westernisation', or through globetrotting, etc.), their ideologies/practices are being shaped by the discourses/constructs of 'westernisation'. This could be seen as part of the process of 'democratisation' of society and individuals that the definition of 'westernisation' refers to.

Interestingly, these web shows have 'westernised' short, crisp English titles, unlike those of popular Indian TV shows and films that have dominantly been in Hindi. This gives these shows a global colour as the OTT platform connects global audiences. Actually, these shows have a hybrid Indo-Western character even when it comes to the use of songs or to the characters speaking heavily in English often, but also speaking in Hindi and sometimes in their mother tongue; it is a natural linguistic amalgamation one perceives in the youth of today.

Little Things (hereafter *LT*) and *Permanent Roommates* (hereafter *PR*) elaborately represent the practice of unmarried live-in relationships or, as it is broadly called, cohabitation. In the former, Dhruv (Dhruv Sehgal) and Kavya (Mithila Palkar) are a young live-in couple in Mumbai, striving to do well in their careers as well as make their lives more 'eventful' or 'happening'. The latter is the story of Mikesh (Sumeet Vyas) and Tanya (Nidhi Singh), who are unsure when it comes to marriage and commitment, but realise that they are much in love, so a live-in relationship remains a better in-between option. When Mikesh arrives in India from the US (after three years of their long-distance relationship) and proposes marriage to Tanya, she is highly unsure. This, in due course of time, shakes Mikesh's firmness about getting married. In Season 2, when they actually live together, Tanya accidentally becomes pregnant and that initially causes even more distress. This distress is not because it is a premarital baby for which she might face social shame (premarital sex or baby traditionally being taboo in the Indian social system). Rather, Tanya is apprehensive about the hindrances that the baby might bring in the path of her career ambitions, her and Mikesh's plans for settling in the US, and in furthering their material aspirations (thus marking her as a liberated woman of modern India). *Adulting* is not about unmarried cohabiting couples but about two young girls, Nikhat (Aisha Ahmed) and Ray (Yashaswini Dayama), with newly started careers. They are in the process of 'adulting' by trying to be more independent and individualistic as they have moved out of their paternal houses and are trying to stand on their own feet in an unfamiliar metropolitan city. Their idea of youth and freedom centres mostly around enjoying themselves, achieving material success, and going on casual dates through Tinder, the global dating app of American origin. The practice of young children necessarily moving out of the parental home in search of freedom, materialistic pursuits and independent living is another contemporary urban trend that has been conventionally considered part of Western mores. So much so that Kavya is unable to 'adjust' with her parents at her parental home when she moves back there after a few years of living in with Dhruv (*LT* S4 E1).[1] Whether it is the couples in live-in relationships or the young girls in the process of 'adulting', they clearly embody the ideals of 'democracy, human rights, individual liberty' which, as Ania Loomba states in the context of postcoloniality/globalisation, have been given to the world by Western civilisation (227). Most often, it is a calculated project of the youth to ascertain their individuality, liberty and rights (a construct/discourse of 'westernisation') by breaking away from conventionality, resulting in sociocultural shifts, though not without hurdles and conflicts.

Some important issues arise from these portrayals: commitment-phobic urban youth are increasingly looking to Western models as a result of which the traditional Indian view of marriage and the structure of the Indian family are undergoing massive changes. The issues of women's individualism, liberty, sexuality and gender roles also arise in discussing this form of 'westernisation'. The Indian family system has undergone a lot of evolution from colonial to postcolonial times and is still evolving. The decline of the joint family system has been due to what Sarah Lamb refers to as the 'force of the four "zations"-modernization, industrialization, urbanization and Westernization' ('Modern Families' 84). Lamb also refers to widespread discourses according to which these 'zations' have brought about a whole new set of ideologies and social forms like 'individualism, materialism, consumerism, self-centredness, a freedom from "traditional" rules and mores ... nuclear families ... a pervasive lack of time' mostly in middle class and upper-middle class urban families (84). Most of these traits are visible in the characters of the web series as they have moved to cities in search of material success. The fast-paced, competitive, professional world allows them very less time outside work (Kavya does not even have time to take her mother around Mumbai in *LT* S2 E4). By either living alone or with partners/roommates, they have further broken down the nuclear family into something more ambivalent, as they hardly form a 'family' per se, and their ageing parents live a life of their own in a separate city or separate household. From a practical point of view, loneliness in a big, unfamiliar city and the stress of professional life makes companionship without the stress and obligations of 'commitment' and marital responsibilities a more lucrative option. This also allows the characters space to focus on their career to fulfil their material aspirations. Dhruv and Kavya have a tense discussion over them not being ready for marriage. Kavya says that she is not ready for unknown reasons while Dhruv assures her that he too does not want marriage at the moment since he cannot multitask. He says that he wants to focus on his career, even though everyone back home in Delhi wants him to get married (*LT* S3 E7). This shows how the urban youth has constructed a space for individual decisions where marriage is only one option—it may not be chosen over career, and there is scope for deferral (or no marriage finally) and non-conformity to conventional norms or familial expectations. The ideals of liberty, individuality and not being trapped by a parochial society's traditional ideas of morality make live-in relationships a comfortable proposition, thus inspiring these youngsters to emulate Western trends, consciously or unconsciously.

Eva Illouz argues that 'a fundamentally capitalist logic of consumer choice' can be an explanation for the difficulties in commitment as there are several choices available and there is always a possibility of something better coming up (qtd. in Titzmann 11). The capitalist logic of market is a 'Western' phenomenon and it is not invalid to argue that the politics of consumerism structures the materialistic mind to keep hunting for the better, to keep questioning relationship choices. Returning from a professional trip, during which Kavya befriended Raunak, she is unsettled by some questions regarding relationship choices. She questions Dhruv if their relationship is the end that they have been looking for; how will they ever know if the current relationship is good enough as there will always be something better; they might feel somebody else is better suited for them. Kavya says: 'It's about making a choice' (*LT* S2 E5). The representation of such complex contemporary sensibilities is a sharp departure from media discourses about unflinching and unquestioning devotion to the partner, constructed in the vein of Indian mythological ideologies that have been the basis of multiple media representations. Such traditional representations had constructed a discourse of 'Indianness' or of a core 'Indian' culture or value system, which is now radically changing.

There are debates regarding the concept of live-in relationships in India which is relatively new in this country. Fritzi-Marie Titzmann observes that even though premarital dating is increasingly acceptable among the urban middle and upper classes in India, 'live-in relationships pose a far bigger threat because they undermine the sanctity of the bond of marriage', while on the other hand, the concept of live-in relationships is regarded as a progressive development 'even though it is considered a "western" concept that has influenced Indian society' (2).

Since there is no marriage in this kind of a cohabitation arrangement, the idea of 'family' and of the roles and relations of each person in the marital or familial institution do not operate in the same way. Perhaps this too gives a sense of freedom and there is less pressure of sustaining the relationship as well. In *LT* S3 E7, Kavya says that a live-in relationship is like 'net practice' (a rehearsal) for marriage. Dhruv says there is a lot of time for marriage, and that they are 'cool' and 'yo' people ('westernised' millennials). He says,

> Out hone ka chance hi nahi hai na, toh bina pressure ke bass khelte raho. ("There's no chance of being out in the game [of relationship], so one can just play on without any pressure'; translation mine.)

The traditional understanding of the Indian faith in the 'sanctity of marriage' (specifically referring to first-time marriage) has evolved with the dominant global discourse on the preference for rehearsing 'marriage' (net practice) not only by way of premarital courtship but by staying together and trying to judge their compatibility. This arrangement may still not be acceptable by a section of urban society, even though courtship and 'love marriages' have been prevalent in India for quite some time now. But it may be argued that 'sanctity' is an ambivalent and relative idea, so the openness and wholehearted conviction for a lifelong, love-filled relationship, and compatible, equal partnership (and therefore the time and trial required before that) could be perceived as parameters of 'sanctity' by modern urban youth. Such ideas could possibly orient them towards considering this kind of 'westernisation' as more natural and rational. In the final season, Dhruv and Kavya discuss marriage but they do not submit to the traditional pressures of the 'system' of marriage, kids, home and household as Indian parents would expect (*LT* S4 E5); they are evolved enough to even think of getting married but remaining childfree if Kavya wishes so (S4 E8). A survey report published in 2004 substantiates the argument:

> Cohabitation before first marriage is now a behavioural norm. Over half of US couples marrying for the first time begin their unions by cohabiting.... In Britain, even higher percentages of first marriages begin as cohabitation.... (Seltzer 922)

But the naturalisation of such relationships and family formations in India, as portrayed by these web shows, corresponds, to some extent, with the changing reality of Indian society. It was in the year 2005 in India that a legal clause first addressed relations 'in the nature of marriage' (Agarwal 50), and in 2015 the Supreme Court validated such relationships as equivalent to marriage, ensuring women in live-in relationships have the same rights as in marriage (Titzmann 1). But social acceptability is still debated as many think 'unmarried cohabitation is incompatible with Indian culture and values' (Titzmann 1). The motif of the sanctity of marriage and its association with family values in India has been the dominant media discourse. This could be a continuation of the anxiety about the 'loosening of ties to what it means to be "Indian"' that the privatisation of television has engendered (Ibrahim 265).

Various Indian courts have given various kinds of judgements in such cases from time to time. The Supreme Court has declared that live-in relationships cannot be designated as illegal. Despite what Titzmann mentions above regarding the Supreme Court's validation, more recent instances show that 'same rights as in marriage' is a dicey and complex proposition in many cases, considering the basic premise of a live-in relationship. Perhaps, then, it would require being more of a personal settlement than legal enforcement since there is no strict legal structure and many areas remain unaddressed. In March 2023, the Supreme Court rejected a PIL for registration of live-in relationships with the centre. The PIL sought registration and guidelines in view of increasing the social security of live-in partners as there are increasing instances of heinous crimes by those in such relationships, but the centre declared it a 'hare-brained idea' (PTI) since it makes no sense to involve the centre which has nothing to do with such relationship choices.

It must be argued that these web programmes encapsulate a very complex intertwining of the modern, urban 'westernised' mindset with those understood as 'core Indian sensibilities'. They portray a moving beyond the 'simple binaries such as tradition and modernity, East and West' (Lamb, *Ageing and the Indian Diaspora* 134), making it difficult to define the constructs of 'Indianness' and 'westernisation'. Shoma A. Chatterji quotes Ahalya Raghuram, a psychologist, who thinks in terms of the social unacceptability of live-in relationships in India and says that the alienation of the couple from their family, parental disapproval and the insecurity of the relationship can create havoc in the psyche of the individuals concerned (257). But no such hiding, insecurity (among the live-in partners or their parents) or parental disapproval is observed in these web series. In fact, when Tanya asks her father if he is sure he has no problem with her and Mikesh's live-in arrangement (which, she clarifies openly, would mean that they might engage in a sexual relationship), her father gives his consent, which rather surprises Tanya. But as a father, he justifies his consent by saying that he has full conviction that nobody can love her better than Mikesh (*PR* S1 E2), which suggests his assuredness that they will ultimately get married. Dhruv and Kavya's parents are fully aware of their live-in relationship. Even if no sign of disapproval regarding live-in relationships is apparent in the parents' psyche, the insecurities, values, sentiments and sensibilities conventionally associated with marriage in India are found lurking beneath in some moments. In *LT* S2 E4, when Kavya's mother visits them in Mumbai and goes around the city with Dhruv in Kavya's absence, she asks him if his parents know about him and Kavya living together. This is a moment of mild insecurity of an Indian mother for her young daughter, as she goes on to ask Dhruv, 'Tum dono serious toh ho, na?' ('I hope you both are serious [about your relationship]'; translation mine). This may be interpreted as a mother's concern who has been brought up in and is part of a larger society that values marriage and the security of 'family' (in the traditional sense) as the culmination of youth, especially for girls. But she is not conservative; she is the embodiment of a fine mixture of modernity (which could partly be a result of India's evolution through 'westernisation'), as she acknowledges the individuality of her daughter, and of traditional 'Indianness', being a loving and concerned 'Indian' mother. In fact, when Mikesh and Tanya's families get to know about the couple's premarital baby, they are perplexed and rush to get the couple married so that the traditional structure of 'family' and society is restored (*PR* S2). The larger society outside the family is not portrayed much in this regard, apart from a few instances of policing by neighbours or security guards.

Bollywood movies or Indian television programmes have rarely glorified or valourised such out-of-marriage relationships, which appear quite normal in the urban settings of these web shows. The dominant discourse of Indian films or soaps has been to insist on marriage and family (though extramarital affairs and sex outside marriage have been portrayed sporadically). If at all the topic of unmarried cohabitation has been touched upon, it is to intensify the drama by making it a sensational non-normativity, a hush-hush affair (as in the 2013 movie *Shudh Desi Romance* or the 2015 web show *Love Bytes*). Nor has it been treated as an almost organically growing trend in the urban space. But *Little Things* and *Permanent Roommates*, in dealing with live-in relationships, or *Adulting*, in dealing with issues like casual dating, do not spin sensational melodrama around it by treating it as immorality or sin, or a case of 'Western' values 'corrupting' the 'purity' of Indian culture.

The changing role of women in such contemporary representations is an important issue that arises out of the discussion of 'westernisation'. The joint family system, with intergenerational relations, gave women the role of 'homemaker' and preserver of 'core Indian values' in the family (mainly by executing the roles of an ideal daughter-in-law, mother and wife), thereby preserving the sanctity of the nation. Partha Chatterjee observes that women in postcolonial times had to maintain the 'traditional' Indian spiritual domain in the domestic sphere as distinguished from an increasingly 'Western', materialist, outer world that engaged the men (qtd. in Lamb, *Ageing and the Indian Diaspora* 50). This has been the media discourse of the family drama or saas–bahu sagas with the popular Indian soap characters Tulsi and Parvati being the icons of 'Indian' family values. This divided gender roles sharply in many ways. But portrayals of gender roles in the three web series under discussion are radically different. With the rise of urbanisation and globalisation, with greater emancipation and mobility, ambitious women with careers have broken the stringent barriers of traditional gender roles, thereby contributing to the global economy. The 'Western', materialist, outer world that Chatterjee mentions is increasingly dominated by career-oriented women like Kavya and Tanya, even Ray and Nikhat, who migrate to metropolitan cities to achieve their aspirations of becoming successful career women. This is their priority over playing traditional gender roles in courtship, marriage or motherhood. Mikesh and Dhruv are representations of modern men who believe in gender equality. This is also a representation of the dismantling of traditional gender roles (generally in the case of marriage), like the woman being expected to cook and feed the family. Kavya hardly ever steps into the kitchen while Dhruv cooks, nor are there any stereotypical expectations from her to play conventional gender roles, not only because they are not married, but because they portray the ideals of liberty and equality which is a by-product of their modern, 'westernised', live-in lifestyle, as contrasted to the postcolonial family system.

The dominant media image of the mother (mostly in family films and soaps) has closely resembled Chatterjee's observations mentioned above. In this context, the portrayal of Nikhat's mother Nafisa as willing to have a drink is pathbreaking. Ray is confused and randomly utters, 'Are moms allowed to drink?' (*Adulting* S1 E2). This utterance bears testimony to the dominant idea of the 'mother' that has persisted in society, family and popular media discourse in India. Nafisa attempts to bridge the generational gap with her daughter by happily allowing her 'controlled drinking' which is a radical shift in the portrayal of the mother figure in popular culture. Both Kavya's and Nikhat's mothers complain about not getting any personal time or space after their fathers retire, in Season 2 of both shows. These mothers assert their individuality, perhaps a result of 'westernisation', unlike the traditional ideal of women's pervasive engagement with family and household chores. The portrayal of female sexuality and assertion of the values of individuality and democracy through sexual choice is another construction of 'westernisation' in the web series. Just a decade ago, there was immense controversy regarding a TV reality show portraying 'pre- or extra-marital sex, practices considered contrary to Indian cultures and value' (Ibrahim 265). But such representations have been celebrated in these web series which is a radical departure from the media discourses that existed a few years ago (much of which still persists). When Mrs Khatri blackmails Tanya that she will tell the whole family about Tanya's premarital pregnancy, suggesting family scandal and defamation, Tanya lashes out at her. She says that she does not care what other people in the extended family say as long as her loved ones are with her (*PR* S2 E4).

Some instances in these web series make it evident that there has been the emergence of an upper/middle class with an evolved value system in the era of globalisation. It may be argued that some ideologies of the young characters' parents closely correspond to the values of 'independence' and 'active life' that Sarah Lamb finds in America with regard to ageing people, in contrast with those she finds in India. Lamb also finds, in North Americans, ideas of boundless prospects of life, of no fixed period when one can be productive, romantic and live life fully (Lamb, *Ageing and the Indian Diaspora* 133–234). Tanya's widowed father embodies a similar ideology as he unabashedly and proudly vocalises his love for Tanya's aunt, his desire to marry her and to explore new prospects in life (*PR* S2 E2).

It is important to analyse how food becomes a major symbol of 'westernisation' in the shows. This also leads to a study of how the capitalist market system dominated by Western market giants has captured the Indian market. Kavya prepares a breakfast spread for Dhruv to make their Sunday special. They have bacon; a waffle is visible on the table; and then there is salad, bread, orange juice, etc. (*LT* S1 E1). The breakfast spread is symbolic of the evolving tastes of Indians and especially of the urban youth, who hardly have time to cook in their busy, career-dominated lives. Many are not experts in cooking proper meals, so they probably find these Western-style breakfast and snack items easier to make. Or it may be plain love for Western food culture. The evolving tastes and love for Western-style food is evident in the way Dhruv and Kavya savour bacon or a salami sandwich, and this 'westernisation' is now a social reality in India. An *Economic Times* article refers to research on 'the pork revolution in India' and the rising demand for pork products like sausages (also popular in America). It mentions how such items had been shunned in Indian culture or only marginally used in the past until they were reintroduced in India by the Portuguese and later by the English. Bacon is a popular British breakfast item. It has attained global popularity and is increasingly available at breakfast buffets in Western-style cafés and restaurants in India. A taste for such meat has developed, thereby increasing the demand for pork/bacon, sausages and salami in the Indian market (Doctor and Sally).

Also visible on the table is some kind of waffle (*LT* S1E1). The waffle is originally from Belgium but is now representative of American cuisine, as waffles are highly popular in American breakfast spreads (Thomson). A *Times of India* article reports how business-oriented youngsters coming back from the West strategically cajoled Indians to try waffles, saying it is like jalebi. Once consumers tried them and the taste developed, there was a boom and a massive change in India's snacking culture (Vishal). It is evident how materialist ventures, better termed the politics of materialism, are gradually cultivating the taste of the urban Indian for European or American food culture which is taking deeper root in India. The article gloats over the fact that 'aspirational young consumers' are more 'international' and global or Western items are rapidly effacing uniquely Indian, traditional ones (Vishal). Western chains are usurping the market, and many indigenous businesses serving Western-style food are also burgeoning. But it must be argued here that if Western culture/tastes or consumer products are replacing the uniquely 'Indian' food culture, rather than trying to make the latter globally popular, then it needs to be seriously questioned as centre–periphery structures may tend to emerge. Globalisation creates new opportunities and global connections while also creating new divisions (Loomba 220).

Another very important food influence (therefore market influence) of the West that has newly colonised the minds and hearts of the urban youth is pizza. Pizza, though it first originated in Italy (Naples), became an integral part of American culture, with the earliest pizza chains booming in the 1950s in the States.

Thus, it became a 'shared cultural obsession' of Italy and America (Daley). Though it is mostly the youth who are obsessed with this Italian/American delicacy, older urban middle/upper class people are also fascinated by it. This would not be expected a couple of decades ago, as the reverse would happen and the elders would stereotypically ask the young to refrain from 'junk food'. But the 'westernised' youth culture seems to have cultivated their taste in the older generation and this phenomenon is reflected in the web content. Mikesh's grandfather constantly creates a fuss for not being given pizza when he craves it and gets irritated at being served roti (Indian bread), milk and banana (*PR* S2 E3), a staple for many from the older generations in India. While this evokes fun, as one would not expect an old man like him to become a cry-baby demanding pizza, his preference for pizza over milk and roti has more implications. It is symptomatic, it may be argued, of a shift in culture/taste (from the more 'Indian' to the 'Western') and class status (suburban/rural to upper middle-class urban) in India. The rapid urbanisation along with migration of many rural residents to the urban areas has gradually brought changes even in the older generations. This generation seems to have become partly absorbed in the 'millennial youth culture', with their children and grandchildren being agents of this cultural shift. This has also been possible in the materialist, post-liberalisation India, with the urban class being increasingly able to afford the 'westernised fast-food culture' both economically and ideologically. This amounts to the 'westernisation' of a larger section of the society.

At the end of their day out on a Sunday when Dhruv and Kavya are too tired to cook the Thai curry they had planned, they decide to order pizza and have some red wine as that would make a 'perfect' dinner (*LT* S1 E1). This shows how pizza has become a preference after a tiring day (even on a non-tiring one when it is a luxury and on sick days as well). Pizza has turned out to be a satisfying, 'perfect', wholesome meal readily available, with multiple pizza outlets in the cities and their quick home-delivery services. In S1 E2 and in S2 E3, again after a long working day, it is an option for them to prepare pasta, another national dish of Italy. A report in the *Hindu Business Line* states:

> Research reports seem to indicate that Indian consumers seem to be patronising Italian cuisine the most, gulping down pizzas and pastas. Chinese comes next. This [is] ... largely fuelled by young consumers.... (Menon)

Ray's prophecy for Nikhat, 'You won't be able to resist pizza' (*Adulting* S1 E3), turns out to be true not only for Nikhat but for most young urban millennials, as these European or American dishes have become a staple and often an obsession for them, despite concerns of health issues that overconsumption may cause.

This leads to the discussion of the opening up of various international fast-food chains across India (and indigenous ones following the foreign models) and the change in food culture and in the Indian consumer market. This phenomenon can be roughly explained by George Ritzer's thesis on the 'McDonaldisation' of society. McDonalds is the foremost American fast-food chain that served as an influence for the fast-food business/culture in the world and probably, later, the fine-dining culture. Ritzer defines 'McDonaldisation' as 'the process by which the principles of the fast-food restaurant are coming to dominate more and more sectors of American society as well as of the rest of the world'. He argues that eating fast food at McDonalds is a 'sign' that the people are in tune with 'contemporary lifestyle' and there is 'a kind of magic or enchantment associated with such food and its settings' (19). It must be argued here that in India, in the post-liberalisation or globalisation period after the 1990s, a culture did emerge with the popularity of and aspiration for foreign brands, with burgeoning mall/supermarket culture and the setting up of international food chains. Moreover, people began to associate this culture with a kind of upscale sophisticated metropolitan life and this gave rise to a materialist–consumerist class. This, in some ways, leads to the idea of 'leisure' and the formation of the 'leisure class'. McDonaldisation, suggests Ritzer, is a system that ensures good quality of product and services, consistency, availability, convenience (to people who lack time due to long work hours, like most of the young characters in these web shows) through their ideals of 'efficiency', 'calculability', 'predictability' and 'control' (23). Some other popular American chains that have driven deeper roots into India are Domino's, Pizza Hut, Subway and KFC. Nikhat is seen relishing 'chicken wings', a dish popularised by KFC, in *Adulting* S2 E3. The way these American giants are taking over the Indian market is clear from an *Economic Times* report in 2014 which says, 'Domino's, the world's largest pizza delivery chain, sells more pizzas in India than anywhere else outside its home country—the US' (Bhushan). This poses serious questions about the rise of another global order/empire dominated by the US through market capitalism. Many foreign chains have incorporated local flavours in their products to 'colonise' the consumers better. This is another ambivalent position; when national/local tastes are absorbed into the products of these foreign brands, should it not be perceived as a 'neo-colonialist' tactic? This can hardly be perceived as 'Indianisation', as it does not amount to a flow of the traditional Indian tastes/culture to the West. The 'neo-colonialist' tactic plays to two factors—people's inclination for the 'Western'/'westernisation' and their love for their own traditional tastes.

Ritzer himself mentions that fast food causes diabetes, obesity, cholesterol and other health problems. It also causes extreme harm to the environment due to excess meat production, fertiliser use, animal waste and so on, which causes climate change, land degradation, air and water pollution, and many more environmental hazards (167–170). It is no exception for India, with its ever-increasing 'westernised' fast-food culture, but this awareness hardly features as a counter-discourse in these shows.

The featuring of 'Indian' food in these web shows seems to be associated with the idea of 'home' and mother, the warmth and comfort associated with a mother's love and care which is often missed when one becomes an adult and gets busy with one's individual life. It also serves as a sort of connection to one's 'roots', 'identity' and the memories of lost days lived before this busy life of materialist pursuits. Traditional food, therefore, may be representative of a lurking sense of 'displacement' from one world (home, family and parental love) to another (busy, wearying professional life). It is also a sort of 'homecoming', metaphorically referring to the seeking of comfort in the traditional Indian 'homely' food when jaded with 'westernised' food. These are the fissures in the practice of a 'westernised' food culture. Dhruv learns how to make the iconic Maharashtrian dish pithla bhakri (pithla is a gram flour curry and bhakri is the Maharashtrian flat bread) from Kavya's mother over phone. He makes great effort to prepare it and surprises Kavya, who had been craving for the pithla bhakri made by her mother. Eating what Dhruv made only reminded her of the taste of her mother's dish (*LT* S2 E5). When Dhruv is in his parental home in Delhi, his mother feeds him an iconic Delhi/Punjabi dish, chhole puri, which he finds extremely tasty with the perfect Indian flavour of hing (asafoetida); he murmurs that he has no idea how long it has been since he has had it. Later he demands some parathas from his mother, saying he has not had them for long (S3 E5). While a sick Kavya loves the stew Dhruv has made for her and a pizza that accompanies it, she fondly remembers how her aayi (mother) had got her into the habit of having khichdi (a sort of Indian porridge/polenta made from cereal) on sick days, which makes her crave it on such days even now. Dhruv again makes an effort to prepare it for dinner (S3 E6). Dhruv's efforts signify the construction of 'home' and a sense of comfort. Part of the love for homemade indigenous food could also be attributed to a sense of saturation with eating out and with fast food, a sort of 'disenchantment' with the McDonaldised culture (Ritzer 165). Another ironical situation arises when Mikesh, a US-returnee, valorises Punjabi food over Italian while Tanya, who has remained in India for long, prefers Italian to impress her guests. Tanya cooks Italian delicacies like

'Alfredo pasta' and 'basil rice' for their housewarming party. On hearing this, Mikesh is surprised and asks her, 'Khaana kahaan hai?' ('Where is the food?'; translation mine), suggesting that whatever Tanya is cooking does not qualify as proper food for him. This is because traditionally he and his paternal family enjoy Punjabi food and Punjabi music, without which a party means nothing to them ("Housewarming", *Permanent Roommates: He Said, She Said*). Tanya, in her insistence on cooking Italian cuisine to impress her guests, may be said to represent, to some extent, the Indian youth which, consciously or unconsciously, casts a longing look at the West. If 'westernisation' emerges as dominant in these shows, it exhibits major fissures with what is traditionally desi, and vice-versa, which makes the constructs of 'westernisation' and 'Indianness' not simply oppositional, rather intersecting and problematic.

The sharp cultural/ideological conflicts of 'Indian' or 'Western' with regards to dressing have changed much with increasing modernisation/globalisation and also with the emergence of concepts like 'Indo-Western'. Dressing/fashion in contemporary urban society is mostly a matter of individual choice, fashion trends and comfort. That which is traditional Indian is occasionally worn by the characters, like Kavya wears either the sari (*LT* S1 E1; S4 E8) or lehenga for weddings (S2 E7) and a salwar-kameez for her father's retirement function (S3 E4). What is problematic is that Ray and Nikhat mock Ray wearing a sari for her cousin's wedding (on her mother's insistence) and how she might trip and fall because of how troublesome it is to drape it (*Adulting* S1 E2). It must also be argued that the way the girls make fun and whine about wearing the sari, it would also amount to a 're-/neo-orientalist' way of demeaning of the Indian cultural symbol that is celebrated even in the West today. Ray, however, finally buys a sari, giving in to her mother's wish.

Tanya encourages Mikesh to find a job, saying that he is a US returnee and therefore highly qualified for a good job in India, as Indians are crazy about imported things ("House Husband",

Permanent Roommates: He Said, She Said). The question arises if this represents a subtle 'neo-orientalist' attitude/mindset which is ridden with a form of 'colonial hangover' of the West. This question must also be asked in view of the market hegemony for products by Western giants. In the case of consumer goods, a hegemonic adulation for Western, especially American, companies and their products can be observed. Tanya works on an Apple laptop (in *PR* S2 promo) while Nikhat wishes that one day Nike (both American multinational corporations) will also recognise and e-mail her for endorsing their brand on social media (*Adulting* S1 E3). These American multinational brands are defining the dreams and aspirations of the youth and at the same time completely capturing the Indian market. Not only goods, but dating apps like Tinder and social-media apps like Instagram (both developed by American multinationals) are pervasively colonising the minds of young people and defining their ideas of 'identity' and fame; like for Nikhat, popularity on Instagram defines a large part of her social aspirations (*Adulting* S2). These 'millennial', young characters, like real-life Indian millennials, have grown up in the post-1990s era of post-liberalisation and globalisation in India amidst the ubiquity of Western brands like McDonalds, Pepsi, Coca-Cola, Lays, Nestlé and Maggi, constantly endorsed by Bollywood stars on television. Nikhat and Ray munch on Lays chips quite often, and Ray makes a Maggi cake for Nikhat's birthday as she cannot get an actual cake (S2). These brands have been here so long and are so loved that they seem as much 'Indian' as belonging to their country of origin, which blurs Western/Indian binaries, as is natural in globalisation. But the point of concern comes up if any form of 'capitalist slavery' to the West arises. A result of the absorption of the Indian market by foreign giants could result in the opposite impacts of globalisation like 'allowing giant foreign corporations to grab larger sectors of the third world's economies', 'suppression of domestic industry' and ruination of small industries as found by an Indian research group called Research Unit for Political Economy (qtd. in Loomba 219). To counter this, a roaring rise of indigenous industries and production framework, and promotion of indigenous items/brands must be the focus of self-reliant India, which is also part of some moves by several governments in the country.

Loomba agrees to the concept of globalisation as explicated by Michael Hardt and Antonio Negri. According to them, globalisation is a new 'empire' which is distinct from the 'imperialist', as the 'empire' 'absorbs them [subject countries] into a new international network' (214). Loomba refers to several thinkers who believe the US to be the new 'empire' (221–227). The analysis of the representation of 'westernisation' in the three web series indicates that America has emerged as a new 'empire' in the global order by dominating the capitalist market system and absorbing the Indian market. In the case of food culture, European and American influences seem to be the most ubiquitous and deep-rooted in India.

Amidst the prevailing discourse of globalisation, these web series do not represent the old anxiety of Western influence and the sentimental lamentation of the loss of 'essential' Indian culture. They portray a more hybridised and globalised society in terms of ideology and social culture, some of which may be considered a progressive change. The changing patterns of the Indian family system, values, position of women, changing gender roles and the dominant media discourses around them have gone through a radical shift which may be seen as a by-product of the 'westernisation'/'globalisation' evident in the web series. This paper has argued that a dominant 'westernisation' or Western hegemony is perceived in the representation of the youth culture and capitalist market, and that tendencies towards 'neo-orientalism' and 'neo-colonialism' must be questioned. But the dominant discourse of 'westernisation' is certainly not without fissures and counter-discourses, as uniquely traditional 'Indian' sensibilities, emotions and tastes surface recurrently. This makes the constructs of 'Indianness' and 'westernisation' intersecting and problematic in today's postcolonial/globalised world.

Note

1. 'S' indicates 'season' and 'E' indicates 'episode'.

Works Cited

Adulting: Season 1. YouTube, uploaded by Dice Media, 18 Apr. 2018, https://www.youtube.com/watch?v=VgyBAtA5yXs&list=PL4x7Of-X4XhjJ60GoQk953MubwDKXq06X.

Adulting: Season 2. YouTube, uploaded by Dice Media, 11 Aug. 2019, https://www.youtube.com/watch?v=TYL6T5FCvA8&list=PL4x7Of-X4XhihdpCA1wCUNB6KEp1FNVms&index=2.

Agarwal, Anuja. 'Law and "Live-in" Relationships in India'. *Economic and Political Weekly*, vol. 47, no. 39, 2012, pp. 50–56.

Bhushan, Ratna. 'India Emerges as Domino's Biggest Market Outside US'. *The Economic Times*, 1 Dec. 2014. https://economictimes.indiatimes.com/industry/cons-products/food/india-emerges-as-dominos-biggest-market-outside-us/articleshow/45329585.cms?from=mdr. Accessed 8 Nov. 2024.

Chatterji, Shoma A. 'The Family in Flux: The Decimated Family in Rituparno Ghosh's Films'. *The Indian Family in Transition: Reading Literary and Cultural Texts*, edited by Sanjukta Dasgupta and Malashri Lal. SAGE Publications, 2007, pp. 243–279.

Daley, Jason. 'The Father of American Pizza is Not Who We Thought He Was'. *Smithsonian Magazine*, 8 Feb. 2019. https://www.smithsonianmag.com/smart-news/father-american-pizza-not-who-we-thought-it-was-180971454/. Accessed 8 Nov. 2024.

Doctor, Vikram, and Madhvi Sally. 'Shedding its Past Poor Image, Pork Slowly Gaining Popularity in India'. *The Economic Times*, 23 June 2017. https://economictimes.indiatimes.com/news/economy/agriculture/shedding-its-past-poor-image-pork-slowly-gaining-popularity-in-india/articleshow/59291205.cms?from=mdr. Accessed 8 Nov. 2024.

Gandhi, Leela. *Postcolonial Theory: A Critical Introduction*. Allen & Unwin, 1998.

'House Husband'. *Permanent Roommates: He Said, She Said*, The Viral Fever, 2020. *Audible*, https://www.audible.in/pd/B09F1M9D3F?source_code=ASSOR150021921000O.

'Housewarming'. *Permanent Roommates: He Said, She Said*, The Viral Fever, 2020. *Audible*, https://www.audible.in/pd/B09F1VJZLC?source_code=ASSOR150021921000O.

Ibrahim, Amrita. 'Voyeurism and the Family on Television'. *The Cambridge Companion to Modern Indian Culture*, edited by Vasudha Dalmia and Rashmi Sadana. Cambridge University Press, 2012, pp. 264–282.

Kok, Jan, and Dalia Leinarte. 'Cohabitation in Europe: A Revenge of History?' *The History of the Family*, vol. 20, no. 4, 2015, pp. 489–514.

Lamb, Sarah. *Ageing and the Indian Diaspora: Cosmopolitan Families in India and Abroad*. Indiana University Press, 2009.

———. 'Modern Families and Independent Living: Reflections on Contemporary Aging'. *The Indian Family in Transition: Reading Literary and Cultural Texts*, edited by Sanjukta Dasgupta and Malashri Lal. SAGE Publications, 2007, pp. 81–102.

Little Things: Season 1. Dice Media, 2016. Netflix, https://www.netflix.com/in/title/81011159.

Little Things: Season 2. Dice Media, 2018. Netflix, https://www.netflix.com/in/title/81011159.

Little Things: Season 3. Dice Media, 2019. Netflix, https://www.netflix.com/in/title/81011159.

Little Things: Season 4. Dice Media, 2021. Netflix, https://www.netflix.com/in/title/81011159.

Loomba, Ania. *Colonialism/Postcolonialism*, 2nd ed. Routledge, 2005.

Menon, Bindu D. 'India's Restaurant Revolution'. *The Hindu Business Line*, 16 May 2013. https://www.thehindubusinessline.com/news/variety/indias-restaurant-revolution/article23029875.ece. Accessed 8 Nov. 2024.

Permanent Roommates: Season 1. The Viral Fever, 2014. Amazon Prime India, https://www.primevideo.com/detail/0PMEGQL9RARKXFWDWBSLJEQ2LF/ref=atv_dp_season_select_s1

Permanent Roommates: Season 2. The Viral Fever, 2014. Amazon Prime India, https://www.primevideo.com/detail/0TEZ4X4KXMCMGL3HMFBFT7K4EA/ref=atv_dp_season_select_s2

PTI. 'Supreme Court Rejects PIL for Registration of Live-in Relationships with Centre; Calls it "Hare-brained" Idea'. *The Indian Express*, 20 Mar. 2023. https://indianexpress.com/article/india/supreme-court-live-in-relationships-registration-centre-hare-brained-idea-8507817/. Accessed 8 Nov. 2024.

Ritzer, George. *The McDonaldization of Society: Into the Digital Age.* SAGE Publications, 2019.

Seltzer, Judith A. 'Cohabitation in the United States and Britain: Demography, Kinship and the Future'. *Journal of Marriage and Family*, vol. 66, no. 4, 2004, pp. 921–928.

Sullivan, Larry E., editor. *The SAGE Glossary of the Social and Behavioural Sciences.* SAGE Publications, 2009.

Thomson, Julie R. 'The History of the Belgian Waffle, Which We've Apparently Been Eating All Wrong'. *Huffpost*, 6 Dec. 2017. https://www.huffpost.com/entry/belgian-waffles-history_n_6535434. Accessed 8 Nov. 2024.

Titzmann, Fritzi-Marie. 'Contesting the Norm? Live-in Relationships in Indian Media Discourses'. *South Asia Multidisciplinary Academic Journal* [Online], vol. 16, 2017.

Vishal, Anoothi. 'Why Waffles are Trending'. *The Times of India*, 6 May 2018. https://timesofindia.indiatimes.com/home/sunday-times/why-waffles-are-trending/articleshow/64045541.cms. Accessed 8 Nov. 2024.

Desirable Femininities as Part of the Hegemonic Nationalist Discourse in Three Contemporary Bollywood Films

Shyaonti Talwar

Introduction

M.K. Raghavendra, while commenting on the structure and the form of the Indian popular film, remarks that there is 'no other cinema in the world that brings "love" as compulsively into its narratives' as Bollywood, and that 'most Indian films are about the triumph of love' (37). It is interesting, therefore, to see how Bollywood films have thematically shifted from the boy-meets-girl love story, or the love triangle where the discourse centres around love, courtship, conflict and revolt, to the dynamics of marriage and a normative socialisation into a married state. This transition can be traced to the 1990s with the emergence of the genre of 'new middle-class films pioneered by Mani Ratnam', which eroticised the marital relationship with the projection of the woman as an active sexual being, moving on to box-office hits like *Hum Aapke Hain Koun...!* (1994) and *Dilwale Dulhania Le Jayenge* (1995), which celebrated the unapologetic and simultaneous presence of 'love, sex and marriage' in the life of a heterosexual couple (John 168–169).

In contemporary times, however, yet another remarkable inflection can be noted in the visual economy of films as the private and libidinal space of a heterosexual couple is now the public and political space of a socially sanctioned, heterosexual marriage that reinforces this hegemonic, patriarchal institution which, like many other recoded institutions, becomes part of the 'development' narrative of the nation state, bolstering Hindu nationalism too in the process (Harriss). On and off screen, the lead female has transitioned from being an object of desire to a model of resilience, with her portrayal as a desiring subject substantially undermined. With her transition from a rebellious lover to a domesticated wife, the underlying plot too has been displaced.

The action of contemporary Bollywood films now takes off from where the action in earlier films ended, to aver 'and they lived happily ever after'. The journey has changed and so has the destination. The expression, pursuit, channelling and culmination of desire in an implicit sexual union is now replaced by some issue of social or political significance. It is not lovers who need to unite now, but marriage that needs to sustain and endure. Marriage is foregrounded and the institution of the family is sacrosanct.

The feminine constructs are women who undertake impossible missions ranging from social reform and the upholding of traditions to rescuing their husbands from the clutches of death and sacrificing their lovers instead. They take on challenges and bring about revolutions in the public space without, however, disturbing the tranquillity of the domestic sphere or dismantling and challenging the patriarchal institution or hegemony of marriage and family, thereby reconceptualising and glamourising regulated sexual relations in tandem with older brahminical codes. In the spirit of Hindu nationalism, the films reconfigure 'the private space of the "home" as a site of Indian culture' where women and their sexualities become 'the repository of Indian identity and tradition, subject to ideologies ... central to the forging ... of the nation' (Panjabi and Chakravarti xix–xx).

Though the representation of women to further the purpose of cultural nationalism (either hegemonic or emergent) is not new, the study of the women protagonists in the three films discussed in this essay is critical in today's times. The women represent archetypal figures and feed into the mythical and religious construct of ideal wifehood, which is the cornerstone of the Hindu right in power and its explicit party ideology that is strategically operating on culturally rather than constitutionally bound edicts, making very deliberate attempts to lay out scripturally inspired, prescriptive and supplementary roles for women which derive support from traditionally constituted upper-caste patriarchal families which are gatekeepers of the status quo.

The femininities taken up for study fit into the mythological construct of the ideal upper-caste Hindu wife who will uphold the family honour but don a reformist garb that will feed into a pseudo-progressive discourse and speak a language spoken by the state without challenging the larger and more entrenched structures of violence and oppression, thereby refraining from disturbing the societal class/caste/gender/religion status quo. This reformist agenda, like a red herring, serves three purposes. First, it is a soft projection of the hard nationalism of the ruling right. It represents some of the right wing's most fundamental discourses that have spelled its victory at the centre, whether it is along the lines of its own dogmatic brahminical religious nationalism (prompted by the two-nation theory) or appropriated discourses of the left liberal savarna/brahminical sensibility (swadeshi and swachhata) that fashioned India's freedom struggle. Third, it attempts a deliberate homogenisation of India's cultural, religious, linguistic and ethnic diversity by making absent from the narrative space real issues of marginalisation and oppression which have intensified in recent years. The constructs are also the conception of savarna minds that have been cultivated in exclusionary spaces of intellectual privilege, which may not be intersectional in nature and therefore reflect only a narrow spectrum of concerns, which is again proof of not much having changed over the years.

Toilet: Ek Prem Katha

Toilet: Ek Prem Katha (2017), set in the Hindi-speaking belt of India, is inspired by a true incident that can likewise be seen as promoting the government of India's Swachh Bharat Abhiyan or nationwide campaign for cleanliness and sanitation ('*Toilet—Ek Prem Katha* a Huge Boost'). Constructing toilets in villages has been a big part of this drive. The real story of the film starts after the boy-meets-girl-and-gets-her part is over.

Keshav (Akshay Kumar), who runs a transport business in a small town, falls in love with the modern and educated Jaya (Bhumi Pednekar) who is literally the poster girl of the English language. Keshav is attracted to Jaya for her smartness and devil-may-care attitude. Keshav's family is steeped in orthodoxy and blind, superstitious beliefs and the fact that this is no secret is evident from his father's (Sudhir Pandey) obsession over Keshav's horoscope and his act of making his son marry a buffalo. Keshav is seen to oblige his father, mostly because he is more of a pacifist than a conformist. Taking the middle path, he convinces Jaya to be part of a plan that will allay his father's superstitions and convince the latter to give his consent to their marriage, which she reluctantly agrees to.

The film gets to the main twist in the plot after a quick romance and clever overcoming of a roadblock that culminates in their marriage. The morning after she is married, Jaya discovers that there is no toilet in her husband's house and that she, like most women in the village, is expected to wake up at the crack of dawn and relieve herself in the open before the world is up and about. Horrified at the prospect and mortified by the fact that her husband could be insensitive enough to endorse this arrangement, Jaya begins a silent protest which manifests as an ideological clash between traditional and progressive worldviews, represented by the father-in-law and the daughter-in-law, respectively. The battle acquires epic proportions as Jaya leaves her husband's house, mobilises the women of the village to fight for toilets and puts her marriage at stake for the cause. Eventually, after a lot of dramatic twists and turns, and efforts mainly on Keshav's part, realisation dawns on the father-in-law who gives in and the daughter-in-law has her way.

Despite being set in contemporary India, the film reflects the early phase of the nationalist struggle which, in its resistance to revivalist nationalism and the colonial rule, also involved a dethroning and evisceration of oppressive customs, superstitions and traditions in Indian society and intersected with women's relative liberation and subsequent entry into the public space. Superstitions and beliefs related to matrimonial alliances, hygiene and civic responsibility, and the personal safety of women are some issues the film addresses. Change is shown to be brought about through a collective movement and a steadfast commitment to the cause of constructing personal toilets, thus privileging a social cause over personal relations. However, while certain mores are refuted and challenged, certain others, which are a part of the culture of compliance, are endorsed and re-essentialised by a brahminical patriarchal agency through Keshav, who stands for the heroic will of the progressive, forward-thinking, soft Hindu and on whose shoulders lies the responsibility of leading the nation towards a modern worldview.

Jaya

The lead female character, Jaya, interestingly contests certain values while ignoring others. Though it is Jaya's liberated, non-conformist and slightly rebellious attitude and appearance, and her modern ways of speaking and bearing that make Keshav promptly fall in love with her and traverse the somewhat rocky and uphill path of courtship, she is quick to don the role of the caretaker of the family immediately after marriage. From a bicycle-riding, jeans-clad, English-speaking, free-spirited young woman into a sari-clad daughter-in-law with the obligatory veil over her head, the spatial and sartorial politics both explicitly relate Jaya's overnight transition and appropriate domestication as she dexterously takes over the kitchen, cooking for and serving three adult men who hitherto were managing their own food. She is yet one more 'Bharatiya nari' or ideal Indian woman, a significant trope in cultural nationalism, who is progressive, but only within the patriarchal framework. She is domesticated enough to be the nurturer, discreet enough to switch from functional to traditional attire, and retains just the right amount of righteousness and progressiveness in her attitude to be the voice of the womenfolk of her small town who either do not realise or cannot articulate the discomfort and embarrassment of relieving themselves in the open.

Jaya is argumentative but not in front of the father-in-law who represents the cultural segment of 'the elders of the house'. Jaya is a feminine construct who challenges the evils in the public space without challenging the subordination of the woman in the domestic space of the family, or disturbing the power relations and the hierarchy between man and woman or husband and wife, or opposing the subservient position of women in the hierarchical institution of the family. This feminine construct shoulders the responsibility of the colonial drive of eradicating social evils that plagued Indian society but retained family values. This kind of femininity that Jaya depicts was partially emancipated and empowered to occupy only a certain niche area in the public sphere of pre-independent India and its nationalist movement. The woman was identified as the marker and upholder of tradition so naturally that she was not expected to challenge the status quo. This is evident from Tanika Sarkar's cultural and historical accounts in which she presents a study of pre-independence upper-caste, middle-class femininities of India that were hegemonised, glorified and iconised by the thinkers and shapers of the Indian freedom movement. These women were a combination of the revivalist and reformist elements and Jaya is one such construct.

Jaya's character has a reformist strain in it as she looks to address a social issue and is seen to be willing to sacrifice even her marriage, a move that, within the filmic narrative, becomes admirable and solicits approval instead of criticism since she is also campaigning for the current government's Swachh Bharat Abhiyan. Thus, Jaya's extreme and radical step of going on the verge of getting a divorce from her husband has the invisible sanction of the foremost patriarchal institution of the nation-state—the Indian government. Apparently, the Indian woman can resort to radical measures in order to address radical issues which are in the larger interest of the nation-state. Even so, the marriage is saved as the father-in-law consents to having a toilet built in the house and the Indian state does not have to be guilty of impairing the institutions of marriage or the joint family system.

The state and its paternalistic intent and authority wins in its endeavours through Jaya, as the orthodoxy of a lesser patriarch (the father-in-law or the head of the family) has to bow down and give way for change to come in. It is thus a struggle between two patriarchal authorities with the woman in a token role with a 'feel-good' element about her characterisation. The womenfolk, who are supposedly suffering because of an age-old tradition that prejudice and superstition will not allow to change, are rescued by the benevolent gesture of the patriarchal state. Besides, the issue becomes appealing to a largely patriarchal sensibility because the concern is made to veer around the 'safety' of the women who go in the open to relieve themselves and their increasing vulnerability to fall prey to 'beasts of lust' (naturally, men), thus foregrounding the imminent threat to their modesty. This 'threat' is actually what makes a convincing case since women have to be protected from being attacked as they are the repositories of family and community honour.

The film, through replicating and reproducing what in many ways resembles a pan-India nationalist struggle for reform and change, presents the nation-state as one homogenous entity (Thapar 36) through womenfolk from the middle-class, upper-caste households whom the film foregrounds, even as the economically deprived, the differently abled, the socially backward and women from other minorities fail to get any screen space.

The upper-caste, middle-class Jaya, her mission accomplished, quite predictably goes back to her daughter-in-law mode and her functional existence as all is well with her marriage and the world. Kumari Jayawardena, in describing the 'new women', observes that they 'unfortunately relapsed into their domestic roles or showed concern only with "equal rights" within the framework of capitalism and the post-colonial state in which the bourgeoisie retained power' (i–ii) and failed to challenge the implicit patterns of exploitation and subordination embedded in social institutions.

Sui Dhaaga

Sui Dhaaga (2018), a phenomenal success at the box office, got a lot of critical attention and appreciation from all quarters, especially for being an inspirational narrative.

The film is structured like a bildungsroman, following the maturing and coming of age of the male protagonist Mauji (Varun Dhawan), who is supported in his journey to self-actualisation and social and professional recognition by his wife Mamta (Anushka Sharma). Mauji is a skilled tailor who belongs to a family of artisans but has to work as a junior employee in a shop that sells sewing machines owing to the financial predicament his family is in. He is married to Mamta, the major part of whose day goes in attending to household chores and the elders in the family.

Mauji's emotional state can be summarily described as disgruntled, with brief periods of contentment and happiness when he is with his wife. The two have a solid companionship and, eventually, Mamta urges him to give up his job, set up his own tailoring shop and choose self-worth over servitude. The couple faces many roadblocks that include opposition from the family and victimisation by the garment manufacturing company they work for, which slyly takes the rights of Mauji's designs and then fires him. Not willing to accept defeat, the couple decide to participate in the annual Raymond Fashion Fund, a fashion competition of considerable repute, and design their own clothes under the brand name 'Sui Dhaaga: Made in India' with the help of the local artisans in the neighbourhood, and go on to win the competition.

Sui Dhaaga addresses the issue of the fast-disappearing handicrafts and cottage industries from the regional landscape of India in the wake of globalisation, rapid industrialisation and increasing mechanisation of production (Dey). Through this couple who have dared to dream the impossible, the narrative enables a filmic revival of the dying and dormant community of weavers and tailors—in other words, indigenous craftsmanship that can create wonders through traditional skills. The film also has a utopian ending when this small-time and small-town couple actually goes on to win the 'best designer' title in a high-profile fashion competition. One witnesses social inclusion and fair and equal representation through the range of clothes the couple designs for the show and through the models that wear them. These are ordinary people with ordinary faces and different body types from all age groups and, as they walk up and down the ramp, they succeed in displacing the 'West-influenced' hegemonic bodies and appearances in the world of fashion.

The 'swadeshi' narrative too courses prominently through an emphasis on the means and resources of production which are purely indigenous, with locally instead of globally inspired designs, patterns and trends. At one level, the film can be read as an alternative discourse or counter-cultural movement to resist the phenomenon called globalisation which has not only changed the objects but also the patterns of consumption, thereby bringing about a huge transformation in the sensibility of the consumer.

This essay, however, is interested in the politics of representation of the female subject, a certain social and culturally constructed femininity which conveniently serves the purpose of strengthening cultural nationalism and exhibits a deceptively feminist agenda that operates well within the hegemonic patriarchal framework. Mamta's character is outlined as and develops on the lines of the 'Bharatiya nari', a consistent trope gaining popularity in recent times with the return of the Hindu right to power. Additionally, the name connotes and invokes images of traditional femininity as 'Mamta', translated as 'maternal affection' in English, which is the pivotal quality, standard and desirability that Indian femininity is expected to embody.

The narrative is cleverly textured so as to make the conformist appear radical, the subservient appear empowered, as one sees a resolute and mature Mamta assisting a dependent, unguided, somewhat belligerent and recalcitrant masculinity bordering on adolescence essayed by Mauji through his journey to self-realisation. Nonetheless, the power equation within the couple and the larger family, and the spatial politics responsible for attributing visibility and voice, contribute to script a subtext radically different from the surface text. Additionally, extreme masculine and feminine characteristics, depicted through Mauji and Mamta respectively, are normalised and go on to entrench attributes normatively associated with each discursively produced gender, further solidifying the gender binary.

Mamta

Mamta, as the unfailing, steadfast companion undeterred by setbacks and unaffected by emotional outbreaks, reflects an extraordinary level of resolve on the one hand and an indefatigable spirit on the other. Her character evokes the archetypal feminine qualities of voiceless endurance and resilience in the face of immense hardships. Mamta seems to belong to the tradition of resolute and determined women who believe in keeping a low profile and harbouring impossible dreams (mostly for their husbands) at the same time. It is Mamta who offers unwavering support and sound counsel on every occasion when her husband faces humiliation and rejection in the external world, represented by the oppressive and hostile figures of his employers and his father. This is evident at all times. For instance, when no one believes in Mauji's gift, his wife does and stands by him; she also goes an extra, unbelievable mile to urge him to procure a sewing machine so that he can start work independently and follow his heart. The actual physical hardship that Mamta endures to procure the machine for her husband is testimony of her devotion and symbolic of the extent to which she is willing to go to make things right for her husband and help him live the life of respectability he deserves.

Mamta is the voice of wisdom and foresight in the film, the entrepreneurial force behind Mauji, who suggests he start his own enterprise and pursue his desires even in the face of adversities and hindrances. And it is she again who urges him to imagine the impossible and participate in the fashion show and helps him garner the talent pool and human resources that will help him materialise this impossible dream. She is also the one who pacifies the people her husband ends up antagonising, hurting or threatening because of his impulsive and tempestuous nature. She seems to be able to do all this—move forward on the path of rebellion—without actually rebelling and without challenging any hierarchies. Her voice is heard only in the space the couple share, either when they are walking to and from work or at the hospital or in the solitary confinement of their room. Within the larger space and in the presence of the whole family, Mamta maintains a studied silence and does not retaliate or voice her protest even when her husband is unfairly treated by his family members.

Though it is tempting to read the film as the reversal of the bildungsroman patterns of films like *Guide* (1965) and *Dangal* (2016), where the man helps the woman in her journey to self-discovery and stardom or where the man assists the woman through an impossible journey, this would be too simplistic an interpretation of *Sui Dhaaga*, which obviously has more intricate threads of discourses woven into it. It is important to problematise the character of Mamta because of her superhuman qualities and abilities. Her love, resolve, sacrifice and silence acquire mythic proportions, reflecting figures from mythology like Sita and Savitri who displayed either unwavering faith in their husbands or went unflinchingly to any extent for the man they loved. The construct of wifehood in the film is complementary to ensure the stability, fame, material well-being and success of the husband.

Mamta is also conservatively draped in a sari with her head covered, to mark her status as a lower middle-class, married woman from a Hindu family. The fact that the role is essayed by Anushka Sharma, a prominent and leading female actor of Bollywood, known for her unconventional roles, her candour and her tomboyish disposition, can be read as the realisation of the utopian dream of taming Sharma which interestingly coincides with her marriage to cricketer and captain of the Indian cricket team, Virat Kohli, a man whose aggression on the field is both valorised and glamorised, a symbol of 'hypermasculinity' in India's 'media-generated culture of the sports industry' (Hari).

Sui Dhaaga thus essays a character who is one more example of the ideal wife and daughter-in-law who contributes phenomenally to the revival of a near-extinct weaver community, and of the art form too. The revival of 'swadeshi' and the need for it to be acknowledged, appreciated and accepted in the free-market economy is brought about by the title that the brand Sui Dhaaga wins in the fashion competition which has competitors and contenders from the highly corporatised and capitalist segment of the industry. The brand becomes an international rage, the family is out of its financial misery, and Mauji and Mamta open a tailoring school and become role models, thus motivating others to follow their example. Seen thus, 'swadeshi' too acquires a new meaning and connotation as it did under the reign of the Hindu right, from being 'defined as an anti-consumerist, economic nationalism that protected markets' to becoming a 'tool and language of globalization' (Sangari 159).

Sui Dhaaga reasserts a unified, homogenised, cultural identity and solidarity against the West and its economic imperialism by conflating the North Indian identity of the Hindi-speaking belt with the identity of the nation-state as the brand beats its closest competitor, its former employer, a probable winner. In beating this competitor, the indigenous artisan has beaten the capitalist who brings Western expertise and capital and exploits Indian labour for economic gains. Interestingly and quite predictably, this capitalist is a single, foreign-educated Indian woman who does not value Indian culture and is certainly not a fan of the institution of marriage held so sacred by her Indian counterpart Mamta, whom she even counsels to leave her husband and join her enterprise. It is imperative that this woman, with her single, moneyed, empowered status, be perceived as a threat and be stereotyped and demonised to a certain extent so that she becomes an appropriate foil to the idealistic and noble enterprise of the married and selfless Mamta who, at all times, puts her husband's concerns and dreams over hers.

Kalank

Kalank (2019) is a multi-starrer historically set in the era preceding the partition in Husnabad, an imaginary neighbourhood in Lahore, in erstwhile northern India, now Pakistan. The film shows the doomed path of star-crossed lovers and is a kind of love triangle with one woman caught between two brothers, one good and one bad, falling in love with the bad one but eventually choosing the good one.

Roop (Alia Bhatt), the daughter of a musician, is married off against her wishes to Dev (Aditya Roy Kapoor) at the entreaties of his terminally ill wife Satya (Sonakshi Sinha), who does not wish her husband to be 'alone' after her death. The very premise of the plot which normalises polygamy, raises an interesting question and makes explicit the overarching patriarchal ideology which determines the trajectory of the narrative for its consumption by a viewership, supposedly conditioned by patriarchy: would the same proposition have been acceptable if it were a dying husband soliciting a match for his soon-to-be-widowed wife, and desiring to groom the future husband to be deserving of her and looking forward to their nuptial bliss, under his very nose?

While Satya tries to sensitise Roop to the ways of the household and groom her into an appropriate wife and a daughter-in-law of the Chaudhary 'khandaan', Roop resists this attempt and instead is drawn to an alternate world of music and dance. Dev, too, on his part, refuses to consummate his marriage with Roop, swearing his loyalty to Satya for which the latter is secretly happy. Roop's insistence to learn music from Bahaarjaan or Bahaar Begam (Madhuri Dixit), a renowned courtesan in Heeramandi, raises authoritarian eyebrows. The father-in-law, Balraj Chaudhary

(Sanjay Dutt), eventually concedes to the arrangement as Roop is sent to Heeramandi to take music lessons under the watchful gaze of the housekeeper Saroj (Achint Kaur).

On her very first day, Roop accosts Zafar (Varun Dhawan), the textbook example of the bad boy of a damned neighbourhood, and feels drawn to him despite his brazen and lecherous advances. Wanting Roop and Dev to develop a rapport, Satya insists that Roop should start working with the newspaper Dev runs. Under the pretext of learning music and writing a story (for the newspaper) on the working-class Muslim community in Heeramandi, Roop meets Zafar a number of times and the attraction between the two intensifies even as Bahaarjaan's concerns increase.

When Bahaarjaan seeks a meeting with Zafar to implore him to stay away from Roop, we come to know that Zafar, in fact, is the illegitimate and abandoned son of Bahaarjaan and Balraj Chaudhary and harbours belligerence towards both his parents for disowning him. He sees procuring Roop as the perfect revenge, a means to sully the family honour. In due course, he truly falls in love with Roop and when Balraj Chaudhary threatens Bahaarjaan and Zafar with dire consequences, the latter beseeches the patriarch to give him his share, as a father would to his son. Only, in this case, by his share, Zafar means Roop. On the other hand, the legitimate son Dev is also estranged from his father as he is unable to forgive the latter for wronging his mother and having an adulterous relationship with Bahaarjaan.

A subplot with increasing communal tension gathers momentum as Abdul (Kunal Khemu), who is seen to mobilise the Muslim working-class community to resist the opening of factories in Husnabad, takes advantage of the complicated situation and deepens the rift between the estranged Balraj and Zafar by creating a series of misunderstandings. Zafar, meanwhile, accidentally runs into Dev and comes to know of his true identity, his belligerence leaving him. With mounting tension and impending threat to the upper-class Hindu community, the Chaudhary family decides to leave Lahore.

When Roop approaches Zafar, he turns her down. Satya succumbs to her illness and Dev proposes the consummation of the marriage, to which Roop mechanically agrees. Meanwhile, the newspaper and the office of the Chaudharys is attacked for endorsing the arrival of factories which would be a big blow to the largely Muslim working-class community. A bloodbath ensues as the employees of the newspaper are killed by a raging Muslim mob and Dev is rescued by Zafar and Roop. Eventually, Zafar is killed by Abdul for helping Roop and Dev escape. While secretly pining for their lost loves, the couple apparently start a new life in Amritsar, trying to find fulfilment in each other, knowing it is the socially appropriate thing to do. A demure and subdued Roop narrates the story to a reporter several years later, blaming herself for having devastated four lives.

The film has a host of female characters who make an interesting study, harkening back to pre-independence India resonating with 'nationalist iconography' which 'reordered notions of feminine virtue and beauty', women showing 'a large measure of self-determination and moral initiative' (Sarkar 264). All the women in the film articulate and enact their reformist, preacher or saviour roles from a high moral ground.

Roop

Stubborn, free-spirited, resolute, with a mind of her own, Roop enters an unenviable matrimonial alliance for the sake of the material security of her younger sisters. The episode highlights but does not address the social predicament and financial burden felt by families to marry off daughters. For Roop, it is a humiliating arrangement which she has to get into for the sake of her two younger sisters, as is made amply clear to her by her father whom Satya has struck a deal with. Satya will ensure the 'security' of Roop's sisters by marrying them off. So, the ultimate goal of a woman's life has to be marriage. It is ironic that even after Roop enters into this unsavoury and hopeless alliance, her father should still consider this kind of an arrangement or deal the best option for his other daughters too, considering that he has been progressive enough to educate Roop and 'give' her freedom. But the normative nature of the discourse and the cryptic allocation of time to this issue, so that the narrative can hurry to the main conflict, is what helps naturalise, for the viewer, the implicit violence which the natal family inflicts on the daughter.

Rejected by the man Roop gets married to, she knows early in the marriage that it is a relationship of compromise. She is shown to want to take her own life but subsequently changes her mind. Roop is partially empowered as she is educated and trained in music. Her desire to go to Bahaar Begam on the very next day of her unconsummated marriage is symbolic of seeking an alternate space, to find meaning in life. To that effect, she does succeed in stepping out of a confined zone and, in fact, enter a space which has a social stigma attached to it. This space, called Heeramandi, which is the most infamous neighbourhood of the city, is, significantly, also home to a lot of Muslims.

Roop does the forbidden by falling in love with Zafar, a man who is an outcaste in every way: a half-Hindu, half-Muslim, bastard child, disowned and abandoned by his parents. Roop, the epitome of the chaste, Hindu virgin, tries to reform Zafar with her virtuousness, attempting to mend the dark and dreadful ways of a Muslim with illegitimate Hindu blood coursing in his veins. In the course of the plot, Roop's chastity is invoked time and again. The platonic nature of her love for Zafar is foregrounded and physical union happens only with the Hindu man and legitimate son Dev, who is the husband. Female sexuality is thus intact as the tradition and honour of the family remain deeply inscribed on Roop's persona.

The tradition of investing family and community honour in a woman and commodifying her manifests in the encounter between Balraj Chaudhary and Zafar, each discussing the claim to Roop in her absence. Zafar pleads with his father to 'give' him Roop just as a father would rightfully bequeath his property to his son, the woman thus reduced to a passive object which can change hands. Interestingly, at this stage Zafar has only an idea of Roop's infatuation for him; she has not explicitly professed her love for him. Balraj, on his part, instead of treating his daughter-in-law as an individual and considering the possibility of asking *her* to stop seeing Zafar, asks Zafar to stay away from Roop. Zafar, though universally loathed, is a man and therefore a subject, has agency and so can 'continue' or 'stop' seeing Roop. Roop, on the other hand, cannot be involved in the discussion because addressing her directly would mean acknowledging her as a sovereign subject with a will of her own.

The marriage is intact as Roop is eventually reunited with her husband and severed from her doomed love. It is apparent, through her interactions with the reporter who is writing her story that, on hindsight, Roop sees her act of going to Heeramandi as a folly which leads to the destruction of four lives. She does not go on to specify which four lives she is referring to.

The film says a few things about 'the ideal woman'. The ideal woman can fall in love but will also need to get over it and make the more socially correct choice. The ideal woman is one who sacrifices what she desires, upholds the norms of the family, is sexually and emotionally restrained, has absolutely no emotional outbursts, is remarkably poised, extraordinarily empathetic and sensitive, willing to fall in love even with the most despised underdog because she is profoundly humane, and epitomises sympathy and love for the disadvantaged. However, sooner or later, wisdom takes precedence over impulsive emotions and she apparently, on her own accord, chooses what is morally right and in the best interest of everyone, prioritising duty over love. She is independent only to the extent that she does not overstep. She does not need to be externally tamed. She brings upon herself her own taming.

All this is depicted through the cinematic language explicitly by sartorial means. Roop's attire changes from a lehenga (Indian skirt) before marriage, exposing her midriff, to a completely covered kurta–sharara (tunic and flowing divided skirt) after marriage, and a sari with a veiled head after Satya's death as she steps into the first wife's shoes as mistress of the house.

Satya

One gets to see the Sita and Savitri archetypes prominently manifesting again through Satya. Satya's concern for her husband takes precedence over her terminal illness. Selfless, sacrificing, restrained, devoted to her husband, upholder of the tradition of the household, the reason why she wants Roop to move in is so that she can familiarise Roop to the ways of her household. One can only marvel at the supremely giving and sacrificing virtues of wifehood which prime stability and uninterrupted running of the household over one's illness and imminent death.

In the process, Satya too, like the men in the film, objectifies Roop, as she enters into a deal with Roop's father to procure her. She deliberately turns a blind eye to Roop's wishes, assigning her an instrumental role in the alliance, largely prompted by the presumption that things will eventually fall in place. She transforms into a mother-in-law-like figure the moment Roop is married to her husband, asking her to learn the ways of the house. Satya encourages Roop to join the office only because of her concern for her husband.

Satya is portrayed as the female authority, uncompromisingly committed to running the household, keeping in place the institution of the family and exercising her agency to this effect. This female authority can support and forgive patriarchy and overlook the injustice done to multiple people. It is Satya who implores her husband to forgive his father for having an affair with another woman. She does not ask her husband to seek his half-brother and get justice for him. Her concerns are restricted to the well-being of the members who fit into the socially approved, normative structure of the patriarchal family.

Bahaar Begam

Though autonomous and firmly established in her own space, Bahaar Begam bears the brunt of the stigma in the larger world governed by patriarchy. She is on the margins, though she would very much have liked to be in the centre and have a marriage and a family. She abandons her son for Balraj Chaudhary, the love of her life. She does not show any of the characteristics of a courtesan or prostitute despite being one all her life. She is shown to pine for a domestic life and not care much for the liberated life of a much-respected singer that she leads at the moment.

Bahaar Begam and Roop have an initial interaction in which the former compliments Roop's voice after hearing her sing but adds critically that it lacks 'namak' or salt, implying spice. Roop's immediate retort is that if there is too much 'namak' or spice, it can mar the taste of the food. 'Namak' becomes a metaphor for a life spiced up, a life full of romantic and sexual adventures which would define and temper one's art. Roop's puritanical rejoinder symbolises a disapproval of this view and the trajectory of the narrative can be foreseen early on from this exchange.

Later, when Roop confides in Bahaarjaan about Zafar, the latter reproaches her for forgetting her wifely duties and obligations. When Roop expresses her disappointment in Bahaarjaan, saying she had expected her to understand her feelings, Bahaarjaan responds sanctimoniously, saying that Roop has misunderstood her and that her being a courtesan does not mean that she is going to support Roop's adulterous inclinations. The courtesan is thus cast in the traditional frame of a mother or elderly woman of the household showing the path of righteousness and emotional restraint to the younger lot that has become wayward. So, interestingly, even the courtesan, though having led an alternative lifestyle all her life, upholds patriarchal family structure and vouches for it, despite being victimised by it and witnessing the victimisation of another woman.

This is a far cry from the courtesan construct that has been part of the nation's imaginary of a certain kind of emancipated 'femininity', albeit on the margins, which films like *Sahib Bibi Aur Ghulam* (1962), *Pakeezah* (1972), *Umrao Jaan* (1981), and even *Utsav* (1984) helped shape. Ruth Vanita in her book *Dancing with the Nation* (2018) looks at the courtesan trope in Hindi cinema and observes how it stands for a liberated female space and comes to be the epicentre of desire and an alternative family structure, revolutionary and radical in its stark difference from the patriarchal family structure, primarily because it is women-centric and has women as decision-makers and heads of the family. Bahaarjaan's construct, on the other hand, seems to gloss over these empowering projections of the courtesan in the pre-globalisation era. In re-invoking the courtesan construct, it reduces her to a diminutive being experiencing a constant 'lack' thus attempting to undercut the liberatory discourse which the courtesan trope has often prompted.

In intimate spaces, when the viewer witnesses Bahaarjaan not as a performer or instructor, she is apologetic and conservative. Her self-deprecation and righteousness when she interacts with the younger generation does not allow even the slightest space to the economically and culturally self-reliant professional and artist in her to come in and make a statement. Particularly interesting is her unquestioning acceptance of her son's venom (he holds his mother entirely responsible for his abandonment issues) and her absolute rejection of him when she comes to know of his forbidden love. Unlike the courtesans of the past, Bahaarjaan's worldview fails to be inclusive and compassionate and seems to be the circumstantially underprivileged righteous alter ego of the entitled savarna woman Satya, who goes around trying to make exclusionary decisions for other people at metaphorical gunpoint, which she thinks is best for them.

The Muslim courtesan Bahaarjan, the sexualised and religious 'other' (woman), the abandoned lover and the imperfect mother, is appropriately juxtaposed with the Hindu wives Satya and Roop, the personifications of altruistic, divine and mythicised feminine attributes who stand in sharp contrast with her. It is therefore only appropriate that as everyone gets ready to flee a volatile Husnabad, Bahaarjaan should remain behind as she cannot be included in the new nation-state that will comprise only wives like Roop who stand for the hegemonic feminine virtues of chastity, sacrifice and suffering and not portray lovers and independent women like Bahaarjaan who are irresponsible mothers and capable of acting out of self-interest.

A moral, authoritarian, patriarchal voice internalised by the female subject, replicating the anxiety-ridden pitch of the colonised Hindu male who located his sense of superiority in the chastity of the Hindu woman dominates the narrative of *Kalank*. This denies the possibility of an alternative feminist voice in Bahaarjaan which could have been a resistance to oppressive patriarchal institutions like marriage and the family and social practices or to spaces like brothels that result from the objectification and commodification of women. Likewise, the narrative places the onus of upholding familial values on the women more than the men.

Dev gives Roop the choice to leave him after he comes to know that she loves someone else; it is Roop who chooses to stay. Balraj Chaudhary, despite threatening dire consequences, does not do anything and removes himself from the situation by leaving town whereas it is Bahaarjaan who actually goes to Roop, and feels morally compelled to expose Zafar. Saroj, the housekeeper, is the one to divulge Roop's whereabouts and her attraction for Zafar to Balraj Chaudhary. It is the women, more than the men, who are shown to take corrective and exigent steps to stop the family from disintegrating and to keep people within socially acceptable confines.

The politics of the narrative is wholly evident from the title; it revolves around the impending threat to the honour of the Chaudhary family through the actions of the daughter-in-law, which naturalises the staunchly patriarchal practice of locating honour in the female subject. Despite Zafar undergoing a change of heart, the tenor of the narrative remains unchanged. It also makes evident another oppressive patriarchal custom: the transition demanded of a woman in her social status and her ontological identity through marriage is a loss of autonomy and choice, and elevation to a position of unimpeachable behaviour.

Though the thread of subversion is maintained till the very end of the film with the alternative space of romantic, heterosexual, illicit/interreligious love foregrounded time and again, it is not adequate since the narrative suggests the futility of inhabiting this space which is manifested in the character of Bahaarjaan. It fails to give us a history of Bahaarjaan's struggle in sustaining herself as an independent woman and instead paints her with similar hues of aspiring wifehood, invisibilising and undermining the possibility of 'alternate non–marriage-based communities' (Menon 49). On the other hand, the very fact that Roop's loveless arrangement of a negotiated marriage turns out alright is a reinforcement of the oppressive version of the patriarchal institution of marriage. It fails to critique the institution and its detrimental and alienating effect on the woman, making it, instead, organic to the female bildungsroman and projecting it as every Indian woman's ultimate objective.

Conclusion

All three films engage in a marked hegemonising and glorification of a certain kind of feminine construct in a postcolonial India that ironically is 'thoroughly colonial' (Sangari 157). The films also celebrate marital conjugality, marking it as synonymous with material and emotional security and privileging it over 'true undying love' that has been the pulse of timeless classics, almost depicting a relief in articulating the 'so-called relative stability and strictness of Hindu rules' (Sarkar 201). A deconstructionist reading of the films, however, foregrounds 'the explosive tensions that are just barely contained within the framework of the family' (Menon 47) and offers an interesting read of the politics behind the representation of these femininities and their manufactured desirability in the cultural imaginary of the Indian viewer.

Works Cited

Dey, Deblina. 'Stitching and Unstitching Labour with *Sui Dhaaga*'. *Economic and Political Weekly*, vol. 53, no. 43, 27 Oct. 2018. www.epw.in/journal/2018/43/postscript/stitching-and-unstitching-labour-sui.html. Accessed 27 Oct. 2024.

Hari, T.N. 'Like Virat Kohli's Aggression, Corporate Toxic Culture is Uncalled For'. *YourStory*, 27 Dec. 2018, yourstory.com/2018/12/virat-kohli-aggression-uncalled. Accessed 27 Oct. 2024.

Harriss, John. 'Hindu Nationalism in Action: The Bharatiya Janata Party and Indian Politics'. *South Asia: Journal of South Asian Studies*, vol. 38, no. 4, 2016, pp. 712–718.

Jayawardena, Kumari. *Feminism and Nationalism in the Third World.* 1986. Verso, 2016.

John, Mary E. 'Globalisation, Sexuality and the Visual Field: Issues and Non-Issues for Cultural Critique'. *Women Contesting Culture: Changing Frames of Gender Politics in India*, edited by Kavita Panjabi and Paromita Chakravarti, School of Women's Studies, Jadavpur University, 2012, pp. 165–180.

Kalank. Directed by Abhishek Varman. Fox Star Studios, 2019.

Menon, Nivedita. *Seeing Like a Feminist.* Zubaan and Penguin Books, 2012.

Panjabi, Kavita and Paromita Chakravarti. Introduction. *Women Contesting Culture: Changing Frames of Gender Politics in India*, edited by Panjabi and Chakravarti, School of Women's Studies, Jadavpur University, 2012, pp. xv–lxxvi.

Raghavendra, M.K. 'Structure and Form in Indian Popular Film Narrative'. *Fingerprinting Popular Culture*, edited by Vinay Lal and Ashis Nandy, Oxford UP, 2007, pp. 24–50.

Sangari, Kumkum. 'New Patriotisms: Beauty and the Bomb'. *From Gender to Nation*, edited by Rada Ivekovic and Julie Mostov, Zubaan, 2006, pp. 153–170.

Sarkar, Tanika. *Hindu Wife, Hindu Nation: Community, Religion and Cultural Nationalism.* Permanent Black, 2001.

Sui Dhaaga. Directed by Sharat Katariya. Yash Raj Films, 2018.

Thapar, Romila. *The Past as Present: Forging Contemporary Identities through History.* Rupa Publications, 2014.

Toilet: Ek Prem Katha. Directed by Shree Narayan Singh. Plan C Studios, Abundantia Entertainment, Friday Filmworks and KriArk Entertainment, 2017.

'*Toilet—Ek Prem Katha* a Huge Boost to the "Swachh Bharat" Journey'. *The Free Press Journal*, 29 May 2019, www.freepressjournal.in/cmcm/toilet-ek-prem-katha-a-huge-boost-to-the-swachh-bharat-journey. Accessed 27 Oct. 2024.

Vanita, Ruth. *Dancing with the Nation*. Bloomsbury, 2018.

'Postcard from Kashmir'

Representations of the Fractured State in Bollywood Films

Somrita Misra

The Kashmiri journalist Basharat Peer has passionately written about his state:

> When pain makes it difficult to articulate coherently, quiet remembrance helps. Like many other Kashmiris, I have been in silence, committing to memory, the deed, the date. The faces of the murdered boys, the colour of their shirts, their grieving fathers.... Kashmir remembers what is done in your name, in the name of your democracy, whether its full import ever reaches your drawing rooms or offices or not. ('Kashmir Unrest' 44)

Peer's words are testament to the hardships and sufferings that the Kashmiri people have been enduring for the last three decades. Since the early 1990s, the state of Kashmir has been in the grip of a conflict between militants fighting for 'freedom' ('azadi') and the Indian security forces, determined to protect 'Indian' interests in Kashmir. The three-decade-old legacy of violence and militancy has led to massive repercussions for the residents of the valley. In 1947, India emerged as a sovereign nation, with dazzling dreams of glory and greatness. Yet, two hundred years of colonial rule had left behind their share of problematic conflicts.

The ownership of the state of Kashmir has, since independence, been the root cause of the animosity between India and Pakistan. India claims Kashmir to be an integral part of its territory, while Pakistan believes that the Muslim-dominated valley 'rightfully' belongs to it. Presently, a portion of the territory of Kashmir lies with Pakistan (Pakistan Occupied Kashmir) and a large area is part of India (Indian Kashmir). The controversial Kashmiri militant movement began at the beginning of the 1990s, with primarily the youth of the state being involved. The Indian army had to resort to swift counter-insurgency measures to deter the separatists and militants. Kashmir is governed by the Armed Forces Special Powers Act, the Disturbed Areas Act, and the Prevention of Terrorism Ordinance, and, until very recently, was given special status under Article 370. The Kashmir conflict has led to the valley being ruled by unrest and arbitrary violence, with bloodshed and blasts becoming part of the normal routine of existence.

When one looks at the representation of Kashmir in Indian popular culture, be it fiction, songs or Bollywood films, it is seen that no justice has been done to this blood-soaked state. Be it popular Indian literature or music, Kashmir, because of its scenic beauty, has always served as a backdrop to romance. The Hindi film industry especially has, by and large, romanticised Kashmir. One need only think of films like *Kashmir Ki Kali* and *Junglee* from the 1960s to understand the truth of this statement. When militancy erupted in the 1990s, bringing Kashmir to the forefront of national attention, Bollywood started another trend, that of depicting Kashmir through patriotic films, blatantly glorifying the army. Again, one need only think of films like *Mission Kashmir*, *Roja* and *Fanaa* to realise this. But in recent years, since the mid-2000s, these trends have been slowly challenged; a few pathbreaking films have astutely and sensitively depicted the nuances of the Kashmir conflict and the deprivations suffered by the residents of the valley. This essay focuses specifically on four films—*Harud*, *Hamid*, *Haider* and *Shikara*—to explore Bollywood's alternative representations of Kashmir.

In 2012, PVR Director's Rare released an offbeat and little-known film, *Harud*, in theatres across the country. Directed by Amir Bashir, *Harud* was filmed in 2010 but would be available for viewing in India two years later. The capitalist politics of multiplexes and the little demand for non-commercial films meant that *Harud* needed the support of the PVR group to be launched in India. What is heartening is that PVR decided to back the project and this simple tale of a lonely Kashmiri boy's struggle reached the Indian masses. *Harud* (literally 'autumn' in Kashmiri) revolves round a teenage Kashmiri boy, Rafiq, whose older brother has gone missing in the war-torn valley. Moving away not only from popular Indian cinematic culture but from the art films of Bollywood as well, Amir Bashir uses influences from Iranian cinema to depict the complex narrative of the Kashmir conflict. We see the Kashmiris struggling with their daily lives and fighting to preserve their belief in the good and the virtuous. The film traverses the ravaged terrain of Srinagar, where Rafiq and his friends try to find meaning in their existence. We see how a fun-filled lunch rendezvous turns into a nightmare of blood and gore for Rafiq and his friends when a blast occurs near the restaurant they are eating at. The alienated state of the Kashmiri youth is never as clear as in this moment when we realise that while the youth in the rest of India can take for granted days of fun and joy, Kashmiri youth can never do so.

Rafiq's empty eyes question the presence of the army in his city; his aimless wanderings across Srinagar show him guns holstered across uniforms, grief-stricken men and women queuing outside police stations to get news of their loved ones, and disillusioned youths like himself who no longer know what to do with their lives and which 'side' to pick. In a state where insurgency abounds and the presence of soldiers loom everywhere, it is easy for youths like Rafiq to believe that their existence will be made meaningful if they go across the border to train as terrorists. Rafiq falls prey to this horrifying trap by militants and it is only because of his poor, law-abiding father that he is brought back in time. One can hear echoes of Peer's words:

> It was the longest, the most eventful winter in Kashmir, a season that still remains. The last two months had changed Kashmir in profound ways.... Along with killing hundreds of pro-India Muslims ranging from political activists to suspected informers for Indian intelligence, the militants killed hundreds of Pandits on similar grounds, or

> without a reason.... Someone would have seen a militant and he would tell us how the militant styled his hair, what clothes and shoes he wore.... The best story was about the magical Kalashnikov.... By the summer of 1990, thousands of young Kashmiri men crossed the Line of Control, for arms training in the Pakistan-controlled part of Kashmir.... Like almost every teenager, I wanted to join them. Fighting and dying for freedom was much desired, like the first kiss on adolescent lips. (*Curfewed Night* 22–24)

In any astute depiction of the Kashmir state, the word 'freedom' resounds. It is clear from Peer's words and from Rafiq's dilemma in *Harud*, that young boys are embroiled in the militant movement without any understanding about or belief in securing the 'freedom' that is preached by the militants. For boys like Rafiq, arms training becomes something which may render purpose to their senseless lives. There is a pivotal moment in the film where a friend who has returned from across the border tells Rafiq: 'Jannat ka rasta kam se kam Pakistan hoke to nahi jata hai' ('The path to paradise does not lie through Pakistan'). We see the young boy's disillusionment with militancy and his helplessness as he struggles to escape the life he has chosen. Bashir conveys the turmoil of Kashmir through abstract images and moments: we feel Rafiq's pain when he discovers his brother's camera and cannot find a scene beautiful enough to capture in the form of a picture; we weep with Yusuf (Rafiq's father) when he breaks down after witnessing the last minutes of a young suicide bomber; and we share the anger of Rafiq's mother as she protests with the other parents of missing children. Amidst all this are ordinary, day-to-day objects—autos, press cars, birds flying in the autumnal sky of Srinagar. *Harud* intersperses the violence and abnormality with the ordinary and the tawdry.

Bashir sets his film in the 2000s when, in a bid to 'streamline' Kashmir, the central government had introduced cellular connectivity in the state. But like everything else, the mobile phone acquires a separate significance for the Kashmiris: while in the rest of India the mobile is a simple communicative device, in Kashmir it becomes a means to remain in contact with one's loved ones and reassure them of one's safety. In an interview with a patronising national TV journalist, a young Kashmiri man gushes his thanks to the government for enabling him to tell his parents every day, wherever he may be, that he is 'alive and safe'. Through each of its scenes and moments, *Harud* shows the dislocation between Kashmir and the rest of the nation. There is a poignant moment in a photo studio in which the song 'Tarif Karu Kya Uski' plays in the background as a forlorn girl mourns a lost lover. The film simmers with wound-up emotions and sentiments; there is minimal dialogue, muted background music and naturally rendered performances, which lead to a complete absence of melodrama. When the violence erupts all around the city in a sudden shower of gunfire and bomb blasts, it is therefore subsumed into the unremarkable everyday life, leaving behind neither tears nor unnatural anguish but a resigned acceptance of what has become 'normal' for Kashmir. In the end, when the ultimate sacrifice is extracted from Rafiq's parents, with a military bullet killing their only other living child, it becomes yet another everyday occurrence, with people sadly watching and comforting Rafiq's sobbing parents. Bashir's film portrays a beleaguered Srinagar rarely seen in Indian films. Shorn of its beauty, Srinagar, in *Harud*, is the city of the mute and the dead, a city which is perpetually on the brink of catastrophe and chaos.

If *Harud* is a muted display of confusion and chaos, Aijaz Khan's *Hamid* (2018) is a poignant plea for help from a small boy who fervently wishes to be reunited with his missing father. Based on the Kashmiri playwright Amin Bhat's *Phone No 786*, *Hamid* tells the story of a seven-year-old Kashmiri boy, Hamid, whose father abruptly disappears one night. After being told that his father is now with 'Allah' and that '786' is God's number, Hamid dials a random number ending with 7-8-6, hoping to speak to 'Allah'. The call goes through to a hardened CRPF jawan who, in a moment of humorous fun, tells Hamid that he is 'Allah'. From here on, the film beautifully portrays the conversations and growing bond between two apparent 'enemies'—a Kashmiri boy whose father may have been killed by the army and a psychologically anguished CRPF jawan who has to cope with his own history of having accidentally killed a young man while chasing a terrorist. In an interview in the *Hindu*, Aijaz Khan revealed that *Hamid* was created because of a chance conversation between him and a friend from Srinagar, who told him about a play he had seen the previous night where a boy dials the numbers 7-8-6 and gets connected with a Kashmiri Pandit. Khan's interest was piqued and he decided to adapt the play into a film.

While talking about the film, both Aijaz Khan and Rasika Dugal (the actress who plays Hamid's mother) spoke of how essential it is to have regular conversations about the Kashmir conflict on national forums. Dugal went on to say:

> There is tons of material on Kashmir. I didn't know which would be the one that would move beyond a political connection or even just an empathetic connection ... I'm hoping that *Hamid* will be that gentle conversation which I haven't heard up till now'. (Naudial)

While *Harud* used the most minimum of dialogues, *Hamid* revolves around the interactions between Hamid and Abhay (the jawan who poses as 'Allah'). Since the film uses a child as its protagonist, it can raise morally pertinent questions with complete innocence. Like all child narrators, Hamid melts the heart of the audience with his simple queries; he earnestly requests 'Allah' to send his father home and to ask him if he is angry because of Hamid's stubbornness in asking for batteries (Hamid's father disappeared the night he went to fetch those batteries). Seven-year-old Hamid has yet to realise that people can go missing without any reason in the violent valley; it is bewildering for him to witness the rapid decline of his mother as she no longer cares for him the way she used to but is now roaming from police stations to hospitals to morgues in search of her husband.

In *Hamid*, like *Harud*, the desolation of Srinagar haunts the audience; Khan, like Bashir, refuses to romanticise the valley as a beauteous landscape in which we can lose ourselves. Rather,

Hamid's young gaze captures the mundane and sordid urbanity of a volatile capital: we meet angry stone-pelters as Hamid walks home from the mosque; we feel Hamid's confusion as he listens to an Islamic cleric advising him to fight for 'azadi' and for Islam; we are moved when he confesses to 'Allah' about his use of a hundred rupees out of his earnings to look for his father; and we share his anger when he picks up a stone to pelt an army vehicle after being told the truth about Abhay. Khan depicts a balanced and holistic view of the Kashmir dispute; while there are the resounding slogans and chants of 'freedom', there is also a fair portrayal of the militants' exploitation of young boys like Hamid. Apart from the central character of Hamid, the film beautifully captures the struggle of a wife looking for her missing husband, in the role of Ishrat, and the trauma of a soldier, battling to overcome emotional imbalance, through the character of Abhay Kumar. The seven-year-old Hamid's antics as he tries to connect with his father conveys the human repercussions of a politically conflicted region in a profoundly heart-wrenching way. At the end of the film, the audience, along with Hamid and Abhay, have an epiphany: that while on the apparent level Hamid and Abhay may perceive each other as enemies, lobbing stones and shells at one another, they are, in reality, both victims of political machinations and therefore share the bond of wronged individuals. The film's poignancy is underlined in one of its singular lines: 'Bachchon ke usulon pe duniya chalti to jannat ban gayi hoti' ('The world would have been a heavenly abode if it were ruled by the principles of children').

Edward Soja writes about the significance of space or territory in a people's psychology or thinking. In his words: 'Understanding how history is made has been the primary source of emancipatory insight.... Today, however, it may be space than time that hides consequences from us....' (1). In the context of Kashmir, Soja's theory of spatial significance becomes especially relevant. In both *Harud* and *Hamid*, we see the space or territory of Kashmir emerge as the most poignant character and the reason for the sufferings of

Rafiq and Hamid; it is because Hamid and Rafiq are residents of the valley that they become victims of the circumstances that engulf their lives. Both boys are constantly conscious of their Kashmiri identity and the space of Kashmir determines their selfhood; they can never be free of their 'Kashmiriness' however much they want, and neither do they themselves desire a denial of their Kashmiri identity. Kashmir engulfs and surrounds the boys; their spatial state determines their lives and their identities. Using Soja to read any narrative of Kashmir is interesting as the spatial identity associated with the state is significant: Kashmir, for India, represents its crown jewel, its integral acquisition; for the inhabitants of the state their being Kashmiri means only the incessant, bitter pill of living in a conflict zone. It is this dual emotion of confused anger and nostalgic longing that we see in Hamid and Rafiq. Kashmir, in its spatial uniqueness, marginalises its residents; the state alienates its people from the rest of the country and fractures their bond with the nation. We see a muted anger in Rafiq; he constantly simmers with resentment when his brother disappears. Studying Rafiq's character in a psychoanalytical context, it is evident that his hurt and anger at the state is displaced into his desire to become a militant. Kashmir, as a space, marginalises and displaces its people; in the wild chase of power, Kashmir is a pawn, a spatial prize that demands the blood of its residents.

Sanjay Kak writes about 'the brazen courage of Kashmiri youth':

> armed with stones in their hands, in groups of no more than a few hundred at a time, taking on Kashmir's much vaunted 'security-grid'.... Over two decades of conflict, Kashmiris have lost their right to speech, assembly and travel; they have all lost all guarantees of their freedom from violence, harassment and unlawful detention. (31, 37)

These words highlight the irreparable gulf between the state of Kashmir and the Indian nation. Gyanendra Pandey comments:

> Like subalternity ... the idea of difference cannot be thought or organized along a single (say cultural or biological) axis....

> Difference becomes a mark of the subordinated or subalternized, measured as it is against the purported mainstream, the 'standard' or the 'normal'.... The proclamation of difference becomes a way of legitimizing and reinforcing existing relations of power. What the disadvantaged, the marginalized and the subordinated ... have done, in response, is to deploy the very category of difference to demand a re-arrangement if not an overturning of prevailing structures of access and privilege. (1, 3)

Pandey's words illustrate the inherent fissures at the heart of any liberal democracy; the very concept of national identity refuses to cede space to people living on the fringes: the minorities, the poor, the dalits, the women. Films like *Hamid* and *Harud* interrogate the idea of conventional nationhood, bringing to the forefront the conflicted reality of our supposedly unified nation.

Postcolonial theoreticians have, time and again, highlighted the marginalisation of ethnic tribes and minorities within the majoritarian space of the nation-state. The desolate images of Kashmir and the resounding protests in the valley are indicative of the widening gulf between majoritarian belief in nationhood and the disillusioned and increasingly rebelling minority living under constant siege. Films like *Harud* and *Hamid* bring this discontentment into the open through the medium of popular cinema. Rafiq's hollowed-out emptiness and Hamid's innocent questions expose the uncomfortable falsehoods of 'national culture' and the exclusionary reality of 'national identity'. For youths like Rafiq and boys like Hamid, there is no 'national identity'; they are struggling for survival in the country that claims to own their land but refuses to listen to their pleas for help. They have no idea whether they are 'Indians', 'Kashmiris' or 'Indian Kashmiris'. In the context of exclusive discourses of nationalism and alternative imaginings of the narrative of Kashmir, it becomes singularly necessary to explore Vishal Bhardwaj's 2014 film, *Haider*. *Haider* has been analysed and explored from numerous angles, including that of Bhardwaj's representation of the state of Kashmir. This essay is interested in exploring *Haider* in comparison with *Hamid* and

Harud, and its significance as one of the major films depicting an alternative version of the Kashmir dispute.

In his interviews on *Haider*, Bhardwaj has spoken about how he chose to set his intended adaptation of Shakespeare's *Hamlet* in Kashmir: how his wife drew his attention to Peer's book *Curfewed Night*, even as he was working on the screenplay for the adaptation of *Hamlet*. Bhardwaj was inspired enough to turn his Hamlet into Haider, a discontented man living in the tumultuous Kashmir of the 1990s. Bhardwaj went on to say: 'I like to fire the shots from Shakespeare's shoulders ... that gives me a lot of license.... In my film, in a way, Kashmir becomes Hamlet' (Singh). *Haider* assumes tremendous significance because as a film by a noted and popular director, it brought the tragic reality of Kashmir to the attention of the most indifferent of audiences. While *Harud* and even *Hamid* struggled to garner multiplex slots and media coverage because of their small budgets and faulty publicity, *Haider* hooked audiences from its very first trailer. As the third film in the Shakespeare series of Bhardwaj, *Haider* promised potentiality and thrills; it was therefore a huge audience which ultimately viewed the film and heard the suppressed cries of the Kashmiri people. In this sense, *Haider* truly became the first 'popular' film in Bollywood to represent the problematic discourses of the Kashmir issue.

Like *Harud*, *Haider* revolves around a young man's traumatic journey across Kashmir; Haider is a student in Aligarh who returns to his home state of Kashmir after his father 'disappears', to find everything in his familiar city changed. However, while *Harud* dealt in abstract images and isolated symbols, *Haider* indulges in blatant Kashmiri motifs: the river Jhelum becomes a metaphor for the keening cries of the families of the 'disappeared' and the dead, and the strains of 'Jhelum, Jhelum dhunde kinara' accompany us as we journey with Haider across Srinagar in his hunt for his father. The famous song 'Gulon Me Rang Bhare' is used sometimes as background score and at other times becomes a poignant recital by Haider's father. *Hamid* and *Harud* are films which are centred around singular protagonists; we see the benighted city of Srinagar from the gaze of Rafiq and Hamid. However, *Haider*, in true Shakespearean style, diverges into multiple characters: while there is the central character of Haider, there are also other stories and other characters with their own perspectives of the conflict. We meet the beautiful and restless Ghazala, Haider's mother, for whom being the wife of a 'disappeared' man means the awful reality of becoming a 'half-widow', a woman who is neither married nor widowed. Terms like 'half-widow' are unique to states like Kashmir where the uncertain political violence leads to many people simply 'disappearing'. We go on to meet Khurram, a man deviously trying to strengthen his own position by selling his loved ones to the authorities. For Khurram, the raging conflict is simply a chance to seize power; he feels no qualms in 'siding' with Indian security forces. Ghazala becomes an unwilling pawn in his game, drawn into the mire of the informers' network through no agency of her own. We also meet Haider's father, who refuses to take a 'side' at all, choosing to save lives as a doctor.

In all three films—*Harud*, *Hamid* and *Haider*—the missing relative becomes a common denominator of loss. We see the presence of the Association of Parents of Disappeared Persons in the films; this is an actual organisation in Kashmir which was founded in 1994 and strives to give voice to the victims of enforced disappearance in the state. All three films, while starkly different in treatment, portray a city that is in perpetual agony: the Srinagar that emerges in *Harud*, *Hamid* and *Haider* is a city that is ravaged by the twin assaults of the security forces and the militants; it is a city which erupts into violence at any moment, senselessly killing and maiming innocent civilians. It is a city where a father can go missing while fetching a present for his child, a brother can vanish without a trace, a husband and parent can be brutally dragged away without any lawful detention procedure, and a cherished home can be blasted into smithereens. *Hamid* and *Harud* deliberately steer clear from the scenic Dal Lake or the sight of snow-capped mountain peaks; *Haider*, however, does project Kashmir's beauty: we see the serenely flowing Jhelum, the snow-filled valley like a postcard, and there is even a musical love sequence between Haider and his girlfriend Arshia. However, the beauty is deceptive and fleeting; we are never sure when the snow may get stained red with blood or bodies will float down the Jhelum. Bhardwaj uses the serene landscape of the valley as an ironic depiction of its hidden turmoil, its chaotic destruction, which is as abrupt as the falling snow.

In one of the most brilliant scenes in *Haider*, the young protagonist stages a street play where he passionately expresses the tragic plight of the Kashmiri people:

> Hum hai ki hum nahi? ... Chutzpah ho gaya hamare sath.... Jiska law hai uska order.... India Pakistan ne milke khela hum se border-border.... Na ab chode hume Hindustan, na ab chode hume Pakistan. Par koi to hum se bhi puchho ki hum kya chahte? ('Do we exist or do we not? We are made to suffer through 'chutzpah'. Lawmakers uphold their own order. India wants us, so does Pakistan. But does anybody care as to what we want?')

Haider, *Hamid* and *Harud* echo with the slogans of 'azadi', a resounding cry that enrages Indian authorities and patriots and stirs the unrest in the valley, fuelling the war of the separatists. Yet it does not alleviate the suffering or grief of the victims of losses in the valley, who have borne the brunt of 'righteous' demands from all 'sides'. The stakes in the Kashmir conflict are too high; there is no resolution that can be easy or unanimous. Haider's wizened grandfather, Hussain Meer, perhaps is prophetic when he says:

> Bada kadim marz hai ... sadio purana. Kitni nasle hazam kar gaya hai hamari.... Jab tak hum apne is intekam se azad nahi honge, tab tak koi azadi hume azad nahi kar sakti.... Intekam se sirf intekam payda hota hai. ('It is a grave problem, and an old one, which has led to the destruction of our generations.... Till we are free of our thirst for revenge, true freedom will never be ours.... Revenge breeds revenge.')

When one analyses the Kashmir dispute, apart from the hardships afflicted upon the residents of the valley, there is another issue that generates a feeling of tragic loss: the exile and eviction of almost 3.5 lakh Kashmiri Pandits from their homes in the valley during the beginning of the militant movement. While films on the insurgency situation in the valley have been few and far between, films about the plight of the exiled Pandits are almost non-existent. However, in 2020, Vidhu Vinod Chopra released *Shikara*, a film that tells the story of Shiv and Shanti, a Pandit couple, who were ousted from their home in the 1990s. Ankur Datta writes about the forced exodus of the Pandits:

> Following mass protests that took place all over the valley in early 1990, large numbers of Kashmiri Pandits began to leave the Kashmir Valley, fleeing to Jammu in the southern part of the state.... Since then, the Kashmiri Pandits have found themselves constituting one of the most distinctive groups of displaced peoples in Indian territory.... How does one address forced migration in a subcontinent where communities have historically been marked by migration? (4, 18)

The dislocation and exile of the Pandits comes under the category of forced migration, and the Pandits are labelled 'internally displaced persons'. Interestingly, the Indian state has renamed and changed the status of the Pandits continuously; they have also been listed as 'migrants' in the last few years.

Chopra's *Shikara* attempts to depict this tragic displacement of the Pandits through the love story of Shiv and Shanti. Shiv and Shanti fall in love in the idyllic setting of the valley and are wedded in typical Kashmiri custom. After their wedding, the couple build a dream home and name it 'Shikara'. However, their blissful life shatters in the winter of 1990 as anger against the Indian nation erupts across the valley. The rising militant movement leads to a tragic outburst of violence one night (the historically significant 19 January 1990), when the homes of several Pandits are set on fire. Shocked and helpless, Shiv and Shanti, along with hundreds of other Pandit families, flee their home overnight and seek shelter in a refugee camp in Jammu. The second half of the film traverses the struggle of the couple in the refugee camp, where the pain of displacement is a constant companion for the camp's inmates. For a film with a theme that is inherently dangerously polarising, *Shikara* gives a refreshingly evocative and balanced representation of the Pandit exodus. Chopra does not vilify an entire community as evil; rather, we see a wonderful depiction of the spirit of 'Kashmiriyat' in the beginning, with a close friendship between the Pandits and the Muslims.

One of Shiv's closest friends is Lateef, a promising Ranji cricketer who celebrates joyously Shanti and Shiv's marriage. Yet, in a tragic turn of events, Lateef becomes embroiled in the armed conflict when his father is murdered by the state for contesting the elections. Lateef warns Shiv to leave Kashmir and go to 'India', clearly underlining the growing divide between the Muslim residents of Kashmir and the majoritarian community of the nation. Years later, when he is captured by the Indian army, Lateef says to the commanding officer words which are reminiscent of Haider's grandfather:

> Apne mere abba ko mara. Badle me maine aapke sou ladke mare. Hum yuhi ek dusre ko marte rahenge, agle sou salo tak. ('You killed my father. In retribution, I killed a hundred of your men. We will go on killing each other for the next hundred years.')

One of the most problematic consequences of the Kashmir dispute is the religious polarisation of victims of violence. For both the displaced Pandits and the imprisoned Muslim residents, their trauma and suffering become a bitterly unique community experience, leading them to hate the 'other' community. Chopra beautifully avoids this trap through his nuanced narration: he ensures that his two major characters, Shiv and Shanti, are devoid of religious bitterness while being nostalgic and sorrowful about their lost home. In one scene, a young boy leads a group of youngsters like himself in a rally in the refugee camp, shouting 'Mandir wahi banayenge' ('We'll build the temple right there'). Shiv immediately intervenes and tells the boy that a true leader never divides communities. Chopra is aware of the divisive trend that his film may take, and takes every measure to avoid it. The pain of the exiled Pandits makes itself felt not through displays of hatred towards Muslims, but through the Pandit community's desire to return to the 'wadi' that is their ancestral land. We see the anguish of an old man in the refugee camp who refuses to budge from his position till he is taken back to Kashmir. His anguished cries of 'Mujhe Kashmir le chalo' ('Take me to Kashmir') haunt the audience long after the film ends. Finally, there is no closure for the Pandits, just as there is no respite for the residents in the valley from the violence: Shiv disperses Shanti's ashes in their native village so that her soul may find peace but their dream house, Shikara, has to be sold. The homecoming that the Pandits dream of will clearly take a long time to be fulfilled.

Pramod K. Nayar has written about the process of anxiety suffered by minorities and fringe communities, who become the 'other' within the nation-state (69–70, 99–113). In the context of the Kashmir conflict, interestingly, both the Muslim residents of the state and the exiled Pandits view the nation with ambivalent emotions. For Kashmiri Pandits, their displacement and pain are a sacrifice that the Indian nation-state has largely ignored. K.N. Pandita angrily writes:

> It is futile to waste our time and energy in running after the Indian political class for the amelioration of our condition.... We are nobody's vote bank because we are numerically insignificant.... The saffronites exploit us, the khadiites despise us, and the reds club us with the bourgeoise. We ask for Homeland.... Does it mean anything to those holding the reins of power? (119–120)

We see a similar questioning of the nation-state in a Kashmiri Muslim writer, Mohamad Junaid:

> In their desire for control over more territory—and the unchallenged right to inflict violence—large and powerful nations run roughshod over legitimate rights of smaller and weaker peoples.. . As Kashmiris, ... caught in the whirlpool of forces of imperialist domination and religious-nationalist chauvinisms ... while the grinding machine of military oppression keeps adding to the long history of our

> suffering—where must we situate ourselves? How must we imagine, think and plan a new life? (280)

For both the Pandit and the Muslim residents of the valley, national pride will always be ambiguous because their nation has failed to include them and their concerns.

Robert Park writes about the destruction of identities of marginal communities. Park believes that marginality is the natural consequence for communities which can no longer return to their original 'home' and who never find acceptance in an alien, dominant culture. The 'marginal man' is trapped in a state of double ambivalence; he can neither return to his original home nor merge with his adapted one (Goldberg). We see how the Pandit community of the valley feels itself marginalised in India in *Shikara*; Shiv and Shanti struggle to maintain their Kashmiri customs in the alien city they have been hurled into. Shanti cooking rogan josh in her small quarters and crying as she remembers the horror of the night of 19 January is one of the most poignant moments in the film; we feel the confusion and sadness within Shiv and Shanti when they are invited to what they assume to be a traditional Kashmiri wedding, and which is simply a parody of a Punjabi marriage celebration. Shiv and Shanti are now 'marginal citizens'; their culture is slowly disappearing in a country that ignores their community.

Marginality, migration and displacement are uncomfortable realities of the twentieth and twenty-first centuries. States like Kashmir are far too common in a neocolonial and 'neo-imperial' world. 'Marginality', as a term, is used to analyse the socio-cultural and economic exclusion of underprivileged groups or communities. For the residents of the valley, marginalisation has become the norm. By their very residence, the Kashmiris are excluded and imprisoned in their own state. Military occupation and its various hazards force the Kashmiris to live in fear and seclusion. People are usually considered migrants when they travel outside their original residence; for the Kashmiri Pandits the label 'migrants' is especially cruel as they never chose to travel outside

Kashmir of their free will. They were ousted from Kashmir one violent night without any wish of theirs and, ever since, they are 'migrants' or, worse still, 'refugees' in their own country. Perhaps 'displacement' is the more apt term for the Pandit community; displacement is a form of migration where individuals are forced to leave their homes against their will. Whatever the terminology, the grief of the Pandit community is ever-present and sharp; they are a people pining for their home and their lost culture.

When one writes on sensitive and emotional issues like the Kashmir conflict, the gravest threat is the creation of binaries. It is believed that if a researcher writes on a text or film showcasing the plight of the Muslim residents in Kashmir, then the question of the exiled Hindu Pandits is sidelined or glossed over. This essay attempts to dismantle this belief: hence it focuses on both the suffering of the Muslim community living in the valley and the displaced Hindu Pandits forced to live in refugee camps. The selection of the four films—*Harud*, *Hamid*, *Haider* and *Shikara*—ensured a holistic and balanced analysis of the Kashmir conflict. The essay could select only one film depicting the pain of the Pandits as there have been virtually no films made on the subject in Bollywood. However, in 2022, Vivek Agnihotri released *The Kashmir Files*, a poignant story of the suffering of the Kashmiri Pandits, which went on to become a national and international success. This essay does not include *The Kashmir Files* in its selection of films because the researcher, after studying the film, feels that it deliberately creates polarising sentiments and also manipulates certain events to depict a one-sided vilification of a particular community.

In the final analysis, all the four films chosen in this essay depict the suffering of Kashmir as a state; when one views all four films together, what emerges is the universality of grief, dissociating it from communities or religions. The films acknowledge that violence, whether perpetrated by a militant, army official or state-sponsored organisation, is the act of that deranged individual; no religion sanctions it and no institution allows it. The poems of the famous Kashmiri poet Agha Shahid Ali interweave within themselves a hope that one day the pristine waters of the Dal Lake will not reek of blood and death. That is the hope that fuels every researcher and scholar who has studied the three-decade-old conflict in Kashmir.

Works Cited

Ali, Agha Shahid. 'Postcard from Kashmir'. *The Veiled Suite*, Penguin, 2010, p. 29.

Datta, Ankur. 'In Place, Out of Place: An Introduction to the Kashmiri Pandits'. *On Uncertain Ground: Displaced Kashmiri Pandits in Jammu and Kashmir*, by Datta, Oxford UP, 2017, pp. 1–36.

Goldberg, Chad Alan. 'Robert Park's Marginal Man: The Career of a Concept in American Sociology'. *Laboratorium*, vol. 4, no. 2, 2012, pp. 199–217, http://soclabo.org/index.php/laboratorium/article/view/4/65. Accessed 10 June 2024.

Haider. Directed by Vishal Bhardwaj. UTV Motion Pictures/VB Pictures, 2014.

Hamid. Directed by Aijaz Khan. Yoodlee Films, 2018.

Harud. Directed by Amir Bashir. ChasingTales, 2012.

Junaid, Mohamad. 'A Letter to Fellow Kashmiris'. *Until My Freedom Has Come: The New Intifada in Kashmir*, edited by Sanjay Kak, Penguin Books, 2011, pp. 279–288.

Kak, Sanjay. 'What Are Kashmir's Stone-pelters Saying to Us?' *Until My Freedom Has Come: The New Intifada in Kashmir*, edited by Kak, Penguin Books, 2011, pp. 31–42.

The Kashmir Files. Directed by Vivek Agnihotri. Zee Studios/Abhishek Agarwal Arts / I Am Buddha, 2022.

Naudial, Svetlana. 'I'm Hoping That Hamid Will Be That Gentle Conversation'. *The Hindu*, 14 Mar. 2019, www.thehindu.com/entertainment/movies/im-hoping-that-hamid-will-be-that-gentle-conversation/article26537331.ece. Accessed 10 June 2024.

Nayar, Pramod K. *Postcolonial Literature: An Introduction*. Pearson Education India, 2008.

Pandey, Gyanendra. 'Introduction: The Difference of Subalternity'. *Subalternity and Difference: Investigations from the North and the South*, edited by Pandey, Routledge, 2012, pp. 1–19.

Pandita, K.N. 'A Moment of Introspection'. *From Home to House: Writings of Kashmiri Pandits in Exile*, edited by Arvind Gigoo, et al., HarperCollins India, 2015, pp. 117–124.

Peer, Basharat. *Curfewed Night*. Random House India, 2009.

———. 'Kashmir Unrest: A Letter to an Unknown Indian'. *Until My Freedom Has Come: The New Intifada in Kashmir*, edited by Sanjay Kak, Penguin Books, 2011, pp. 43–46.

Shikara. Directed by Vidhu Vinod Chopra. Vinod Chopra Films, 2020.

Singh, Harneet. 'Kashmir Is the Hamlet of My Film'. *The Indian Express*, 5 Oct. 2014, indianexpress.com/article/entertainment/bollywood/kashmir-is-the-hamlet-of-my-film. Accessed 10 June 2024.

Soja, Edward W. 'Preface and Postscript'. *Postmodern Geographies: The Reassertion of Space in Critical Social Theory*, by Soja, Verso, 1989, pp. 1–9.

Tonight, What the Nation Wanted to Know but Never Listened To!

'Info-Perennis' and Popular Public Arena

Anindya Sekhar Purakayastha

> [T]he study of popular culture points us to modern acts of discernment, identity-formation, and passionate activism ... It is through popular cultural artifacts that historians may trace evidence of the ways in which the agency of viewers/consumers impels a civil society to grapple with change, to process change through indigenous sociologies of knowledge so that it can be naturalised and accommodated. I would argue that the visual realm is an absolutely critical component in this process in South Asia ...
>
> —Sandria B. Freitag
> 'The Realm of the Visual: Agency and Modern Civil Society'

> The dissolution of TV into life, the dissolution of life into TV.
>
> —Jean Baudrillard
> *Simulacra and Simulation*

This essay comes within the ambit of popular visual culture in India. To be precise, it takes as its empirical archive the burgeoning presence and surging clout of everyday 24×7 television news channels and their convivial intertextuality with numerous social-media networks. South Asian scholars have earlier engaged with popular forms of Indian visual culture such as photographs of deities, freedom fighters or of family frames, calendars, Bollywood films or even popular television shows such as *Indian Idol*, *Ramayana* and *Mahabharata*. However, of late, multiple private news channels (both vernacular and English), online news portals, news clips, news images, WhatsApp news and Twitter news have unprecedentedly widened the field. This essay locates the birth of a new info-nation, fed with and fanned by this constant inflow of news stories. This is what is called a state of 'info-perennis'—a perennial supply of information on all things and their uninterrupted everyday influx into Indian drawing rooms, producing a new category called the tele-publics or the cyber-publics who are always informed through headline stories, and are armed with readily available info clips to be forwarded through WhatsApp, Twitter or Facebook. All of these have radically transformed the Indian public space, offering fresh insights on popular cultural studies. This journey from the state-owned Doordarshan channel to privately run popular channels like Republic TV in India provides a staggering trajectory, an incredible shift in terms of cultural semiology and hermeneutics, rendering new interpretations of popular culture. One seldom comes across serious new studies on this emerging visual space which are modelled on existing templates of Western news channels—dress codes and stylistics of news anchors, optics, studio décor, newsroom debates, breaking-news style, glossy semiotics of bold headlines, the beaming simulacrum of reinforced reportage and so on. Yet, despite these Euro-American inflexions, Indian TV news channels are unique sites of popular culture, distinct in their elementary aspects and functioning mechanisms. My argument in this essay is to examine whether the mushrooming of television news channels in India in the last decade and its convivial symbiosis with social-media platforms is largely democratising the Indian public sphere, enfranchising the dispossessed populace to articulate their voice or enabling people to have access to news and information, thus reinforcing greater public participation and agency. Recent scholarship in global media theory has unanimously agreed on the democratising role of media. Even though we confront terminologies like 'fake news' and 'paid media', digital media today has, by and large, opened up new frontiers of public discourse, introducing new possibilities for democratic deliberation. Some specimens of recent work on media and democracy such as Ravish Kumar's *The Free Voice: On Democracy, Culture and the Nation*; Jan Zielonka's *Media and Politics in New Democracies: Europe in Comparative*

Perspective; Stephen Cushion and Justin Lewis's edited anthology *The Rise of 24-Hour News Television: "Global Perspectives"*; Natalie Fenton's edited *New Media, Old News: Journalism and Democracy in the Digital Age*; and Herbert J. Gans's *Democracy and the News* testify to the growing contribution of digital media and news channels in forging democratic public opinion. Notwithstanding the abysmal records of Indian-television news media when it comes to the authenticity of news and its political neutrality, television news channels are becoming a great source of popular mobilisation and engaging everyday culture in India. Despite the loud and chaotic nature of Indian media debate, the future of an 'argumentative Indian' or the possibility of an agonistic Indian civil society is perhaps being slowly cradled into a reality. Initially, I focus on the flip side of tele-news in India but subsequently my argumentative schema underscores the limitations of traditional theories of popular culture that deny it any claims for people's power. I show how the cacophony of Indian news debate, though scandalous and intimidating, is a site of future possibilities for civic, democratic interactions. Borrowing from South Asian scholar Sandra Freitag, I classify the existing raucous phase of Indian news channel debates as the virtual 'public arena', where primitive habits of fierce antagonism survive and are yet being slowly challenged, yielding place to saner debates. In what follows, I initially dwell on the hegemonic presence of digital news-media platforms in India in recent years. Through a comparative frame and literary analogy, I attempt to demonstrate how digitalisation of the news space has turned it into a powerful site of public-opinion building and a quasi-sacred space of popular consciousness.

Newsroom 'Fire Sermon' or What the Nine o'Clock News Said!

Seen through the lens of popular culture, Indian 24×7 news channels offer the perfect domain for public culture and mass behaviour. They also offer fresh explorations of social anthropology as deliberations in news-channel debates provide scope for closer analysis of public opinion and perception gathering. Some primetime news shows are highly popular, and vocabularies and cultural attitudes promoted and practised in these shows have larger cultural hegemonic acceptance. Looking at regular verbal skirmishes and boisterous verbal brickbats used during television news, cynics might say that had T.S. Eliot been alive today, he perhaps would have rescripted and rechristened *The Waste Land* as the *The Popular Land*, conceding an ideological summersault to hide his 'liberal', 'progressive' positions. My hunch is that he would have renamed the final section as 'What the Republic TV 9 o'Clock News Said'.

According to Indian scriptures and as enunciated by Eliot, the godly figure Prajapati donned the mantle of the divine oracle in the ur-text of *The Waste Land* (1922), pronouncing the sacral 'three Ds' as the prescribed ethical survival toolkit for the early twentieth century. The original poem ended with those lofty, divine injunctions for righteousness and altruism. In this speculative and popularly fictive post-2015 remake of Eliot's Nobel Prize-winning poem, the cosmic battle between the gods (read the nationalists/patriots/consumers/regular watchers of popular Indian TV shows like *Didi No. 1* or *Dada Giri*, *The Hero Honda Sare Ga Ma Pa*, etc.) and the prototypical ashsuras (the progressives/critical thinkers/liberals/'Macauley putras' [English-speaking westernised intellectuals], etc.), might be solved through a one-liner: 'And tonight what the nation wants to know…'. For almost all Indian tele-citizens, this polemical dramaturgy of posing a televised question, highly pitched and spiced with suspense and thrill and subsequently exploding with wild allegations, prefiguring the direction of the answer before the debate on what the 'nation wants to know' can actually begin, is very well-known courtesy Mr Goswami, the irrepressible anchor of Republic TV who subjects the entire Indian nation every night to encounter this question during the 9 o'clock news. The entire Indian nation, he presupposes, gets glued to his nationalist chastisements and rebukes routinely delivered in his popular primetime news show.

The subsequent thundering chaos and shouts that ensue in the name of television debate as it happens every day on Republic TV and also on various other vernacular and English news channels in India remind us of what Freitag succinctly argued years ago—that in India you do not have the Habermasian 'public sphere'. Rather, in its place, India witnesses its evolution from a 'public arena' to the civic system of public sphere—a space where all are allowed to speak and are heard instead of one loud voice shouting down the others. However, despite their limitations and gross misuse, popular visual platforms such as news channels are crucial to understand grounded issues related to the democratic category of the 'public'.

> For the realm of the visual remains, even after 25 years, largely unconnected to analyses of 'the public', despite its centrality to the ways in which public issues, enactments and interests are expressed and debated. To provide overarching ways to think about how... [to] treat 'the public', as well as to draw attention to issues still not addressed that offer future challenges, ... conceptualising the subject around four aspects that emerged ... the public as enacted; the public as envisioned; public space, both rhetorical and actual; and concepts of the public expressed as belief, interpretation, understandings, values and 'public opinion'—that is, as concepts understood to motivate and influence their audiences. (Freitag, 2015, 512)

Freitag's essay 'The Realm of the Visual: Agency and Modern Civil Society' is a perfect specimen of research on popular visual culture in India. According to her, various acts of seeing and knowing help ordinary people at the popular level to constitute their identity and construct meaning from their world, and make them active participants in shaping their society and scrutinising their nation-state. This allows the tracing of the meaning-making procedure through popular culture. These are precursors of modem acts of discernment, identity formation and passionate activism. One can understand how prescient Freitag has been in tracing this agential role of the visual space as far as popular subjectivation and empowerment is concerned in South Asia or India, to be precise.

For the lack of a better word, I would argue that, since 2015, India has witnessed a mad popular rush for this Goswamification of the preexisting public arena. Thus Eliot's sectional subtitle 'What the Thunder Said' frantically runs away towards this new caption of 'What Arnab Goswami Thundered' and, subsequently, unlike in Eliot's 'liberal' original text, the national battle in the popular televisual arena does not conclude with 'Shanti, shanti, shanti'. The cacophonous verbal skirmish in replying to Goswami's seminal nationalist ontological query does not offer any concrete answer, as high-decibel garrulity, coupled with rhetorical pitch, verbal threats and the entire dramaturgy of the Arnab Goswami show, mutate into a traditional Indian wrestling match where questions are raised and a political scapegoat is roped in, blackened, tarnished, humiliated and villainised to elicit slovenly verbal assaults.

Argumentative or Shouting Indian?

Jurgen Habermas's contention of communicative reason being the cornerstone of civil-society debates and popular democracy or of a people's nation begs for an exit route when it is placed beside Goswami's regular show at 9 o'clock. Needless to say, Goswami's talk show is very popular and this essay examines this new phenomenon of 24×7 television news as popular entertainment and a site of popular empowerment. Its phenomenal power to influence public opinion on the nation and narration or on the pedagogies of the nation has few parallels in Indian television history. Earlier, the state-controlled Doordarshan was envisaged as a powerful machinery to disseminate state-ordained narratives of national unity and national loyalty, but Goswami's verbal salvo and his arena-esque transformation of the television newsroom have catapulted him into a household name. People make fun of him and yet they like him; in other words, his shows are extremely popular and his sound bites or telecast videos are immediately forwarded as WhatsApp messages. It is an open secret that Goswami evinces overt advocacy for a particular political ideology and occasionally some of the news items, stories or reports shown in his channel have been directly accused of being 'fake news'. Even new terminologies such as 'paid news' or 'sopari news' (paid to tele-visually target a political opponent) have also come into the popular Indian public domain today. Invited speakers opposing this biased or inaccurate dissemination of news and reports have alleged that they received threat calls or are trolled by organised 'troll armies' which are cyber assaulters, threatening people on Twitter, WhatsApp or other virtual platforms. These neologisms have entered the popular Indian lexicon for regular mass use and yet, despite all this, Goswami's popularity keeps soaring. How do we explain this phenomenal impact of a TV show in which every night the entire nation is sermonised on what they should think, act and imagine, prefiguring for all of us who is the enemy and who is the saviour. Apart from that, post-Goswami news has ceased to be news; it has become pure popular entertainment, offering a staple diet for popular purchase such as verbal violence, suspense, sensationalism, scandal reporting, yellow journalism, tabloid-ification, thrill and cheap humour. This provides us scope to examine this transformation in the current political economy of the signs. Even though there are critics who would argue that popular social media does more harm than good and 24x7 news channels are nothing but pure marketisation of Newspeak, feeding on a gullible info glut for higher TRP ratings, one can explore the possibility of analysing all these new media-related activities through the theoretical perspectives of the 'public arena' or the public empowered to act as the bricoleur, negotiating through this semiotic guerrilla warfare being enacted through headlines and news images. Is the popular following of noisy Indian news channels a sign of the Indian public arena slowly graduating towards a public sphere? Is there, in other words, a public sphere in the making in India? Television news debates in India throw up a fascinating domain of new research in popular behaviour, popular consumption tendencies and new areas of popular opinion making. India is fast becoming a network society—a version of the information society where people are subjected to a continuous inflow of news and 'breaking stories'—entities which are immediately shared and circulated among all by each member of the Indian society. This massive circulation and the subsequent debates, although not enriched by rational rigour and civic norms, are still early signs of a civilised agon, where popular opinion and decision making are integrally connected. The social-media boom in India and the growing technologisation of Indian public spaces have sustained the popular use of social media, something that demands immediate examination in the light of recent theories of media culture, consumption and user culture.

WhatsApp University, Troll Army in Semiotic Democracy

By some accounts, India currently has 400 million users of WhatsApp and the highest number of Facebook users in the world. This is how we can characterise the biggest democracy of the world because this growing, mediatised surge of a digital public sphere of India has turned it into what scholars would describe as an info-nation, a popular condition in which people are fed WhatsApp messages and social media posts on Facebook, Twitter, Instagram, etc. The most popular form of political tool doing the rounds to checkmate the political rival is the troll army, another bizarre and new coinage that implies how political and cultural vitriol is played out through this digital space of popular usage. This is the techno-capitalist India of the 2020s, a far cry from the timid affective agony of the 'midnight's children'. If populism in early postcolonial India adopted the shape of nationalist fervour in terms of a Gandhian culture of austerity and the early discourses of Mother India spawned by Bollywood movies, populism and what we call popular culture have witnessed unprecedented transformations in the last one decade. In a way, the pedagogies of nation-making were part of the postcolonial popular and the lexicon of popular culture was suffused with issues related to unity and national integration. In contrast, the popular culture in contemporary Indian public space is to scathingly argue for fragmentation, separate identities, individual and group rights, and territorial rights. The fierce crudeness of these battles led to violence, asking for the speedy growth of a civil society that functions in the Habermasian public sphere, marked by civic and rationalised debate as performed by civil-society actors in European society. Placed against this view, Amartya Sen's idea of the 'Argumentative Indian' stands beholden to a distant past of glorious debates and dialogues among Indian seers. Contrary to this glorious tradition, news on television channels today is no longer read or telecast; news happens and all news is participatory news, box-office news, or breaking stories. The metaphors of Bollywood are transferable now to the domain of news channels. This pervasive clout of news channels has generated a form of delirium nation that goes wild and rhizomic in the wrong sense of the term. Recent scholarship on cultural theory has argued for a Deleuze–Guattari turn to cultural study (Wiley and Wise). Deploying Deleuze and Guattari in the Indian context, I argue for promising signs of re-territorialisation in popular participation in public debates on Indian news platforms. A thousand digital plateaus are virtually opening up in India in terms of new options, news portals and news platforms to articulate one's desires and grievances. Indian popular news media has ushered in actual 'nomadology' in audience behaviour; one can shift from one to the other channel in search of authenticity and a better show. Visual media has generally been critiqued and compared with possible conditions of imprisonment and closure of Plato's Cave, a site that provides mere reflection and illusory distortion and not the truth. The media has also been accused of helping in the formation of a society of control. But in spite of all these apprehensions, digital news media in India is perhaps showing early signs of liberating promises through public participation and popular opinion making. WhatsApp has become so powerful in India today that it has created terms like 'WhatsApp university', demonstrating its popular clout and influence over the masses. One particular political party in India is being currently critiqued by its opponents for their strategic use of WhatsApp university, or the production of manufactured false news which has immediate popular purchase. However, even though such allegations and counter-allegations continue to afflict the Indian public space, the fact remains that all political and popular stakeholders are resorting to media and news media platforms to articulate their views. This corroborates my initial point, which is that despite terrible loopholes, news channels are emerging as significant sites of popular public culture, something we as cultural studies scholars can seldom ignore.

Sahana Udupa develops, in her book *Making News in Global India: Media, Publics, Politics*, a rich and complex analysis of the news media through her field surveys conducted at Bengaluru in the context of urban neoliberal transformation. Through her meticulous ethnography of the Bengaluru edition of *The Times of India*, Udupa demonstrates how various forms of new media serve as 'a means of constituting (and challenging) the multiple desires generated by Bangalore's emergence as a global city, desires centred around commodities, urban revival, civic activism and social mobility' (Hasty 232). Udupa's case study reinforces that neoliberal globalising forces comprehensively determine everyday practices of journalism in today's new India. She introduces the useful concept of 'bhasha media' to describe the 'self-reflective and performative realm' of news practice that produces forms of cultural and linguistic locality that is in constant dialectical engagement with neoliberal forces (Hasty 234). Thus, her study analyses the functionality of media in the context of neoliberal transnational and class domination, showing how the media acts as a site of local cultural expression and resistance by showing the implications and co-production of those two realms.

To Question or Not to Question? That Is the Question

Renowned scholar and historian Romila Thapar in her book *The Public Intellectual in India* focuses on the overall climate of intolerance and violence in contemporary India. Any opposition or critique of governmental policies in recent years has been immediately branded as anti-national, prompting Thapar to say 'to Question or not to Question that is the Question' for Indians now. Even if some media houses have shown political bias or collusion with the powers that be, there are hundreds of news portals and channels which are offering counter-views, helping in the formation of what Nancy Fraser describes as the 'counter-publics' (67). If one switches on the television set at 9 pm in India and opts for the Republic TV channel, which currently has the highest viewership among English news channels, one would encounter a beaming Mr Goswami, the overly agitated TV anchor yelling at the top of his voice and beginning his 9 pm TV news with the rhetorical question, 'And tonight the nation wants to know…' TV news has metamorphosed into nationalist pedagogy through Goswami, where the audience is drilled into a one-hour course on nation and narration, something even Homi K. Bhabha would be unable to emulate. But Goswami has a steady target audience who like this rabblerousing and demagoguery in the name of TV anchoring, this overdose of nationalist emotion and choreographed orchestration of news debates in which all liberals and English-speaking intellectuals are rebuked as pseudo-scholars or pseudo-nationalists. When in 2017 a military officer in Kashmir roped in a local Kashmiri youth in front of a military vehicle to ward off protesting stone pelters in Kashmir, renowned postcolonial scholar Partha Chatterjee compared Major Gogoi's act, who took that decision to rope the Kashmiri youth, as the 'General Dyer moment' of independent India. Republic TV blasted out at Chatterjee that night, going to the extent of asking, 'Who the hell is Partha Chatterjee?' and querying whether he was nationalist enough: in other words, whether he had any business to speak on India and Indian affairs. All he was reduced to was a Western-educated, liberal, postcolonial scholar who has no heart for India. Even if this had popular following and support, it failed to stop the debate; the Kashmir episode evoked much furore on other channels and the debate continues even though current political hegemonies are not in favour of these pro-people opinions on Kashmir. This leads us to revisit existing theories of cultural studies because empirical archives on new media and public participation demonstrate new energies of active involvement, and previous theoretic models of interpellation, hegemony or ideological state apparatuses, while largely remaining true, are found to be challenged through the micro-politics of popular everyday struggle and public negotiation.

Mass Culture as *Compromise Equilibrium* or the Carnivalesque?

Antonio Gramsci's notion of the 'compromise equilibrium' (Storey 90) perceives the popular cultural field as a site of constant contestation and adjustment; it is synchronic, moving perpetually between resistance and incorporation at any given historical moment. This leaves room for individual agency and not complete subjugation. Theorists like John Fiske have wedded the idea of the 'carnivalesque' with popular culture, hinting how they locate the cultural space as a field populated with spectacles where they can articulate their wild and repressed voices, can shout, tolerate or even enjoy an overdose of histrionics or delirium. On the contrary, those who are opposed to the paradigm of popular culture have situated it only within a horizon of bondage or subordination. Dwight Macdonald, in his essay 'A Theory of Mass Culture', argues:

> Mass culture is imposed from above. It is fabricated by technicians hired by businessmen; its audience are passive consumers, their participation limited to the choice between buying and not buying. The Lords of Kitsch, in short, exploit the cultural needs of the masses in order to make a profit … (Macdonald 83)

In a similar vein, the Frankfurt School too developed the idea of the 'culture industry' to launch its critique of mass culture; however, its line of argument was radically different from what Matthew Arnold viewed as the anarchic ways of mass or low culture. Both Max Horkheimer and Theodor Adorno coined the term 'culture industry' to designate the process and mechanism of mass culture production, arguing that the products of cultural industry are characterised by two features, namely, 'cultural homogeneity' and 'cultural predictability'. Evidently, they could not see any agential opening to be provided by mass or popular culture as it is purely imbricated in the logic of the market and spawns a homogeneity of consumer-centric cultural conformism to fashionable templates of culture predetermined by the market. Because it is homogenous, it is predictable and does not offer any scope for creative hermeneutic possibilities. For Arnold, popular culture poses a threat to social and cultural authority and social order whereas for the Frankfurt School, popular culture exerts social authority as it is completely inscribed in the logic of global capital and therefore its agenda is to replicate the hegemonic order of the market economy (Storey 85). Subsequently, cultural theorists like Jean Baudrillard refuse to comply with what they would call economic reductionism, looking at all social phenomenon as the product of economic relations and systems of production or as the fallout of the ideological state apparatus. Baudrillard argues about the economy of signs, something that locates the importance of visual culture as the domain of popular participation.

> In the modern era, the problems of industry, production, use of labour, exploitation, and accumulation dominated the organization of the economy and society. In the current period there is 'a new era of simulation in which computerization, information processing, media, cybernetic control systems, and the organization of society according to simulation codes and models replace production as the organizing principle of society'. (Best and Kellner 118)

This is a passage

> 'from a *metallurgic* into a *semiurgic* society' ... in which signs take on a life of their own and constitute a new social order structured by models, codes, and signs. (Best and Kellner 118)

Semiotics refers to the theory of signs; the structures, types, significations and relationships among signs and semiology plays a crucial role in popular visual culture. What Baudrillard argues is that the signs, simulations and codes that characterise the current era have developed to a point that it is these that structure society and make it difficult to distinguish these signs and symbols from social reality, or social reality becomes the signs and simulations and these structure the social world. In developing this analysis, Baudrillard develops several new concepts like simulacrum or virtual reality in which the virtual supplants the actual.

Advocates of popular culture therefore adopt a different approach, positing how popular culture widens the spectrum and generates a 'semiotic democracy' where all can participate. I argue that scholars of Indian popular culture can apply this notion of semiotic democracy when it comes to our analysis of modern digital news platforms in India. Popular culture is expected to produce 'sophisticated bricoleurs' (Collins 254) who enjoy the eclectic expanse of popular culture, marked by polysemy and a plurality of options. With that argumentative transformation, there is a paradigm shift from the perspectival mode grounded in theories of hegemony and political economy to the hermeneutic mode of cultural studies. John Storey, in his analysis of the 'cultural field' in the parlance of popular cultural studies, argues that if the financial economy is predicated on exchange values, the cultural economy hinges on use value. The economy of popular culture is concerned with the use of 'meanings, pleasures, and social identities' and in a cultural economy, the television show ceases to be a mere commodity and emerges as a site for the production of meanings and pleasure for the audience. Audiences are not passive consumers, rather:

> ordinary people use the symbolic resources available to them under present conditions for meaningful activity in both manifest and endlessly elaborated upon by new revisionism ... if such writers as John Fiske and Paul Willis are to be believed, they cope very well indeed, making valid sense of the world and obtaining grateful pleasure from what they receive. Apparently, there is so much action in the micro-politics of everyday life ... (Storey 173)

Conclusion: From Arena to the Public Space

This theoretical claim brings us, once again, back to the possibility of the evolution of the postcolonial public sphere through a mediatised transformation of technological use and rise of public debate. Even though these early trends show signs of premodern tendencies of violence and crude uncivility, a new public sphere in contemporary techno-capitalist India is on the rise. The postcolonial public space is significant for the actualisation of democracy, decoloniality and ultimate liberty. During colonial rule, anti-colonial mobilisation was galvanised within the public space through a massive and intelligent use of public deliberation, nationalist pedagogy and liberation imaginary that aroused mass response among the disenfranchised population living under foreign rule. In the Indian context, the clever use of nationalist or mythological symbols, images, popular public narratives, public addresses and public debates streamlined a nearly uniform opinion for a united battle against the coloniser. Gandhi and the Indian National Congress or the 'nationalist elite', to borrow from Partha Chatterjee, used the public space or public sphere for national political mobilisation. They also capitalised on the popularity of religious myths and images and used them for political mobilisation. At that time, the media was not available the way it is present today but in a certain way, today's media is deploying that anti-colonial phase of populist drives, props and measures of public attention. During the nineteenth century, under the impact of Western education, there developed in Bengal a strong rationalist or intellectual climate that fuelled the trend of rationalist thinking and critique of traditionalist sects or community structures. This fomented a long array of social-reform measures in India. Public intellectuals like Rammohun Roy, Vidyasagar, Akhay Kumar Datta or Bhudev Mukhapadhyay came up with views on various social issues in their writings. This rationalist public sphere, however, declined with the rise of patriotic nationalist trajectories spearheaded by extremist nationalist figures.

Scholarly opinion argues that in India we do not have a public sphere; what we have, instead, is what Freitag calls a public arena or arenas, dominated by various communities and there is a long history of the evolution of these public arenas. The Indian public is different from Habermas's idea of the public sphere; it is more akin to Fraser's notion of 'counter-publics'. I argue that while Freitag and others are to be kept in mind, post-2011, with the rise of social media and countless news channels and blogs, a distinct Indian public sphere has been on the rise that has tried to shape public opinion. Of late, this same public sphere has been rife with discussion on various issues; prominent among them are issues of nation, Hindutva, secularism, non-secularism, minorities and religion. This conflation of the civic with the public or the modern with the rogue element under the same rubric of the political as it happens in India has facticity, but one needs to be careful about this analysis sliding into the zone of the familiar narratives of oriental irrationality. Such an analytical frame, while correct in many ways, fails to provide a way out.

I move to Thomas Blom Hansen et al. to engage with the analysis of public violence manifesting as popular sovereignty in India today. This reifies the public-arena hypothesis which, though largely correct, has a long historical background that dates back to colonial policies of bifurcating their governmentality structures under the domain of the inside (cultural sphere) and the outside (public, official or governmental sphere) of Indian life. Most colonial historians have proved how this British policy of leaving the cultural spheres of India untouched by governmental control spawned a domain of religious and cultural performance to show off intercommunity competition of performative strengths and cultural supremacy. Freitag has argued how various fictive community identities, distinct from what Sudipta Kaviraj (99), in his study of civil society in India, calls pre-colonial 'fuzzy identities', emerged in colonial India. This conflation of street violence and community claims spearheaded by various strongmen or patrons also had deep colonial roots. The colonisers allowed it to grow until it went beyond its limits and assumed communal overtones, resulting in internecine battles. Subaltern historians like Shahid Amin and Gyanendra Pandey have meticulously shown in their studies how popular discourses on community identities were forged in that colonial zone of cultural assertion that was not intervened into—a legacy that we continue to experience in various complex forms as this cultural or communal identity is being politicised today for modern electoral gains. This offers a new area for postcolonial research.

Today, the mightiest sociopolitical force in India is neither the state nor the law but deeply embedded vernacular ideas of popular sovereignty. Notions of the right to rule by the people (swatantra rajya or lokshahi) have taken deep hold. But unlike the specificity of precisely delineated caste and religious communities that play such a large role in everyday life, 'the people' or majority who are invoked in public performances remain a more open category and are never entirely pre-given. They need to be continuously filled and performed in order to remain potent (Hansen 39).

This prompts one to focus on the dynamics and operative principles in the public sphere, and this essay concludes by raising certain key questions which are crucial for the future of Indian cultural study. The questions are:

- Despite the fact that the Indian public sphere is different from norm-centric ones, an active, mediatised public sphere is surely emerging. How robust is that new public sphere going to be? Will it be distinct from its European counterparts? If yes, how can we demarcate that? Can there be a separate domain of Indian media studies?
- What suffuses the new mediatised public sphere—noise, issues, visuals, images, sounds, manipulations, narrative formations, social media skirmishes or conventional media? Or do we also have strong signs of agonism being enacted through indigenous modes?

- What are the issues being debated or shouted at—nation, religion, minority, secularism, corruption, national integrity, NRC? How does it expand further?

New frontiers of Indian popular cultural research can be hinged on these queries as the future ahead will experience greater consolidation of this new domain of public and popular participation in the digital domain of news and news making.

Works Cited

Amin, Shahid. *Event, Metaphor, Memory: Chauri Chaura, 1922–1992.* University of California Press, 1995.

Baudrillard, Jean. *Simulacra and Simulation.* Semiotext(e), 1983.

Best, Steven, and Douglas Kellner. *Postmodern Theory: Critical Interrogations.* The Guilford Press, 1991.

Collins, Jim. 'Television and Postmodernism'. *Channels of Discourse, Reassembled*, edited by Robert Allen, Routledge, 1992.

Cushion, Stephen, and Justin Lewis, editors. *The Rise of 24-Hour News Television: 'Global Perspectives'.* Peter Lang Publishing, 2010.

Fraser, Nancy. 'Rethinking the Public Sphere: A Contribution to the Critique of Actually Existing Democracy'. *Social Text*, no. 25/26, 1990, pp. 56–80.

Fenton, Natalie, editor. *New Media, Old News: Journalism and Democracy in the Digital Age.* SAGE Publications, 2009.

Freitag, Sandria B. 'The Realm of the Visual: Agency and Modern Civil Society'. *Indian Sociology*, vol. 36, no. 1–2, 2002, pp. 365–397.

———. 'Postscript: Exploring Aspects of "the Public" from 1991 to 2014'. *South Asia: Journal of South Asian Studies*, vol. 28, no. 3, 2015, pp. 512–523.

Gans, Herbert J. *Democracy and the News.* Oxford University Press, 2004.

Hansen, Thomas Blom, et al., editors. *Majoritarian State: How Hindu Nationalism Is Changing India.* Oxford UP, 2019.

Hasty, Jennifer. Review of *Making News in Global India: Media, Publics, Politics* by Sahana Udupa. *South Asia: Journal of South Asian Studies*, vol. 41, no. 1, 2018, pp. 232–234.

Kaviraj, Sudipta. *The Imaginary Institution of India: Politics and Ideas*. Columbia University Press, 2010.

Kumar, Ravish. *The Free Voice: On Democracy, Culture and the Nation*. Speaking Tiger, 2018.

Macdonald, Dwight. 'A Theory of Mass Culture'. *Diogenes*, vol. 1, no. 3, 1953, pp. 1–17.

Pandey, Gyanendra. *The Construction of Communalism in Colonial North India*. Oxford University Press, 1997.

Sen, Amartya. *The Argumentative Indian: Writings on Indian History, Culture and Identity*. Penguin, 2006.

Storey, John. *Cultural Theory and Popular Culture: An Introduction*. Pearson, 2001.

Udupa, Sahana. *Making News in Global India: Media, Publics, Politics*. Cambridge University Press, 2015.

Wiley, Stephen B. Crofts, and J. Macgregor Wise. 'Guattari, Deleuze and *Cultural Studies*'. *Cultural Studies*, vol. 33, no. 1, 2019, pp. 75–97.

Zielonka, Jan. *Media and Politics in New Democracies: Europe in Comparative Perspective*. Oxford UP, 2015.

Global Desi

Indian Beauty-Pageant Winners on the American Stage

Sarbani Banerjee

Introduction

In India, the avatar of the 'Indian Barbie', who is dark and lean and dons quintessentially traditional Indian outfits and jewellery, became the rage in the closing decades of the twentieth century. She was seen as the 'ideal' combination of East-meets-West that turned the imagination about the 'global Indian woman' into a reality. It was also around this time that a number of Indian women had paraded away with beauty-pageant trophies. A study of the rich history of Indian beauty queens and pop culture icons reveals their diverse images on screen. Persis Khambatta, Miss India 1965, heralded a campy appeal through her appearance in abstract pastel-colour videos and shaved head for the 1979 American science-fiction film *Star Trek* (Hamamoto and Liu 227). In the 1970s and 1980s, Zeenat Aman, Juhi Chawla and Sonu Walia had been successful pageant contestants before embarking on acting careers in Bollywood. Zeenat Aman, Femina Miss India Asia Pacific 1970, is associated with redefining the screen heroine's identity with her westernised image, and for launching a new form of sexual politics and grey shades of femininity in 1970s Bollywood (Jhunjhunwala 22; Rajadhyaksha and Willemen 41; Gehlawat 51). She was a harbinger of cine-sexuality through item numbers that refashioned Bollywood's commercial cinema and the middle-class gaze. Swaroop Sampat, Miss India 1979, is remembered for endorsing Shingar kumkum and upholding the middle-class aesthetic. Sampat appeared in television shows that projected the ordinary lives of commoners. The early 1990s brought in the trend of New Queer Cinema, which addressed the fantasies and experiences of LGBTQ Asian-American artists (Rich 32). Situated in this movement, artists such as Pratibha Parmar discover the 'diverse aesthetic influences, from Indian cinema and cultural iconography to pop promos and 70s avant-garde films' that informed their screen image (Parmar 35). The Indi-pop culture of the 1990s was inaugurated by Alisha Chinai, Baba Sehgal and Remo Fernandes, among others, and offered a parallel industry and alternate imagination to Bollywood music.

The trend of beauty queens that started with Sushmita Sen, Aishwarya Rai and Yukta Mookhey suggests that they were the Indian Barbies of the 1990s. At the turn of the twentieth century, Lara Dutta, Priyanka Chopra and Diya Mirza brought laurels to the country by winning Miss Universe, Miss World and Miss Asia Pacific, respectively. Endorsed by commercial sponsors, the triumph of the Indian beauty queen was perceived as India's feat at an international level, which bolstered the country's economic and cultural position and created new interfaces with postcolonial popular culture. She became a curious navigation of the global with the local, a combination of Indian cultural heritage with Western body politics and consumer culture. As Shoma Munshi notes:

> What is new in this rapidly changing urban socio-economic climate is how representations of the body of the woman in particular span both the national and international as a site of identification, being instilled with notions of India's 'modernity' and increasing visibility on the international arena. (163)

The editorial of the *Indian Express* lauds: 'After the plague when India's modernising image took a nose-dive, Sushmita and Aishwarya have come forward to redeem the image of modernising India' (qtd. in Manchanda 85). The twenty-first century saw global Indianness as a gendered development. *Newsweek*, *TIME* and *National Geographic* depicted the country's entrée into global modernity and its representation as a corporate brand through the faces and bodies of cosmopolitan Indian women (Reddy 30).

International brands such as Benetton, Levi's and Nike launched outlets in India and instantly became successful, with Indian models and beauty queens promoting these products. Sushmita Sen and Aishwarya Rai's appearance in Coca-Cola advertisements on Indian television indulged the scheme of Cocacolonisation. Their success reinforced the fact that beauty pageants and fashion shows go hand in hand with advertising hyperbole, imposing norms of consumption and feminine beauty. These events opened up opportunities and platforms for an entrepreneurial culture.

Set against this backdrop, this essay understands the role of Indian beauty-pageant winners and actors in carrying India to the 'globe' and back, with their bodies. It examines the business of glamour in American talk shows, and discusses how these shows present 'India' through the complex, hegemonic grids of fashion, stereotypical meanings of culture, and public relations. In particular, the essay reads the participation of illustrious personalities in specific episodes of American talk shows and entertainment web series such as *The Oprah Winfrey Show*, *The Wendy Williams Show* and *Worth It*. It studies how the chatty style of conversation in these shows connects the personal with the public and the commercial. By observing the audience both within and outside the virtual frame, it probes how these shows commoditise 'candour' and 'privacy' for their saleable quality.

Cover Girls and Showstoppers: Carrying the Utopia on the Body

Fashion lies at the crossroads of matters such as 'collective and personal identity dynamics, production and consumption patterns, and social distinction and imitation mechanisms' (Aspers and Godart 172). In Europe, fashion became a significant social force with the emergence of the bourgeoisie and capitalism, especially with the transitions brought about by the European Renaissance in the fourteenth century (Davis; Steele). Pioneer fashionistas such as Lady Duff-Gordon maintained that fantasy, consumption and altruism are interrelated, making a parallel between philanthropy and patriotism, and fashion and theatrical spectatorship. She persuaded women to give vent to their idiosyncrasies and self-expressions through consumer habits, and termed her creations 'personality dresses' and 'gowns of emotions' (Schweitzer 585, 599). A champion of fashion nationalism, she urged American women to style their own gowns as a way of articulating their independence from Paris. Post 9/11, George W. Bush legitimised this attitude through associating dutiful citizenship with active trading for attaining a stable national economy (Schweitzer 586). Duff-Gordon's and Bush's views draw on 'radical consumerism', which advocates 'that consumption is a creative and potentially liberatory process and that the ability both to influence and to reflect global style is, in fact, an important public power' (Thomas 250).

Beauty-pageant winners are associated with modernity and development, and in the after years of winning the title they play an inspirational figure on different platforms of social activism, 'stag[ing], expos[ing] and resolv[ing] crises in group representation in the flesh' (Hoad 57). Pageants give birth to the 'material subject' or persona developed through staged self-awareness. Such a subject appears in carnivals, parades and shows, creating a 'magnetic pole ... attract[ing] ... the visions, desires, and expectations of people participating in the event' and emerges as 'a temporary tool for newness, for possible futures, even small utopias' (Sjorslev 218). The subject's demonstration of beauty engenders affects such as estrangement, identification and need, which speak to questions of citizenship and belonging (Reddy 33). She props up spectacles and performances that assume an important role in levelling global discrepancy in the same capacity as the multinational corporate world. In other words, she 'offer[s] a useful shorthand for the representational relation between deeply unequal countries and apparently equal contestants' (Hoad 57, 64).

Brinda Karat remarks that, in India, the imagining of beauty queens as role models aims at creating a homogeneous market of consumers comprising chiefly the Indian middle class (qtd. in

Manchanda 88).[1] While Karat states that beauty contests bring out 'an element of assertiveness, of greater self-confidence' in the participants, Madhu Kishwar had earlier campaigned against beauty contests, perceiving them as the celebration of a westernised, elitist culture that commoditised women's bodies.[2] Afterwards, Kishwar observed that in an Indian setting, these contests are better alternatives to a 'repressive karva chauth culture and Khomeinivad for women' (qtd. in Manchanda 88). According to Arjun Appadurai, even as the pageant's rituals are (unimaginatively) indigenised, the participants function within racial, gender and class parameters that follow White middle-class femininity (139–157).

On the other hand, Colleen Cohen, Richard Wilk and Beverly Stoeltje observe that the pageants

> showcase values, concepts, and behavior that exist at the center of a group's sense of itself and exhibit values of morality, gender, and place.... The beauty contest stage is where these identities and cultures can be—and frequently are—made public and visible. (2)

In the past, beauty pageants have often been associated with the question of chastity. Helen Morgan resigned after the revelation of her being an unmarried mother. The Chinese American beauty queen's progress is stereotypically symbolised in her departure from cultural practices, such as bound feet to wearing stiletto heels. It suggests that the woman has gained an economic foothold and access to modern commodities, and become a part of the commercialised world (Wu 8). Paradoxically, the Chinatown 'queen' is also expected to uphold the ancient virtues of (Chinese) womanhood, such as respectful submissiveness towards her family patriarchs. Similarly, 2009 Miss British Virgin Islands pageant winner Josefina Nunez's 'Barbie persona' referenced both '"a true Virgin Islander" and a self-fashioned subjectivity based on consumption, entrepreneurial savvy, and malleable affiliations' (Cohen 691). Her performance evoked the conventional cultural practice of self-fashioning of the Caribbean woman as well as the emerging Caribbean middle-class affect (Freeman; Miller).

In the South Asian context, women's bodies acquire a baggage of conservative notions of community and culture in nationalist and neo-orientalist discourses, both in the countries of origin and in the diaspora (Gopinath; Lal).

American Talk Shows: The Business of Fashion, Beauty and Stardom

In most American talk shows, the stage converts into a space of intentionally held-out secrets, where the audience assumes the roles of the voyeur, the buyer and the judge. Ironically, the audience imbibes only plastic privacy that the host and her guests pander for its consumption. Oprah Winfrey turns her fluctuating weight into an industry and speaks in public about her life in an apparently uninhibited manner, but hardly discusses her fiancé Stedman Graham. In this, she betrays a contemplated stage persona that is glossed over by a façade of spontaneity. Most of the talk shows' feminist component is balanced on the (female) host's capacity of being effusive and playing the confidant to her guests. The invited icons discuss break-ups, scandals, peer pressure, and other awkward moments with the host. While accentuating emotional discharge, these shows also link self-value with the possession of goods. The pedagogy of consumerism in talk shows comprises an exhibition and legitimating of products. To fulfil the consumerist dreams of the audience, hosts frequently give away expensive prizes, such as home makeovers or vacation tours. Winfrey is known to have gifted cars to her studio audience (Halper 5). Wendy Williams cajoles her audience to extend their loyalty to the posh designers who create the props and decor on her stage. The host's acts of gifting, vouching for brands and inculcating habits in her audience are connected with an affirmation of taste and sentiment. Referring to Winfrey's show, Harris and Watson state:

> [The] message of uplift via consumption is one that can be directed only at those classes with the financial ability to realize it.... [T]he underlying message of her biography and show demonstrates one of the fundamental principles of the American Dream: if I am

> self-actualized and work hard, good things will come to me.... [M]irroring her purchasing habits will bring [the audience] closer to her and, ... the success she represents. (8–9)

The nature of American talk shows compels the audience to imagine a parasocial relationship with the host. It happens through the latter's powerful oratory skills and a conscious practice of verbal identification. Jane M. Shattuc observes the following:

> Winfrey slowly invokes the audience as a larger social collectivity. She directs the debate toward social issues through her selection of questioners and specifically through the rhetorical use of pronouns 'you', 'I', and 'we'. To illustrate she says ... 'The question we all have, I am speaking for the audience here and the audience around the world listening'. (95–96)

The 'Oprah Effect' or 'Oprah Factor' is explained in the host's name transforming from subject to verb to adjective (Smith-Shomade 149). Winfrey's power-woman image, duly boosted by her monthly *O: The Oprah Magazine* and the show, draws as much on her female fandom as on her modest origin and personal experiences of sexual abuse. In like manner, many beauty queens and celebrities discuss their journey from rags (or ordinary roots) to riches, and subscribe to a myth of 'middle-class' belonging. The populist appeal of such a journey essentially rests on the power of affect. In the process of enacting the role of a global power, the Indian beauty queen's public persona encompasses 'the unbridled aspirations of the Indian middle class' (Mitra 6). Radhika Parameswaran refers to the important role that the image of a successful beauty queen plays in shaping the hybrid taste of the global Indian consumer who celebrates patriotism and nationalist affiliation by vouching for a cosmopolitan material culture (366). However, the definition of 'middle-class-ness' coined by celebrities often refers to an unreal social allocation and a set of standardised (in India: Bollywoodised) practices, which cannot contain the disparate layers of the middle-class population. This kind of imaging is observable in the case of Priyanka Chopra, who emphasises her non-glamorous background, and Meghan Markle, who has prevailed in her journey from being an ordinary film star to becoming the Duchess of Sussex. Amitabh Bachchan discusses Aishwarya Rai's 'domesticated' and 'traditional' image as qualities that make her a suitable daughter-in-law (Bharadwaj).

Global Desi: Indian Beauty-Pageant Winners on the American Stage

Oprah Winfrey's fans commend her talk show as an unbeaten self-help programme, whereas critics perceive harmful body-shaming ideas in the famous host repeatedly confessing how she starved herself to lose weight and resorted to slimming supplements and VLCDs, even comparing food with dope (Howard 106–107). The participation of beauty-pageant winners in Winfrey's show burgeons a two-way desire of 'being with her' to 'become her'.[3] This point is illustrated in Winfrey's episode with Aishwarya Rai ('Episode dated 24 April 2005'). As Winfrey walks around in a pink chiffon sari that the former Miss World drapes her in, the host's discomfort about her bodily 'flaws' is balanced out by a moment of self-love. On the other hand, the guest, who is hitherto associated with physical beauty, finds a platform for promoting her feminist views.

The deliberate language used for welcoming the stars in the show is significant. Winfrey introduces Rai as 'the most beautiful woman on the planet', 'the number-one box-office film star in the world', yet also as someone that she decides the American viewers probably have never before heard of. Here, the American talk show plays the role of public relations in promoting the beauty queen, presumably at her behest, but also establishes the American superiority and privilege underlying the audience's ignorance about a big star from India. Winfrey contextualises Rai's presence on the American stage by mentioning that she is the 'international face' of L'Oréal, Coca-Cola and De Beers diamonds, suggesting the marketable connections that the beauty queen heralds.

Intriguingly, Rai's 'respect for Indian traditions' is understood from her choice of living with her parents. She is presented as a 'deeply religious' person, and one who never kisses on screen. The questions that Winfrey asks Rai follow the trail of this introduction: Do Indian women choose their own partners? Is sex outside of marriage considered a cultural taboo in India? And, do Indians use a lot of skin-lightening products?[4] Winfrey's introduction to Rai sets the ground for a predictable conversation, as the audience within and outside of the television space perceives the latter as carrying 'authentic middle-class' Indian values on her body. Contrarily, in Winfrey offering to flaunt her lingerie with the sari, there is an assertion of her difference from Rai's Indianness. Winfrey wearing a sari suggests Indian ethnicity being repositioned in a multicultural American milieu, where the garment's localised sense of 'propriety' is restyled for new meanings.

While Rai is avowedly on a mission to dispel myths about the Indian woman,[5] the beauty queen's profile feeds on romanticised notions about her. She plays along with her 'tropical' image by reminding the audience that she is from the land of the *Kamasutra*, however not forgetting to bring up that she speaks English like an American subject. Rai acts with the same facility as that of a 're-orientalist' who presumes the role of keeper of a typified global South Asian image, 'imposing the culture, values, attitudes, etc., of a select minority as representative of the diverse majority' (Lau 573). In Winfrey using the appellation of 'mystery woman' for Rai, who hails from the 'faraway exotic land ... of Taj Mahal and Bollywood', there is a dual suggestion—of the show taking place, physically and psychically, at the heart of America; and Rai's parameters of success being defined in terms of her having arrived from a 'developing' country to the nucleus of show business. While Rai is a specimen of enquiry in her geographical membership as an Indian, she is produced as a diva through her Indian self being parcelled off as a commodity on the global dais.

The entertainment web series *Worth It* by L'Oréal Paris showcased Rai, its brand ambassador, in the light of her success in different fields—from a model and actress to a mother and Cannes jury member ('The Worth It Show'). The show, the guest, the brand, and Cannes Film Festival share a symbiotic relationship, making each other more mass marketed. L'Oréal's slogan 'Because I'm worth it' brings in a sense of women's empowerment through being able to play with makeup. In point of fact, however, the kind of female agency that is celebrated is problematic. Creative workshops, cosmetics artists and art designers enjoy an upper hand over real women. L'Oréal advertises its products through sending the message that the 'right' makeup can make any woman look like Aishwarya Rai, which is a way of aggrandising the merchandise at the expense of diminishing the representative.

In *The Wendy Williams Show*, Williams projects Priyanka Chopra and Nick Jonas's 'Hindu wedding' as a bizarre museum item that is synonymous with gaudy clothes, palaces, extravagant gold jewellery and loud music ('Hot Topics Hour'). Her comments, such as the wedding is a 'steal', the entertainment programmes centring the wedding are 'annoying', and 'Who is spending for all that?', are xenophobic.

In an earlier episode with Chopra ('Priyanka Chopra'), the host treats the beauty queen as a pricey package by focusing attention to her costume, part by part. Chopra pushes the agenda of the show by playing an advertiser of exclusive brands. She flaunts her feet before the shoe cam and announces the name of the brand, Francesco Russo. Triggering a sense of alienation and identification alternately, the show, in the process of amusing the audience, aims at controlling their preferences. When asked if the American paparazzi makes her want to go back home, Chopra retorts that she 'live[s] on a plane', is 'extremely nomadic' and even quips that the 'world is too small to contain [her]'. There is a chauvinistic attempt on Williams's part to pin Chopra down solely within the lines of her Indian identity, whereas the latter dodges her effort through insisting that she is a transnational public figure who shifts base according to the nature of her work. Chopra, then, is not on the American stage only as a stooge to fit into the shoes of the Indian Barbie. She is cognisant of her share in the globalised market, so she not only takes back foreign brands to India, but also burdens the multicultural American stage with Indian baggage. As Williams puts it rightly, Chopra is 'okay just staying in Jersey'.

Conclusion

Since its origin in the early 1920s, the talk show in America has played a momentous role in shaping public discourse. It has exposed people to different perspectives and made their opinions heard. The idea behind such a programme was to make an individual viewer feel included and relevant (Halper 78). Such an ecosystem bears a socio-political onus, where the ordinary and the famous share a common space. In an ideal situation, it replicates the foundation of a thriving democracy. On the other hand, with the progress of time, the commercial aspect of talk shows has become overriding enough to ebb the audience's position. The talk-show programme, bought and sold in the communications marketplace, popularises a culture based on commodity fetishism. It emphasises the exchange value of a product over its pleasure value, benefitting the ideology of the 'free market' and propelling capitalist expansion into different domains of society (Quail et al. 30, 31). Even as the setting of the conversation in these shows evokes a comfortable niche that is supposed to bring the audience in, the latter is not an active contributor, only a patron. The materialistic dialogues that make talk shows trendy suggest that the idea of a niche is, in fact, a chimera aiming at higher ratings and bigger sponsors. As this essay demonstrates, many talk shows have opinionated hosts who direct the audience's predilections in a certain way.

In this regard, illustrious figures from India such as Rai and Chopra hold the positionality of power as re-orientalists, identifying simultaneously as the insider and the outsider. In their own proclamation of authenticity and the American stage's exaction of truth claims in their images, there is a problem of totalisation, even vulgarisation, which 'seek less to negotiate… the complications and nuances of identities ... [depicting] South Asian women and culture oversimplistically, stereotypically, and often sensationally' (Lau 572, 581). In many instances, Indian celebrities also steal the spotlight through etching their unconventional viewpoints in contrast to a definitive Indian culture. Their agency as beauty queens is primarily self-referential, which perpetuates as well as subverts stereotypes, depending on what is received well on a global stage.

It suffices that the audience consider that even as they emulate the famed stars' lifestyles and punch lines, they themselves do not matter; their act of spending does. In an age of hyper-reality, it would be a vain attempt to distinguish a star's performance from her life; one can hardly tell where fiction ends and life begins or if there is a life apart from fiction. Spinning yarns in the air is an art and craft that all stars who have walked on the American stage learned early on in their lives.

Notes

1. In America, the notion of fashion shows as an elite spectacle changed in the early 1900s, resulting in women from the middle and working classes being able to afford the costumes on display. During this time, several shows in New York and Philadelphia were made free to the public.
2. Protesters at the 1996 Miss World pageant in Bangalore 'wore caps for Miss Illness, Miss Poverty, and Miss Unemployment' as a way of pointing to the real coordinates of the Indian society (Hoad 56). Since the 1970s, feminist protestors have commonly referred to beauty pageants as 'cattle shows'.
3. This can be compared with Berlant's reading of the mutual gazing between two mulatta women, Clare Kendry and Irene Redfield, in Nella Larsen's novel *Passing*. Irene's desire for the 'erotic, sensational', bourgeois White femininity that Clare embodies also enables her to suppress her black body in negotiating with the market. Irene's xenophilia is not to make love or enjoy the privileges of Clare's body, but wear her body like a fetish (Berlant 108–109).

4. Women of colour have been repeatedly accused of skin lightening in magazines and publicity photos. The United Kingdom singer and former *X Factor* contestant Rebecca Ferguson was accused of digitally lightening her promotional photographs ('What Have They Done to Rebecca?'). Aishwarya Rai Bachchan allegedly looked much lighter on the cover of *Elle* (Abraham).
5. Rai refers to her Miss World experience as a 'mission' to clear people's misconceptions and enlighten them about the new, global India ('The Most Beautiful Woman').

Works Cited

Abraham, Tamara. 'Bollywood Star Furious Over Elle Magazine Cover "Skin-whitening" Scandal'. *MailOnline*, 31 Dec. 2010, www.dailymail.co.uk/femail/article-1343026/Bollywood-star-Aishwarya-Rai-Bachchan-left-furious-alleged-skin-whitening-Elle-magazine-cover.html. Accessed 18 Apr. 2024.

Appadurai, Arjun. *Modernity at Large: Cultural Dimensions of Globalization*. Minnesota UP, 1996.

Aspers, Patrik, and Frédéric Godart. 'Sociology of Fashion: Order and Change'. *Annual Review of Sociology*, vol. 39, 2013, pp. 171–192.

Berlant, Lauren. *The Female Complaint: The Unfinished Business of Sentimentality in American Culture*. Duke UP, 2008.

Bharadwaj, Vinita. 'The Rise and Stepping Behind of Aishwarya'. *Gulf News*, 20 Apr. 2007, gulfnews.com/opinion/thinkers/the-rise-and-stepping-behind-of-aishwarya-1.107172. Accessed 18 Apr. 2024.

Cohen, Colleen, et al., editors. *Beauty Queens on the Global Stage: Gender, Contests, and Power*. Routledge, 1996.

Cohen, Colleen. 'BVI Barbie: Materializing Subjectivity on the Beauty Pageant Stage'. *Anthropological Quarterly*, vol. 89, no. 3, summer 2016, pp. 689–721.

Davis, Fred. *Fashion, Culture, and Identity*. Chicago UP, 1992.

'Episode dated 24 April 2005'. *The Oprah Winfrey Show*, Aishwarya Rai interviewed by Oprah Winfrey ('Women Across the Globe'), Harpo Productions, 24 Apr. 2005.

Freeman, Carla. *High Tech and High Heels in the Global Economy: Women, Work, and Pink-Collar Identities in the Caribbean*. Duke UP, 2000.

Gehlawat, Ajay. 'The Construction of 1970s Femininity, or Why Zeenat Aman Sings the Same Song Twice'. *South Asian Popular Culture*, vol. 10, no. 1, 2012, pp. 51–62.

Gopinath, Gayatri. *Impossible Desires: Queer Diasporas and South Asian Public Cultures*. Duke UP, 2005.

Halper, Donna L. 'How the Talk Show Was Born: The History of a Genre'. *Icons of Talk: The Media Mouths that Changed America*, by Donna L. Halper, Greenwood, 2008, pp. 1–78.

Hamamoto, Darrell Y., and Sandra Liu, editors. *Countervisions: Asian American Film Criticism*. Temple UP, 2000.

Harris, Jennifer, and Elwood Watson. 'Introduction: Oprah Winfrey as Subject and Spectacle'. *The Oprah Phenomenon*, edited by Jennifer Harris and Elwood Watson, University Press of Kentucky, 2007, pp. 1–31.

Hoad, Neville. 'World Piece: What the Miss World Pageant Can Teach about Globalization'. *Cultural Critique*, vol. 58, autumn 2004, pp. 56–81.

'Hot Topics Hour! #9'. *The Wendy Williams Show*, season 11, episode 61, Wendy Williams Productions, 3 Dec. 2018.

Howard, Ella. 'From Fasting toward Self-Acceptance: Oprah Winfrey and Weight Loss in American Culture'. *The Oprah Phenomenon*, edited by Jennifer Harris and Elwood Watson, University Press of Kentucky, 2007, pp. 101–123.

Jhunjhunwala, Udita. 'The Elegant Zeenat Aman'. *Women in Indian Film*, edited by Nasreen Munni Kabir, Zubaan, 2009, pp. 9–32.

Lal, Vinay. *The Other Indians: A Political and Cultural History of South Asians in America*, edited by Don T. Nakanishi and Russell C. Leong, UCLA Asian American Studies Center, 2008.

Larsen, Nella. *Passing*. Albatross Publishers, 2017.

Lau, Lisa. 'Re-Orientalism: The Perpetration and Development of Orientalism by Orientals'. *Modern Asian Studies*, vol. 43, no. 2, Mar. 2009, pp. 571–590.

Manchanda, Rita. 'Icons of Indian Womanhood'. *India International Centre Quarterly*, vol. 23, no. 2, summer 1996, pp. 84–94.

Miller, Daniel. 'Why Clothing Is Not Superficial'. *Stuff*, by Daniel Miller, Polity Press, 2010, pp. 12–41.

Mitra, Sreya. '"Miss World" Meets "Dutiful Daughter-in-Law": Modernity, Marriage, Motherhood and the Bollywood Female Star'. *Celebrity Studies*, 5 July 2018, pp. 1–19.

'The Most Beautiful Woman in the World'. *60 Minutes*, Aishwarya Rai interviewed by Bob Simon, produced by Neeraj Khemlani, CBS, 29 Dec. 2004.

Munshi, Shoma. 'A Perfect 10—"Modern and Indian": Representations of the Body in Beauty Pageants and the Visual Media in Contemporary India'. *Confronting the Body: The Politics of Physicality in Colonial and Post-colonial India*, edited by J.H. Mill and S. Sen, Anthem Press, 2004, pp. 162–182.

Parameswaran, Radhika. 'Global Queens, National Celebrities: Tales of Feminine Triumph in Post-liberalization India'. *Critical Studies in Media Communication*, vol. 21, no. 4, 2004, pp. 346–370.

Parmar, Pratibha. 'Queer Questions'. *Sight and Sound*, Sept. 1992, p. 35.

'Priyanka Chopra'. *The Wendy Williams Show*, Priyanka Chopra interviewed by Wendy Williams, season 9, episode 152, Wendy Williams Productions, 23 May 2017.

Quail, Christine M., et al. 'The Commodification of Talk Show Culture'. *Counterpoints*, vol. 152, 2005, pp. 29–45.

Rajadhyaksha, Ashish, and Paul Willemen. *Encyclopaedia of Indian Cinema*, rev. ed., Fitzroy Dearborn, 1999.

Reddy, Vanita. 'Jhumpa Lahiri's Feminist Cosmopolitics and the Transnational Beauty Assemblage'. *Meridians*, vol. 11, no. 2, 2011, pp. 29–59.

Rich, B. Ruby. 'New Queer Cinema'. *Sight and Sound*, Sept. 1992, pp. 30–34.

Schweitzer, Marlis. 'Patriotic Acts of Consumption: Lucile (Lady Duff Gordon) and the Vaudeville Fashion Show Craze'. *Theatre Journal*, vol. 60, no. 4, Dec. 2008, pp. 585–608.

Shattuc, Jane M. *The Talking Cure: TV Talk Shows and Women*. Routledge, 1996.

Sjorslev, Inger. 'The Material Subject as Political: Style and Pointing in Public Performance'. *Anthropological Theory*, vol. 12, no. 209, 2012, pp. 209–228.

Smith-Shomade, Beretta E. *Shaded Lives: African-American Women and Television*. Rutgers UP, 2002.

Steele, Valerie. *Paris Fashion: A Cultural History*. Oxford UP, 1998, p. 327.

Thomas, Deborah. *Modern Blackness: Nationalism, Globalization, and the Politics of Culture in Jamaica*. Duke UP, 2004.

'What Have They Done to Rebecca? Former X Factor Star Ferguson's Skin Noticeably Lighter in New Promo Shots'. *MailOnline*, 1 Dec. 2011, www.dailymail.co.uk/tvshowbiz/article-2068258/X-Factor-star-Rebecca-Ferguson-noticeably-lighter-skin-new-promo-shots.html. Accessed 18 Apr. 2024.

'The Worth It Show'. *YouTube*, uploaded by Aishwarya Net, 14 May 2018, www.youtube.com/watch?v=T4YPlYiLeMY. Accessed 18 Apr. 2024.

Wu, Judy Tzu-Chun. '"Loveliest Daughter of Our Ancient Cathay!": Representations of Ethnic and Gender Identity in the Miss Chinatown U.S.A. Beauty Pageant'. *Journal of Social History*, vol. 31, no. 1, autumn 1997, pp. 5–31.

Home and Away

Refugees, East Bengal FC and Evolving Fandoms in Calcutta

Rajarshi Roy and Shirsho Dasgupta

> [F]or us, the ultimate metaphor was Calcutta, where all that was remote, unknown and cherished, converged.
>
> —Manas Ray
> 'Growing Up Refugee: On Memory and Locality'

> Searching for a roof over their heads … and a fistful of rice twice a day, they began their struggle for survival under conditions of unbearable hardship. Lost and impoverished, in an unknown territory and hostile environment, faced with severe adversities … the road to life was the one that led to the football field where East Bengal was playing.
>
> —Moti Nandy and Shampa Banerjee
> 'Football and Nationalism'

On 17 August 1980, the leading Bengali daily *Ananda Bazaar Patrika* ran a front-page story with the headline 'Football: The New Killer in Calcutta!' The previous day, a league match of little importance between rivals Mohun Bagan, the team associated with the native Indian Bengalis, and East Bengal, the team associated with migrants from former East Pakistan (present-day Bangladesh) bore witness to clashes between the fans of the two clubs and widespread violence in the stands, precipitating a stampede. Thirteen fans died and hundreds were injured. This rivalry between East Bengal and Mohun Bagan dates back to nearly a century and the Calcutta Derby is, according to FIFA (the sport's international governing body), one of world football's most absorbing rivalries ('India's All-Consuming Rivalry').

However, according to Paul Dimeo, 'Before partition, East Bengal and Mohun Bagan had a friendly relationship.... [East Bengal] shared a ground with Mohun Bagan and, until the cataclysmic political changes of 1947, the two clubs saw each other as siblings' (111). Even contemporary culture portrays the rivalry as respectful competition. For example, the Bengali film *Dhanyee Meye* (Brave Girl) has an extremely popular song in which a sequence has the members of the same football team—belonging to a small neighbourhood club—affirming their support for either of the two clubs. *Mohan Baganer Meye* (The Girl from Mohan Bagan), released just four years before the tragedy of 1980, portrays the rivalry in a comic vein—the fathers of the bride and the groom are opposed to the match since one supports East Bengal and the other, Mohun Bagan.

How then did this supposedly 'healthy' rivalry become bitter and violent? While football unites communities and (re) produces collective identities, it is also about social differentiation (Armstrong and Young). What exactly does it mean to be a fan of either club and how are they different from each other? To answer this, we must go back to the history of the two clubs and of Calcutta itself.

I

Football came to India with the British East India Company and the early pioneers of the game in the country were 'civil servants ... officers of the trading firms, members of the regimental battalions ... European teachers from the educational institutions ... and sailors from the merchant navy' (Nandy and Banerjee 241–242). In Calcutta—then the seat of power of the British Raj—Anglo-Indian schools had sports as an integral element of their school curriculum. For these early missionaries, football was a tool to inculcate the ethics of hard work, perseverance, team loyalty, obedience to authorities, correct physical development and 'manliness' (Bandyopadhyay 378). From the mid-nineteenth century onwards, with the rise of the 'martial races' theory, Bengalis were stereotyped by the British colonisers as weak and inferior. The Bengali response to this profiling was uniquely cultural. In Kausik Bandyopadhyay's words:

> The Bengali people reacted to the stereotype through the promotion of a 'neo-traditional physical culture' to efface the 'self-image of effeteness' ... This movement ... began to promote the rejuvenation of the ancient Hindu principle of physical culture. However ... even if rigorous physical exercise was looked upon as a plausible weapon to counter British stereotypes ... it did not afford Bengalis the opportunity to compete with their colonizers on even terms.... Bengalis ... sought new ways to reassert their physical prowess and redeem their masculinity. Western sports, and especially football, provided the ideal tools. (378)

As nationalist sentiments gripped Bengal, especially in the wake of the political crisis precipitated by Lord Curzon's decision to partition the province of Bengal in 1905, football came to be seen as a cultural weapon to fight imperialism. The sight of barefoot Bengalis matching up against better-equipped European sides would become an image ingrained in the cultural memory of Bengalis. In the 1961 romantic film *Saptapadi* (Seven Steps), for example, the Christian, Anglo-Indian Rina Brown (Suchitra Sen) first meets the Bengali brahmin Krishnendu (Uttam Kumar) during a football match where a barefoot Krishnendu is playing against a heavily booted European side (Chowdhury-Sengupta 298).

The establishment of Mohun Bagan Club can be read only in this context. Founded in 1889 by a few idealistic affluent men from north Calcutta, it was an institution which aimed not only to produce skilled sportsmen but also to impart moral and social values. As Bengal reeled under political and social unrest, Bagan won a string of trophies from 1904 to 1910. In 1911, the club defeated multiple European civil and military teams to march into the finals of the Indian Football Association (IFA) Shield. On 29 July 1911, in front of a crowd estimated to be between 60,000 to 100,000 strong, Mohun Bagan came back from being a goal down to scoring twice, beating East Yorkshire Regiment 2–1, to lift the coveted IFA Shield. For European scholars like Paul Dimeo and Tony Mason, Bagan's victory did little to fight against British imperialism (Dimeo 107). They argue that since football, after all, was the game of the white masters—the sahibs—adopting the sport as a cultural weapon meant adopting the discourse of the colonisers themselves and was thus little more than mimicry (Mason).

However, mimicry does not necessarily connote subservience. In *The Location of Culture*, Homi K. Bhaba writes:

> Mimicry is, thus the sign of a double articulation; a complex strategy of reform, regulation and discipline, which 'appropriates' the Other as it visualizes power.... The effect of mimicry on the authority of colonial discourse is profoundly disturbing. For in 'normalizing' the colonial state or subject, the dream of post-Enlightenment civility alienates its own language and produces another knowledge of its norms. (86)

It is the production of the gap resulting from the alienation of the colonial discourse from itself that gives mimicry a potent, subversive edge. Mohun Bagan's victory was an actualisation of this other language speaking back to the language of colonialism. As Rudrangshu Mukherjee notes, 'For Bengalis ... the win over a white team in football seemed a moment of national pride.' One must note here that although the 1905 Partition of Bengal province was supported by the Muslims of East Bengal due to their poor economic conditions as well as the perceived dominance of Hindu businessmen and landlords, resulting in communal tension in the region, Bagan's victory in the IFA Shield provided an occasion for communal amity in Calcutta.

Neither Mohun Bagan's dominance nor this communal amity would last. As the independence movement gained momentum, so did communal tensions between Hindus and Muslims. The rise of the Muslim League, with Bengal as one of its strongholds, also happened to coincide with a string of trophies won by Mohammedan Sporting Club. Then of course there was the rapid rise to prominence of another football club, one associated with the immigrant community from the eastern part of the province—East Bengal.

II

The dominant discourse in India post-1947 portrays the country as a land which, despite its difficulties, has always been welcoming to migrants and refugees. In January 2018, for instance, Martand Jha penned an article for *Mint* with the self-explanatory headline 'India's Refugee Saga, from 1947 to 2017'. Jha ends his piece with the words:

> [O]ver the years India has received wave after wave refugees from many of its neighbours.... India has generally followed the principle of non-refoulement, refusing to send refugees back to a place where they face a threat to their life. For a country of India's resources, this is an achievement of no small magnitude.

The most popular examples given by the proponents of this discourse are, of course, that of the Dalai Lama and Tibetans, and of the immigrants from East Pakistan. In 2017, Ranjeev Dubey, in a *Business Today* opinion piece on another persecuted ethnic minority seeking asylum in India unwittingly (or perhaps not) betrayed the other side of this discourse. Of the Rohingyas, whom he refers to as 'the additional unwashed million', he writes:

> [T]he incontrovertible fact of the matter remains that these guys are illiterate, unskilled, do not speak the local lingo and basically hang around markets aggressively harassing visitors for handouts. Their nocturnal activities are also the subject of much complaint.

This xenophobic attitude towards migrants is nothing new. Nandy notes that the native Calcutta populace had treated East Bengalis with condescension right from the beginning of the nineteenth century—for the original settlers of Calcutta, the migrants were little more than 'country bumpkins', and on stage and on screen, comic characters were almost always East Bengalis (Nandy 249). To openly express their contempt, the migrants were referred to as 'bangaal' by the Bengalis of Calcutta, and bangaals in turn started to refer to the West Bengalis as 'ghoti' (Majumdar 287–288).

In 1947, West Bengal went to India and East Bengal went to Pakistan. However, West Bengal's size was a third of the size of the erstwhile Bengal province pre-independence. At the same time, the new state was saddled with a huge population exacerbated by the influx of Hindu refugees from the East. Besides a severe reduction in revenue, the then chief minister of West Bengal, Dr B.C. Roy, declared that the state faced a food deficit of 2 million tonnes of rice and cereal. Moreover, the Marwari community in Calcutta gradually managed to not only carve out a niche for itself in the commercial sector but also to push out older Bengali traders. In this backdrop, the Bengalis of Calcutta viewed the bangaal refugees as an economic liability and their rehabilitation as something that jeopardised the prosperity and future development of the state.

The disdain, often bordering on hatred, and the exploitative attitude of many of the locals are also revealed in popular Bengali novels of the era. In Bimal Mitra's 1963 novel *Ekak, Dashak, Shatak* (Year, Decade, Century), for instance, the character of Shibaprasad Gupta maintains a facade of sympathy towards the refugees but does not hesitate to raze their makeshift shacks to the ground to cash in on the surging price of real estate. In Shirshendu Mukhopadhyay's 1987 novel *Madhab O Taar Pariparshik* (Madhab and His Surroundings), when Madhab, a young refugee, goes to the house of his local landlord to seek help, he is driven out from the premises, and the courtyard where Madhab had stood is thoroughly washed since he had 'defiled' the place and it needed to be purified again. Government efforts at rehabilitating the refugees, more often than not, faltered when faced with local hostility. To the migrants, therefore, Calcutta seemed to be a hostile city devoid of any compassion and love. Subhasri Ghosh, in her study, cites a migrant who wrote:

> All I crave for is a roof above my head and a decent livelihood that would allow me to live like a human being.... After all, I am not

> a native of Calcutta, I am a sharanarthi, an udbastu (refugee).... Leaving my prosperous village homeland, I now spend my nights on pavements of Calcutta in abject poverty roaming from door to door with my infant son begging for food.

Ghosh goes on:

> A refugee from the Sabhar area of Dacca district compared himself to a fallen star. Another unfortunate soul from Dhamrai lamented that by a strange twist of fate the Bangals—the connoisseurs of good food—who took great pleasure in throwing lavish feasts, were themselves knocking from door to door with their begging bowls to gather two square meals a day.

The migrants who had the worst experience were perhaps the squatters. Dissatisfied at the Indian and West Bengal governments' negligible efforts at rehabilitation, many came together and took initiatives at self-rehabilitation through the forcible seizure of vacant plots of land. The majority of these 'jabardokhol' (illegal encroachment) colonies came up between 1949 and 1950 and the squatters came in direct conflict with the local people and the absentee landlords of the plots on which they erected their makeshift tenements (Ghosh).

One must remember that the vast majority, if not all, of these refugee colonies and settlements—whether established by squatters or sanctioned by the government—sprang up either outside the then limits of the city proper or on its outskirts, like Baghajatin and Netaji Nagar in present-day 'south Kolkata' and the settlements in the Rajarhat area in the 24 Parganas. These refugee colonies were detestable to the native residents of Calcutta. Within these colonies, too, there were internal divisions and conflicts. If life outside the colony was difficult, society inside it was neither homogeneous nor one where everyone enjoyed the same status. It was rife with internal tensions in class, caste and dialect—the local dialects of the districts were homogenised by the Dhaka dialect, which in turn was at the mercy of the Bengali spoken by the Calcutta natives. Just like the native settlers of Calcutta who shunted the migrants off to the peripheries of the metropolis, inside the colony itself, the relatively more affluent pushed the people from poorer backgrounds to the outskirts of the colony proper. Opposed to this space in the margins of the city—a space which, for the East Bengali migrants, was a veritable charnel house of seething discontent—lay the Maidan.

III

In the words of Sarmistha De and Bidisha Chakraborty:

> In Calcutta, nothing symbolizes urban growth and planning under British rule more than the Maidan and its surrounding areas—it may be said that the city grew around this open space ... as the traders' economic and political power grew and humble hamlets and trading posts surrounded by dense jungle became transformed into the City of Palaces, the nerve-centre of a vast and mighty empire. (3)

From the nineteenth century onwards, along with the Fort and the offices of power and administration, the institutional structures of 'colonial knowledge' found its place around the Maidan. Since the vitality of this power rested primarily on sharpening the difference between the coloniser and the colonised, its disciplinary institutions and knowledge zones were confined within a carefully protected area of physical exclusiveness. The Maidan, which was initially an appendage to the Fort, was placed at the centre of this physical exclusiveness. By 1911, several clubs that catered to the recreation of the Europeans gained a foothold in the Maidan. When the maiden Calcutta Football League was kicked off, many of these clubs took part in it. Thus, the Maidan was, for a long time, perceived as a metaphor for British occupation and the space was, likewise, identified with the European way of living.

However, with time, the Maidan also started being frequented by civilian Indians. It became the site for a leisurely promenade, a coach ride, watching the Europeans play cricket, and enjoying circus shows and bioscopes (De and Chakraborty 17). Considered to be the heart around which Calcutta grew, the Maidan became a symbol of the city itself. Sporting contestations between European clubs and Indian ones became a symbolic battle for the city. This symbolic meaning attributed to the Maidan would, however, gradually change with time.

The Bengali nonsense writer and poet Sukumar Ray once associated the Maidan with the merry mode of life. It was this meaning that got attributed to the space post-independence. The Maidan and its surrounding areas house restaurants, pubs and nightclubs frequented by the affluent elite of the city and, at the same time, the offices of administration which were hardly sympathetic to the plight of the migrants from the eastern side of the border. The oppressor–oppressed sentiment already associated with the Maidan remained but the communities identified with each side changed. Where before independence Indian nationalist clubs waged war against European football clubs, in the sporting sphere post-independence, East Bengal, the club of the bangaals, was seen as battling for the city against Mohun Bagan, a club whose identity was forged around the idea of nationalist India.

IV

In 1919, Sailesh Basu, a footballer from Dhaka, made a name for himself at Jorabagan Club. However, in a crucial tie against Mohun Bagan at the Coochbehar Cup the next year, Basu was dropped from the team. He alleged that it was his ethnicity that cost him his place and complained to the club's vice-president Suresh Chaudhuri who, despite his best efforts, failed to find a remedy to this situation. In protest, Chaudhuri, himself an influential businessman from East Bengal, resigned from his position at Jorabagan Club and, with the help of Basu and a few others, founded a football club that would appeal to the East Bengali population living in Calcutta. Thus was born East Bengal Club on 1 August 1920.

From the very beginning, much to the pleasant surprise of the club's founders, East Bengal attracted an enthusiastic support base. The club was made an affiliate to the Indian Football Association, allowed to play in the Second Division League and given a ground on the Maidan. Its meteoric rise was, however, not looked upon favourably by some. In 1925, with a string of victories, East Bengal was deservingly promoted to the First Division of the Calcutta Football League, although amidst much controversy. Before that year, the official rules only allowed two Indian clubs to play in the league. Interestingly, while the representatives of all the European clubs in the league voted to overturn this rule and allow East Bengal to compete in the tournament in the interest of the development of the sport in the country, the only two clubs which opposed the move were the Indian ones, among them Mohun Bagan (Majumdar 289–290). This was the start of the now-legendary ghoti–bangaal rivalry between Mohun Bagan and East Bengal.

East Bengal grew from strength to strength and soon found itself in a three-way battle with Mohun Bagan and Mohammedan Sporting for domination over the city's footballing sphere. East Bengal achieved its maiden League triumph in 1942, was crowned champion of the IFA Shield the next year and, in 1945, won both the trophies in a single footballing season. Meanwhile, West Bengal witnessed a huge influx of refugees from its eastern counterpart during Partition and again during Bangladesh's war for independence from Pakistan in 1971. As thousands poured in from across the border, East Bengal's support swelled. It is interesting to note that both of East Bengal's 'golden ages' (periods in which they enjoyed unrivalled success) came during these moments—in 1949–53 and again in 1970–75.

The refugees, as already documented, were confined to a life of squalor, impoverishment and governmental neglect. It was in such circumstances that they discovered East Bengal—a club that was founded to represent them and carried the name of their lost homeland. Struggling for survival in a hostile environment, amongst an unwelcoming local populace who openly showed their contempt, they found that East Bengal was:

> fighting another battle in the field and winning! They all ran in frenzied haste, to assemble under the club's red and yellow banner.

> The victory of East Bengal stood for the triumph of their dreams. (Nandy 250)

According to Amitava Chatterjee:

> The spectator adds to the possibilities of sport (as subaltern practice) as … it is the presence of the spectator that turns an event into a performance: for this reason historians argue that 'the spectacle has always been a potent political weapon'. The relationship between player and spectators can often be based on the identification of the crowd with the competitor, who comes to represent the crowd; his physical trials are seen as manifestations of their daily struggles and difficulties. (690)

A similar identification undoubtedly unfolded between the refugees and East Bengal Football Club.

For these supporters of the red-and-gold, Mohun Bagan—the club of the ghotis—was naturally the antagonist and although it occasionally reared its head, East Bengal repeatedly managed to wrestle back supremacy on the football pitch. Each victory of East Bengal over their bitter rivals became a cultural weapon for the bangaals to fight the discrimination they experienced in their daily lives. As Nandy notes, 'East Bengal brought anger … in the backdrop of a hostile social, economic, and political environment (250). These sentiments are echoed by journalist Arnab Ghosh as well who observes:

> All those down-trodden people, who had no money, and who left everything, their landed properties, their home, etc. etc. They started identifying themselves with the East Bengal club because of their defeat in the social life.… And if East Bengal become victorious they feel themselves at least they have established something. (qtd. in Dimeo 113)

Against Paul Dimeo's contention that the East Bengal–Mohun Bagan rivalry is one that is based upon ethnic identities, Madhuja Mukherjee posits that the rivalry was the result of an expression of subnationalism on the part of East Bengal—an expression that was naturally opposed to the very identity of Mohun Bagan as a nationalistic Indian club. According to her, ethnic identity hardly mattered since many popular and even legendary players of both the clubs actually ethnically belonged to the other side or were not even remotely Bengali. Both analyses, however, are based on truth value and fail to take note of the fact that, at the end of the day, what is being discussed is a football club. Rex Nash argues that fan cultures should be seen as 'imagined communities' and their nature is hardly every subject to consideration of truth validity (468). Moreover, according to Anthony King, these fan cultures are an 'amalgam of historical episodes, myths, traditions, and plain inaccuracies' (436). For the supporters, it is thus hardly of any relevance where their players hail from. This 'mythic culture', as it were, is also especially important for East Bengal, as we shall shortly see.

Arriving in India, the general reaction of most migrants was one of shock and disbelief. East Bengalis had reputation of being 'home birds' and they struggled to come to terms with the fact that they were permanently cut off from their bhita-maati (home and hearth) and that which was once their desh (homeland) was now bidesh (foreign country). The identity of the bangaal in Calcutta was thus one which centred around the idea of a lost homeland. This homeland was perhaps not a 'real' geographical place but a reconstruction of an idyllic lost utopia—a space which was 'psycho-geographical', as it were.

As Manas Ray notes, 'Stories upon stories—the sense of place took a nostalgic aura.... The landscape was a landscape of nostalgia' (126). It was this nostalgia and longing for an unattainable lost homeland that was invested in East Bengal Club. The club provided a reassuring sense of permanence to a people struggling to deal with a life that had radically changed almost overnight. It 'offered a telos, a meaning beyond the play of the merely accidental. The displacement was bearable' (Ray 126).

Let us pause for a moment and briefly take stock of what we have seen so far in the (changing) nature of football fandom in Calcutta. The identity of the original Mohun Bagan fans is based on nationalist cultures and begins with the idea of a unified, nationalist India—at the time still not in existence—while for East Bengal it is the aspiration to return to the sunny green paddy fields and beautiful rivulets—a land lost forever. In both cases it revolves around psycho-geographical spaces, a fantasy land that either never existed or can never be regained. It is apparent that the latter, in a way, subverts the former; the dream of a unified, independent Bengal, let alone India, is never achieved. The region is divided into two. One half is irrevocably lost and its people do not readily see themselves as 'belonging' to Calcutta, in turn giving rise to an uncanny presence in the city's culture and polity.

But what does this mean for third- or fourth-generation East Bengal fans who have, by now, been assimilated into Indian society? What is the unchanging kernel around which ideas of Calcutta fandoms are constructed? To understand this, it becomes necessary to read the Calcutta Derby as a sort of historical text and to study the traditions of the fan bases and support groups and even the in-stadium celebrations or choreography.

V

One of the most interesting facts about the Calcutta Derby is perhaps the fact that, since the 1990s, both the teams have been using the same stadium for their national league matches, thus bringing the use of 'contention' to the very surface. When we interviewed the match-day regulars of both the clubs, we came up with two disparate opinions which could perhaps in a way be attributed to the demographics of the fanbase. Those individuals who have been attending matches for over thirty years attached a sense of nostalgia with playing another club in their own backyard.

Perhaps Karl Marx's conceptualisation of nostalgia should be read in order to make proper sense of this sentiment: 'In order to arrive at its own content, the revolution of the nineteenth century must let the dead bury their dead' ('The Eighteenth Brumaire').

This sentence has reverberated through more than 150 years of revolutionary thought and practice. For Marx, nostalgia was an unhealthy ailment within political life. His concerns were sharpened by the fact that popular struggles in England in the mid-nineteenth century often combined anti-capitalism with an antagonism to industrialisation. The tendency of the masses to look backwards was met head-on by Marx:

> [W]e say to the workers and the petty bourgeois: it is better to suffer in the contemporary bourgeois society, whose industry creates the means for the foundation of a new society that will liberate you all, than to revert to a bygone society, which, on the pretext of saving your classes, thrusts the entire nation back into medieval barbarism. ('Montesquieu LVI')

The equation of the 'bygone' to 'barbarism' is given impetus by the pathological undertones of nostalgia. In essence, however, it rests on the assumption that to be rational is to be forward-looking. Although the persistent tendency of working-class movements to look to the past for models of social freedom has been overcome by Marxists in a variety of ways, the most common and most indicative response has been to represent nostalgia as an irritant on the body of a maturing class sensibility. Opposed to this, today we have a comparatively newer 'brand' of fans who choose to identify themselves as the 'ultras'.

The behavioural tendency of ultras groups includes the use of flares, vocal support in large groups and the display of banners at football stadiums, all of which are designed to create an atmosphere which encourages their own team and intimidates opposing players and supporters. Their opinions about the shifting of matches from their home ground in the Maidan to the new Yuva Bharati Krirangan (or Salt Lake Stadium) is largely welcoming. The stadium, in their conceptualisation, is no different from the idea of 'turf war'—vestiges of which was evident in the interviews of the older fans. It is entirely possible that between the generations of these fans—ones who perhaps had firsthand experiences of refugee colonies and perhaps even migration, and those who imbued the sensibilities of rivalries of the game from YouTube videos and match-day stadium recordings—there exists a strain of inherited memory that has undergone massive cultural dislocation owing to media coverage and over-sensationalising of the ghoti–bangaal phenomenon.

A key point of distinction is to be noticed in the nature of the fandom related to both clubs. It could be argued, in a slight modification to Amitav Chatterjee's point which tries to find a rudimentary analogy between popular fandoms and 'ritualized warfare' (693), that modern fandom relating to both the clubs has moved beyond their all-consuming rivalry and nostalgia towards a project of self-preservation in the age of late capitalism. Likewise, the rivalry today is not a simple Derby Day 'law and order' issue; it is something that has remained ever more vigilant in the face of ceaseless transformation of Indian football clubs into brands and franchises and unilateral decision-making by club officials. The word 'fandom' thus comes closer, in one sense, to a form of football activism. If history and nativist sentiments remained central to the fostering of the rivalry, the present age of 'fandom' boasts of a form of solidarity between the rival fans that finds activism necessary in issues like the 'One Nation One League' and the anti NRC–CAA movement.

This is evident from the fact that fans from both the clubs came together to protest against the newly passed Citizenship (Amendment) Act (CAA) and the National Register of Citizens (NRC), which many argue will strip Indian citizenship off certain minority groups, mainly Bangladeshi Muslim immigrants. This event constitutes an interesting political moment in the history of the Calcutta Derby. A match report of the Derby carries the following description:

> Mohun Bagan supporters unfurled a banner with a message similar to that of East Bengal. 'Respect our history, heritage and tradition', read the banner in English, while the Bengali one noted, 'Ever since the sun set over the fields of Plassey, it is we who have taught you

> to fight looking the enemy in the eye.' Another banner read, 'When we were here, there were no documents.' ('CAA')

This report marks a curious antinomian point in the history of the Derby, wherein the history of the rivalry that had started in the 1920s has now found a new sense of political maturity in the face of an imposed national identity. While such spontaneous moments of political expression have been absolutely rare in the history of the clubs and their shared rivalry, we do not know whether these moments are perhaps enough to qualify it to be an anti-fascist stance. But what we can say for sure is the community of the fan, or the 'fandom', has moved out of the surrogacy of mutual rivalry and solicits presence in the womb of mutual identification through each other's history. The lessons learnt from Partition, migration and several other defining moments has led to the genesis of a new 'community' of fans, whose solidarity outlasts the ninety minutes and goes beyond the turnpikes of the Salt Lake stadium.

This new 'community' of fans may be products of a rivalry that goes beyond their generation, to a historic native–refugee conflict. However, late capitalism imbues their fanhood with a tremendous need for 'football activism' that reflects the issues pertaining to the realpolitik within the arc of the stadium. Memory and solidarity thus constitute the two distinct historical antinomies in the history of fandom related to the East Bengal–Mohun Bagan rivalry. The essence of community spirit has developed the memory of this rivalry into a sense of social responsibility towards the game and its stakeholders. It has come a long way from being just a form of 'ritualized warfare'.

Works Cited

Ananda Bazaar Patrika (Calcutta), 17 Aug. 1980.

Armstrong, Gary, and Malcolm Young. 'Fanatical Football Chants: Creating and Controlling the Carnival'. *Culture, Sport, Society*, vol. 2, no. 3, 2007, pp. 173–211.

Bandyopadhyay, Kausik. '"The Nation and Its Fragments": Football and Community in India'. *Soccer & Society*, vol. 9, no. 3, 2008, pp. 377–393.

Bhabha, Homi K. 'Of Mimicry and Man: The Ambivalence of Colonial Discourse'. *The Location of Culture*, Routledge, 1994, pp. 85–92.

'CAA Brings East Bengal and Mohun Bagan Fans Under One Banner, First Time in 100 Years'. *The Hindu*, 21 Jan. 2020, www.thehindu.com/news/cities/kolkata/caa-brings-east-bengal-and-mohun-bagan-fans-under-one-banner-first-time-in-100-years/article30616925.ece. Accessed 27 Oct. 2024.

Chatterjee, Amitava. 'Spectator and Violence: Football in Colonial and Postcolonial Calcutta'. *Soccer & Society*, vol. 12, no. 5, 2011, pp. 689–700.

Chowdhury-Sengupta, Indira. 'The Effeminate and the Masculine: Nationalism and the Concept of Race in Colonial Bengal'. *The Concept of Race in South Asia*, edited by Peter Robb, Oxford UP, 1995, pp. 282–303.

De, Sarmistha, and Bidisha Chakraborty. 'Maidan: The Open Space in History'. *Social Scientist*, vol. 38, no. ½, 2010, pp. 3–22.

Dhanyee Meye. Directed by Arabinda Mukhopadhyay. Shree Productions, 1971.

Dimeo, Paul. '"Team Loyalty Splits the City into Two": Football, Ethnicity and Rivalry in Calcutta'. *Fear and Loathing in World Football*, edited by Gary Armstrong and Richard Giulianotti, Berg, 2001, pp. 105–118.

Dubey, Ranjeev C. 'Why India Can't Afford Rohingya Refugees'. *Business Today*, 9 Nov. 2017, www.businesstoday.in/opinion/fineprint/story/rohingya-refugee-crisis-india-bengal-rakhine-myanmar-bangladesh-jammu-settlement-90233-2017-11-09. Accessed 27 Oct. 2024.

Ghosh, Subhasri. 'Representation of Forced Migrants: A Case Study of East Bengali Migrants to West Bengal'. *Conserveries mémorielles: Revue transdisciplinaire de jeunes chercheurs*, no. 13, 2013, journals.openedition.org/cm/1490. Accessed 27 Oct. 2024.

'India's All-Consuming Rivalry'. *FIFA*, 8 Apr. 2011, www.fifa.com/news/y=2011/m=4/news=india-all-consuming-rivalry-1414458.html. Accessed 18 Apr. 2023.

Jha, Martand. 'India's Refugee Saga, from 1947 to 2017'. *Mint*, 9 Jan. 2018, www.livemint.com/Sundayapp/clQnX60MIR2LhCitpMmMWO/

Indias-refugee-saga-from-1947-to-2017.html. Accessed 27 Oct. 2024.

King, Anthony. 'Football Fandom and Post-National Identity in the New Europe'. *The British Journal of Sociology*, vol. 51, no. 3, 2003, pp. 419–442.

Majumdar, Boria. 'Ghati-Bangal on the Maidan: Subregionalism, Club Rivalry and Fan Culture in Indian Football'. *Soccer & Society*, vol. 9, no. 2, 2008, pp. 286–299.

Marx, Karl. 'Montesquieu LVI'. *Neue Rheinische Zeitung*, no. 202, 21 Jan. 1849, www.marxists.org/archive/marx/works/1849/01/22.htm. Accessed 27 Oct. 2024.

———. 'The Eighteenth Brumaire of Louis Bonaparte'. *Die Revolution*, 1852, www.marxists.org/archive/marx/works/1852/18th-brumaire/ch01.htm. Accessed 27 Oct. 2024.

Mason, Tony. 'Football on the Maidan: Cultural Imperialism in Calcutta'. *The International Journal of the History of Sport*, vol. 7, no. 1, 2007, pp. 85–96.

Mohan Baganer Meye. Directed by Manu Sen. Kalimata Productions, 1976.

Mukherjee, Madhuja. 'The Otherness of Self: Football, Fandom and Fragmented (Sub)nationalism in Bengal'. *Soccer & Society*, vol. 14, no. 5, 2013, pp. 652–669.

Mukherjee, Rudrangshu. 'Elegy on the Maidan'. *The Telegraph* (Calcutta), 5 Mar. 2002.

Nandy, Moti and Shampa Banerjee. 'Football and Nationalism'. *India International Centre Quarterly*, vol. 17, no. ¾, 1990, pp. 240–254.

Nash, Rex. 'Contestations in Modern English Professional Football'. *International Review for the Sociology of Sport*, vol. 35, no. 4, 2000, pp. 465–486.

Ray, Manas. 'Growing Up Refugee: On Memory and Locality'. *India International Centre Quarterly*, vol. 28, no. 2, 2001, pp. 119–137.

Saptapadi. Directed by Ajoy Kar, performances by Uttam Kumar and Suchitra Sen. Alochhaya Productions, 1961.

Contributors

E. Dawson Varughese is Associate Professor at Manipal Centre for Humanities (MAHE), Karnataka. She is the author of the seminal text *Reading New India* (2013) and *Visuality and Identity in Post-millennial Indian Graphic Narratives* (2018). Forthcoming in 2024 is *Post-millennial Indian Speculative Fiction in English.* She is currently editing *The Routledge Companion to Twenty-First Century Indian Fiction in English.*

Rishi Ghosh does research in modern Bengali poetry, social science-oriented interdisciplinary studies, and culture studies. He is Associate Professor at Gour Mahavidyalaya, Malda. He also works as Honorary Correspondent at the daily newspaper *Uttar Banga Sangbad.*

Oindrila Mitra is Assistant Professor at the Department of English, Sree Chaitanya College, Habra, West Bengal. Her research interests are children's literature, popular literature, Indian English fiction, and postcolonial studies. She completed her MPhil from Visva Bharati University, Shantiniketan.

Puja Sen Majumdar completed her MPhil in social sciences in 2019 from the Centre for Studies in Social Sciences. She was interested in continental philosophy, queer and feminist theory, history of religions, and art history.

Rini P. Kujur completed her MPhil in social sciences in 2019 from the Centre for Studies in Social Sciences. Her research interests are visual texts/cultures, social movements, legal histories, and the anthropology of religion.

Puja Chakraborty is a faculty member in the Department of English, Malda Women's College. She is pursuing her PhD from the Department of English and Culture Studies, University of

Burdwan. Her areas of interest include gender studies, postcolonial studies, contemporary Indian writing in English, and popular culture. Her essays have been published in *Rupkatha Journal on Interdisciplinary Studies in Humanities*, *Muse India*, and *Cafe Dissensus*, among others.

Suchetana Banerjee teaches literature, theatre, and research methodologies at the Symbiosis School for Liberal Arts, Symbiosis International University, Pune. She is a comparatist, a translator, and a theatre maker. Her research interests include comparative literature, literary and performative traditions, literatures of Africa, South Asian devotionalism, and theatre studies. She has published on cross-cultural literary transactions, theatre studies, and African literatures and cultures.

Medha Bhadra Chowdhury is Assistant Professor in the Department of English, St Xavier's University, Kolkata. She completed her PhD from Jadavpur University, Kolkata, on the oral histories of women survivors of the Bangladesh Liberation War. Her areas of specialisation include gender and memory studies, women's writing, and feminist theory.

Siddhartha Chakraborti is Assistant Professor in the Department of English, Aligarh Muslim University. His PhD thesis was on decolonisation in the Indian context. He is one of the founding members of DHARTI and has recently bagged a GIAN project at AMU, in the area of digital literatures, with the University of Alberta. In his spare time, he enjoys photography and computer games.

Ananya Chatterjee is Assistant Professor of English at Balurghat College. She completed her master's degree in English from the University of Calcutta. She is a PhD research scholar at Techno India University, Kolkata. She was Assistant Professor in English at JIS College of Engineering, Kalyani. She has contributed research articles to several books and journals.

Nisarga Bhattacharjee is a PhD research scholar at the Department of English Literature, EFL University, Hyderabad. He has been a part-time lecturer at Seth Anandram Jaipuria College (Day) and at Achrya Prafulla Chandra College. He completed his MPhil in English from the University of Calcutta. He has published several articles in journals and books. His area of interest is late-Modernist and postmodern literature (poetry in particular).

Mita Bandyopadhyay is Assistant Professor of English at Techno India University, Kolkata. Her research areas include film studies and communication studies.

Arindam Modak is Associate Professor of English in the Department of Humanities and Social Sciences at the National Institute of Technology Durgapur. He carried out research on literary theory and criticism. He regularly presents papers at national and international conferences, and has published a number of scholarly articles in peer-reviewed and Scopus-indexed international journals.

Jayati Ganguly teaches in the Department of English, Bidhan Chandra College, Asansol, West Bengal. She is pursuing her PhD at the Department of English, Diamond Harbour Women's University, West Bengal. Her research interests include culture studies, feminist studies, and motherhood studies, among others.

Shyaonti Talwar is an ELT trainer and Assistant Professor of English at RNC Arts, JDB Commerce and NSC Science College, affiliated to SP University, Pune.

Somrita Misra is Assistant Professor of English at Chanchal College, Malda, West Bengal. She is passionate about Harry Potter and is interested in the analysis of children's literature.

Anindya Sekhar Purakayastha, currently with the School of Translation and Cultural Studies, Institute of Language Studies and

Research, Kolkata, has been Professor of English at Kazi Nazrul University. Previously, he taught at Sidho Kanho Birsha University, West Bengal, and the Central University of Odisha. His research focuses on critical theory, literary and cultural representations, and postcolonial interventions from the global south. He looks into recent ideas of decoloniality, literary and cultural translation, and postcolonial politics.

Sarbani Banerjee teaches in the Department of Humanities and Social Sciences at IIT Roorkee. She earned her PhD in comparative literature from the University of Western Ontario. Her areas of specialisation include postcolonial literatures and theory, alternative spiritualities, post-Partition Bengali literature and cinema, diasporic literatures, and women's studies. She has published in journals of international repute, including *Interventions*, *South Asian Review*, *Journal of Postcolonial Writing*, *Journal for Cultural Research* and *Feminist Media Studies*.

Rajarshi Roy is Assistant Professor of English at Vivekananda Satavarshiki Mahavidyalaya, West Bengal. He is pursuing his PhD at the Department of English, Jadavpur University. He was a recipient of the UGC-RUSA 2.0 fellowship (2019–2020) to translate Prasanta Kumar Paul's *Rabijibani* from Bangla to English during his tenure as an MPhil scholar at Jadavpur University.

Shirsho Dasgupta is a journalist at the Washington DC bureau of the *Miami Herald*/McClatchy newspapers where he works on projects and investigations. He began his journalism career as a football writer. He holds a master's degree in English from Jadavpur University and another in journalism from the University of Southern California. The views expressed in his essay are not the opinions of his employers.

Communicative English—I

A.P. Girdhar
Faculty
B.K. Birla Institute of Engineering & Technology
Pilani, Rajasthan (India)

TECHSAR™
NEW DELHI

Published and Printed by
Techsar Pvt. Ltd.
4435–36/7, Ansari Road, Daryaganj
New Delhi-110002 (India)
E-mail: tech_info@techsarworld.com
Website: www.techsarworld.com

ISBN 978-93-82332-06-0

Reprint 2025

Preface

This book is especially designed for the students of B. Tech pursuing their studies from the institutions affiliated to Rajasthan Technical University Kota. The book covers the syllabus of the subject "Communicative English" prescribed for the students of first semester of first year.

Unit 1 contains a comprehensive discussion of all major grammatical concepts and their applications for communication purposes. Unit 2 deals with all major forms of writing. The material is designed to help the learners acquire writing skills required for performing academic tasks, since the approach is practical, the material included would also inculcate communicative competence needed in the professional world. Each lesson in units 3, 4 and 5 is followed by a summary, glossary, very short questions, short questions and essay type questions.

Every effort has been made to present the material in the simplest possible language so that students can understand it easily and they feel encouraged to write their answers in their own language.

A.P. GIRDHAR

Preface

[illegible] designed for the [illegible] from the [illegible] [illegible] Communicative English [illegible] for the students of first semester of first year.

[illegible] comprehensive [illegible] communication purposes. Unit 2 [illegible] The material is designed [illegible] required for professional [illegible] practical [illegible] communicative competence [illegible] Each [illegible] glossary, very short questions, short questions and essay type questions.

[illegible] has been made to present the material in [illegible] language [illegible]

[illegible]

Acknowledgements

It is my sacred duty to express my sense of gratitude to Dr. P. S. Bhatnagar, Director, B K Birla Institute of Engineering & Technology, Pilani for his great motivation, valuable guidance and constant support without which I would not have ventured to undertake this task. My thanks are also due to the two Deans of the Institute, Prof. S. B. Dandin and Prof. L. Solanki for their kind support and encouragement.

I shall be failing in my duty if I do not express my thankfulness to my great and most valuable friends Dr. S. R. Yadav, Dr. Vipin Kumar, Dr. A. K. Malik and Ms. Ruchi Sharma for their valuable suggestions from time to time writing of this book.

A.P. GIRDHAR

Contents

UNIT 1

Grammar

1

Tenses

INTRODUCTION TO TENSES

What do we mean by tenses?

1) Verb is an important component of a sentence. There are several forms of a verb (12 forms). We have to choose the correct forms of the verbs in our sentences. We choose the correct forms of the verbs on the basis of the time of the action and the nature of activity. We can say that choosing the correct form of the verb is the function (meaning of the tenses). By learning tenses, we learn to use the correct form of the verb in a sentence in relation to time and aspect.

Examples

Tense period	Aspect (Nature of activity)	Form of the tense (first plain verb)	Example
Present	Habitual and current, universal truth, etc.	Plain verbs like, teach, go, show, keep, etc.	I teach English.

The first consideration is the time. Time can be present, past or future.

The second consideration is aspect, i.e., the nature of the activity. For example, in the following sentences the time is present but each sentence has different aspect.

1. He goes to school everyday.	(action takes place regularly, it is habitual)
2. He is going to school now.	(continuing at present)
3. He has gone to school.	(perfect, finished, work is complete.)
4. He has been going to school since 2008.	(work started in the past and is still continuing)

When we consider tenses we have the following points to consider:

1. Period (present, past or future)
2. Aspect (habitual, continuous, perfect and perfect continuous)
3. The form of the verb
4. Adverbs (denoting the time of the action)

Present Indefinite or Present Simple Tense

Period	Aspect	Form of the verbs	Adverbs
Present	Habitual, recurrent, universal truth, verbs of departure or arrival, historical presence	First form. Important- inflection of the verb, with 's' or 'es' (only in this tense when the subject is of 3rd person singular)	Every day, daily, regularly, usually, generally, rarely, scarcely, never, seldom, often, always etc.

Examples

1. I go for a walk daily.
2. He goes to school every day.

Negatives

Formation of negatives – General rule for transforming the sentences into negatives.

We put 'not' after the helping verb. Since there are no helping verbs in the present indefinite tense, we use 'do' or 'does'.

Examples

Affirmatives	Negatives
He goes to school every day.	He does not go to school. (Since we have put 'es' after 'do', inflection will not be done to 'go').
I help my students after the classes.	I do not help my students after the classes.
You smoke in the presence of your elders.	You do not smoke in the presence of your elders.

Interrogatives

How to form interrogative sentences?

General rule – Interrogative sentences start with helping verbs.

In this tense there is no helping verb. Therefore, start your interrogative sentences with 'do' or 'does'.

Examples

Affirmatives	Negatives
I like reading books.	Do I like reading books?
You need some medical attention.	Do you need any medical attention?

WH questions

Wh questions start with 'wh' word and a helping verb.

Formation

Wh + Aux. + S + V

Examples

Where does he live?

When do they return from work?

Normally 'wh' questions answer the following things:

When, where, how, whose and why.

Examples

When do you get up in the morning?
Where do you live?
How do you reach your office?
Whose book do you want?
Why did you misbehave?

Present Continuous Tense

Period	Aspect	Word formation	Adverbs
Present Continuous	We use this tense when some action is in progress (Some work is going on at the time of speaking)	Be form Is, am, are + Main verb + ing	Now, at present or after some clause

Examples

1. Diya is writing a letter now.
2. I am talking on the phone.

II. For immediate future – He is going to Bombay tomorrow.

Some more examples
1. He is working in the field now.
2. I am writing a novel at present.

Negative: Negatives are made by putting 'not' after the 'be' verb.

Examples

He is not working in the field now.
I am not writing a novel at present.

Simple Questions

Formation—Be + S + V + ing.
Is he working in the field now?
Are you going to Bombay tomorrow?

Wh Questions

Formation of the sentence—Wh + be verb + Main Verb + ing + (adverb)

1. Who is coming to tea tomorrow?
2. Where are you going now?
3. How is he feeling now?

Perfect Tense

Its uses

1. **Simple perfect:** Work completed but its result is felt in the present.

Examples

I have completed my work. —Now I am free.
I have taken my lunch. —I am not hungry now.

2. **Continuative use**
   Work started at some definite point of time in the past but is continuing in the present.

1. I have worked in this college since 1982.
   or
   I have been working in this college since 1990.
2. I have lived in the house for 10 years.
   or
   I have been living in this house for 10 years.

Important

Never use the adverbs of the past with the present perfect tense.

Wrong	Right
I have bought this pen yesterday.	I bought this pen yesterday.
My brother has come to see me last night.	My brother came to see me last night.

Present Perfect Continuous

Use: We use this tense to state an activity that started at some definite point of time in the past and is continuing in the present.

Examples

1. He has been learning English since his childhood.
2. He has been waiting for him for 5 minutes.

Use of 'since' and 'for'

1. We use since for point of time, example, since morning, since 1982, since Monday, since evening.
2. We use "for" for period of time, for example, for 5 minutes, for an hour, for a week, for a decade, for 10 years.

Past Tense

Past Indefinite

Use: We use past indefinite tense:

1. to denote an action that took place at some definite point of time in the past.
   "The Minister tendered his resignation last week."
2. to denote a habitual action in the past.
   "He played football when he was young.
   Or
   He used to play football when he was young."

Time	Verb	Adverbs of the past
Past	(Second form of the verb)	yesterday, ago, last month, last week, last year, etc.

Examples

He went home yesterday.

He passed the examination last year.

Negative

Use 'did' as helping verbs + the first form of the verb

Examples

He went to London last month.	He did not go to London last month.
He failed to qualify for the final.	He did not fail to qualify for the final.

Questions/Interrogatives
Did + S + verb first form + Object + (adverb)

Did he ask you for anything?

Did they warn you about the damage?

Past Continuous

Use: To state/describe an action that was continuing at some definite point of time in the past.

Aspect	Time
Action continuous	past

Examples

He was smoking a pipe. When I saw him yesterday.

When I saw him yesterday he was smoking a pipe.

Formation/Structure of the verb

Be (was/were) + main verb + ing

Example

He was running after the bus.

Past Perfect

Use: Two actions take place. Both these actions take place in the past. But these actions do not take place at the same time. One action takes place earlier than the other. The action that takes place earlier may be called pre-past. We use past perfect for the action that took place earlier.

Example

The bell had rung at 10.45 am. Before I reached the college (11.00 am)

The bell rang at 10.45 am (pre-past).
I reached the college at 11.00 am - past.
The bell had been rung before I reached the college.
We can change the order of the clauses.

When I reached the college the bell had been rung.

Verb in the past perfect tense
Had + past participle (3rd form)

Adverbial = a clause in the past indefinite tense.

Past Perfect Continuous

Example

It had been raining for two hours when I reached home.

Use: We use this tense to state an action that remained continuous for some time at some definite point of time in the past.

Verb

Had been + MV + ing
Adverb: an adverbial clause in the past indefinite tense.

Future Indefinite

We use various tenses to refer to some future action/event.

1. For immediate future	Present Continuous Tense	She is going to Bombay tomorrow.
2. Shall/will I/we – shall He/she/it/they – will	I shall go to Germany next year. He will accompany me.	
3. For intention	Going to form	

In this case the emphasis is on intention.

Example

I am going to buy a car next week.

Present Indefinite

With the verbs of arrival/departure.

Example

The train leaves at 9.00 p.m.

Use	Example	Verb
Future continuous To refer to some action that will be continuous at some definite period of time in the future	I shall be travelling in a bus at this time tomorrow	Shall/will/be + MV + ing
Future perfect	I shall have completed my work by this time tomorrow	Will/shall have + past participle

EXERCISES

I Supply the correct form of the verbs:

1. A baby ________ when it is hungry. (cry)
2. We ____ newspapers to know about the world affairs. (read)
3. Honesty ________ in the long run. (pay)
4. We ______ tea in the morning. (drink)
5. She ________ not _____ tea. (like).
6. Women in India ________ not ______. (smoke)
7. Fish ______ in water. (swim)
8. Birds _______ in the sky. (fly)
9. A mother _______ her children very much. (like)
10. _____ he _____ admission in this institute? (want)

II Transform the following sentences into negatives.

1. She goes to temple every Sunday.
2. I like my shirts clean.
3. Kapil Dev throws the ball very fast.
4. Gavaskar plays 20-20 matches.
5. Ram and Shyam live together.
6. The earth revolves round the sun.
7. Our English teacher explains every point clearly.
8. The moon shines during the night.
9. The law takes its own course.
10. They worship Lord Hanuman.

III Transform the following sentences into interrogative sentences.

1. She washes her clothes everyday.
2. They want to learn English
3. My wife knows how to sew and knit.
4. The Principal wishes everybody well.
5. You drink boiled water to keep fit.
6. People use computer network for faster results.
7. His mother milks cows.
8. A good teacher revises all the lessons.
9. Students always behave nicely.

IV Use the correct form of the verbs given in brackets.

1. He usually _________ to school on foot(go)
2. Take an umbrella. It _________ now (rain).
3. We can play now because we __________ (finish) our work.

4. He ______ (learn) English for 5 years but he ______ (not learn) much.
5. Do you know where Mohan _____ (live).
6. Pakistan ________(try) to build long range missiles for long but _______ (not succeed) yet.
7. _______he _______ (tell) you anything about the girl he wants to marry?
8. ________she ________ (not go) to temple everyday?
9. What ________ the workman _________ (do) at present?
10. Vote for the candidate who _____ (talk) about the development of the country.

V Change the following sentences into negative sentences.

1. He appeared in the I.P.S. examination last year.
2. Mohan applied for the post of a stenographer.
3. She asked me to stay for lunch.
4. Deepika invited me for dinner last night.
5. The Principal dismissed him from service.

VI Present Tense

Supply the correct forms of the verbs given in brackets.

1. I –– (go) for a walk everyday. My mother also –– (go) with me.
2. My mother –– (cook) meals during the day. I –– (help) her in the kitchen.
3. She –– (teach) in a school. I –– (teach) in a college.
4. Sunita –– (work) in an office. Her cousin –– (work) in the same office.
5. My brother –– (play) tennis. My sister –– (play) badminton. They –– (practise) in the evening.
6. He –– (preach) charity but –– (not practise) it.
7. She –– (not like) flattery. Her sister –– (not like) self praise. They –– (not like) falsehood.
8. –– you –– (like) dancing? She –– (not like) dancing but she –– (like) singing.
9. Diya –– (love) birds but she –– (not love) animals.

10. I –– (work) very hard but my wife –– (not appreciate) it.

VII Convert the following sentences into singular sentences.

1. They go to office in a taxi but come back in a bus.
2. Girls always like to dress well.
3. Carpenters make furniture.
4. Babies cry when they are hungry.
5. Do old men irritate their children?
6. Classrooms have blackboards.
7. Lions are brave animals.
8. Cats like to live alone
9. My sons go to school on their bikes.
10. Teachers are kind persons.

VIII Fill in the blanks by supplying the correct forms of the verbs given in the brackets.

1. We –– (come) to this house in 1935 and –– (live) here ever since.
2. We –– (stay) at the Taj whenever we –– (go) to London.
3. I –– (write) to him last week but he –– (not reply) yet.
4. Thousands of people –– (die) before the war –– (end).
5. The child –– (go) to sleep before its mother –– (arrive).

IX Complete the following sentences by inserting the correct forms of the verbs given in brackets (either the present simple or present continuous).

1. My mother –– (cook) breakfast in the morning. She –– (cook) breakfast now.
2. My father –– (go) to his work everyday. He –– (go) to his work now.
3. Deepika cannot come out to play now. She –– (cook) meal for her father.
4. It was cloudy yesterday, but the sun –– (shine) today.

5. Normally he –– (travel) by air but today he –– (go) to Bombay by car.
6. My brother –– (spend) his holidays with us every year.
7. I –– (like) Deepika very much. She too –– (like) me.
8. We –– (go) to New York to spend our holidays. We often –– (go) there for fun.
9. Your car will be ready in an hour. The mechanic –– (repair) it even now.
10. She is –– (dry) her hair in the sun now. She –– (do it) every Sunday.

X Complete the following sentences by inserting suitable forms of the verb given in brackets.

1. –– Mohan –– (attend) the classes regularly?
2. –– the workmen –– (repair) the road now?
3. –– they –– (obey) their teachers?
4. –– the child –– (sleep) now?
5. –– he –– (bowl) faster than he does usually?
6. –– these girls –– (learn) cookery in school?
7. –– she –– (work) hard now?
8. Who –– (know) what is going to happen tomorrow?
9. –– the bungalow –– (lie) vacant now?
10. –– they –– (mind) my calling on them so often?

XI Complete the following sentences by supplying the correct forms of the verbs given in the brackets.

1. Shakespeare –– (be born) at Stratford-on-Avon but –– (spend) most of his time in London.
2. As he –– (run) after the bus, he –– (fall) and –– (break) his leg.
3. They –– (eat) some fruits after they –– (finish) dinner.
4. I –– (see) you yesterday. You –– (drink) a cup of tea, but you –– (not see) me.
5. He already –– (design) some important buildings and now he –– (design) a hotel.

XII Complete the following sentences by supplying the correct forms of the verbs given in brackets.

1. While I — — — (walk) through the park with Dipika last night a man — — — (snatch) her bag and — — — (run) away. I could not run after him because it — — (be) too dark to leave her alone. The police — — (not catch) him yet.
2. I — — — (see) that you — — (buy) a new hay. How much — — (pay) for it.
3. They — (walk) across the road when a motorcycle — — — (hit) them.
4. We — — — (buy) the car a year ago.
5. By the time we reached the airport, the plane — — (leave), so we couldn't meet her.
6. How long you — — (travel)? You look tired.

XIII Complete the following sentences by supplying the correct forms of the verbs given in brackets.

1. It — — — (rain) since 5 O'clock. (be).
2. He — — — here since 2004. (live)
3. Who has — —lunch today. (prepare)
4. He will catch the bus if he — — — early. (start)
5. He had — — an accident last month. (have)
6. She — — bread and butter this morning. (have)
7. We — — to college at 10 O' clock everyday. (go)
8. No sooner did the teacher come in then the students — — making a noise. (stop)

SOLUTIONS KEY

(I) (1) cries (2) read (3) pays (4) drink (5) does, like (6) do, smoke (7) swim (8) fly (9) likes (10) does, want.

(II) (1) does not go (2) do not like (3) does not throw (4) does not play (5) do not live (6) does not revolve (7) does not explain (8) does not shine (9) does not take (10) do not worship.

(III) (1) Does she wash (2) Does he want (3) Does my wife know (4) Does the Principal wish (5) Do you drink (6) Do people use (7) Does his mother milk (8) Do students always behave.

(IV) (1) goes (2) is raining (3) have finished (4) has been learning, has not learnt (5) lives (6) has been trying, has not succeeded (7) Has, told (8) does not go (9) is doing (10) talks.

(V) (1) did not appear (2) did not apply (3) did not ask (4) did not invite (5) did not dismiss.

(VI) (1) go, goes (2) cooks, help (3) teaches, teach (4) works, works (5) plays, plays, practise (6) preaches, do not practise (7) does not, does not, do not (8) Do, like, does not, likes (9) loves, does not (10) work, does not appreciate.

(VII) (1) He goes to school in a taxi and comes back in a bus. (2) A girl always likes to dress well. (3) A carpenter makes furniture. (4) A baby cries when it is hungry. (5) Does an old man irritate his children? (6) A classroom has a blackboard. (7) A lion is a brave animal. (8) A cat likes to live alone. (9) My son goes to school on his bike. (10) A teacher is a kind person.

(VIII) (1) came, have lived (2) stay, go (3) wrote, has not replied (4) had died, ended (5) had gone, arrived.

(IX) (1) cooks, is cooking (2) goes, is going (3) is cooking (4) is shining (5) travels, is going (6) spends (7) like, likes (8) are going, go (9) is repairing (10) is drying, dries.

(X) (1) Does, attend (2) Are, repairing (3) Do, obey (4) Is, sleeping (5) Is, bowling (6) Do, learn (7) Is, working (8) knows (9) Is, lying (10) Do, mind.

(XI) (1) was born, spent (2) was running, fell, broke (3) ate, had finished (4) saw, were drinking, did not see (5) has designed, is designing.

(XII) (1) was, snatches, ran, was, have not caught (2) see, have bought, did you (3) were walking, hit (4) bought (5) had left (6) have you been.

(XIII) (1) has been (2) has been living (3) has prepared (4) starts (5) Had (6) Had (7) Go (8) stopped

2

Passive Voice

There are two ways of reporting an action. They are:

a. Active Voice: He is cutting a tree.

b. Passive Voice: A tree is being cut by him.

Choice of Active Voice and Passive Voice

I. Active voice is always preferred because:
   i. It is more polite.
   ii. It is informal and friendly.
   iii. It gives more importance to the 'doer'/the agent.

II. The use of the Passive Voice
   1. Passive voice is used when the 'agent'/the doer of the action is not known.

Examples

i. My pocket has been picked. (I do not know who has picked my pocket.)

ii. The ship has been sunk. (We do not know who has sunk the ship.)

2. Passive Voice is used when action is more important. (We are interested in the action, not in the agent.)

Examples

i. The food has been cooked. (We are interested only in the cooking of the food. Who cooked it is not important.)

ii. The shoes are being polished. (We are not interested in the agent—as to who is polishing the shoes.)

Rules for the transformation of Active Voice sentences into Passive Voice

Example

Active Voice : He is reading a book.

Passive Voice : A book is being read by him.

Rules

1. Bring the object in place of the subject (with some modification if necessary).

Example

Active Voice : I told them the truth.

Passive Voice : They were told the truth by me.

(In this case one of the objects is them. When put into the place of the subject it becomes they.)

2. Take the subject to the place of object (with some modification if necessary).

Example

Active Voice : They kicked Ram.

Passive Voice : Ram was kicked by them.

(When the subject 'they' is put in the place of object it becomes 'them'.)

3. Put 'by' before the new object, i.e., by them, by Mohan.
4. Change the main verb into past participle (third form of the verb). In the passive voice the main verb is always in the past participle.

Examples

Active Voice : I have completed the work.
Passive Voice : The work has been completed by me.
Active Voice : She opens the windows in the morning.
Passive Voice : Windows are opened by her in the morning.

The choice of an auxiliary verb (helping verb)

Passive voice is not possible without a helping verb. The choice of the helping verb depends on the tense of the sentence in the active voice.

The following table explains the choice of the auxiliary

Tense in the active voice sentence	Auxiliary	Examples	
		Active Voice	Passive voice
Present Indefinite	be (present) is, am, are	I teach English.	English is taught by me.
Present Continuous	is, am, are + being	He is learning English.	English is being learnt by him.
Present Perfect	has, have + been	Kapil Dev has scored a century	A century has been scored by Kapil Dev.
Present Perfect Continuous		No Passive Voice is possible	
Past Indefinite	was, were	He gave me a book.	I was given a book by him.
Past Continuous	was, were + being	They were eating mangoes	Mangoes were being eaten by them.
Past Perfect	had + been	She had eaten her breakfast before 10 am.	Her breakfast had been taken by her before 10 am.
Past Perfect Continuous		No Passive Voice is possible.	
Future Indefinite or Modals	will, shall, can, may, must, would, should, might + be	She will repent her action.	Her action will be repented by her
		She may open an account in the bank.	An account may be opened by her in the bank.
Future Perefect	will have, shall have + been	He will have run a race.	A race will have been run by him.

Problems

1. How to make negatives?
   For making negatives put 'not' after the helping verb.

Examples

i. He does not like mangoes.
   Mangoes are not liked by him.
ii. He is not reading a book.
   A book is not being read by him.
iii. The President did not give away the prizes.
   Prizes were not given away by the President.

Interrogatives

Interrogative sentences start with auxiliaries.

Examples

i. Does he obey his father?
   Is his father obeyed by him?
ii. Have you phoned him?
   Has he been phoned by you?
iii. Was he learning motor driving?
   Was motor driving being learnt by him?
iv. Will the police target the criminals?
   Will the criminals be targeted by the police?
v. Should he consult a senior lawyer?
   Should a senior lawyer be consulted by him?

The problem of two objects

Some sentences have two objects. In such cases one of the objects may be used as the subject.

Examples

Active Voice	Passive Voice	
	Option 1	Option 2
I teach you English.	You are taught English by me.	English is taught to you by me.
I told them the truth.	They were told the truth by me.	The truth was told to them by me.
The teacher has told us the story.	We have been told the story by the teacher.	The story has been told to us by the teacher.

Important

Option 1 is better. It is often preferred to option 2. In the first option a person becomes the subject. In the second option non-living thing becomes the subject.

Imperative Sentences

For imperative sentences we use the following construction.
Let + Object + be + third form of the verb + by + subject

Examples

1. Bring a chair.
   Let a chair be brought by you.
2. Arrest the thief.
   Let the thief be arrested by you.
3. Close the account.
   Let the account be closed.

Questions starting with 'who' in the active voice are started with "By whom" in the passive voice.

Examples

1. Who looks after the patients?
   By whom are the patients looked after?
2. Who taught you English?
   By whom were you taught English?

EXERCISES

I. Turn the following sentences into passive voice.

1. Good people always admire good behaviour.
2. He hurt his arm in an accident.
3. Did they build Rome in a day?
4. He is doing this exercise carefully.
5. They have not opened this box for the last fifty years.
6. Did the servant break any plates?
7. They may ask some important questions.
8. Students must write their answers on one side of the paper.
9. Who pushed the table into the corner?

II. Change the following sentences into passive voice.

1. Good students keep discipline.
2. A good batsman meddling the ball.
3. Hawkers are selling apples.
4. Girls are knitting sweaters.
5. The farmers have ploughed the land.
6. She has already cooked breakfast.
7. He caught the ball on the boundary line.
8. They removed their shoes.
9. The farmers were digging the earth.
10. The women were combing their hair.
11. They had caught the train.
12. The driver had stopped the bus.
13. They may move the high court.
14. I shall read the letter aloud.
15. He will speak the truth.

III. Change the following sentences into passive voice.

1. He does not like smoking.
2. Does he like swimming?
3. I do not like a white collar job.
4. Do you read novels in your spare time?
5. He is not improving his language.
6. Are they supporting the Congress party?

7. Are women fighting elections?
8. Children are not doing much work.
9. They have not paid their fees.
10. Has Kapil Dev scored a century recently?
11. They did not favour my candidature.
12. Did he put some eggs into the basket?
13. They were not singing songs at the party.
14. Was he teasing girls?
15. Will he teach this course next year?
16. He may not like the hot coffee.

IV. Change the following sentences into passive voice.

1. Who stole my pen?
2. Who performs the last rites of a dead person?
3. Who is supporting the BJP?
4. Who has scored a century?
5. Who had led the winning team?
6. Who will compeer the show?
7. Clean the table.
8. Show him the way to BITS.
9. Fetch your sister.
10. Buy some vegetables from the market.

V. Put the following into passive voice:

1. They are flying in reinforcements.
2. My father gave me a five hundred rupee note.
3. All the ministers will see him off at the airport.
4. The police killed a terrorist.
5. I can answer the question.
6. Is she watering the flowers?
7. Julia rescued three cats.
8. The teacher is not going to complete the exercise.

SOLUTIONS

I

1. Good behaviour is always admired by good people.
2. His arm was hurt in an accident.
3. Was Rome built in a day?

4. This exercise is being done carefully by him.
5. This box has not been opened by them for the last fifty years.
6. Were any plates broken by the servant?
7. Some important questions may be asked by them.
8. Answers must be written on one side of the paper by the students.
9. By whom was the table pushed into the corner?

II

1. Discipline is kept by good students.
2. The ball is meddling by a good batsman.
3. Apples are being sold by hawkers.
4. Sweaters are being knit by girls.
5. The land has been ploughed by the farmers.
6. Breakfast has already been cooked by her.
7. The ball was caught by him on the boundary line.
8. Their shoes were removed by them.
9. The earth was being dug by the farmers.
10. Their hair were being combed by women.
11. The train was caught by them.
12. The bus had been stopped by the driver.
13. The Hight Court may be moved by them.
14. The letter will be read aloud by me.
15. The truth will be spoken by him.

III

1. Smoking is not liked by him.
2. Is swimming liked by him?
3. A white collar job is not liked by me.
4. Are novels read by you in your spare time?
5. His language is not being improved by him.
6. Is the Congress party being supported by them?
7. Are elections being fought by women?
8. Much work is not being done by children.
9. Their fees have not been paid by them.
10. Has a century been scored recently by Kapil Dev?
11. My candidature was not favoured by them.

12. Were any eggs put into the basket by him?
13. Songs were not being sung by them at the party.
14. Were girls being teased by them?
15. Will this course be taught by him next year?
16. The hot coffee may not be liked by him.

IV

1. By whom was my pen stolen?
2. By whom are the last rites of a person performed?
3. By whom is the BJP being supported?
4. By whom has a century been scored?
5. By whom had the winning team been led?
6. By whom will the show be compeered?
7. Let the table be cleaned by you.

   Or

   You are required to clean the table.
8. Let the way to BITS be shown to him.

   Or

   You are required to show him the way to BITS.
9. Let your sister be fetched by you.
10. Let some vegetables be bought from the market.

V

1. Reinforcements are being flown in by them.
2. I was given a five hundred rupee note by my father.
3. He will be seen off at the airport by all the ministers.
4. A terrorist was killed by the police.
5. The question can be answered by me.
6. Are the plants being watered by her?
7. Three cats were rescued by Julia.
8. The exercise is not going to be completed by the teacher.

3

Reported Speech or Indirect Speech

Sometimes we have to report what someone has said or thought. We can use one of the following two ways for this.

1. Reproducing the actual words spoken by the speaker. These words are put within inverted commas. This kind of speech is called "Direct Speech."

Example

My mother said to me, "I am going home."

The above information may also be reported by the speaker in his own words.

My mother told me that she was going home.

The change of speech from direct into indirect requires some changes. Now we shall study the required changes. Let us take one more sentence in direct speech and change it into indirect speech.

Example

Direct Speech: Deepika said to me, "I am getting married tomorrow."

Indirect Speech: Deepika told me that she was getting married the next day.

Changes Involved

From the above-mentioned example we find the following changes in the indirect speech:

1. The change of the reporting verb "said".
2. Removal of commas after the reported verb, i.e., said.
3. Use of a conjuction like that, if, whether, etc.
4. Change of pronouns.
5. Change of the tense of the verb in the reported speech.
6. Change of adverbs of time and place.

Rules for Various Changes

1. Change of the reporting verb, i.e., "said"
   The change of reporting verb depends on the kind of sentence in the reported clause. A direct speech has two clauses: a reporting clause and a reported clause.

Example

My teacher said to me, "Work hard and you will succeed."

Reporting clause: My teacher said to me,

Reported clause: "Work hard and you will succeed."

If the reported caluse is a statement, the verb "said" is changed into "told". We can also use words like 'informed' etc. If the statement in the reported clause is interrogative the verb 'said' is changed into "asked". If the clause is 'imperrative' the verb 'said' is changed into 'ordered', 'commanded', 'told', 'requested' according to the nature of the imperative, i.e., order, request, etc.

Examples

1. The teacher said to me, "Sit down"
   The teacher commanded me to sit down.
2. My friend said to me, "Please lend me your books."
   My friend requested me to lend him my books.

In the case of exclamatory sentences we use the following method:

He exclaimed with sorrow/pleasure/surprise and said and make the reported clause a simple clause.

Examples

1. The police officer said, "What a terrible accident!"
   The police officer exclaimed with sorrow and said that it was a terrible accident.
2. My friends said, "Hurrah, we have won the match!"
   My friends exclaimed with joy and said that they had won the match.

Introduction of Conjuctions

Simple sentences in the reported clause require the conjunction 'that'.

Interrogative sentences: 'require' 'if' or 'whether'.

Imperative sentences: We use 'to' infinitive for imperative sentences.

For exclamatory or optative sentences we use 'that'.

Change of Pronouns

When converting direct speech into indirect speech some pronouns are changed.

1. Pronouns of the third person (he, she, it, they) do not change.
2. Pronouns of the first person (I, we) change according to the person of the subject of the reporting clause.

Example

He said to me, "I want to join BITS."
He told me that he wanted to join BITS.
In the above reported speech 'I' has been changed into 'he'.

3. Pronouns of the second person (you, your) change according to the object of the reporting clause.

Example

He said to me, "You must join BITS to ensure good placement."

He said to me that I must join BITS to ensure good placement.

In the reported speech 'you' has been changed into 'I' as per the object of the reporting clause

Change of Adverbs

Adverbs of nearness change into adverbs of distance.

Direct Speech	*Indirect Speech*
Now	Then
This	That
Here	There
These	Those
Hence	Thence
Ago	Before
Today	That day
Tomorrow	The next day
Yesterday	The previous day
Last night	The previous night
Last week	The previous week
The next day	The following day

Change of Forms of the Verbs

When are forms of the verbs not changed in the reported speech?

1. If the verb of the direct speech is in the present tense (say, has said)

Example

He says, "I am going home."
He says that he is going home.

2. When the reporting verb is in the simple future tense, i.e., will
3. When the statement in the reported clause refers to something universally true or it is of habitual nature.

Examples

My teacher said to us, "The earth revolves round the sun."
My teacher told us that the earth revolves round the sun.

Change of Tenses

If the reporting verb is in the past tense, the verb in the reported speech will be changed in the following manner.

Direct Speech	*Indirect Speech*
Present Indefinite	Past Indefinite
Present Continuous	Past Continuous
Present Perfect	Past Perfect
Present Perfect Continuous	Past Perfect Continuous
Past Indefinite	Past Perfect
Past Continuous	Past Perfect Continuous
Shall	Should
Will	Would
Can	Could
May	Might

Note: Modals like must, should, ought to, do not change.

Examples

1. She said to me, "You always waste your time."
   She told me that I always wasted my time.
2. My teacher said to me, "You are wasting my time."
   My teacher told me that I was wasting his time.
3. The master said to the servant, "You have broken all my crockery."
   The master told the servant that he had broken all his crockery.
4. My father said, "I have been waiting for a long time."
   My father told that he had been waiting for a long time.
5. The woman said, "My son worked hard last year."

The woman told that her son had worked hard the previous year.

6. I said to my son, "You were smoking a cigarette yesterday."
   I told my son that he had been smoking a cigarette the previous day.
7. I said, "I shall not waste my time in future."
   I said that I would not waste my time in future.
8. He said, "It may rain."
   He told that it might rain.
9. He said, "I can run fast."
   He said that he could run fast.

EXERCISES

I. Change the following sentences into reported speech.

1. He said to me, "I shall see you tomorrow."
2. He says to Lalit, "You are not a good singer."
3. His mother will say to him, "You are a good boy."
4. The teacher said, "Honesty always pays in the long run."
5. Ram said to his wife, "I shall bring a present for you today."
6. The teacher said to Ganesh, "What are you doing?"
7. The officer said to the clerk, "When will you go home?"
8. Jack said to Jill, "Why are you climbing the hill?"
9. Jill said to Jack, "I want to fetch a pail of water."
10. The teacher said to his students, "Do all the planets keep moving all the time?"

II. Change the following sentences into indirect speech.

1. He said to the servant, "Go away."
2. Shila said to me, "Please help me to solve my problems."
3. The teacher said to one of the students, "Bring a piece of chalk from the office."

4. My mother said to me, "Work hard for the examinations."
5. My father said to me, "Do not waste your time."
6. I said to her, "May you succeed in your endeavours!"
7. The boys said, "Hurrah! We have won the match."
8. Yuvraj said, "Oh! I am undone."
9. "What a crushing defeat!", Raju remarked.
10. She said to Deepika, "What a naughty child you are!"

III. Change the following sentences into indirect speech.

1. He said to his son, "Do not worry about anything."
2. I said, "I do not care for anyone."
3. He said, "I do not know. I may not come back."
4. He said to me, "What can I do for you, dear?"
5. The little girl said, "O, that I were a princess!"

IV. Change the following sentences into indirect speech.

1. She said to him, "What do you want?"
2. He said to me, "Can you solve this problem?"
3. Christine said to Ronaldo, "I saw Amy at the bank two hours ago".
4. James said to Lisa, "Don't eat so much junk food".
5. The teacher said, "I am busy now".
6. He said to me, "I do not think I can oblige you again in this way".
7. I said, "I shall finish my work as quickly as I can".
8. He said to me, "I have never seen such a lazy boy as you are".

SOLUTIONS

I

1. He told me that he would see me the following day.

2. He says to Lalit that he is not a good singer.
3. His mother will tell him that he is a good boy.
4. The teacher said that honesty always pays in the long run.
5. Ram told his wife that he would bring a present for her that day.
6. The teacher asked Ganesh what he was doing.
7. The officer asked the clerk when he would go home.
8. Jack asked Jill why he was climbing the hill.
9. Jill told Jack that he wanted to fetch a pail of water.
10. The teacher asked his students if all the planets keep moving all the time.

II

1. He ordered the servant to go away.
2. Shila requested me to help her solve her problems.
3. The teacher ordered (asked) one of his students to bring a piece of chalk from the office.
4. My mother advised me to work hard for the examinations.
5. My father advised me not to waste my time.
6. I prayed to God that she might succeed in her endeavours.
7. The boys exclaimed with joy and said that they had won the match.
8. Yuvraj exclaimed with sorrow and said that he was undone.
9. Raju exclaimed with sorrow and said that it was a crushing defeat.
10. She exclaimed with sorrow and told Deepika that she was a naughty child.

III

1. He told his son not to worry about anything.
2. I said that I did not care for anything.
3. He said that he did not know. He might not come back.
4. He asked me endearingly what he could do for me.

5. The little girl wished to be a princess.

   Or

   The little girl said that she wished she were a princess.

IV

1. She asked me what I wanted.
2. He asked me if I could solve that problem.
3. Christine told Ronaldo that she had seen Amy at the bank two hours before.
4. James advised Lisa not to eat so much junk food.
5. The teacher said that he was busy then.
6. He told me that he did not think he could oblige me again in that way.
7. I said that I would finish my work as quickly as I could.
8. He told me that he had never been such a lazy boy as I was.

4

Conditional Sentences

What are conditional sentences?

1. A conditional sentence has two clauses:
    1. A conditional clause or If clause
    2. Main clause

Main clause is also called the principal clause or the resultant clause.

The conditional clause states the condition.

The main clause states the result.

Conditional Clause: If I get first class marks in my examination.

The main clause states the result if the condition is fulfilled.

I shall join engineering courses.

The main clause:

The most important thing to learn in the conditional sentences is the form of the verb to be used in both the clauses.

The choice of the form of the verb depends on the type of condition in the conditional clause.

Types of Conditional Sentences

There are three types of conditional sentences.
They are sentences with-

1. **Open condition**

   Open condition is a condition that is likely to be fulfilled in the future.

For example:

"If I go to France next year I shall study French.

It means there is a chance or likelihood of my going to France ___ the condition is open.

2. **Rejected Condition**
   Rejected condition is a condition that was not fulfilled in the past and so the result was not achieved.

Example

If I had got 90 per cent marks in my senior secondary examination I would have joined BITS, Pilani.

"It means the condition of obtaining 90 per cent marks was not fulfilled, so the result of joining BITS was not achieved.

3. **Imaginary or impossible**
   This condition is either impossible or imaginary.

Examples

Impossible/Unread
If I were you,
If I became an animal,

Imaginary

If I were the Prime Minster,
If I became the President of India.

The following table explains the forms of the verbs to be used in the various types of conditional sentences.

Type of condition	*Tense in the conditional clause*	*Tense in the main clause*
Open condition	Present Indefinite Example – If I go to Jaipur	Future Indefinite Example – I shall bring some books for you.

Rejected condition	Past Indefinite If I had gone to Jaipur	Future Indefinite I would have brought
		some books for you
Impossible or imaginary	Past Indefinite (were or became) If I were you, If I became the P.M.,	Future Indefinite Would + first form of the verb I would teach him a lesson. I would remove poverty.

Notes:

(1) In the case of impossible or imaginary condition 'would' in the main clause can be replaced by 'might', 'should', etc.

(2) In the case of rejected condition 'if' can be removed from the conditional clause.
If I had gone to Jaipur, or Had I gone to Jaipur.........

(3) A conditional sentence can begin with either of the two clauses, i.e., the conditional clause or the main clause.

Example

If I go to Jaipur, I shall bring some books for you.

Or

I shall bring some books for you if I go to Jaipur.

EXERCISES

I. Fill in the blanks with the correct forms of the verbs given in brackets.

1. If Mohan applies I __________ (offer) him the job.
2. If we go to Agra we __________ (visit) the Taj Mahal.
3. If my son gets 80 per cent marks in his examination he _______ (join) BITS.
4. If I were a god I __________ (grant) him his prayers.
5. Had I received a call from him in time I _________ (save) his life.

6. If I became the President of India, I ______ (make) it strong.
7. If we catch the dacoit we ______ (hand) him over to the police.
8. If we had been careful we ______ (avoid) the accident.
9. I ______ (go) to Jaipur if I get leave.
10. If he ______ (save) money he would have led a comfortable retired life.

II. Fill in the blanks with the correct forms of the verbs given in brackets.

1. The plate would have broken if you ______ (throw) it.
2. If it ______ (be) fine. I shall go for a swim.
3. You would be silly if you ______ (not take) this opportunity.
4. If it rains they ______ (get) wet.
5. You ______ (meet) him if you had wanted.
6. If I were you, I ______ (go) home.
7. I will help you, if you ______ (need) it.
8. You ______ (catch) the train if you hurry.
9. You would be ill if you ______ (eat) to much.
10. He will succeed if he ______ (try).

III. Fill in the blanks with the correct forms of the verbs given in brackets.

1. If you ______ (try) you would have succeeded.
2. If you are good, the principal ______ (reward) you.
3. If the rain ______ (fail) to come there will be a famine.
4. If you worked hard, you ______ (succeed).
5. If you send a message now he ______ (get) it this evening.
6. If he ______ (not work) hard, he will not learn much.
7. He ______ (come) if you invited him.
8. He will certainly do it, if it ______ (be) possible.

9. If he recovers from his illness, he ______ (join) duty soon.
10. If I ________ (be) the P.M. I would improve the condition of women.

SOLUTIONS

(I)

(1) shall (2) shall (3) will (4) would (5) would have saved (6) would (7) shall (8) would have avoided (9) shall (10) had saved

(II)

(1) had thrown (2) is (3) did not take (4) will (5) would have met (6) would go (7) need (8) will catch (9) ate (10) tries

(III)

(1) had tried (2) will reward (3) fails (4) would succeed (5) will get (6) does not work (7) would come (8) is (9) will join (10) were

5

Modal Verbs

What are modal verbs?
Modal verbs are small words like *can, could, may, might, must, shall, should, will, could* and *ought to.*

Modal verbs come before main verbs. They modify the meaning of the main verbs. They are used to express opinions, ideas, to give advice, suggestions, threats, etc.

Detailed Consideration of Modal Verbs

Various uses of Can

I. Can is used
to state ability, capability, capacity, knowledge.

Examples

1. He can run fast. (ability)
2. This room can accommodate ten persons. (capacity)
3. She can read and write English. (knowledge)

II. to seek or give permission
The modal 'can'may be used to seek and give permission. But in formal English the use of may is preferred because it is formal and polite.

Examples

1. You have finished your home work. Now you can go and play.

2. You can leave the place after completing your work.

III. Can is also used to express possibility or likelihood. But in modern English the use of may is preferred.

Examples

1. There are heavy clouds. It can rain.
   Or
   It may rain.
2. There are some holidays. My son can come.
   Or
   My son may come.

Could

I. Past ability
Could is used to express ability in the past.

Examples

1. When I was a boy I could run fast.
2. She could dance very well when she was young.

II. Could is also used to make polite requests.

Example

Could you lend me some money, please?

May

I. May is used to seek or give permission.

Examples

1. May I come in, sir?
2. Yes, you may.

II. The modal 'may' is used to express the concepts of likelihood/possibility.

Examples

1. Indian batting line is strong. It may win the final.
2. He is working hard. He may pass the examination.

III. May is used to express wish or give blessings.

Examples

1. May you prosper in life!
2. May you live long!

IV. May is used to state the purpose of an action.

Examples

1. He is working hard so that he may succeed.
2. She is going to some hill station so that she may improve her health.

Might

I. We use might to express slight possibility.

Examples

1. There are thin clouds. It might rain.
2. There are only few holidays. My son might come.

II. We can also use might to express the concept of suggestion.

Examples

1. You might consult a good dictionary.
2. You might try some Ayurvedic medicine.

Should

I. We use should to give advice or make a suggestion.

Examples

1. You should go for long walks for good health.
2. You should improve your English.

II. We use should to express the concept of moral obligation.

Examples

1. Students should respect their teachers.
2. Children should obey their parents.

III. Should is also used to express the concept of desirability.

Examples

1. We should keep our houses clean.
2. We should adopt hygienic habits.

Ought to

The modal ought is used to express the idea of moral obligation. In this sense 'ought to' and 'should' have the same meaning.

Examples

1. We ought to obey our elders.
2. Students ought to keep discipline in the classroom.

Must

I 'Must' expresses the concept of strong necessity. When some action is essential to obtain result we use the modal 'must'.

Examples

1. If you want to catch the bus, you must run. (If you do not run you will not catch the bus.)

2. If you do not join the coaching center, you will not succeed.

II. Strong obligation

We use the modal must to express strong obligation.

Examples

1. In Delhi scooter drivers must wear helmets.
   (If they do not wear helmets they will be punished.)
2. The morning session is only for girl students. Boys must keep away from the campus.
   (If they not do so, they will be punished.)

III. Logical deduction

We use the modal must to come to some logical deduction.

Examples

1. He is looking pale and weak. He must be ill.
2. She comes to the college in her own luxury car. She must be rich.

Mustn't

We use mustn't to express the concept of prohibition.

Examples

1. Students mustn't pluck flowers.
2. Students mustn't sit on the college boundary wall.

Needn't

We use 'needn't' to express the idea of absence of necessity, i.e., when some action is not necessary.

Examples

1. There is lot of time. You needn't run.
2. All problems will be solved in due course. You needn't worry.

Will

Will is used with second and third person pronouns in the future tense. But when the auxiliary will is used with first person pronouns i.e. 'I' and 'We' it becomes a modal. As a modal it expresses the concepts of strong determination, promise or threat.

Strong Determination

Example

I will marry Sita and no other girl.

Promise

Example

I will stand by you through thick and thin.

Or

I will help you.

Threat

Examples

1. I will see you.
2. If you misbehave I will teach you a lesson.

Would

The auxiliary, 'would' is used to express past habits.

Example

1. Often he would walk in lonely places in search of peace.

2. We also use 'would' to make polite requests.

Examples

1. Would you please pass on the salt?
2. Would you mind my sitting here?

Shall

Shall is an auxiliary used with first person pronouns in the future tense. But when we use 'shall' with second or third person pronouns 'shall' becomes a modal and it expresses the following concepts.

1. Strong determination
2. Promise
3. Threat

Examples

1. You shall join only MBBS classes and no other branch of study. (strong determination)
   (It is strong determination of the speaker about HIS son or daughter on whom he can exercise his authority.)
2. No matter how much it costs, you shall have the best education. (promise)
3. Your son shall not enter my house again. (threat)

EXERCISES

I. Fill in the blanks with appropriate modals with the help of the concepts given in brackets.

1. You are ill. You – – see a doctor. (strong necessity)
2. She – – speak Hindi, English and French. (ability)
3. If you want a successful career in industry, you – – improve your communication skills. (advice)
4. Cars – – be parked in front of the gate. (prohibition)
5. We – – respect all religions. (moral obligation)

6. She — — go to Bombay next week. (possibility)
7. You — — to respect your elders. (moral obligation)
8. Everyone — — obey the rules of traffic. (strong obligation)
9. I do not want to listen anything against my joining army. I — — join it. (strong determination)
10. He — —lift the box even with one hand. (ability)

II. Rewrite the following sentences using modals.

1. He is able to ride a horse.
2. I suggest that you may consult a doctor.
3. He is likely to join our party.
4. I am determined to marry that girl.
5. You are warned not to play dirty politics with us.
6. She is looking pale and weak. Certainly she is ill.
7. He was able to run fast when he was young.
8. It is our moral duty to help the poor.
9. Are you able to teach me how to read and write?
10. I pray God for her long life.

III. Supply the correct modals in the following sentences from the modals given in brackets.

1. I — — teach you good manners if you misbehave. (will/shall)
2. Your son — — have the best education. (will/shall)
3. You — — consult a good dictionary. (must/should)
4. The night is dark and cloudy. He — — lose his way. (may/should)
5. He — — run fast on a slippery ground. (may/can)

SOLUTIONS

I.

(1) must (2) can (3) should (4) mustn't (5) should (6) may (7) ought (8) must (9) will (10) Can.

II.

1. He can ride a horse.
2. You should consult a doctor.
3. He may join our party.
4. I will marry that girl.
5. You shall not play dirty politics with us.
6. She must be ill.
7. He could run fast when he was young.
8. We should help the poor.
9. Can you teach me how to read and write?
10. May she live long!

    or

    May she have long life!

III.

(1) will (2) shall (3) should (4) may (5) Can.

UNIT 2

Composition

6

Dialogue Writing

In today's highly competitive world of business employers attach great importance to the conversational ability of the candidates appearing for job interviews. As a first step students must familiarize themselves and practise courtesy words like 'excuse me', 'thank you' 'welcome', 'sorry', 'Its all right', etc.

Whenever they have to start a conversation they should start it with greeting the other party by saying Good morning, Good afternoon, etc. Naturally the receptionist at the desk or the officer concerned will say "What can I do for you?." The speaker can straightaway tell the purpose of his visit. In a bank he may say "Sir, I want to open an account." In a school or college he may say "I want an application form for admission." At the reservation centre he may say "I want to book a seat for Bombay." In this way the conversation gets started.

Solved Examples

1. Suppose you are Priyanshu. After passing Secondary Examination you want to get admission in a city college. So you go to the Principal for admission. You may start your dialogue like this:

Priyanshu : May I come in, Sir?
Principal : Yes, you may.
Priyanshu : Good morning, Sir.
Principal : What can I do for you?

Priyanshu : Sir, I have passed my Senior Secondary Examination. I want admission in your college.

Principal : We accept only first divisioners. What is your percentage of marks?

Priyanshu : Sir, I have secured 75 percent marks in my Sr. Sec. Exam.

Principal : In which faculty do you want admission?

Priyanshu : Sir, I had commerce subjects in my Senior Sec. Exam. I want admission in B.Com Part I.

Principal : You are eligible for admission. You may get the admission form and prospectus from the office and apply.

Priyanshu : Thank you, Sir.

2. Suppose you are Mahesh. You want to apply for a loan to buy a plot of land. Write an imaginary dialogue between you and the Bank Manager. You may start your dialogue like this:

Mahesh : Good morning, Sir.

Bank Manager : Good morning. How can I help you?

This is how the dialogue should continue:

Mahesh : Sir, I want to apply for a loan to buy a plot of land.

Manager : How much money do you want?

Mahesh : Sir, I want a loan of rupees one lakh.

Manager : Have you an account with this bank?

Mahesh : Yes, Sir. My bank account number is 5108961520.

Manager : We offer loan only against surety by our account holders. Can you arrange two persons who can stand surety for this loan?

Mahesh : Yes, Sir, I have some friends who have account in your bank. They are ready to stand surety for me.

Manager : Okay. This is the form for applying loans. Please complete all the formalities.
Mahesh : Thank you, Sir.

3. A patient who has been unwell for some time goes to his doctor. Write an imaginary dialogue which may take place between the patient and the doctor.

Doctor : What is your ailment?
Patient : I have a high fever.

The dialogue may continue like this

Doctor : How long have you been suffering from fever?
Patient : Sir, for the last two days.
Doctor : Have you taken any medicines.
Patient : I took aspirin. It gave me some relief.
Doctor : Show me your tongue. (The patient shows his tongue. After examining the chest and feeling the pulse.)
Doctor : You are suffering from cold. Nothing serious. Take these tablets as described in the prescription slip and you will be quite okay in two or three days.
Patient : Thank you, Sir.

4. Two friends Anil and Abdul Razzak meet at the railway station. Anil informs him about his success in I.I.T. Examination. He has been called for counselling. Write a brief dialogue between them. You may begin like this:

Anil : Hello Abdul. How are you?
Abdul : Hello Anil. How are you? (both shake hands)

The Dialogue may proceed like this

Anil : Where are you going?
Abdul : I am not going anywhere. I have come here to book a seat for my uncle who is going to Bombay for some business purpose. But where are you going?

Anil : I am going to Delhi for counselling. I have been selected in I.I.T.

Abdul : My heartiest congratulations. So you have made to I.I.T. Which branch will you prefer?

Anil : I will opt for Computer Science in I.I.T. Kanpur.

Abdul : My good wishes to you.

5. You are Babita. Your friend Saroj has come to invite you to her birthday party which is going to take place on 15th October 2012. You are unable to attend the party owing to some important engagement. You may begin like this:

Saroj : Good morning, Babita.

Babita : Good morning, Saroj What are you up to these days?

The dialogue should proceed like this

Saroj : I am busy with preparation for my birthday party. I am sure you have not forgotten my birthday.

Babita : Of course, not. How can I forget the birthday of my dearest friend?

Saroj : Okay. The party is at 5.00 pm. I have especially come to invite you for the party.

Babita : I am sorry. I shall not by able to attend it. My cousin is to be married on the same day. I must go to Agra to attend it.

Saroj : Can't you skip the marriage ceremony for my sake?

Babita : Sorry, I can't do this. But my congratulations to you. And my best wishes for many happy returns of the day.

Here are some exercises on simple everyday affairs for practice.

First meeting between two freshers

Mohan	:	(On seeing another student on the campus) Good morning. I'm Mohan. I'd like to have the pleasure of your acquaintance.
Ramesh	:	I'm Ramesh. I'm a fresher here.
Mohan	:	I'm also a fresher.
Sohan	:	Which is your stream of study?
Mohan	:	It is CSE. Which is yours?
Sohan	:	Mine is ECE.
Mohan	:	By the way, why did you prefer this institute over so many others?
Sohan	:	It has good reputation. My father came here to know about its merits. He met some of the staff members. He also met some senior students who told him there was nothing fake 'farziwada' in this institute.
Mohan	:	Now, you have been studying here for a few weeks. What's your opinion about the staff here?
Sohan	:	Frankly speaking, the faculty here is quite good. Some of the staff members are quite young and inexperienced but they are dedicated and hard working and this compensates.

On going to a canteen

(A meets his friend B outside the class)

A	:	Good' morning. How are you?
B	:	Good' morning. I am fine. Thank you.
A	:	You are most welcome. How is it that you are not in the class?
B	:	We have a vacant period after two classes.
A	:	It's quite good. It is quite refreshing. Where are you going?
B	:	I am going to the canteen for a cup of tea. I am sure you would like to join me.

A	:	Of course, I would like it very much. But I would like a cup of coffee. Tea does not suit me.
B	:	You can have coffee. Would you like to eat anything, snack etc. I am feeling a bit hungry.
A	:	What can we get here?
B	:	We can have biscuits, samosas and sandwiches.
A	:	I don't like fried things. I would have some biscuits. You can have anything you like.
B	:	Waiter! Bring a cup of tea, a coffee, a packet of biscuits and two sandwiches.
Waiter	:	Vegetarian or non-vegetarian.
B	:	Vegetarian
B	:	(After they have finished they call the waiter for the bill. A wants to pay but B says) It's my pleasure. Let me leave this pleasure.
B	:	(to the waiter) How much is the bill?
Waiter	:	Rs. 40/-
B	:	(gives him Rs. 50/- and says) You can keep the change waiter. Thank you.

7

Paragraph and Précis Writing

Writing is an art which can be cultivated by practice. A paragraph is a short composition. It is brief and to the point. It has no illustrations. Important features of a paragraph are:

(i) Content, i.e., the ideas to be expressed.

(ii) Language should be simple, grammatically correct and suit the topic of the essay.

(iii) Style. It is said that 'style' is the man. It means every man has a different style. As far as possible writer should write in his own way and should not copy the style of any other author.

A composition has a beginning, a middle and an end. The beginning introduces the topic. The middle develops and exemplifies the same. The end gives a logical conclusion.

SOME PARAGRAPHS

1. Books are our best Friends
Or
The importance of Books

Books are the best friend of man. In the first place they are always available. Living friends can be insincere. They can deceive us. Books are never insincere. But one should be very careful in selecting the books. Some friends can be good friends and some friends can be bad friends. In the same manner good

books are good company and bad books are bad company. Good books inspire us for good deeds. Books give us delight. They also give us wisdom. They almost cost us nothing.

One should be very careful in selecting books. There are so many books. We cannot read all of them. One should avoid dull and uninteresting books. They kill our interest in reading.

Choice of subjects is also important. One should not read whatever one finds by chance. The reader should try to get books on the subject of his choice. In this way his reading will be delightful and useful.

In the modern world people are losing interest in books. They are still interested in stories but they look toward to cinema and T.V. They forget that cinema and T.V. can never take the place of books. Books have always been the best friend of man. They will always remain the best friend of man. One's character is known from the company one keeps. A man's culture and social status are known from the books he reads.

2. The Best Student of my class

Or

My Best Friend

Man is a social animal. He cannot live without society. We come across so many people in life. We like some of them and we do not like some. We like the company of some and we make them our friends.

Deepak is my best friend. He is also the best student of my class. He is good in studies and always stands first in the examinations. But he is also very sincere, honest and humble. He is very polite and kind. All the teachers like him. All the students of my class admire him and look to him for guidance and inspiration.

Deepak is good not only in studies but he is a great sportsman. His hobbies are reading and playing

games. He plays hockey and table tennis. He is a good player of hockey. He is also the champion of table tennis.

Deepak is of very helpful nature. He likes to help all his friends in many ways. He helps the weak students in their studies. He even extends financial help to poor students. If somebody is ill Deepak becomes a nurse for him. He looks after the ill with care and devotion.

We are proud to have Deepak in our class. I am very lucky that I have got a friend like Deepak.

3. Television: its uses and abuses

(The same matter can be used for the topic Cinema: its uses and abuses)

Television is the most important invention of the twentieth century. But people have different views about it. Some people like it and call it a great blessing. Others consider it a great evil. In fact television is good if it is used for good purposes. But it is an evil if it is used only as a pass-time.

Television provides us amusement. It can also be used for education. As a source of entertainment it offers unique opportunities. Today life is not easy. It is full of doubts, tension and disappointments. A healthy entertainment relieves us of tension for sometime. Moreover, it is easily available. As a medium of education television can be of great use. It can bring revolution in the spread of education. It is a great source for the spread of information. It is already being used by the U.G.C for teaching purposes. Lectures from the best teachers on different subjects can be televised for vast number of learners.

Television has also its abuses. Cable T.V. provides cheap and unhealthy entertainment. Some of these programmes can spoil the youth. They are in bad taste. Moreover, some young people watch too much television and ignore their studies. They become so

fond of T.V. that they neglect all other important works. In conclusion we can say that television is good but one should make a judicious use of it.

4. A visit to a place of historical interest
Or
A visit to the Taj Mahal

A visit to a place of historical interest serves two purposes. Such a visit gives us a lot of pleasure. It also teaches us. In India there are so many places of historical interest. Agra is one such place. It is mostly remembered for its beautiful Taj Mahal.

Our school arranged a tour of Agra last month. I also joined the tour. Our main attraction was the Taj Mahal. We reached Agra in the morning. From Delhi we travelled to Agra by the Taj Express. We enjoyed this train journey very much.

The Taj Majal is known as the symbol of pure love. It was built by the emperor Shahjahan in memory of his beloved wife Mumtaj. He loved his wife very much and he built this monument as an eternal memorial of her.

The Taj Mahal is the most beautiful structure in the world. It is one of the great wonders of the world. It is situated on the bank of the Yamuna. The entire building is made of pure white marble. It is surrounded by four lofty minarets. Verses from the holy Koran are engraved on the main gate.

The Taj Mahal is so beautiful that it attracts thousands of visitors every month from all over the world.

Our visit to this historical place proved very useful. Our history teacher was with us. He explained to us the historical significance of the place. He also explained to us the architecture of the structure.

5. A visit to a zoo

A visit to a zoo is very important for a student. It increases his knowledge of the animal world. Real

education does not come only from books. Visiting places like zoo is also important for education.

A zoo is a place where all kinds of beasts and birds are kept. In a zoo efforts are made to construct their natural habitats. In their natural habitats they feel more comfortable.

A few days ago I visited the zoo in New Delhi with my friends. It is the biggest zoo in Asia. It has beasts and birds from all over the world. We saw tigers, lions and leopards. We also saw different kinds of monkeys and apes. Apes have wonderfully adopted themselves to the environment of the zoo. They have learnt to be friendly. We shook hands with apes and offered them ice creams which they enjoyed very much.

We also saw some white bears. These have been brought from Canada. They are much bigger than the black bears of India. We also enjoyed the sight of various kinds of snakes. They look very beautiful in their bright black or brown colours.

We saw some beautiful sparrows of different varieties with beautiful shining colours. We heard them singing their charming songs.

This visit to the zoo provided us a lot of fun. But it also increased our knowledge of the universe.

6. Importance of computers

Or

The role of computers in the present age

Computer is one of the greatest inventions of the modern world. It has changed man's life. It is playing very significant role in the society. It has made governance very efficient and speedy. It has brought a revolution in the concept of management.

Computer is a man-made machine. It follows man's commands and produces desired results. It was invented by man. But it can work faster than man. It is more efficient than man.

The first computer was made by Blais Pascal of France in 1642. But the real computer was made by an English man in the nineteenth century. Since then many improved types of computers have come which have made man's work easier and smoother.

Computers are being used in every field of life. Computers have become essential for the various branches of engineering. Computers are being used for addition, subtraction, multiplication, division, etc. In the medical field computers are being used for diagnosing the various diseases. Computers have proved very useful for banks, railways and post office departments. Even petty shopkeepers do their business with the help of computers.

Computers have some disadvantages also. They have increased unemployment. A computer can do the work of many persons. So it has reduced the need for manpower. Moreover, it has made man a bit lazy. Nevertheless the modern world cannot go on without computers.

7. Mahatma Gandhi - the father of the nation

Or

My favourite leader

Mahatma Gandhi is my favourite leader. He is the most favourite leader of a vast number of persons in the world. He is known all over the world as an apostle of peace and love. He was a great teacher. He taught people the way of life. He taught people to love each other and help each other. He showed the world the path of "Ahinsa" — the path of non-violence. He also taught the right way to achieve the goals, i.e., "Satyagrah". It means to achieve your goals by following the path of truth.

Gandhiji was born at Porbander in Gujarat on 2nd October 1869. His father's name is Karam Chand Gandhi and his mother's name is Putlibai.

Gandhiji went to Engand to study law. He started practising law in Bombay High Court. He went to

South Africa to fight a law case. But the conditions of Indian people moved him. He made up his mind to fight for the rights of people.

Gandhiji fought for India's freedom. He undertook Dandi March to fight for the rights of Indians. He gave a call to the BrItish Government to "Quit India". He fought for human dignity. He fought against social evils and untouchability. He brought a revolution in the thinking of the people and their way of life. He helped India get its freedom. But he did much more than that. He roused the conscience of the country.

I love Gandhiji for his love of India. I like Gandhiji's ideals. He is my favourite leader. He is admired by many millions of people of the world.

8. If I were the Prime Minister of India

Life is made of wishes. Everyone has his own wishes. Some wishes are easy to fulfil. Others are almost impossible. One such wish is to be the Prime Minister of a great country like India. But if I were the Prime Minister of India I would bring revolution in the country. I would make it a country of my dreams—a strong India without corruption, without injustice and without exploitation.

I shall take necessary steps to remove child abuse. Our country got freedom more than sixty years ago. Still our children are being maltreated. There is the curse of child labour and child marriage. I will send every child to school to get decent education and decent employment. I shall take steps to stop exploitation of women. They must get their right to lead an honourable life. I shall abolish the dowry system.

The greatest evil in India is corruption. I shall root out corruption from India. In this way India can become strong. I shall ensure education for all. I shall make "Yoga" compulsory in schools and colleges. In

this way every person will enjoy physical and spiritual health. If Indian youth is strong India is strong.

9. The importance of newspapers

In the present age newspapers have become very important. In a democratic country free Press is one of the pillars of democracy. Democracy cannot survive without free Press.

The world is developing fast. It is also becoming smaller and smaller as far as travel time is concerned. No country can afford to live in isolation. No person can afford to live in ignorance of what is happening in his own country and what is happening in his neighbouring countries.

Newspapers keep our knowledge of current affairs up-to-date. They also increase our knowledge of the language. They widen our mental horizon. They change our attitude towards life by making us aware of the new trends in public life.

Newspapers serve the interests of different classes of people. There are political news and political commentaries. There are news from the business world. There are news about sports and games. There are magazines for literary news and the entertainment world.

Newspapers can serve as instruments of social change. They can act as guides of our social and moral conduct. But the newspapers should not have vested interests. They should not have narrow aims. They should act as a watchdog of justice and human rights.

10. My favourite book

Or

The book I like most

Books are the best friends of man. In the present age no man can live without books. Books give us pleasure and wisdom. They keep us constant company.

In life an educated person reads a number of

books. But one or two books become his favourite. This book leaves a lasting impression on his mind. It influences him very much.

I have also read a number of books in English and Hindi. I have liked the works of authors like William Shakespeare and Ravindranath Tagore. But the book that has left a permanent impression on my mind is *Godan*. It is a novel in Hindi by Munshi Prem Chand. He is the greatest novelist in Hindi. He is called "Upanyas Samrat."

Godan is the story of a poor farmer of a village. His name is Hori. He is a victim of social evils. He is also a victim of man's greed. He goes on fighting for his values of life and dies in the process.

Godan is a great novel for many reasons. The character of Hori has been portrayed beautifully and realistically.

Godan brings before our eyes a real picture of village life of the nineteenth century. We see a world torn by human greed. It is an ugly world yet it is charming. It is charming because of the emotional ties of the people. Indeed, *Godan* is a great work of Munshi Prem Chand. It is as immortal as its writer.

11. The best use of leisure time
Or
My favourite hobby

A hobby helps us to make the best use of our leisure time. A hobby is an activity that we do in our spare time. It gives us pleasure. But a good hobby is a creative activity. It helps in the proper development of a man's personality. Some common hobbies are: reading books, listening music, painting and drawing and gardening.

My hobby is gardening. I have a small piece of land in front of my house. I grow flowers and fruit trees in this garden. I get fresh air from the plants and flowers. I get fresh fruit from the fruit trees.

I keep by graden neat and clean. I remove the weeds from the plants. I water the plants regularly. I also use proper manure for the plants. In this way my hobby gives me good exercise for the body. I get a lot of pleasure when I see the plants growing bigger and bigger. This pleasure takes care of my mental health. In this way I am able to make the best use of my leisure time. Whenever a friend visits my house I take him to my garden. All my friends enjoy visiting my little garden. They like the smell of beautiful flowers and the taste of juicy fruits. I am very proud of my hobby and I love it very much.

12. The teacher I like most

A good teacher is a demigod. He moulds the minds of his students. He is a great source of inspiration. His influence spreads everywhere. Good teachers build the nation. There are so many teachers in my school but I like my English teacher the most. All the other students of the school also like him and admire his way of teaching. His name is Dr. Krishan Mohan.

Dr. Krishan Mohan is the master of his subject. He is a first class M.A. in English literature. He has obtained his Ph.D. degree from Agra University, Agra. His method of teaching is very good. He explains everything in lucid and simple language. His class is quite entertaining. There is never a dull moment in his class.

All the students like Dr. Krishan Mohan because he is a thorough gentleman. He is very honest, sincere and punctual. He is sweet-tempered and he never loses his cool. It is simply impossible to provoke him. He welcomes all the joys and sorrows of life with a sweet smile.

Dr. Krishan Mohan is very impartial. He does not show any favour to anyone. But he treats all his students with equal love and affection.

Dr. Krishan Mohan is a very dedicated teacher. Any student can go to him at any time for any guidance. He leads a very simple life. He believes in simple living and high thinking. He is an ideal teacher. We are proud that we are students of such a great teacher.

13. The T.V. serial I like the most

Today television has become the greatest source of entertainment. It is also a source of imparting knowledge.Nowadays there are so many T.V channels. They show movies, reality shows, serials, etc. Some of the serials have become very popular and nobody wants to miss them. One of these serials is *Ramayan*. I like this serial the most.

Ramayan serial is not just a story. It presents the philosophy of life. It deals with human relationship.It shows how a brother should deal with his brother and what kind of relationship should be there between husband and wife. It also highlights the duties of a king. A king's personal life is not important. His sole concern is to give consideration to the feelings of his people.

The story of *Ramayan* is very old but it has not lost its charm. The serial *Ramayan* has been directed very ably. All the characters have played their roles expertly. Its photography is very beautiful and its music is charming.

Ramayan is important not only for its story. It has a great message for humanity. It symbolizes the triumph of good over evil. It stands for the victory of humility over pride. Lord Ram represents the forces of good. The demon king Ravana represents the forces of evil. He is the personification of pride and arrogance. Naturally the forces of evil are defeated and the forces of good triumph.

14. An accident

Or

Give an account of the accident witnessed by you

A serious accident took place near Triveni Piao (a place of drinking water) yesterday. A young man was coming from the CEERI side on his motor-bike. His bike slipped and he fell on the ground. He was not wearing a helmet. His head hit the wall and he started bleeding profusely. A big crowd gathered there. But nobody was willing to help this unfortunate man. Then suddenly a young man came there. He shouted "someone give a towel". But nobody responded. He took off his own shirt and tied it around the bleeding head. He immediately halted a passing three-wheeler and put the wounded man into it. He look him to the Birla Sarvajanik Hospital, Pilani. It was about 1.30 p.m and all the doctors were going for lunch. He caugut hold of one of the doctors and requested him to take care of the wounded man. When the doctor asked as to who will sign the papers, the man told him to be quick with his work. Rest of the formalities will be takan care of in due course. In the meantime he got the mobile phone of the wounded person and phoned to all his relatives whose numbers had been fed into it. This timely help saved the life of a young man. Later it was learnt that the young man was a teacher and he was returning from school.

Another interesting fact was known about this good Samaritan. He was distributing the wedding invitations of his own marriage. Three cheers to this young hero and with good wishes for his happy married life.

15. An election scene

In a democratic country elections are held to choose representatives of the people. India is the biggest democracy in the world. In India elections are held to elect Members of Parliament and Members of

Legislative Assemblies. Elections are also held to choose members of committees, councils and Gram Panchayats.

In India people take a lot of interest in elections. Elections are like fairs and festivals. It is more so in small villages. Women go to the polling booths wearing their best dresses and singing song. There are long queues before the polling booths. There is a mood of fun and festivity.

Preparations for the elections start much ahead of the election date. Candidates organize public meetings and rallies. There is also door-to-door canvassing. Candidates spend a lot of money to win the people.

Of late a lot of violence is seen during elections. Antisocial elements have joined politics and their aim is to win the elections by hook or by crook. Money and muscle power are being used to win the elections. There is nexus between politicians and criminals. This is threatening the survival of democracy. Of course the government is doing its best to arrange free and fair elections.

PRÉCIS WRITING

A précis is a brief account of some event. Normally, it is about one-third of the original passage. In the précis only the central idea is given. All examples, metaphors, similes, etc., are omitted. It does not contain any extra or superfluous words. As far as possible a précis should be in your own language. The first requirement of a good précis is the clear understanding of the passage. The next is the ability to reproduce main ideas of the text effectively. Therefore précis writing involves an excuse in comprehensive and effective writing.

A good précis must have the qualities of completeness, clarity and brevity.

What to avoid in a précis

1. Avoid all kinds of repetitions.
2. Avoid all expressions such as: it is thus clear, I think, I suppose, as far as I know, it is a known fact, it goes without saying, it should be borne in mind.

For example

As far as I think he should be able to get admission in MBA.

- He should be able to get admission in MBA.

Some solved examples of summaries are given here.

1. Read the following passage carefully and summarise it to its one-third.

   "A fair weather friend is like a shoe with a hole in it. Both become undependable with change of season. But there is difference between the two. A bad shoe is bad you know it. A bad friend is bad but you do not know. The friend follows you like a shadow if it pleases him or dogs your steps if it pays him. But when trouble or sorrow comes, he turns his back on you, he acts as though he never knew you. A good dog is always more faithful and you can trust him better. (97 words)

PRÉCIS

A selfish friend is as bad and undependable as a bad shoe although we do not know it. He keeps you company in good days and leaves you during your bad days. A dog is more faithful and trustworthy. (39 words)

2. Read the following passage carefully and summarise it to its one-third.

   "Patience is better than wisdom. An ounce of patience is worth a pound of brains. All men praise patience, but only a few practise it. It is a medicine which is good for all diseases but it is not every garden that grows the herbs to make it from. Many people are

born crying, live complaining and die disappointed. They think every other person's burden to be light and their own feathers to be heavy as lead, and yet, if the truth were known, it is their fancy rather than their fate that makes things go so hard with them."(100 words)

PRÉCIS

Patience is better than wisdom though few people practise it. It is a cure for all diseases though found in rarity. Many people grumble that their misfortunes are greater than others' but fancy not fate makes things hard. (37words).

3. Read the following passage, mention the main points and write a summary based on them in English.
"In India, value of life lies in morality and spirituality. Life is soul force, not matter. In the Western countries, people are very much after material gains. For them, life is mainly worldly. Materialism is the basis of life for the Western people. They don't realize the moral and spiritual value of life." (53 words)
The main points
(i) For Indians life is soul force and they value morality and spirituality.
(ii) For the Western people life is worldly and they run after material gains.

PRÉCIS

Value of life for Indian people lies in morality and spirituality whereas Western people run after material gains. (18 words)

4. Read the following passage carefully and summarise it into one-third.
"A lot of improvement is needed in our educational system. In our Secondary Schools, the courses are to be changed, to bring in practical training. In this way, when a student passes out of school he can go straight into the job for which he has been trained. It will mean

too that fewer students will go to the universities. This is all to the good, for at present our colleges are overcrowded. If there are fewer students in them, we can also improve our university education. (90 words)

PRÉCIS

For improvement in education courses in schools must include practical training so that students go to jobs after schooling. This will reduce rush in colleges. This will improve quality of university education. (32 words)

5. Read the following passage and make a summary of it in one-third.

"There is a well known story of how an old farmer called his three idle sons around him when on his death-bed, to impart to them an important secret. "My sons" said he, "a great treasure lies hidden in the estate which I am about to leave to you". The man gasped. "Where is it hidden?" exclaimed the sons in a breath, "I am about to tell you", said the old man. "You will have to dig for it", but his breath failed him before he could impart the weighty secret, and he died.

Forthwith the sons set to work with spade and mattock upon the fields, and they turned up every sod and clod upon the estate. They discovered no treasure. But they learnt to work, and when the fields were sown, and the harvest came, lo ! the yield was prodigious. Then it was that they discovered the treasure concealed in the estate, of which their father had advised them. (160 words)

PRÉCIS

An old man on his death-bed told his three idle sons that there was a great treasure in his estate and died. The sons dug out the whole estate but found no treasure. When sowed, the estate produced great harvest. The sons learnt the secret of success and value of hard work. (53 words)

8

Report, its Importance and Report Writing

What is a Report?

A report is an account of an event or an accident that has already taken place.

What is the Importance of Report Writing?

A report is a description of an event for the benefit of some who was not present on the scene. In this sense many memorandums, letters or news items are reports. An analysis of examination results, preparation of absentees, readings taken from a measurement instruments are reports. But the reports of scientists, engineers and business executives are very important. These reports are about the work they have done or about the activities of their organizations.

Reports should be the result of careful investigation, sound thinking and logical organization. Clarity is the most important feature of a good report. The writing should be very clear and easy to understand. A report is presented in a more or less conventional from established by long and varied experience.

Various Types of Reports

Reports can be

(1) Oral

(2) Written

They may be informal or formal. Then there are three kinds of reports. They are:

(i) Informational
(ii) Interpretive
(iii) Routine.

Essence of a Good Report

1. A report must have clarity. It should be clear in meaning. It should be easy to understand. There should be no chance of any confusion or misunderstanding.
2. A report should be brief and to the point.
3. It must have logical progression of events.
4. The language of the report must be simple and without any mistake of spelling or grammar.

Some Solved Examples

1. Points

1. A house on fire
2. cries and shrieks
3. people assemble
4. use of water
5. rescue of an injured old woman and a child

or

A house on fire

Report

A house in Ward No. 12 of Chirawa town caught fire. The people in the house started crying. A large number of people came out from their houses. They started throwing water with buckets and pitchers. The fire was brought under control within half an hour. Luckily there were no casualties. An old woman and child were rescued from the burning house by youths of the area. They were immediately taken to the Government hospital. They are reported to be out of danger.

2. Points

1. Hockey match last Sunday
2. between our school eleven and college eleven.
3. school eleven defeated the college eleven by one goal
4. a large number of students
5. very interesting match

Or

Report of a hockey match

Report

A hockey match was played between our school eleven and Government College, Sikar. A large number of students had gathered to witness the match. The first goal was scored by the captain of our school team in the fifth minute of the first half. But the college team scored an equaliser within 3 minutes. Our school team scored the winning goal in the second half of extra time. The match was very interesting. It was highly enjoyed by the spectators.

3. Points

1. An accident on the highway
2. a truck collided with a car
3. the truck driver tried to escape but arrested
4. the car driver wounded
5. taken to hospital

Or

Report of an accident

Report

A serious accident took place on highway No. 9 yesterday. A truck was coming at high speed from Rewari. It hit a car coming from Delhi. The truck driver lost control of his vehicle. It appeared that he was drunk. He tried to escape but he was caught by the people and handed over to the police. The car driver was wounded. He was taken to a nearby hospital for treatment. The role played by the men gathered there was highly commendable.

4. Points

1. Free eye operation camp
2. health minister inaugurates
3. social workers extend services
4. doctors, nurses perform efficiently
5. 200 patients operated upon

Or

Write a report an eye operation camp

Report

A free eye operation camp was organized in Buhana by Haldwani Charitable Trust from 15th March to 20th March, 2009. It was inaugurated by the Health Minister of Rajasthan. The social workers of the area extended free services to the patients. The doctors and the nurses performed their duties very efficiently. A record number of 200 patients were successfully operated upon. The patients were given medicines free of cost.

5. Points

1. A rich couple
2. thieves break into the house
3. take away box full of ornaments
4. dogs bark
5. neighbours wake up
6. thieves run
7. people chase
8. telephone to police

Or

Report on a robbery

Report

Yesterday an attempt was made to rob a house in Prem Nagar. The thieves broke into the house of a rich couple. They tried to take away a box full of ornaments. But the dogs started barking and woke up the neighbours. The thieves started running. They were chased by the young

men of the locality. They also phoned the police. The thieves were caught. In this way the attempt of robbery was foiled.

6. Points

1. A bank robbery in the Punjab National Bank of the city
2. cries and shrieks
3. robbers threaten the staff
4. run away with money

Or

Report on a bank robbery

Report

A robbery took place in the Punjab National Bank, Patiala yesterday. Five armed robbers entered the bank through the main gate after overpowering its guard. A large number of people were there in the bank. They started crying. The staff of the bank tried to resist. But they were threatened of dire consequences. The robbers ran away with a lot of cash before the police arrived.

UNIT 3

Short Stories

9

The Luncheon

W. Somerset Maugham

W. Somerset Maugham was born in Paris in the year 1874. He was the youngest son of the Solicitor to the British Embassy. Orphaned at the age of 10 Maugham started living with his uncle, the Vicar of Whitestable. He was educated at King's School, Canterbury and Heidelberg University in Germany. After studying medicine for six years and qualifying as a doctor, he developed interest in literature and started writing fiction. His first novel "Liza of Lambert" appeared in 1897. His most important novel is "Of Human Bondage" which appeared in 1915. This novel is considered as his outstanding achievement. Maugham formed a bridge between the Victorian England and the modern world of invention and enterprise.

He died on December 16th 1965 at the ripe age of 91 leaving behind his great literary output.

* * * * *

I caught sight of her at the play and in answer to her beckoning I went over during the interval and sat down beside her. It was long since I had last seen her and if someone had not mentioned her name I hardly think I would have recognised her. She addressed me brightly.

"Well, it's many years since we first met. How time does fly! We're none of us getting any younger. Do you remember the first time I saw you? You asked me to luncheon." Did I remember?

It was twenty years ago and I was living in Paris. I had a tiny apartment in the Latin Quarter overlooking a cemetery and I was earning barely enough money to keep body and soul together. She had read a book of mine and had written to me about it. I answered, thanking her, and presently I received from her another letter saying she was passing through Paris and would like to have a chat with me; but her time was limited and the only free moment she had was on the following Thursday; she was spending the morning at the Luxembourg and would I give her a little luncheon at Foyot's afterwards? Foyot's is a restaurant at which the French senators eat and it was so far beyond my means that I had never even thought of going there. But I was flattered and I was too young to have learned to say no to a woman. (Few men, I may add, learn this until they are too old to make it of any consequence to a woman what they say.) I had eighty francs (gold francs) to last me the rest of the month and a modest luncheon should not cost more than fifteen. If I cut out coffee for the next two weeks I could manage well enough.

I answered that I would meet my friend—by correspondence—at Foyot's on Thursday at half-past twelve. She was not so young as I expected and in appearance imposing rather than attractive. She was in fact a woman of forty (a charming age, but not one that excites a sudden and devastating passion at first sight), and she gave me the impression of having more teeth, white and large and even, than were necessary for any practical purpose. She was ' talkative, but since she seemed inclined to talk about me I was prepared to be an attentive listener.

I was startled when the bill of fare was brought, for the prices were a great deal higher than I had anticipated. But she reassured me,

"I never eat anything for luncheon", she said.

"Oh, don't say that!" I answered generously.

"I never eat more than one thing. I think people eat far too much nowadays. A little fish, perhaps. I wonder if they have any salmon."

Well, it was early in the year for salmon and it was not on the bill of fare, but I asked the waiter if there was, any. Yes, a beautiful salmon had just come in, it was the first they had had. I ordered it for my guest. The waiter asked her if she would have something while it was being cooked. "No", she answered, "I never eat more than one thing. Unless you had a little caviare. I never mind caviare."

My heart sank a little. I knew I could not afford caviare, but I could not very well tell her that. I told the waiter by all means to bring caviare. For myself I chose the cheapest dish on the menu and that was a mutton chop.

"I think you're unwise to eat meat," she said. "I don't know how you can expect to work after eating heavy things like chops. I don't believe in overloading my stomach."

Then came the question of drink.

"I never drink anything for luncheon," she said.

"Neither do I," I answered promptly.

"Except white wine," she proceeded as though I had not spoken. "These French white wines are so light. They're wonderful for the digestion."

"What would you like?" I asked, hospitable still, but not exactly effusive.

She gave me a bright and amicable flash of her white teeth.

"My doctor won't let me drink anything but champagne."

I fancy I turned a trifle pale. I ordered half a bottle. I mentioned casually that my doctor had absolutely forbidden me to drink champagne.

"What are you going to drink, then?"

"Water."

She ate the caviare and she ate the salmon. She talked gaily of art and literature and music. But I wondered what the bill would come to. When my mutton chop arrived she took me quite seriously to task.

"I see that you're in the habit of eating a heavy luncheon. I'm sure it's a mistake. Why don't you follow my example and just eat one thing? I'm sure you'd feel ever so much better for it."

"I *am* only going to eat one thing," I said as the waiter came again with the bill of fare.

She waved him aside with an airy gesture.

"No, no, I never eat anything for luncheon. Just a bite, I never want more than that, and I eat that more as an excuse for conversation than anything else. I couldn't possibly eat anything more—unless they had some of those giant asparagus. I should be sorry to leave Paris without having some of them."

My heart sank. I had seen them in the shops and I knew that they were horribly expensive. My mouth had often watered at the sight of them.

"Madame wants to know if you have any of those giant asparagus," I asked the waiter.

I tried with all my might to will him to say no. A happy smile spread over his broad, priest-like face, and he assured me that they had some so large, so splendid, so tender, that it was a marvel.

"I'm not in the least hungry," my guest sighed, "but if you insist I don't mind having some asparagus." I ordered them.

"Aren't you going to have any?" "No, I never eat asparagus."

"I know there are people who don't like them. The fact is, you ruin your palate by all the meat you eat."

We waited for the asparagus to be cooked. Panic seized me. It was not a question now how much money I should have left over for the rest of the month, but whether I had enough to pay the bill. It would be mortifying to find myself ten francs short and be obliged to borrow from my guest. I could not bring myself to do that. I knew exactly how much I had and if the bill came to more I made up my mind that I would put my hand in my pocket and with a dramatic cry start up and say it had been picked. Of course it would be 'awkward if she had not money enough either to pay the bill. Then the only thing would be to leave my watch and say I would come back and pay later.

The asparagus appeared. They were enormous, succulent and appetising. The smell of the melted butter tickled my nostrils as the nostrils of Jehovah were tickled by the burned offerings of the virtuous Semites. I watched the abandoned woman thrust them down her throat in large voluptuous mouthful and in my polite way I discoursed on the condition of the drama in the Balkans. At last she finished.

"Coffee?" I said.

"Yes, just an ice-cream and coffee," she answered.

I was past caring now, so I ordered coffee for myself and an ice-cream and coffee for her.

"You know, there's one thing I thoroughly believe in", she said, as she ate the ice-cream. "One should always get up from a meal feeling one could eat a little more."

"Are you still hungry?" I asked faintly.

"Oh, no, I'm not hungry; you see, I don't eat luncheon. I have a cup of coffee in the morning and then dinner, but I never eat more than one thing for luncheon. I was speaking for you."

"Oh, I see"

Then a terrible thing happened. While we were waiting for the coffee, the head waiter, with an ingratiating smile on his false face, came up to us bearing a large basket full of huge peaches. They had the blush of an innocent girl; they had the rich tone of an Italian landscape. But surely peaches were not in season then? Lord knew what they cost. I knew too—a little later, for my guest, going on with her conversation, absentmindedly took one.

"You see, you've filled your stomach with a lot of meat"—my one miserable little chop—"and you can't eat any more. But I've just had a snack and I shall enjoy a peach."

The bill came and when I paid it I found that I had only enough for a quite inadequate tip. Her eyes rested for an instant on the three francs I left for the waiter and I knew that she thought me mean. But when I walked out of the restaurant I had the whole month before me and not a penny in my pocket.

"Follow my example," she said as we shook hands, "and never eat more than one thing for luncheon."

"I'll do better than that," I retorted, "I'll eat nothing for dinner to-night."

"Humorist!" she cried gaily, jumping into a cab. "You're quite a humorist!"

But I have had my revenge at last. I do not believe that I am a vindictive man, but when the immortal gods take a hand in the matter it is pardonable to observe the result with complacency. Today she weighs twenty-one stone.

SUMMARY

'The Luncheon' by W. Somerset Maugham is a story of hypocrisy and affectation. It also deals with the exploitation of innocence and simplicity.

The story is in the subjective mode. It is narrated by the protagonist (the main character). He had met an old acquaintance of his at the play. During the interval in answer to her beckoning he had gone over and sat beside her. He had met her after a long time and had almost forgotten her name. She reminded him of the past years.

It happened twenty years ago when he was living in Paris. He had a small apartment. He was earning enough to keep body and soul together. She had read his books and he had written to her thanking her.

Presently he received another letter from her. She was passing through Paris and asked him if he would give her a little luncheon at Foyat's. It was a restaurant far beyond his means. But he was young and felt flattered and he had not learnt to say "No" to a woman. He had only eighty francs to last him the rest of the month. He thought that a modest lunch would not cost more than fifteen francs. He could cut coffee for two weeks to manage well. He agreed to meet her at Foyat on Thursday at 12.30. When he met her he found that she was not young. She was about forty, not attractive but imposing. She seemed inclined to talk and he became an attentive listener.

From the menu he found out that prices were a great deal higher than he had expected. But her friend assured him she never ate anything for luncheon. She never ate more than one thing for lunch. She would like to eat fish preferably a salmon which was out of season at that time. So it was very costly. When the Salmon was being cooked she expressed her desire to eat caviar, another delicacy all the time repeating that she ate only one thing for luncheon.

To keep the bill in limit the author ordered Muttonchops, the cheapest dish, for himself. When it came to the question of drinks she said she did not drink anything except white wine. She told him that her doctor would not let her drink anything except champagne. The author became white with fear of the mounting bill. He pretended that his doctors had forbidden him to drink champagne. She ate delicacies like salmon, caviare all the time repeating that she ate one thing at a time.

She said that she could not eat anything except asparagus if they had got these. She said it would be sin to leave Paris without tasting asparagus. She was enjoying the best fare but the heart of the narrator was sinking in anticipation of a heavy bill.

Now the narrator was not worried as to how will he spend the rest of the month without money. He was worried whether he had enough money to pay the bill. He thought about feigning that his pocked had been picked, He was also thinking whether the lady had enough money to pay the bill. He may have to pawn his watch or something else if there was not enough money.

After the asparagus she ordered coffee with the ice cream all the time saying that she ate only one thing at the lunch. Finally the waiter brought peaches and the lady took one. When he had paid the bill he had only enough for a small tip. Her eyes rested on the three francs he left for the waiter she thought that it was mean on his part. When he walked out of the restaurant he had the whole month before him and not a penny in his pocket.

Before parting the lady advised him to follow her example and never eat more than one thing for luncheon. He retorted that he would eat nothing for dinner that night. Before jumping into a cab she told him that he was quite a humorist.

The narrator said that he had his revenge. He was not a vindictive man and immortal gods would pardon him when he observed the result with complacency. That day she weighed twenty one-stone a very ungainly weight for a woman. That she became over weight was his revenge.

GLOSSARY (WORD MEANINGS)

Luncheon : a formal lunch or a formal word for a lunch
Becoking : to give somebody a signal to move, to come near
Recognize : to know who somebody is or what something is
Tiny : Very small in size or amount
Apartment : a set of rooms for living in usually on one floor of a building
Cemetery : an area of land used for burying people
Barely : just, certainly not more than a particular amount
Chat : talk in a friendly informal way to somebody
Foyat : the a name of a famous restaurant in Paris
Restaurant : a place where one can buy and eat a meal
Flattered : feel pleased and special
Consequence : a result of something that has happened.
Francs : Unit of money in Switzerland and several other countries (like rupee in India)
Correspondence : exchange of letters
Appearance : the way somebody looks
Imposing : impressive to look at, making a strong impression
Charming : very pleasant or attractive
Excite : feeling of pleasure, enthusiasm or emotion

Devastating : destructive
Passion : strong feeling of love, hatred, anger, enthusiasm
Impression : an idea, opinion or feeling that you get about somebody or something
Talkative : a person who talks too much
Inclined : wanting to do something
Fare : food that is offered as a meal
Anticipated : to expect something; to see what might happen in the future
Generously : willing to give freely, liberally
Salmon : a large fish with silver skin used for food
Caviare : the eggs of some type of fish
Dish : food prepared in a particular way.
Menu : a list of the food that is available at a restaurant
Mutton : meat from a fully grown sheep
Chop : a thick slice of meat with a bone attached to it
Overloading : to eat too much of something
Promptly : without delay, exactly at the correct time
Expect : apart from, not including
Proceeded : to continue doing something, to go ahead
Digestion : the process of digesting food, the ability to digest
Hospitable : One who is pleased to welcome, generous and friendly to visitors
Effusive : showing too much emotion
Amicable : agreeable, pleasant, friendly
Flash : shine brightly for a short time
Champagne : French sparking white wine
Gaily : in a cheerful way, in a bright way
Wave : to move your hand or arm in order to attract attention
Aside : to one side, out of the way
Sink : to be in a state of unhappiness, to lose heart
Horribly : very badly, shocked, frightened
Expensive : Costing too much, costly

Giant	: very big in size
Asparagus	: a kind of vegetable
Splendid	: excellent, very good, great
Tender	: easy to bite through and cut
Pallate	: the ability to recognize and enjoy food
Mortifying	: humiliating, causing shame or embarrassment
Awkward	: difficult, odd, bad, inconvenient
Enormous	: huge, extremely large
Succulent	: containing a lot of juice and tasting good
Appetizing	: something that makes you hungry or thirsty
Nostrils	: either of the two openings at the end of the nose
Voluptuous	: attractive in a sexual way
Abandoned	: left and no longer wanted
Thoroughly	: completely
Faintly	: weakly, not enthusiastically
Ingratiating	: try too hard to please somebody
Peaches	: a kind of fruit
Absent mindedly	: tending to forget things
Miserable	: very unhappy, uncomfortable
Snack	: a small meal or amount of food eaten hastily
Inadequate	: not sufficient, not much
Mean	: unkind, low, not willing to give much
Retort	: to reply quickly in an angry, offended manner
Humorist	: one who has the ability to cause humour (laughter)
Revenge	: punish somebody for causing hurt to you
Vindictive	: spiteful, determined to take revenge
Immortal	: that lives or lasts for ever
Pardonable	: which can be pardoned, excused, forgiven
Complacency	: a feeling of satisfaction

QUESTIONS REQUIRING VERY SHORT ANSWERS

Q. 1. Where had the author caught sight of the lady?
Ans. He had caught sight of the lady at the play.

Q.2. What did the lady remind the narrator?
Ans. The lady reminded him that he had asked her to luncheon.

Q.3. When did the incident of the luncheon take place?
Ans. It took place twenty years ago when the author was living in Paris.

Q.4. How much was the narrator earning at that time?
Ans. He was earning barely enough to keep body and soul together.

Q. 5. What did the lady write to him?
Ans. She wrote that she was passing through Paris and thought if he could give her a little luncheon at Foyat.

Q.6. Why could the narrator not say "no" to the lady?
Ans. He was young and felt flattered and at that time he had not learnt to say "no" to a woman.

Q.7. How much money had he at that time?
Ans. He had only eighty francs to last him the rest of the month.

Q.8. How much did he think the luncheon would cost?
Ans. He thought that a modest lunch would not cost more than fifteen francs.

Q.9. How would he make up for the loss of fifteen francs?
Ans. He thought he would make up for the fifteen francs by cutting coffee for two weeks.

Q.10. How did the lady look when she met the narrator for the luncheon?
Ans. She looked more imposing than attractive.

Q.11. What did the author find after looking at the menu?
Ans. He felt that the prices were much higher than he had expected.

Q.12. Why did the author feel reassured?
Ans. The author felt reassured because the lady said that she never ate anything for lunch.

Q.13. Did the lady follow her own advice that one should not eat more than one thing for the Luncheon?
Ans. No, she did not follow this principle.

QUESTIONS REQUIRING SHORT ANSWERS

Q.1. What did the woman eat and drink for the luncheon?
Ans. The woman ate and drank the following

i) Salmon
ii) Cavarie
iii) Asparagus
iv) Peaches
v) Champagne
vi) Coffee with ice cream

Q.2. What principle did the lady profess about eating?
Ans. The lady professed that she had some principle about eating at a luncheon. She said that when one would get up from lunch one should have the feeling that one could eat something more.

Q.3. What incongruity do you find in the character of the lady?
Ans. We find incongruity in the character of the lady in so far as she never did what she professed. She professed

that she never ate more than one thing for the luncheon. But in practice she ate a number of things. She said that she never ate anything for the lunch but she ate a lot.

Q.4. What contentment does the author feel. How does he justify that he has taken his revenge?

Ans. The author had been cheated of whatever money he possessed. He says that he is not vindictive. But he has a feeling of contentment and a feeling that he has taken his revenge. The lady had eaten a lot. After eating so much she might weigh twenty-one stone. This is something very bad for a woman. This was his revenge.

Q.5. What final advice did the lady give to the author?

Ans. The lady advised the author to follow her example of not eating more than one thing at the luncheon.

Q.6. Do you find the title: "The Luncheon" a suitable one?

Ans. The title "The Luncheon" is quite suitable. The story is about the lunch. If the narrator had not invited the lady for the luncheon there would not have been any story

ESSAY TYPE QUESTIONS

Q.1. Write a critical appreciation of the story "The Luncheon" by W. Somerset Maugham.

Q.2. How does the lady in the story "The Luncheon" exploit the simplicity and gentlemanly conduct of the narrator?

Q.3. Attempt characterization of the main characters of the story "The Luncheon".

Answer:

"The Luncheon" is a very delightful, entertaining and instructive story by W. Somerset Maugham. In this story

Maugham has juxtaposed the hypocrisy, affectation and cunning of a woman with the gentlemanly conduct of the narrator. It is the story of exploitation of the simplicity and innocence of a gentleman by a clever woman. The story is in the subjective mode and it has been told by the narrator himself.

The author caught sight of the woman at the play. In answer to her beckoning he went over to her during the interval and sat beside her. He had met her after a long time: she reminded him how he had invited her for the luncheon. She had read a book by him and had written to him.

Presently he received a letter from her. She wrote to him that she was passing through Paris and could he give her a little luncheon at Fayot's, a restaurant where normally French senators ate. He knew that it was far beyond his means. But he felt flattered and he had not learnt to say "no" to a woman.

He had only eighty francs to last him for the rest of the month. But he thought a modest luncheon would cost not more than fifteen francs and he could save that amount by cutting coffee for the next two weeks.

They agreed to meet at Fayot on Thursday at half past twelve. He found that she was not so young. In appearance she was more imposing than attractive. When the menu was brought he found that the prices were a great deal higher than he had expected but he felt re-assured when the lady said that she never ate anything for lunch. She went on repeating the two sentences that she never ate anything for lunch and that she never ate more than one thing at lunch. But she chose the finest delicacies like salmon fish which was out of season and so cost too much. When the waiter asked her if she would like to eat anything while the salmon was being cooked she said that she never ate more than one thing for lunch but would like to have a little caviare, a very expensive dish. The author's heart sank because he knew he could not afford caviare. To cut costs he ordered mutton chop for himself which was the cheapest dish.

When the question of drinks came, she chose champagne, the costliest drink. When the waiter approached again with the menu she said she could not eat anything except asparagus.

Now the question was not as to how he would spend the month without any money but how would he pay the bill which would be enormous. He was thinking of some strategy to face this unpleasant situation. He thought he might pretend that his pocket had been picked. He might leave his watch there. Then he asked her about coffee and she ordered coffee with ice cream for herself and plain coffee for him. After eating so much she talked about her principle that one should always get up from a meal feeling that one could eat a little more. When the narrator asked her whether she was still hungry she replied that she never ate anything for lunch. She never ate more than one thing for lunch. They were waiting for the coffee when the waiter brought some peaches and the guest took one. When he had paid the bill he had only three francs which he left as a small tip for the waiter. The woman thought it a mean act.

Before jumping into the cab she advised the narrator to follow her example of never eating more than one thing for lunch. The narrator retorted that he would not eat anything for dinner that night. She called him a humorist and left.

The narrator felt a sense of complacency. He was not vindictive but he felt he had taken his revenge. He observed the result with satisfaction. After eating so much she might weigh twenty-one stone – not a good weight for a woman.

This is how the author had dealt with the theme of greed and hypocrisy in his story "The Luncheon". He has portrayed the characters very realistically and beautifully.

The story is remarkable for its wit, humour and satire. It is also remarkable for the excellent portrayal of the characters in the story. Another distinctive feature of the story is the art of dramatic narration. The whole story has been told in short beautiful dialogues in simple language and colloquial diction.

He has presented two characters who stand in naked contrast to each other and who expose their character through what they say.

10

How Much Land Does a Man Need?

Leo Tolstoy

Leo Tolstoy is one of the greatest story tellers the world has produced. He was born in Russia in the year 1828 and died in 1910. As a writer of fiction he can hardly be compared with any other figure in the world of literature. He wrote a lot of fiction and his writings cover novels, novellas, short stories etc.

Tolstoy's novels powerfully reflect the life of Russia with all its truth, complexity and its contradictions. His most important works are:

1) *War and Peace*

2) *Anna Kaemina*, and

3) *A Confession*

War and Peace is generally regarded to be one of the greatest novels written.

The most important feature of his fiction is the psyo-analysis of the soul. He delves deep into the souls and reveals the innermost thoughts of his characters.

* * * * *

There once was a peasant named Pahom who worked hard and honestly for his family, but who had no land of his own, so he always remained as poor as the next man. "Busy

as we are from childhood tilling mother earth," he often thought, "we peasants will always die as we are living, with nothing of our own. If only we had our own land, it would be different."

Now, close to Pahom's village there lived a lady, a small landowner, who had an estate of about three hundred acres. One winter the news got about that the lady was going to sell her land. Pahom heard that a neighbor of his was buying fifty acres and that the lady had consented to accept one half in cash and to wait a year for the other half.

"Look at that," Pahom thought. "The land is being sold, and I shall get none of it." So he spoke to his wife. "Other people are buying it, and we must also buy twenty acres or so. Life is becoming impossible without land of our own."

So they put their heads together and considered how they could manage to buy it. They had one hundred rubles laid by. They sold a colt, and one half of their bees, hired out one of their sons as a laborer, and took his wages in advance. They borrowed the rest from a brother-in-law, and so scraped together half the purchase money. Having done this, Pahom chose a farm of forty acres, some of it wooded, and went to the lady and bought it.

So now Pahom had land of his own. He borrowed seed, and sowed it, and the harvest was a good one. Within a year he had managed to pay off his debts to the lady and his brother-in-law. So he became a landowner, plowing and sowing his own land, making hay on his own land, cutting his own trees, and feeding his cattle on his own pasture. When he went out to plow his fields, or to look at his growing corn, or at his meadows, his heart would fill with joy. The grass that grew and the flowers that bloomed there seemed to him unlike any that grew elsewhere. Formerly, when he had passed by that land, it had appeared the same as any other land, but now it seemed quite different.

Then one day Pahom was sitting at home when a peasant, passing through the village, happened to stop in. Pahom asked him where he came from, and the stranger answered that he came from beyond the Volga, where he had been

working. One word led to another, and the man went on to say that much land was for sale there, and that many people were moving there to buy it. The land was so good, he said, that the rye sown on it grew as high as a horse, and so thick that five cuts of a sickle made a sheaf. One peasant, he said, had brought nothing with him but his bare hands, and now he had six horses and two cows of his own. Pahom's heart was filled with desire. "Why should I suffer in this narrow hole," he thought, "if one can live so well elsewhere? I will sell my land and my homestead here, and with the money I will start fresh over there and get everything new."

So Pahom sold his land and homestead and cattle, all at a profit, and moved his family to the new settlement. Everything the peasant had told him was true, and Pahom was ten times better off than he had been. He bought plenty of arable land and pasture, and could keep as many head of cattle as he liked.

At first, in the bustle of building and settling down, Pahom. was pleased with it all, but when he got used to it he began to think that even here he was not satisfied. He wanted to sow more wheat, but had not enough land of his own for the purpose, so he rented extra land for three years. The seasons turned out well and the crops were good, so that he began to lay money by. He might have gone on living comfortably, but he grew tired of having to rent other people's land every year, and having to scramble to pay for it.

"If it were all my own land," Pahom. thought, "I should be independent, and there would not be all this unpleasantness."

Then one day a passing land dealer said he was just returning from the land of Bashkirs, far away, where he had bought thirteen thousand acres of land, all for only one thousand rubles.

"All one need do is to make friends with the chiefs," he said. "I gave away about one hundred rubles' worth of dressing gowns and carpets, besides a case of tea, and I gave wine to those who would drink it, and I got the land for less than two pence an acre."

"There now," thought Pahom, "out there I can get more than ten times as much land as I have now. I must try it."

So Pahom left his family to look after the homestead and started on the journey, taking his servant with him. They stopped at a town on their way, and bought a case of tea, some wine, and other presents, as the tradesman had advised him. On and on they went until they had gone more than three hundred miles, and on the seventh day they came to a place where the Bashkirs had pitched their tents.

As soon as they saw Pahom, they came out of their tents and gathered around their visitor. They gave him tea and kumiss, and had a sheep killed, and gave him mutton to eat. Pahom took presents out of his cart and distributed them, and told them he had come about some land. The Bashkirs seemed very glad, and told him he must talk to their chief about it. So they sent for him and explained to him why Pahom had come.

The chief listened for a while, then made a sign with his head for them to be silent, and addressing himself to Pahom, said:

"Well, let it be so. Choose whatever piece of land you like. We have plenty of it."

"And what will be the price?" asked Pahom.

"Our price is always the same: one thousand rubles a day."

Pahom did not understand.

"A day? What measure is that? How many acres would that be?"

"We do not know how to reckon it out," said the chief. "We sell it by the day, as much as you can go round on your feet in a day is yours, and the price is one thousand rubles a day."

Pahom was surprised.

"But in a day you can get round a large tract of land," he said.

The chief laughed.

"It will all be yours!" said he. "But there is one condition: if you don't return on the same day to the spot whence you started, your money is lost."

"But how am I to mark the way that I have gone?"

"Why, we shall go to any spot you like, and stay there. You must start from that spot and make your round, taking a spade with you.

Wherever you think necessary, make a mark. At every turning, dig a hole and pile up the turf, then afterward we will go round with a plow from hole to hole. You may make as large a circuit as you please, but before the sun sets you must return to the place you started from. All the land you cover will be yours."

Pahom was delighted. It was decided to start early next morning. They talked awhile, and after drinking some more kumiss and eating some more mutton, they had tea again, and then the night came on. They gave Pahom a featherbed to sleep on, and the Bashkirs dispersed for the night, promising to assemble the next morning at daybreak and ride out before sunrise to the appointed spot.

Pahom lay on the featherbed, but could not sleep. He kept thinking about the land.

"What a large tract I will mark off!" thought he. "I can easily do thirty-five miles in a day. The days are long now, and within a circuit of thirty-five miles what a lot of land there will be! I will sell the poorer land, or let it to peasants, but I'll pick out the best and farm it. I will buy two ox teams, and hire two more laborers. About a hundred and fifty acres shall be plow land, and I will pasture cattle on the rest."

Looking round he saw through the open door that the dawn was breaking.

"It's time to wake them up," thought he. "We ought to be starting."

He got up, roused his man (who was sleeping in his cart), bade him harness; and went to call the Bashkirs.

"It's time to go to the steppe to measure the land," he said.

The Bashkirs rose and assembled, and the chief came too. Then they began drinking kumiss again, and offered Pahom some tea, but he would not wait.

"If we are to go, let us go. It is high time," said he.

The Bashkirs got ready and they all started: some mounted on horses, and some in carts. Pahom drove in his own small cart with his servant, and took a spade with him. When they reached the steppe, the morning red was beginning to kindle. They ascended a hillock and, dismounting from their carts and their horses, gathered in one spot. The chief came up to Pahom and stretched out his arm toward the plain.

"See," said he, "all this, as far as your eye can reach, is ours. You may have any part of it you like."

Pahom's eyes glistened: it was all virgin soil, as flat as the palm of your hand, as black as the seed of a poppy, and in the hollows different kinds of grasses grew breast high.

The chief took off his fox fur cap, placed it on the ground and said:

"This will be the mark. Start from here, and return here again. All the land you go round shall be yours."

Pahom took out his money and put it on the cap. Then he took off his outer coat, remaining in his sleeveless undercoat. He unfastened his girdle and tied it tight below his stomach, put a little bag of bread into the breast of his coat, and tying a flask of water to his girdle, he drew up the tops of his boots, took the spade from his man, and stood ready to start. He considered for some moments which way he had better go - it was tempting everywhere.

"No matter, " he concluded, " I will go toward the rising sun."

He turned his face to the east, stretched himself, and waited for the sun to appear above the rim.

"I must lose no time," he thought, "and it is easier walking while it is still cool."

The sun's rays had hardly flashed above the horizon, before Pahom, carrying the spade over his shoulder, went down into the steppe.

Pahom started walking neither slowly nor quickly. After having gone a thousand yards he stopped, dug a hole, and placed pieces of turf one on another to make it more visible.

Then he went on; and now that he had walked off his stiffness he quickened his pace. After a while he dug another hole.

Pahom looked back. The hillock could be distinctly seen in the sunlight, with the people on it, and the glittering tires of the cart wheels. At a rough guess Pahom concluded that he had walked three miles. It was growing warmer; he took off his undercoat, flung it across his shoulder, and went on again. It had grown quite warm now; he looked at the sun, it was time to think of breakfast.

"The first shift is done, but there are four in a day, and it is too soon yet to turn. But I will just take off my boots," said he to himself.

He sat down, took off his boots, stuck them into his girdle, and went on. It was easy walking now.

"I will go on for another three miles," thought he, "and then turn to the left. This spot is so fine, that it would be a pity to lose it. The further one goes, the better the land seems."

He went straight on for a while, and when he looked round, the hillock was scarcely visible and the people on it looked like black ants, and he could just see something glistening there in the sun.

"Ah," thought Pahom, "I have gone far enough in this direction, it is time to turn. Besides I am in a regular sweat, and very thirsty."

He stopped, dug a large hole, and heaped up pieces of turf. Next he untied his flask, had a drink, and then turned sharply to the left. He went on and on; the grass was high, and it was very hot.

Pahom began to grow tired: he looked at the sun and saw that it was noon.

"Well," he thought, "I must have a rest."

He sat down, and ate some bread and drank some water; but he did not lie down, thinking that if he did he might fall asleep. After sitting a little while, he went on again. At first he walked easily: the food had strengthened him; but it had become terribly hot, and he felt sleepy; still he went on, thinking: "An hour to suffer, a lifetime to live."

He went a long way in this direction also, and was about to turn to the left again, when he perceived a damp hollow: "It would be a pity to leave that out," he thought. "Flax would do well there." So he went on past the hollow, and dug a hole on the other side of it before he turned the corner. Pahom looked toward the hillock. The heat made the air hazy: it seemed to be quivering, and through the haze the people on the hillock could scarcely be seen.

"Ah!" thought Pahom, "I have made the sides too long; I must make this one shorter." And he went along the third side, stepping faster. He looked at the sun: it was nearly halfway to the horizon, and he had not yet done two miles of the third side of the square. He was still ten miles from the goal.

"No," he thought, "though it will make my land lopsided, I must hurry back in a straight line now. I might go too far, and as it is I have a great deal of land."

So Pahom hurriedly dug a hole, and turned straight toward the hillock.

Pahom went straight toward the hillock, but he now walked with difficulty. He was done up with the heat, his bare feet were cut and bruised, and his legs began to fail. He longed to rest, but it was impossible if he meant to get back before sunset. The sun waits for no man, and it was sinking lower and lower.

"Oh dear," he thought, "if only I have not blundered trying for too much! What if I am too late?"

He looked toward the hillock and at the sun. He was still far from his goal, and the sun was already near the rim.

Pahom walked on and on; it was very hard walking, but he went quicker and quicker. He pressed on, but was still far from the place. He began running, threw away his coat, his boots, his flask, and his cap, and kept only the spade, which he used as a support.

"What shall I do," he thought again. "I have grasped too much, and ruined the whole affair. I can't get there before the sun sets."

And this fear made him still more breathless. Pahom went on running, his soaking shirt and trousers stuck to him, and his mouth was parched. His breast was working like a blacksmith's bellows, his heart was beating like a hammer, and his legs were giving way as if they did not belong to him. Pahom was seized with terror lest he should die of the strain.

Though afraid of death, he could not stop. "After having run all that way they will call me a fool if I stop now," thought he. And he ran on and on, and drew near and heard the Bashkirs yelling and shouting to him, and their cries inflamed his heart still more. He gathered his last strength and ran on.

The sun was close to the rim, and cloaked in mist looked large, and red as blood. Now, yes now, it was about to set! The sun was quite low, but he was also quite near his aim. Pahom could already see the people on the hillock waving their arms to hurry him up. He could see the fox fur cap on the ground, and the money on it, and the chief sitting on the ground holding his sides.

"There is plenty of land," thought he, "but will God let me live on it? I have lost my life, I have lost my life! I shall never reach that spot!"

Pahom looked at the sun, which had reached the earth; one side of it had already disappeared. With all his remaining strength he rushed on, bending his body forward so that his legs could hardly follow fast enough to keep him from falling. just as he reached the hillock it suddenly grew dark. He looked up—the sun had already set! He gave a cry: "All my labor has been in vain," thought he, and was about to stop, but he heard the Bashkirs still shouting, and remembered that though to him, from below, the sun seemed to have set, they on the hillock could still see it. He took a long breath and ran up the hillock. It was still light there. He reached the top and saw the cap. Before it sat the chief laughing and holding his sides. Pahom uttered a cry: his legs gave way beneath him, he fell forward and reached the cap with his hands.

"Ah, that's a fine fellow!" exclaimed the chief. "He has gained much land!"

Pahom's servant came running up and tried to raise him, but he saw that blood was flowing from his mouth. Pahom was dead!

The Bashkirs clicked their tongues to show their pity.

His servant picked up the spade and dug a grave long enough for Pahom to lie in, and buried him in it.

Six feet from his head to his heels was all he needed.

SUMMARY

How Much Land Does a Man Need? is a story of human greed and discontentment. It is the story of a man who in his lust for land loses everything.

It is the story of Pahom who worked hard and honestly but had no land. He wanted to own land for happiness.

Close to his village there lived a lady who owned about 300 acres of land. She was selling her land and Pahom bought some land from her. He had one thousand rubles, borrowed some money from his brother-in-law, sold a colt and even hired out one of his sons as labourer and took his wages in advance. Within a short space of time he was able to pay off his debts. Now he had his own land but he was not satisfied. He wanted more and more land and he was not contended.

One day when Pahom was sitting at home he met a peasant who was passing through his village. He had a long conversation with him. The peasant told him that he came from beyond the Volga river. There was much land for sale and so many people were moving there to buy land. The land there was very fertile and the crops were very good and people became prosperous. Pahom thought why should he suffer in that narrow hole. He sold his land, homestead and cattle and moved his family to the new settlement. At first he felt quite satisfied. But soon be became unhappy and discontented. He wanted more and more land to grow wheat and other crops.

One day he met a passing land dealer. He was returning from the land of Bashkirs where he had bought thirteen thousand acres of land for only one thousand rubles. He told Pahom that what one needs to do is to make friends with the chiefs by offering them gifts of dressing gowns carpets, tea etc. Pahom felt tempted. He thought he could get more than ten times land. Pahom left his family to look after his homestead and started on his journey with his servant. They reached the land of Bashkirs where Bashkirs had pitched their tents. Bhahkirs gave him tea and Kumiss and gave him mutton to eat. Pahom took presents out of his cart and distributed them. He told them that he had come about some land. Bashkirs seemed very glad and told him that he must talk to their chief. So they sent for their chief and explained to him why Pahom had come.

The chief told Pahom that he could get as much land as he wanted. Pahom asked the price and the chief told him that their price was always the same i.e. one thousand rubles a day. Pahom did not understand this. So the chief explained to him that for one thousand rubles he would get as much land as he could get round. But there was a condition. He must return to the same spot from where he started on the same day. If he did not return the same day he will not get any land and he will lose his money.

Pahom was not able to sleep peacefully that night. He was full of anxiety. He wanted to cover as much land as possible. He woke up early in the morning and also woke up the Bashkirs.

The chief put his fur cap on the ground and put one thousand rubles on it. This was the place from where Pahom had to start his walk. Pahom took some food and water. He carried a spade with him for digging marks for the land covered by him. He was walking at a brisk pace. The more land he covered, the greedier he became. The land was virgin and it was very good for crops. He did not rest. He wanted to cover as much land as possible.

Pahom felt tired and thirsty. He had gone too far. Now he had the fear that he might not be able to return in time.

He started running towards the hillock where the Bashkirs were waiting for him and beckoning to him. He was totally exhausted. But he did not stop. He must reach the place before the setting of the sun.

Pahom looked at the sun. It reached the earth. It had already disappeared on one side of it. With all his remaining strength Pahom rushed on. Just as he reached the hillock it suddenly grew dark. He thought that the sun had already set. But he heard the shouting of Bashkirs. He thought that though from below the sun seemed to have set, the Bashkirs on the hillock could see it. He took a long breath and ran up the hill. It was still light there. He reached the top and saw the cap.

There sat the chief laughing and holding his sides. Pahom uttered a cry. His legs gave way beneath him. He fell forward and touched the cap with his hand.

The chief admired Pahom's effort and called him a fine fellow. Pahom's servant came there to raise him. But he saw that blood was coming from his mouth. Pahom was dead. He picked up the spade and dug a grave for Pahom to lie in and buried him in it.

How much land did Pahom need? He needed only six feet of land from his head to heels.

GLOSSARY (WORD MEANINGS)

Peasant : a person who works on a farm
Tilling : preparing the land for growing crops.
Estate : a large area of land that is owned by one person or family.
Consent : permission to do something
Rubles : the unit of money in Russia
Colt : a young male horse upto the age of 4 or 5
Scraped : to manage to win or do something with difficulty
Harvest : cutting of crops
Plowing : plough, to dig and turn over land for farming

Sowing	:	to plant or spread seeds
Pasture	:	area where animals can graze
Bloom	:	blossoming, flowering
Formerly	:	earlier, previously
Stranger	:	a person that you do not know.
Volga	:	a famous river in Russia
Rye	:	a plant grown for food for animals
Sheaf	:	a bunch of plants tied together after they have been cut
Arable	:	suitable for growing crops
Bustle	:	to move around in a busy way
Scramble	:	manage to achieve something with difficulty
Kumiss	:	a drink popular in some parts of Russia
Mutton	:	meat of a sheep or a goat
Reckon	:	to calculate an amount or numbers
Track	:	an area of land, especially a large one
Spade	:	a tool for digging
Circuit	:	a line, route, journey around a place
Dispersed	:	to move apart and go into different directions
Assemble	:	to come together as a group
Farm	:	an area of land used for growing crops
Rouse	:	to make somebody wake up
Mount	:	go up, ascend, climb
Steppe	:	a large area of land with grass but few trees
Ascend	:	go up, climb
Stretch	:	area of land or water
Glisten	:	to shine
Virgin	:	(of land) pure, original, natural condition, not cultivated
Soil	:	the top layer of the earth in which plants grow
Unfasten	:	to undo something that is fastened
Girdle	:	a belt fastened around the waist
Flask	:	a bottle with a narrow top
Horizon	:	the place where earth seems to meet the sky
Stiffness	:	hard, difficult to bend

Hillock	: a small hill
Terribly	: very badly
Perceived	: noticed, to become aware of something
Damp	: slightly wet
Hollow	: having a hole or empty space inside
Hazy	: not clear because of haze
Quivering	: shaking trembling
Lopsided	: having one side lower, smaller than the other.
Blunder	: stupid or serious mistake
Soak	: to put something in liquid to become completely wet
Parch	: an area of land very dry
Utter	: something complete
Click	: make short, sharp sound

VERY SHORT ANSWERS

Q.1. Who told Pahom about the land of Bhaskirs and what did he tell?

Ans. A passing land dealer told Pahom about the land of Bhaskirs. He told Pahom that he had bought 13,000 acres of land for one thousand rubles.

Q. 2. What did Pahom do after hearing about the land of Bhaskirs?

Ans. Pahom left his family to look after the homestead and started his journey for the land of Bhaskirs.

Q.3. Who did Pahom take with him.

Ans. Pahom took his servant with him.

Q.4. What did he buy for the Bhaskirs?

Ans. He bought some wine and other gifts.

Q.5. How did the Bashkirs welcome Pahom?

Ans. The Bashkirs welcomed Pahom by offering him tea, kumiss and mutton.

Q.6. What was the price of the land quoted by the Chief of the Bashkirs?

Ans. The Chief said that the price was the same, i.e., one thousand rubles a day.

Q.7. What was the meaning of one thousand rubles a day?

Ans. The meaning of one thousand rubles a day was that for 1000 rubles Pahom could get as much land as he could walk over a day.

Q.8. How did Pahom undo himself?

Ans. Pahom tried to cover much more land than he could possibly do.

Q.9. What happened to Pahom when he came back?

Ans. Pahom fell down and died.

Q.10. How much land did Pahom need?

Ans. Pahom needed only six feet of land from his head to toes.

Q. 11. What is the irony in the story?

Ans. Pahom wanted more and more land whereas he needed only six feet of land.

QUESTIONS REQUIRING SHORT ANSWERS

Q.1. How did Pahom arrange money to buy the land from the lady?

Ans. Pahom had one thousand rubles. He borrowed some money from his brother-in-law. He sold a colt. He hired one of his sons as a labourer and got his wages in advance.

Q.2. How did Pahom feel when he became the land owner?

Ans. Pahom became happy ploughing his own land, cutting his own trees and feeding his cattle on his own

pastures. He felt great when he ploughed his own land.

Q.3. What did the peasant tell him about the land beyond the Volga?

Ans. The peasant told him that much land was for sale beyond the Volga. Many people were moving there to buy it. The land was very good and it gave good crops. It was cheap.

Q. 4. What did Pahom do to move to the land beyond the Volga?

Ans. Pahom sold his land, homestead and cattle at a good profit and moved to the land beyond the Volga.

Q.5. How was the land dealer able to buy land so cheaply from the Bashkirs?

Ans. The land owner gave away about a hundred rubles worth of dressing gowns, and carpets. He gave them a case of tea. He gave wine to those who would drink.

Q.6. Write a brief note on the characterization of Pahom. Discuss the role played by him.

Ans. Pahom is the most important character in the story, *How Much Land Does a Man Need*? He is the protagonist and other characters play minor roles. It is through the character of Pahom that Leo Tolstoy answers the question "how much land does a man need?"

Pahom is not an individual but he is also a type. He is the representative of vast humanity. It is not the question before Pahom only. It pertains to all human beings.

It is the story of Pahom's greed and unbounded ambition but it is also the story of all human beings. It is the flaw in the character of Pahom but this flaw is a common phenomenon. Pahom is the representative of humanity. So his character is very important.

Q.7. Write a brief note on the appropriateness of the title *How Much Land Does a Man Need?*

Ans. Writers choose the titles for their books very carefully. Either they take the titles after the names of protagonists (main characters) or after the names of important places or events. But Leo Tostoy has chosen his title from the question which he wants to answer as to how much land does a man need?

A man does not need more than six feet of land although he craves for more and more.

Man's whole life is wasted in accumulating although it is a universal truth that he does not need to accumulate. He has to leave everything behind. Since the story's aim is to highlight this simple fact that one does not need to accumulate the title is most appropriate.

ESSAY TYPE QUESTIONS

(1) Write a critical summary/appreciation of the story *How Much Land Does a Man Need?* by Leo Tolstoy.

(2) How does Leo Tolstoy work out the theme of human greed and temptations in his story *How Much Land Does a Man Need?*

(3) Write a note about the appropriateness of the title *How Much Land Does a Man Need?*

Answer:

How Much Land Does a Man Need? is one of the most popular stories by Leo Tolstoy. It is the most anthologized story by Tolstoy. He is the master of the art of story telling. His stories are not only entertaining but they are also instructive. His stories are based on realism and they give an insight into basic human nature. They make criticism of life and in that way increase our understanding of life on this earth.

How much land does a man need is a story of human greed. It shows how one temptation leads to another and finally temptations lead to destruction. The story has a tinge of irony. Man wants more land whereas he needs only six feet of land. This is a universal truth but it is easily forgotten.

Pahom is the protagonist of the story. He needed just six feet land from head to toes but he ran from place to place as he wanted more and more land.

The title of the story is most significant. It is appropriate. Though it is Pahom's story but it applies to all human beings. Man may accumulate as much wealth as he wants but finally all roads lead but to the grave. This universal truth is lost sight of and the result is unhappiness and discontentment.

At the start Pahom is an honest, hard-working man. He has no land of his own. He thinks that more and more land would make his life happy. When he gets an opportunity he buys land from a lady who owns a lot of land. He had some money and borrows some money from his brother-in-law. He sells a colt and hires out one of his sons as a labourer taking his wages in advance. He pays off his debts and he has plenty of fertile land. But he is satisfied only for a short time. Peasants trespass on his meadows and cornfields. Disputes with neighbours and court battles make his life miserable.

One day he hears of a place where land is cheap. It is beyond the river Volga. He sells all his land, homestead, and goes to the land beyond the Volga. He feels contentment for some time but soon he begins to want more and more land.

A tradesman passing through his place tells him about the land of Bashkirs where he can get a lot of land for nearly no money. He will get almost ten times as much land. He leaves the place with his servant. The place is three hundred miles away and it takes them seven days to reach there. He has bought some presents for the Bashkirs. He meets the chief and tells him about his desire to buy land from them. Their offer is very unusual. Their price is one thousand rubles for a day. It means for one thousand rubles Pahom can get

as much land as he can cover by walking in one day, i.e. from the sun-rise to the sunset. This is a golden opportunity to own a lot of land. But here again Pahom becomes a victim of his own greed. He is tempted to walk over more and more land.

He stays out as long as possible marking out land with the spade. Towards the end he realizes that he is far away from the starting point. He rushes back to the hillock. Bashkirs cheer his good fortune. But he drops dead exhausted from the run. His servant tries to raise him but to no avail. He digs his grave and buries him there.

Leo Tolstoy has beautifully and realistically analyzed human nature. It is the basic instinct of man to want more and more and invite upon himself his own doom. Man is never content with his life no matter how well off he is.

This is how Leo Tolstoy has worked out the theme of human greed. He has shown how one temptation leads to another and finally it proves fatal.

Leo Tolstoy's stories have some messages to convey and some morals to teach. *How Much Land Does a Man Need* is remarkable both for its contents as also for the art of dramatic narration. The whole story has been told through dialogues and the diction is simple and colloquial.

Leo Tolstoy chose the titles for his stories very carefully and these titles are always relevant and appropriate. The title *How Much Land Does a Man Need* is most appropriate. There is a tinge of irony in the story and its title. Trying to possess more and more the protagonist loses his life.

11

The Last Leaf

O. Henry

O. Henry is one of the greatest story tellers of America. His real name is William Sydney Porter. He was born in 1862 and died in the year 1910.

Henry's stories are remarkable in so far as they provide an insight into the myriad experiences of life. He has deep understanding of human nature. His characters are drawn from every field of life. He is quite comfortable in portraying lives of good people like authors, sales men as well as people like burglars, drug-addicts etc.

In his stories we find the mixture of humour and pathos. There is reversal of fortune in his stories and there is sudden twist in the plot. Some of his more important stories are:

i) *The Last Leaf*

ii) *The Gift of Magi*

iii) *After Twenty Years*

* * * * *

In the 1890s, many artists lived in Greenwich Village, in New York City.

Sue and Johnsy were artists. The two girls met each other in the month of May, at a restaurant in Greenwich Village.

'I'm from the State of Maine,' Sue said to Johnsy. 'I draw pictures for stories in magazines.'

'I'm from California,' Johnsy said to Sue. 'But I want to go to Italy. I want to paint a picture of the Bay of Naples!'

The two girls talked happily for an hour – about art, about clothes, about food.

Soon after their first meeting, Sue and Johnsy moved into a studio apartment together. Their rooms were at the top of an old brick house in Greenwich Village.

In December, it was very cold in New York. Snow fell and there was ice in the ground. Many people in the city became ill. The illness was called pneumonia. The doctors tried to help the sick people, but many of them died.

That month, Johnsy had pneumonia. She was very ill. She lay in her bed and she did not move. A doctor visited her every day. But Johnsy was not getting better. One morning, the doctor spoke quietly to Sue outside Johnsy's room.

'I can't help her,' the doctor said. 'She is very sad. She doesn't want to live. Someone must make her happy again. What is she interested in?'

'She's an artist,' Sue replied. 'She wants to paint a picture of the Bay of Naples.'

'Painting!' said the doctor. 'That won't help her!'

The doctor left the apartment.

Sue went into her own room and she cried quietly for a few minutes. Then she picked up her drawing board and some pencils. She started to sing a happy song and walked into Johnsy's room.

Johnsy lay silently in her bed. Her face was thin and white. She was looking towards the window.

'Johnsy is asleep,' Sue thought.

She stopped singing and she sat down in a corner of the room. Then she started to draw a picture for a magazine. Suddenly, Sue heard a quiet sound. She went quickly to the side of the bed. Johnsy's eyes were open. She was looking out of the window and she was speaking quietly.

'Twelve,' Johnsy said. A little later, she said 'eleven'. Then she said 'ten'. Then 'nine'. And then she said 'eight' and 'seven' almost together. She was counting backwards.

What was Johnsy looking at? What was she counting? Sue looked out of the window.

Outside the window, Sue saw the brick wall of the next house. An old vine grew against the wall. There were very few leaves on its branches.

'Six,' Johnsy said. 'They're falling faster. Three days ago, there was almost a hundred. Ah, there goes another! There are only five now.'

'Five? What are you talking about, Johnsy?' Sue asked. 'Please tell me.'

'There are only five leaves on the vine now,' said Johnsy. 'The last leaf will fall soon and then I'll die. Didn't the doctor tell you about the leaves?'

'Don't say that! You're not going to die!' Sue said. 'You're going to get better. The doctor told me that this morning. I'll bring you some soup and I'll draw my picture. The magazine will pay me quickly. Then I'll buy us some nice food.'

Johnsy was still looking at the vine. 'There are only four leaves now,' she said. 'I don't want any soup. The last leaf will fall soon.'

'Johnsy, dear,' Sue said. 'Please close your eyes and go to sleep. I have to finish this drawing by tomorrow. And I don't want you to look at those leaves any more.' Johnsy closed her eyes. 'But I want to watch the last leaf,' she said again. 'It will fall soon. The leaves are tired. I'm tired too. I want to die.'

'Please try to sleep,' Sue said. 'I'm going to talk to Behrman for a minute. I must have a model for my drawing. Behrman will be my model.'

Old Behrman lived downstairs. He was also an artist, but he had never painted a good picture. He was sad about this and he was angry about it too.

'One day, I will paint a wonderful picture,' Behrman often said. 'One day, I will paint a masterpiece.'

But he had never painted a masterpiece. And he was more than sixty years old.

Sue found the little old man in his dark room. She told him about Johnsy and the vine leaves.

Oh, the foolish girl!' Behrman shouted. 'An old vine can't kill people!'

'But the vine is killing her,' said Sue. 'She's very ill and weak. She sees the vine dying. Now she wants to die too.'

Behrman was angry, but he loved the two young artists very much.

'Ah, little Miss Johnsy,' he said quietly. 'She's too good for this place. One day, I will paint a masterpiece. Then we will all go to Italy. We will go to Naples. Yes! But today, I'll be your model.'

Together, they went upstairs. Johnsy was sleeping. Sue pulled the shade down over her friend's bedroom window. Then she took Behrman into her own room. They both looked at the vine. Cold rain was falling.

'Soon there will be snow,' Sue thought.

Behrman sat down and Sue started to draw a picture of him.

That night, there was a storm. The rain fell heavily and the wind was very strong.

Johnsy woke early the next morning. 'Pull up the shade,' she said to Sue.

Sue pulled up the shade. There was still one leaf on the vine! The leaf was dark green and yellow. And it hung from a branch twenty feet above the ground.

'That's the last leaf,' said Johnsy. 'It will fall today. I'll die at the same time.'

Sue put her face close to her friend's face.

'Don't say that, Johnsy,' she said quietly. 'I don't want you to die.'

Johnsy did not answer.

The leaf stayed on the vine all day. That night, there was more wind and rain.

In the morning, Johnsy woke early again. 'Pull up the shade,' she said.

The leaf was still on the vine. Johnsy lay in her bed and she looked at it for a long time. Then she called to Sue.

'I've been a very foolish girl, Sue,' she said. 'I wanted to die. But the last leaf has stayed on the vine. It has taught me a lesson. Please, bring me a bowl of soup now.'

An hour later, Johnsy spoke again.

Sue, my dear,' she said. 'One day, I'm going to paint a picture of the Bay of Naples!'

The doctor visited the girls in the afternoon. He looked at Johnsy carefully and he held Sue's thin hand.

'Take good care of your friend,' he said. 'She is going to get well. Now I have to go downstairs. I have to visit Mr Behrman. He has pneumonia too. I must send him to the hospital.'

The next day, the doctor spoke to Sue again.

'Your friend will soon be well,' he said. Then he told her some other news.

That afternoon, Sue went into Johnsy's room and she put her arm around her friend's shoulders. 'Mr Behrman died this morning, in the hospital,' she said. 'Two days ago, one of the neighbours found him in his bedroom. Behrman was very ill. His shoes and clothes were cold and wet. The neighbour sent for the doctor. Later, the neighbour found a ladder outside in the yard. There was a lamp next to it. And there were brushes, and some yellow and green paint.'

'Johnsy, look out of the window,' Sue said quietly. 'Look at the last leaf on the vine. It's still there. It has never moved in the wind. Didn't that surprise you? It's Behrman's masterpiece, dear. He painted it on the night of the storm.'

SUMMARY OF THE STORY

O. Henry's story *The Last Leaf* is set in Greenwich village in New York city. It is set in the years 1890s. It is the story of two young female artists. Their names are Sue and Johnsy. They had met each other in the month May at a restaurant. Sue was from the state of Maine. She drew pictures for stories in magazines. Johnsy was from California. She wanted to go to Itlay to paint a picture of the Bay of Naples. Soon

after their meeting they started living together in a studio apartment. Their rooms were at the top of an old brick house in Greenwich village.

In December New York became cold with the ground full of ice. Many people died from a disease known as pneumonia. Johnsy also got pneumonia. She lay in bed and did not move. A doctor visited her everyday but she did not get better. She was sad and she did not want to live. The doctor said that somebody must make her interested in something. Johnsy was a painter and she wanted to paint a picture of the Bay of Naples. But the doctor said that it won't help.

Sue became sad. She picked up her drawing board and some pencils. She started to sing a happy song and went into Johnsy's room. Johnsy woke up. She was looking out of the window and she was speaking quietly. She was counting twelve, eleven ..... She was counting downward.

There was an old vine tree against the wall of the next door. Johnsy felt that the leaves were falling fast. Three days ago there were almost a hundred leaves. Now there were only five.

Johnsy had got an idea in her head. She thought that her life was also going away with the falling of leaves. She will die when the last leaf falls. She told this to Sue. Sue told Johnsy that she would recover. She told Johnsy that she would bring soup for her. She will draw some pictures. The magazines will pay her quickly and she will buy some nice food.

There were only four leaves left on the vine. They will fall soon and Johnsy thought she would die. Sue told Johnsy not to look at the vine. But Johnsy wanted to watch the falling of the last leaf. She will also fall with the last leaf.

There is another important character in the story. His name is Behrman. He is sad because he has never been able to paint a good picture. He wanted to paint a masterpiece.

Sue went down to see Behrman. She told him about the fears of Johnsy about the falling of the leaves. He called Johnsy a foolish girl. An old vine could not kill her. Behrman

exclaimed "She is too good for this place". He told Sue that one day he will paint a masterpiece and go to Naples.

Behrman and Sue went to Sue's room where he acted as a model for Sue's picture.

That night experienced a storm. There was rain. Johnsy woke up in the morning and asked Sue to pull up the shade. She saw the leaf. It was dark green and yellow. It hung from a branch twenty feet above the ground. Johnsy had thought that the leaf would fall and she would die that night but the leaf had stayed on. This gave hope to Johnsy and she lived on.

The doctor visited Johnsy and assured Sue that Johnsy was getting better.

The doctor had one more patient downstairs. It was Behrman. Johnsy became quite well but there was a sad news. Behrman died in the hospital. Two days ago the neighbour of Behrman found him ill in his room. His shoes and clothes were wet. There was a ladder outside the house and there was a lamp, some paint and brushes.

The last leaf never moved. It was not the real leaf. The real leaf had fallen. It was the leaf painted by Behram in the cold wet night. He did this to save the life of Johnsy. This leaf gave hope to Johnsy. This was the masterpiece painted by Behrman. Finally he was able to paint a masterpiece. He gave his own life to save the life of another artist

GLOSSARY (WORD MEANINGS)

Artist	: a person who creates works of art especially painting or drawing
Restaurant	: a place where one can buy and eat a meal
Bay	: a part of the sea surrounded by a wide curve of land
Studio	: a place where radio or television programmes are recorded
Apartment	: a set of rooms for living
Pneumonia	: a serious illness of lungs that makes breathing difficult

Drawingboard : a hard strong wooden material used for drawing pictures
Backward : move in the opposite direction
Vine : any climbing plant with long thin stems
Model : a person who is employed to be painted, drawn or photographed
Downstairs : a lower floor of a house or building especially the one at ground level
Masterpiece : a work of art such as painting that is the best example of the artist's work

SHORT QUESTIONS AND ANSWERS
VERY SHORT QUESTIONS

Q.1. Where did the two artists live?
Ans. The two artists lived in an apartment in the village Greenwich

Q.2. What are the names of the two female artists?
Ans. The names of the two artists are Sue and Johnsy.

Q.3. What did Sue do for a living?
Ans. Sue drew pictures for stories for magazine

Q. 4. Where did Sue come from?
Ans. Sue came from the State of Maine.

Q.5. Where did Johnsy come from?
Ans. Johnsy came from Califronia.

Q.6. What did Johnsy want to do?
Ans. Johnsy wanted to paint a picture of the Bay of Naples.

Q.7. Where did the two girls move after the breakfast?
Ans. They moved to a studio apartment.

Q.8. From which disease were the people suffering?
Ans. The people were suffering from pneumonia.

Q.9. From which disease was Johnsy suffering?
Ans. Johnsy was suffering from pneumonia.

Q. 10. Why was Johnsy not recovering?
Ans. Johnsy had lost hope in life and she wanted to die.

Q. 11. What did the doctor suggest to Sue about the recovery of Johnsy?
Ans. The doctor suggested that someone must make her happy again.

Q.12. What was Johnsy doing when Sue went into her room?
Ans. Johnsy was looking towards the window.

SHORT QUESTIONS AND ANSWERS

Q. 1. What belief had got fixed in Johnsy's mind?
Ans Johnsy looked at the failing leaves of the vine. Everyday some leaves were falling. A few days ago there were hundreds of leaves. Now there were only nine or ten. She got the belief that she was also dying with the falling leaves. She believed that when the last leaf fell she would die with the last leaf.

Q.2. How does Johnsy compare herself with the leaves?
Ans. Johnsy compares herself with the falling leaves by saying that the leaves were tired and she was also tired. The leaves would die and she would die with the falling of the last leaf.

Q.3. Who was Behrman? What did he want? Was he able to fulfil his wish?
Ans. Behrman was an artist. He was an old man. He wanted to paint a masterpiece. But he was not able to paint his masterpiece. Finally he painted a leaf on the Vine tree which saved the life of Johnsy. This painting was his masterpiece.

Q.4. Did the last leaf fall?

Ans. Yes, the last leaf fell. But it was not noticed by Johnsy. She looked at the leaf painted by Behrman and took it for the real last leaf.

Q.5. What is the lesson we learn from this story?

Ans. The message of the story is that hope is the best medicine. Hope is the greatest gift that one can give because hope gives life.

Q.6. Comment on the great sacrifice made by Behrman.

Ans. Behrman is a very important character of the story. He is an old artist. He wants to paint his masterpiece. But he is not successful.

He is told by Sue about Johnsy who is suffering from pneumonia. He is also told about the belief of Johnsy that she will die with the falling of the last leaf. He goes out during the night when the ground is full of ice. He paints a leaf on the vine tree. Johnsy looks at this leaf which never falls. She gets hope and survives. But Behrman gets pneumonia for working in the cold night. He dies from this pneumonia. This last painting was his masterpiece as it saved the life of Johnsy. This is how he sacrificed his life and saved the life of Johnsy.

ESSAY TYPE QUESTIONS

1. Critically appreciate O. Henry's story *The Last Leaf*.
2. How does O. Henry establish the supremacy of hope over depression in his story *The Last Leaf*.
3. What threatened the life of Johnsy and what saved her life in the story *The Last Leaf*.
4. How was Behrman able to paint his masterpiece and how it saved the life of Johnsy?

Answer:

The Last Leaf is one of the most popular stories by O. Henry. This story has all the features of a good story like the

reversal of fortunes, the most unexpected turn of events, etc.

The Last Leaf is the story of the triumph of hope over depression. It is the story of two young female artists who had met each other in the month of May in the village Greenwich. Their names were Sue and Johnsy. Sue was from the State of Maine and she drew pictures for stories in magazines. Johnsy was from California. Her ambition was to go to Itlay and paint a picture of the Bay of Naples. They started living in an apartment in Greenwich.

In December it was very cold and the snow fell. Many people died from a disease known as pneumonia. Johnsy also got an attack of pneumonia. A doctor visited her but she was not getting any better. One morning the doctor told Sue that Johnsy had lost the will to live and she was suffering from depression. She must be made interested in something. Sue told the doctor that Johnsy was an artist and she wanted to paint a picture of the Bay of Naples. But the doctor said that it won't help.

Sue went into the room of Johnsy. Sue found Johnsy looking out of the window. She was looking at the vine tree. She was counting the leaves of the vine tree. She was counting backward twelve, eleven... She had got the belief that she was also dying with the dying of the leaves of the vine. A few days ago there were about a hundred leaves. Now there were only five. She felt that she would die when the last leaf fell.

Sue kept assuring Johnsy that she was not dying and brought some soup for her which Johnsy refused to drink.

Downstairs lived another artist. He was old and his name was Behrman. He wanted to paint a masterpiece which he was never able to do. Sue went to his room and told him about the problem of Johnsy. He said that Johnsy was a foolish girl. Nobody died from the falling of leaves from a vine tree. He went into Sue's room and served as a model for her picture.

That night there was a storm. Rain fell heavily and the wind was very strong. Johnsy got up very early next morning

and asked Sue to pull up the shade. She looked at the vine tree. There was still one leaf on the branch of the vine tree. It was hanging twenty feet above the ground. Johnsy felt that the last leaf would fall soon and she would die but this did not happen. Johnsy lived on. The doctor visited Johnsy and found that she was getting better and she would live. But there was a sad news. Behrman died the same morning in the hospital. Two days ago neighbours found him ill in his bedroom. His shoes and clothes were cold and wet. There was a ladder outside. There was a lamp next to it. There was a brush and yellow and green paint.

The last leaf on the vine was still there. It had never moved in the wind. It was not the real leaf. It was the leaf painted by the old artist. It was Behraman's masterpiece painted on the night of the storm. It gave hope to the dying spirit of Johnsy. This is how O. Henry has dealt with the theme of the triumph of hope over depression.

The Last Leaf is remarkable for many reasons. It is remarkable for the beautiful characterisation of the three characters. They represent the spirit of love, kindness and sacrifice. They are very endearing characters.

The story is also remarkable for the art of narration which is dramatic.

The title of the story *The Last Leaf* is also most suitable because the whole story revolves around it.

UNIT 4

Essays

12

On the Rule of the Road

A.G. Gardiner

A.G. Gardiner is a great essayist who has the ability to teach the basic truths of life in a language which is both graceful and witty.

Gardiner was born in 1865 in England and died in the year 1946. He earned his reputation as a journalist editor and author. Today he is known for his great essays on the subjects most relevant to all ages. His essays are written in a graceful style. They are uniformly elegant and humorous. In his essays he teaches the basic truths of life. His important works are:

i) Pillars of Society

ii) Life of Goerge Cadbury

iii) The Life of Sir William Harcourt

iv) Portraits and Portents

v) Many Furrows

vi) Certain People of Importance

*****

A stout old lady was walking with her basket down the middle of a street in Petrograd to the great confusion of the traffic and with no small peril to herself. It was pointed out to her that the pavement was the place for pedestrians, but she replied "I'm going to walk where I like. We've got liberty

now." It did not occur to the dear old lady that if liberty entitled the pedestrian to walk down the middle of the road, then the end of such liberty would be universal chaos. Everybody would be getting in everybody else's way and nobody would get anywhere. Individual liberty would have become social anarchy.

There is a danger of the world getting liberty-drunk in these days like the old lady with the basket, and it is just as well to remind ourselves of what the rule of the road means. It means that in order that the liberties of all may be preserved, the liberties of everybody must be curtailed. When the policeman, say, the Piccadilly Circus steps into the middle of the road and puts out his hand, he is the symbol not of tyranny, but of liberty. You may not think so. You may, being in a hurry, and seeing your car pulled up by this insolence of office, feel that your liberty has been outraged. How dare this fellow interfere with your free use of the public highway? Then, if you are a reasonable person, you will reflect that if he did not interfere with you, he would interfere with no one, and the result would be that Piccadilly Circus would be a maelstrom that you would never cross at all. You have submitted to a curtailment of private liberty in order that you may enjoy a social order which makes your liberty a reality.

Liberty is not a personal affair only, but a social contract. It is an accommodation of interests. In matters which do not touch anybody else's liberty, of course, I may be as free as I like. If I choose to go down the road in a dressing-gown who shall say me nay? You have liberty to laugh at me, but I have liberty to be indifferent to you. And if I have a fancy for dyeing my hair, or waxing my moustache (which heaven forbid), or wearing an overcoat and sandals, or going to bed late or getting up early, I shall follow my fancy and ask no man's permission. I shall not inquire of you whether I may eat mustard with my mutton. And you will not ask me whether you may follow this religion or that, whether you may prefer Ella Wheeler Wilcox to Wordsworth, or champagne to shandy.

In all these and a thousand other details you and I please ourselves and ask no one's leave. We have a whole kingdom in which we rule alone, can do what we choose, be wise or ridiculous, harsh or easy, conventional or odd. But directly we step out of that kingdom, our personal liberty of action becomes qualified by other people's liberty. I might like to practise on the trombone from midnight till three the morning. If I went on to the top of Everest to do it, I could please myself, but if I do it in my bedroom my family will object, and if I do it out in the streets the neighbours will remind me that my liberty to blow the trombone must not interfere with their liberty to sleep in quiet. There are a lot of people in the world and I have to accommodate my liberty to their liberties.

We are all liable to forget this, and unfortunately we are much more conscious of the imperfections of others in this respect than of our own. A reasonable consideration for the rights or feelings of others is the foundation of social conduct.

It is in the small matters of conduct, in the observance of the rule of the road, that we pass judgment upon ourselves, and declare that we are civilized or uncivilized. The great moments of heroism and sacrifice are rare. It is the little habits of commonplace intercourse that make up the great sum of life and sweeten or make bitter the journey.

SUMMARY OF THE ESSAY

A.G. Gardiner's essay deals with the importance of following the traffic rules. No excuses, no pretexts are acceptable for ignoring the traffic rules. No one can be allowed to break the traffic rules on the pretext of personal liberty.

The author has also discussed the concept of liberty. Liberty does not mean one can behave as one likes. An individual's liberty should not interfere with the liberty of others.

Gardiner has started the essay with the example of a stout woman walking with her basket down the middle of a street in Petrograd. When she was told that she should walk on the pavement she replied that she was going to walk where she liked because she had liberty. The lady did not understand that if liberty allowed her to walk down the middle of the road there would be universal chaos. This kind of liberty is no liberty but social anarchy.

There is the danger of the world going "liberty drunk". We must remind ourselves of what the rule of the road means. The simple rule is to preserve liberty of all everybody's liberty must be curtailed. When a policeman performs his duty on a road crossing and puts out his hand he is the symbol of liberty and not of tyranny.

When somebody's car is stopped he may feel bad and think that his liberty has been outraged. But if the policeman does not interfere with you he may not interfere with anyone leading to anarchy. It means by stopping his car he has submitted to a curtailment of his personal liberty to enjoy a social order. It makes his liberty real.

One may be free to do as one likes in matters which do not touch anybody else' liberty. If one goes down the road in a dressing gown, no body bothers. People have the liberty to laugh at him. The same applies to the personal habits like dyeing hair or waxing moustache. Such liberties do not interfere with the liberties of other people. People have freedom in so many such matters. But one's liberty should not interfere with the liberty of others. Suppose one likes to practice on the trombone during odd hours. If he does this in an isolated lonely place, no body bothers. But if one does on the road, his neighbours may remind him not to interfere with their liberty to sleep in the quiet.

One has to accommodate one's liberty to the liberty of others. Unfortunately people are more conscious of the imperfections of others but not of their own.

A reasonable consideration for the rights and feelings of others is the foundation of social conduct. Observance of the rule of the road is the test whether we are civilized or not.

Leave aside the great moments of heroism and sacrifice which are rare, it is small commonplace habits that make the sum of life. It is these habits that make the journey of life sweet or bitter.

GLOSSARY (WORD MEANINGS)

Stout : fat, plump
Petrograd : name of a city
Confusion : a state of not being certain about what is happening
Peril : serious danger
Pavement : side walk, a flat part of the side of a road for people to walk on
Pedestrian : a person walking in the street, not travelling in a vehicle
Liberty : freedom to live as you choose
Entitle : to give somebody the right to have or do something
Chaos : a state of complete confusion and lack of order
Anarchy : a situation in a country or organization without order or control
Drunk : in a great state of excitement because of a particular emotion
Preserve : Save, to keep something in its original position
Curtail : to limit something
Piccadily Circus : name of a place
Insolence : extremely rude, showing lack of respect
Outrage : to cause shock or anger, a cruel or violent act
Dare : to have the courage to do something
Reasonable : fair, sensible
Reflect : to think carefully and sensibly about something
Maelstrom : a situation full of strong emotions that makes you frightened

Accommodation : an agreement or arrangement between two people which is acceptable to every one
Indifferent : having or showing no interest in something
Dyeing : colouring
Moustache : a line of hair that a man allows to grow on his upper lip
Fancy : special liking
Mustard : a thick cold yellow or brown sauce
Mutton : meat of a goat or a sheep
Champagne : a French sparkling white wine
Shandy : A drink made by mixing beer with lemonade
Ridiculous : causing laughter
Conventional : to follow what is considered acceptable
Trombone : a large brass musical instrument
Quiet : making very little noise
Liable : likely to do something
Conscious : aware of something
Imperfection : a fault or weakness in somebody
Consideration : something that must be thought about
Intercourse : communication between people, countries

QUESTIONS REQUIRING VERY SHORT ANSWERS

Q. 1. Where was the stout old lady walking?
Ans. The stout old lady was walking down the middle of the street.

Q. 2. What would be the result of her walking down the middle of the street?
Ans. There would be great confusion and there would be peril to herself.

Q.3. What did the old lady say when she was told that the pavement was the place for pedestrians?
Ans. The old lady replied that she was going to walk where she liked because she had liberty.

Q.4. What did not occur to the lady?
Ans. It did not occur to the lady that if liberty entitled people to walk down the middle of the road there would be universal chaos.

Q. 5. What would you think of the policeman if he stopped your car if you were reasonable?
Ans. You will reflect that if he interfered with no one the whole traffic would be held up.

Q.6. About what are we much more conscious?
Ans. We are conscious about the imperfections of others.

Q.7. What is the foundation of social conduct?
Ans. A reasonable consideration for the rights or feelings of others is the foundation of social conduct.

Q.8. What are rare things in this world.
Ans. The great moments of heroism and sacrifice are rare

QUESTIONS REQUIRING SHORT ANSWERS

Q.1. What does the rule of the road mean?
Ans. The rule of the road means that in order that the liberties of all may be preserved the liberty of everybody must be curtailed.

Q.2. What happens when one submits to the curtailment of one's private liberty?
Ans. When one submits to the curtailment of one's personal liberty one enjoys a social order which makes one's liberty real.

Q.3. What is the real meaning of liberty?
Ans. Liberty is not a personal affair only. It is a social conduct. It involves the accommodation of interests.

Q. 4. What kind of personal liberty is not objectionable?

Ans. If one goes down the road in a dressing gown nobody will object. One may dye his hair the way he likes or wax one's moustache. No body will object though some may laugh at such a conduct. This kind of liberty does not interfere with the liberties of others.

Q.5. How do we know whether somebody is civilized or not?

Ans. It is in the small matters of conduct that we know whether somebody is civilized or not. It is in the observance of the rule of the road that we know whether somebody is civilized or not.

Q. 6. What makes up the great sum of life and what makes life's journey sweet or bitter?

Ans. It is the little commonplace habits and dealings with others which make up the great sum of life and they make the journey of life sweet or bitter.

ESSAY TYPE QUESTIONS

Q.1. How does Gardiner emphasize the importance of curtailment of the liberties of everybody to preserve the liberties of all in his essay "On the Rule of the Road".

Q.2. In his essay "On the Rule of the Road" Gardiner says "Liberty is the accommodation of interests" Substantiate.

Answer:

"On the Rule of the Road" is a very well-known essay by A.G. Gardiner. He is a great essayist whose essays are elegant, graceful and humorous. In his essays he teaches the basic truths of life in an easy and amusing manner. His teachings are relevant for all the people of all ages.

In the essay "On the Rule of the Road" Gardiner has emphasized the importance of following the rules of the road.

He points out that the traffic rules do not interfere with the personal liberty of an individual. They rather ensure the preservation of the liberty of others. He emphasizes that the curtailment of the liberty of everybody is necessary to ensure the liberty of all. Liberty is not a personal affair only. It is a social contract. It is an accommodation of interests.

In matters which do not affect the liberty of others one is free to do what one likes. One has the liberty to dye one's hair the way one likes. One has the liberty to wax one's moustache. These acts of liberty do not interfere with the liberties of others. So nobody bothers about liberties of this kind. But if somebody wants to play trombone he has to be careful about the rights of others. If he goes to a mountainous area and plays there, nobody bothers. But if he plays this trombone in the sreet, his neighbours may feel disturbed and may complain. This kind of liberty is no liberty because it interferes with the liberty of others who want to sleep in quiet. In this regard the author says that most of us are conscious of the imperfections of others and we are not aware of our own imperfections.

Gardiner says that a reasonable consideration for the rights and feelings of others is the foundation of social contract. It is not right to think that observance of traffic rules interferes with the liberty of people. Rules of the road ensure greater liberty.

What is the test to find whether a person is civilized or not? The answer to this question lies in small matters of conduct. The observance of the rules of the road may declare whether we are civilized or not. It is the common habits of men that make up the sum of life. These habits can make the journey of life sweet or bitter.

This is how Gardiner has emphasized the importance of the rules of the road on which depends our happiness. Gardiner is a great teacher and he teaches the art of living in his essays. He does this in a style which is graceful and humorous. In this essay he has taught the basic truths of life in a language which is simple but very graceful and dignified.

13

The Gandhian Outlook

S. Radhakrishnan

> S. Radhakrishnan was a great teacher, scholar and statesman. He was regarded as India's most influential scholar of comparative religion.
>
> He was born on 5th September 1888 and died in April 1975. He was a great scholar and a great statesman who influenced the whole world with his thoughts and ideas. He was the Vice President of India from 1952-1962 and President of India from 1962 to 1967.
>
> He was honoured with many national and international awards. Among the many honours he received were a knighthood (1931) and the Bharat Ratna (1954).
>
> Though he is an internationally acclaimed scholar and ideal statesman, he is more remembered as a great teacher. His birthday is celebrated all over India as Teachers' Day on 5th September.

*****

Gandhiji was essentially a religious man. A religious man, when he is authentically religious, rises above all the particular group loyalties and becomes a universal man. The great point about Gandhiji is that he realized in practice the theoretical implications of religions that have been with us from the beginning of religions. Hindus talk about *Abhaya and Ahimsa, fearlessness* and love; Budhists talk about wisdom and love or compassion, Prajna and Karuna: Christians talk

about truth and freedom, Muslims speak to us of one God and one family on earth. But what distinguishes a prophetic nature like Gandhiji is the seriousness with which he implements these ideals and lives for them. We talk about them. The knowledge is in us, but not the deed which answers to knowledge.

So far as Gandhiji is concerned his greatest contribution is to make us understand that even in this world of narrow loyalties and artifices, it is possible for us to incarnate these great ideals of truth and love. Whenever he had to do a particular action, take up some line of conduct, he questioned himself, he fasted, he prayed, and he ransacked his brains till at last he was able to say: 'This is the line of conduct on which to proceed.' In that sense, as a religious man, he was essentially a universal man, an internationalist.

He took up the causes of India to demonstrate to the world that the weapons which he was employing in this smaller compass could be extended to the whole: 'If I am able to establish the validity of non violence in India, it could as well be applied to the whole world. That is how he argued. He argued that political freedom could be won by non-violent methods. He wanted to demonstrate to the world that the method sanctified by history—violence, deceit and cunning—was not the only way to achieve political objectives. Winning of freedom by non-violent methods would be a lesson to the rest of the world. So he took up the Indian cause, not out of any narrow patriotism, not only because he happened to belong to India, but because of his intense love for humanity and in order to enable humanity to adopt a different outlook, a different attitude, with regard to the problems which faced humanity. In that sense, he was first and foremost an internationalist and only then a nationalist in its narrow sense. His nationalism was a means to internationalism.

His whole attitude was one of universalism. If we have conflict with Englishmen let us not hate the Englishmen, because both Englishmen and Indians are offspring of the same Divinity.

If we happen to be estranged for a time, we must feel that even though we have differences, we are still all brothers. That would enable us to love the evil-doer while hating the evil that was in his methods. Gandhiji's whole attitude was to understand the opponent, any particular kind of evil. In that way he felt that all strife, even civil strife, could be more or less eliminated.

It is the same attitude of love that made him feel that other religions are also to be regarded as valid as his own. The belief that your religion is supreme and the talk of exclusive monopoly of truth seemed to him a kind of spiritual pride. If he wanted us to be humble, and to understand and respect other religions, as he himself did, it was because his standpoint was that truth happens to be the essence of all religions. He wanted that everyone should practice this both in mind and spirit, and he believed that one who is able to do it will reach the goal. If the Constitution of our country embodies that principle, it is largely due to Gandhiji's teaching—it is the expression of his sentiment of love and understanding for other people and creeds.

If we have today so much of uncertainty, so much of fear, so much of confusion, it is because our goals are not clear. We have not given to the human mind something to satisfy its hunger, hunger for truth and something that creates universal brotherhood. Gandhi wished us to love and sympathize with other people. He did not want to divide them into minor compartments and say: you are Hindu, you are Muslim, you are Boer, you are South African. If we want to get real human unity in this world, we must take our religion more seriously. Our primary loyalty must be to the human race.

It this sense of a common humanity that is lacking today. If we take the advanced nations of the last decade or two, we see abundance of natural resources, great intellectual penetration, wonderful scientific achievement, even great development of discipline and leadership. These qualities are not enough. Something deeper, something more universal in appeal to man is necessary. Unless we are able to train

our young men and women in this sense of world citizenship and make them understand that national loyalties must be subordinate just as we today subordinate family loyalties to the nation—the world cannot escape disaster. We talk of the United Nations. It is symbol of this growing unity of the world order. It is unfortunately the séance of conflicts at the present moments, but it can still be saved for achieving through its medium the goal of the future world, the international society, if Gandhi's philosophy and ideals could be adopted.

If Gandhi had lived longer, he would have worked to build a world state; a world state of which, the different nations are merely branches. He would have given to that world state a kind of executive authority, a kind of police force, not military power but only a police force to maintain the normal civil life. He visualized such a world state in which rivalries among nations will have been set aside like rivalries between individuals of the same nation through the development of the nation state.

If a happier world order has to be evolved for the good of the future generations, we must declare right here that we believe in universal brotherhood, that we will respect one another, whether it be individuals or nations, that we will not apply two different methods of criticism, one to ourselves and a different one to others. All that is necessary is to transform these theoretical beliefs of one family, one God etc. into practical realities. I realize that we cannot overnight bring about this change. But it is necessary to bring about, may be slowly, this transformation of our society with good-will and understanding amongst us keeping in view always that the role of self-denial is the best medium for educating others.

Of course, if we go back to the prehistoric ages, we find each man followed his own dictates and that he was the sole judge of what is right and what is wrong. Gradually community life was evolved and we have given ourselves the rule of law: these law courts, the judges and so on by means of which wrong is sought to be redressed in the

community. Again we have some individuals who place themselves above all these laws, the sanyasis, who have neither desires nor belongings and who can go and sit in far-off mountains. They need not bother about these national governments and world governments; but for ordinary people trying to be saintly and as yet not fully so, we do require a world organization, a world police, a world court, a world bank and so on, so far as nations are concerned. We have to put theories into practice and demilitarize ourselves and employ police only for purposes of maintaining internal order. All this is practicable if there are people who can make non-violence their creed. We have seen that military might offer no solution for our disputes. Therefore, it becomes incumbent upon us to find out means by which solutions to the complex problems of the day can be offered on a more permanent basis. In this connection I would only add that Gandhi was anxious that means must be as pure as the end itself.

SUMMARY

In this great essay S. Radhaakrishnan has emphasized the importance of Truth and Non-violence advocated by Gandhiji for the solution of the problems of the world.

Radhakrishnan says that Gandhiji was an authentically religious man who rose above all narrow group loyalties and became a universal man. He realized in practice the theoretical implication of religions. In essence all religions have great ideals like Abhay, Ahimsa, love and compassion and the concept of one God and one family. We know all these ideals but we do not practice them.

Gandhiji made us understand that even in this world of narrow loyalties it was possible to follow these great ideals of truth and love. Before doing any action it is important to know whether it is right or wrong. Before doing any action Gandhiji tried to find out through prayers and fasting the right line of conduct. In this sense he was a universal man. He was an internationalist.

Gandhiji advocated the weapons of non-violence and truth. He argued that if these weapons could be used in India they could be used all over the world.

Gandhiji wanted to show that the method of deceit and cunning was not the only way to achieve political objectives. He wanted to win freedom for India through non-violent methods to show to the world that this was possible. He took up this cause not out of narrow patriotism but because of his intense love for humanity. He was an internationalist. His nationalism was a means to internationalism.

Gandhiji's whole attitude is one of universalism. People of different nations may have differences but they are all brothers and the children of the same Divinity.

Gandhiji's attitude of love made him feel that all religions were to be regarded as valid as any other. He believed that truth happened to be the essence of all religions. And no religion is greater than the other.

Gandhiji did not believe in the division of people into small compartments of Hinduism, Islam or Christianity. We must understand our religions and over primary loyalty must be to the human race.

In the last one or two decades the world has progressed too much in the matter of natural resources, intellectual penetration and wonderful scientific achievements but this is not enough. We have to train our young men and women in this sense of world citizenship. They must learn to subordinate national loyalties to international loyalties.

The author says that if Gandhiji had lived longer he would have worked to build a world state with executive authority with a kind of police force, not the military force, to maintain normal social life.

Radhakrishnan says that we must declare that we believe in universal brotherhood. We cannot have different principles or rules for different persons. We must transform these theoretical beliefs of one family, one God into practical realities.

Things were quite different in pre-historic days. In those days man followed his own dictates to the question of what

was right and what was wrong. Now we have the rule of law which all of us must follow. But there are some people who place themselves above law like saints. They need not bother about national governments or international governments. But for the common people we need the world organization, the world police and the world bank.

We have to demilitarize ourselves and employ police only for the maintenance of internal peace. This is possible only if we make non-violence our creed. We have to find out means by which solutions to the complex problems can be found. Gandhiji laid great emphasis on the purity of means. Means must be a pure as the ends.

GLOSSARY (WORD MEANINGS)

Authentically : in a real and genuine way
Loyalty : the quality of being faithful in your support
Universal : involving all the people of the world
Theoretical : based on some formalized ideas
Implications : a possible effect or result of an action or a decision
Compassion : a strong feeling of sympathy for people who are suffering
Distinguish : recognize the difference between two people or two things.
Prophetic : things proving to be correct, say correctly what will happen in the future
Implement : carry out, make something start to happen
Contribution : an action or a service that helps a cause
Incarnate : to give a definite or human form to a particular idea or quality
Ransack : turn upside down, cause damage
Internationalist : a person who believes that countries should work together in a friendly way
Demonstrate : show something clearly by giving proof or evidence

Compass	:	range or extent of what can be achieved in a particular situation
Validity	:	the sate of being legally or officially acceptable
Sanctify	:	to make something seem legal or right
Decent	:	dishonest behaviour
Patriotism	:	love of your country and willingness to defend it
Intense	:	very great, very strong
Humanity	:	people in general
Universalism	:	involving all the people in the world
Conflict	:	a situation in which there are opposing ideas, feelings, wishes
Offspring	:	a child of a particular person or couple
Divinity	:	a god or goddess (here it means God)
Strife	:	conflict, serious disagreement between two persons
Eliminate	:	to remove, to get rid of
Valid	:	legally or officially acceptable
Exclusive	:	Only given to one particular person or group
Monopoly	:	complete control or possession of something
Constitution	:	the system of laws and basic principles
Embody	:	to include or contain something
Component	:	a separate section (here a group, division)
Abundance	:	too much, sufficient
Resources	:	supply of something that a country needs
Subordinate	:	to treat something as less important than something else, situation or events
Philosophy	:	a set of beliefs or an attitude to life that guides behaviour
Adopt	:	to start to use a particular method
Visualize	:	to form a picture of something in your mind, imagine
Transformation	:	complete change in something
Pre-historic	:	connected with the time before history was written down

Community	:	all the people who live in a particular country or area
Evolve	:	to develop gradually from a simple to a more complicated form
Sought	:	past tense of seek to (look for something)
Redress	:	to correct something that is wrong, put right
Demilitarize	:	to remove military forces from an area
Incumbent	:	a person who has an official position

QUESTIONS REQUIRING VERY SHORT ANSWERS

Q.1. How does the author define an authentically religious man?

Ans. An authentically religious person rises above all the particular loyalties and becomes a Universal man.

Q.2. What is the great point about Gandhiji?

Ans. Gandhiji realized in practice the theoretical implications of religion.

Q.3. What made Gandhiji believe that all religions were valid?

Ans. Gandhiji's attitude of love towards humanity made him believe in the validity of all religions.

Q.4. How can a happier world order be evolved?

Ans. We must declare our faith in universal brotherhood and respect sone another.

Q.5. How can lasting peace be ensured in the world?

Ans. Lasting peace can be ensured by demilitarizing ourselves. Police should be there for the purpose of maintaining of internal order. We should make non-violence our creed. We should find out means of solving complex problems.

QUESTIONS REQUIRING SHORT ANSWERS

Q.1. What is Gandhiji's greatest contribution?

Ans. Gandhiji made us understand that even in the world of narrow loyalties and artifices it was possible to follow these great ideals of truth and love.

Q. 2. Why did Gandhiji take up the Indian cause?

Ans. Gandhiji took up the Indian cause not out of narrow patriotism. He did not take up this cause because he belonged to India. He took up this cause because of his intense love for humanity. He took up this cause to enable humanity to adopt a different outlook, a different attitude with regard to problems of humanity.

Q.3. Why is there so much uncertainty, fear and confusion in the world?

Ans. There is so much fear, confusion and uncertainty in the world because our goals are not clear. We have not satisfied the hunger of the mind for truth. We have not done something that creates universal brotherhood.

Q.4. How, according to Rathakrishnan, can the world escape disaster?

Ans. The world can escape disaster if we train our young men and women in the sense of world citizenship. We should make them understand that national loyalties must be subordinated to international loyalties.

ESSAY TYPE QUESTIONS

1. How, according to Radhakrishnan, Gandhiji was essentially a universal man, an internationalist?

Answer?

In this essay "The Gandhian outlook", S. Radhakrishnan has called Gandhiji an essentially universal man, an internationalist. He has said so because of the most liberal views of Gandhiji about religion. Gandhiji was authentically religious. He rose above particular group loyalties. He realized in practice the theoretical implications of religions. For him all the religions were good. Hindus believed in Abhay and Ahimsa. Budhists believed in love and compassion. Christians believed in truth and Muslims spoke of one God and one family.

Gandhiji thought that it was possible for us to follow the great ideals of truth and non-violence. He always laid emphasis on choosing the right course of action. In that sense he was a religious man. Whenever he had any problem in deciding what was the right course of action, he prayed and fasted to find the right line of conduct. Since Gandhiji respected all religions, loved all the people of the world without any prejudice or narrow barriers, he was a universal man, an internationalist.

2. What is Gandhiji's attitude towards religion as described in the essay "The Gadhian Outlook" S Radhakrishnan?

Answer

In his "The Gandhian Outlook" S. Radhakrishnan has described Gandhiji's attitude towards religion.

Gandhiji was a man of love. He was totally against hatred. If we have conflict with Englishmen we should not hate the Englishmen because all of us are the offsprings of the same Divinity.

Gandhiji had the same attitude of love in the matter of religion. He regarded the other religions as valid as of his own religion. He believed that truth was the essence of all religions. If one says that his religion is supreme he is showing spiritual pride in his conduct. Gandhiji taught us to be humble to understand and respect other religions. He

believed that if we want real unity in the world we must take our religion more seriously. He preached that our primary loyalty must be to the human race.

3. For what would have Gandhiji worked if he had lived longer?

Answer

If Gandhiji had lived longer, he would have worked to build a world state. He would have given a kind of executive authority to this world state. He would have given it a police force, not the military power. Police force would have been there to maintain the normal civil life. He would have established a world without rivalries.

This could have been possible only if all the people declared their faith in universal brotherhood. It would have needed the transformation of our theoretical beliefs like one God, one family into realities. It would have needed the demilitarization and employment of police force only for purposes of maintaining internal peace.

Military might does not offer any solutions to our disputes. So it would have been necessary for the world to find out means by which solution to complex problems could be found. Means must be as pure as the end itself.

14

Our Own Civilization

C.E.M. Joad

C.E.M. Joad was a great English philosopher and writer. He was also a great broadcasting personality. He became very famous for his appearance in a serial "The Brains Trust". The Brains Trust was an extremely popular B.B.C. wartime discussion. This made him a celebrity.

Joad was born in Durham in 1891 and died in 1953. He was educated at Balliol College, Oxford. Here he developed his skills as a philosopher and debater. He completed his course of study at Balliol College earning John Locke Scholarship. After completion of his studies he joined civil service. But he continued to write his great essays. His two very well known books are:

i) *Guide to Modern Thought* (1933)

ii) *Guide to Philosophy* (1936)

These two books made him a well known figure in public society.

* * * * *

First and foremost there are order and safety. If today I have a quarrel with another man, I do not get beaten merely because I am physically weaker and he can knock me down. I go to law, and the law will decide as fairly as it can between the two of us. Thus in disputes between man and man right has taken the place of might. Moreover the law protects me from robbery and violence. Nobody may come

and break into my house steal my goods or run off with my children. Of course there are burglars, but they are very rare, and the law punishes them whenever it catches them.

It is difficult for us to realize how much this safety means. Without safety those higher activities of mankind which make up civilization could not go on. The inventor could not invent, the scientist find out or the artist make beautiful things. Hence order and safety, although they are not themselves civilization, are things without which civilization would be impossible. They are as necessary to our civilization as the air, we breathe, is to us and we have grown so used to them that we do not notice them any more than we notice the air. For all that, they are both new things and rare things. Except for a short period under the Roman Empire there have been order and safety in Europe only during the last two hundred years, and even during that time there have been several revolutions and a great many wars, thus it is a great achievement of our civilization that today civilized men should in their ordinary daily lives be practically free from fear of violence. They are also largely free from the fear of pain. They still feel ill, but since the use of anaesthetics became common illness is no longer the terrible thing it used to be. And people from all over the world know that for the first time the world is becoming a single place, instead of lot of separate places shut off from one another. One might say that for centuries the nations of mankind lived in a number of separate boxes holding no communication with each other except when the people in one box invaded those in the next and some of the boxes were never opened at all. Then came a time when there was constant coming and going between the boxes so much so that the sides of the boxes were breaking down and the world was beginning to look more like one enormous box. Wars and revolutions in this century unhappily put a stop to this, and the sides of some of the most important boxes have again been firmly closed. Russia and the countries under the same system are now shut in behind what is often called the iron curtain. Nevertheless

all the world's boxes have at some time been opened so that there is no danger of any unknown people breaking in upon our civilization from outside and destroying it. The danger comes rather from within, it is a danger from among ourselves. This brings me to our defects.

DEFECTS OF OUR CIVILIZATION

In democratic countries men are equal before the law and have a voice in deciding how and by whom they shall be governed. But sharing out of money—which means the sharing-out of food and clothing and houses and books and so on - is still very unfair, while some few people live in luxury, many have not even enough to eat and drink and wear. Even in the finest of the world's cities thousands of people live in dreadful surroundings. There are many families of five or six persons who live in a single room, in this room they sleep and dress and wash and eat their meals, in this same room they are born and in this same room they die. And they live like this not for fun, but because they are too poor to afford another room.

It is, I think, clear that until everyone gets his proper share of necessary and delightful things, our civilization will be far from perfect.

A still greater danger comes from war. Although, so far as the buying and selling and exchanging of goods are concerned, the world could and should be a single whole, across its surface there still run the frontiers of different states. Many of these were fixed in the distant past, some even of the most recent go back a couple of hundred years, go back that is to say, to a period before the train and the motor car, the steamship and the aeroplane were invented. Yet these inventions by making the world so small that I today in England am nearer in travelling time to somebody in Scotland, have made nonsense of these national frontiers by which it is still divided. These divisions, the political divisions, which run between mankind, would not matter greatly, if it were not for the fact of war. Twice already in my lifetime, from 1941 to 1918 and again from 1939 to 1948

almost the whole of world has been torn by war. Moreover, in the conditions of the present day, any war that starts anywhere is more and more likely to spread everywhere. In 1953 we are faced with the fact that the world has fallen as under into two great 'Power Blocs". What is called the Western Bloc, including most of Europe and America and Eastern Bloc including Russia and the nations of Eastern Europe and supported by China. These two blocs are bitterly opposed and mutually suspicious. Each is frightened of the other, and because of their fear they spend great quantities of money in making terrible weapons, in building aeroplanes and in training soldiers and airmen, until today a great part of the world is like a big armed camp. A single match will set a hay-rick ablaze, and with all this war material lying about, the world is again like a hay-rick waiting for that match. You might say that all through history there have been wars and that mankind has survived in spite of them. It has even developed and become civilized in spite of them. This is true, but unfortunately as part of his development man has enormously increased his power over nature. He has learned to tap the hidden forces of our planet and use them for his purposes. Now if his purposes are those of destruction, each fresh advance in his mastery of nature only increases the danger from war, as men learn to destroy one another in even greater numbers from even greater distances and in ever more varied and ingenious ways. Man has now discovered how to release the colossal forces locked up in the atom. In consequence the leading nations of the world are now making atom bombs which if another war comes, would almost certainly be widely used. Nobody knows what the effect of dropping atom bombs on a large scale would be, but it is quite possible that the total destruction of the civilization of West, and even of other parts of the world, might ensue. As somebody has jokingly remarked in the next war men will fight with atom bombs and in the war after that with bows and arrows.

In the opinion of many the only way to prevent this is to set up some sort of government for the whole world.

Two attempts have already been made in this direction. The first which succeded the first world war, was called the League of Nations, the second which followed the second world war, the United Nations. The purpose of both organizations was to provide a sort of law court for nations who had previously gone to war to settle their disputes, would now go to the League of the Nations or the U.N. instead. Neither organization has had much success. The League nations no longer exists, and the U.N. at the time of writing cannot yet act as a world authority because of the great gulf, which, as mentioned above runs across the world between the western nations on the one hand and the Russian bloc of powers on the other. It is nevertheless, clear that the chief hope of the world in the future depends upon our ability to set up some form of world government. Yet another great defect of our civilization is that it does not know what to do with its knowledge. Science, as we have seen, has given us power fit for the gods,, yet we use them like small children.

For example we do not know how to manage our machines. Machines, as I have already explained, were made to be man's servants, yet he has grown so dependent on them that they are in fair way to become his masters. Already most men spend most of their lives looking after and waiting upon machines. And the machines are very stern masters. They must be fed with coal and given petrol to drink and oil to wash with, and must be kept at the right temperature.

SUMMARY

In the essay "Our Own Civilization" C.E.M. Joad has discussed the virtues and defects of our civilization.

The first praise of our civilization is order and safety. Today if two persons quarrel one is not beaten up because he is physically weak. He can go to the law and law will decide as fairly as it can between two of them. So 'right' has taken the place of 'might'. Law also protects the citizens from robberies and violence as far as possible.

The author has emphasized the value of safety and order. Scientists and inventors perform higher activities. The higher activities of scientists could not go on without order and safety. These higher activities of scientists and engineers make up our civilization. Without order and safety civilization would be impossible. They are as necessary as the air we breathe.

Order and safety were not always there. They have been there in Europe only for the last 200 years with occasional revolutions and wars which disturbed order and safety.

One great blessing of our civilization is freedom from pain because illness is not so painful because of the invention of anaesthetics.

Another blessing of our civilization is that for the first time the world is becoming a single place instead of separate places shut off from one another. Earlier people lived in isolation in separate boxes holding no communication with each other.

DEFECTS OF OUR CIVILIZATION

Our civilization has some defects. In a democratic country men are equal before Law. But the sharing of money and sharing of necessities of life like food is not fair. Some people live in luxuries while others live in extremely poor conditions. Some families live in single rooms, using the same room as the living room, bed room etc. Our civilization will not be perfect till everyone gets his fair share of things.

Another defect of our civilization is threat of war. The world has become one as far as selling and buying is concerned. But there are still political frontiers and therefore there is danger of war. The invention of cars and aeroplanes has made the world smaller as far as travelling time is concerned. The national frontiers have become meaningless but the world is still divided by these boundaries. These political boundaries would not mean much if there was no threat of war. Already the world has seen two great world wars from 1914 to 1918 and from 1939 to 1943. Today any war that starts from anywhere is likely to spread

everywhere. The world has been divided into two power blocs, i.e., the Western bloc and the Eastern bloc. Because of the fear of each other they are spending great quantities of money in building aeroplanes and training of soldiers. The world is like a hay-rick waiting for a matchstick. Today war is more dangerous. Unfortunately as part of his development man has enormously increased his power over nature. Each fresh advance in man's mastery over nature makes the war more dangerous as men are learning to destroy men in greater numbers and in more clever ways. Man has learnt to use the forces of atom and more and more nations are making atom bombs which can cause the total destruction of the West and some other parts of the world.

HOW TO PREVENT THIS DESTRUCTION?

The only way to prevent this destruction is the setting up of some sort of Government for the whole world. Two attempts have already been made in this direction. The first was the formation of the League of Nations after the first world war. The second was the formation of the United Nations Organization after the second world war. But unfortunately the U.N.O. cannot still act as a world authority because of the gulf between the European nations and Russian bloc of power.

Another defect of our civilization is that it does not know what to do with its knowledge. We do not know how to manage our machines. Man is so much dependent on machines that they have become man's master. Man has to spend too much time on waiting upon them and feeding them with coal or petrol and to keep them in right temperature.

GLOSSARY (WORD MEANINGS)

Knock down	: cause to fall down
Fairly	: in a just manner
Break into	: to enter a building by force

Burglar	:	a person who enters a building illegally to steal
Rare	:	not happening very often
Empire	:	a group of countries that are controlled by one ruler
Revolutions	:	great change, an attempt to change the government by violent means
Anaesthetics	:	a drug that makes a person unable to feel anything, especially pain.
Communication	:	a process of expressing ideas or feelings, giving information
Iron curtain	:	a very well guarded border between the Western Europe and Communist countries
Dreadful	:	very bad, unpleasant
Afford	:	to be able to pay
Steamship	:	a ship driven by steam
Frontier	:	a line that separates two countries
Hay-rick	:	a large pile of hay
Enormously	:	huge, immense, in a big way
Planet	:	used to mean the world
Varied	:	of many different types
Ingenious	:	very suitable for a particular purpose, resulting from clever, new ideas
Consequence	:	the result of something that has happened
Jokingly	:	to say something that is not true because you think it is funny
Prevent	:	stop something from happening
Gulf	:	A large difference between two people or groups
Dependent	:	needing something to survive or be successful
Stern	:	strict, serious or difficult

QUESTIONS REQUIRING VERY SHORT ANSWERS

Q.1. What is the first and foremost praise of our civilization?

Ans. In our civilization there are order and safety.

Q.2. From what does law protect the citizens?
Ans. Law protects the citizens from violence and robbery.

Q.3. Why does the author call order and safety new and rare things?
Ans. Order and safety are new and rare because these have been in Europe only during the last 200 years.

Q.4. What is the second praise of our civilization?
Ans. Our civilization has made man free from the fear of pain of illness

Q.5. What has made man free from the pain of illness?
Ans. The use of anaesthetics has made man free from illness.

Q.6. What is the first defect of our civilization?
Ans. In a democratic country man is equal before law. But there is no equality in the sharing of money which means sharing of food, clothing, housing etc.

Q.7. What is the greatest danger to our civilization?
Ans. The danger of war is the greatest threat to our civilization.

Q.8. What is the most important reason for the danger of war?
Ans. The world is divided into two power blocs - the European block and the Russian bloc

QUESTIONS REQUIRING SHORT ANSWERS

Q. 1. What is the meaning of order and safety?
Ans. If one is knocked down by another person because he is physically weak, he can go to Law to seek justice. Law will decide fairly between these two persons. So "right" has taken the place of "might".

Q.2. What is the significance of order and safety for civilization?

Ans. Order and safety are very significant for civilization. They are as necessary as the air we breathe. Without order and safety the higher activities of man could not go on. Scientists will not be able to find new things. Inventors will not be able to invent. Artists will not be able to make beautiful things.

Q.3. What does the author mean when he says that for a number of years mankind remained in a number of boxes?

Ans. The author wants to say that countries were isolated and cut off from each other. There was no communication among them. Some of the countries had not been discovered.

Q.4. Why is there greater threat of war and why has war become more destructive?

Ans. Most of the countries are spending their enormous resources on training of soldiers and airmen. They are spending their resources on the manufacture of weapons of mass destruction.

Q.5. How can mankind prevent war?

Ans. Mankind can prevent war if it is able to set up world government with executive authority. It must demilitarize the world. There should be police only for the maintenance of internal security.

ESSAY TYPE QUESTIONS

Q.1. What does Joad say in praise of our civilization in his essay "Our Own Civilization"

Ans. In his great essay "Our Own Civilization" C.E.M. Joad has discussed the advantages of our civilization.

The first and foremost advantage of our civilization is order and safety. He says that if he has a quarrel with someone, he does not get beaten because he is physically weaker. He can go to law and the law will

decide as fairly as it can between the two of them. So "right" has taken the place of "might". There are less chances of getting robbed because law protects us from violence and robbery. So man is free from fear. Order and safety enable scientists to find and inventors can invent and artists can make beautiful things. These higher activities of scientists, inventors and artists cannot go on without order and safety.

Another advantage of our civilization is freedom from pain of illness people still fall ill but illness is no longer painful because of the use of anaesthetics.

For the first time the world is becoming a single place instead of lot of separate places shut off from each other.

Q.2. What, according to C.E.M. Joad, are the defects of our civilization?

Ans. In his essay "Our Own Civilization" C.E.M. Joad has described some of the defects of our civilization. These defects threaten the existence of our civilization.

In a democratic country men are equal before the law. They have a voice in deciding how they will be governed. But the sharing of money is not fair. Sharing of money means the sharing out of food, clothing, houses, books etc. Some people live in great luxuries while others live in extreme poverty.

Another great defect of our civilization is threat from war. The world has become one as far as buying and selling of goods is concerned. But still there are political boundaries. The world has become small as far as travelling time is concerned. Modern scientific inventions have made war very dangerous.

Man has increased his power over nature. Men have learnt to destroy one another in greater number. Leading nations of the world are making atom bombs. The use of these bombs may bring the total destruction of our civilization.

Q.3. How, according to Joad, can mankind prevent war?

Ans. Many people think that the only way to prevent war is to set up some kind of world government. Two attempts have already been made. The first was the setting up of League of Nations after the first world war. The second was the setting up of the United Nations Organization. The idea was to provide a sort of law court for nations who had previously gone to war to settle their disputes. But they have not succeeded in preventing wars. U.N.O. cannot act as a world authority.

It is clear that the chief hope of survival of the world lies in our ability to set up some form of world government.

UNIT 5

Poems

15

The Unknown Citizen

W.H. Auden

W.H. Auden is a great modern poet. He represents the spirit of his age in his poetry. The modern age is the age of spiritual waste. Modern man is the victim of boredom and loneliness. He is lonely in the crowd.

Auden was born in 1907 and died in 1973. His first volume of poems was published in 1928. He continued to write up to the end of his days. His span of actual production extends over a period of more than thirty-five years. During this period he wrote almost every kind of verse like lyrics, sonnets, odes, ballads, etc. He also wrote plays. His literary output is voluminous. He was not only a voracious reader but he had passion for travel. He spent a lot of time in Germany. He visited Spain and China. He went to the U.S.A. and settled down there and became its citizen.

W.H. Auden is one of the greatest poets of the 20th century standing next only to T. S. Eliot and W. B. Yeats. His poetry is a mirror of the spirit of the twentieth century and in this sense makes a criticism of life.

*****

(To JS/07 M378
This marble monument
Is Erected by the State)

He was found by the Bureau of Statistics to be
One against whom there was no official complaint,

And all the reports on his conduct agree
That, in the modern sense of an Old-fashioned word, he was a saint,
For in everything he did he served the Greater Community.
Except for the War till the day he retired
He worked in a factory and never got fired,
But satisfied his employers, Fudge motors Inc.
Yet he wasn't a scab or odd in his views,
For his Union reports that he paid his dues.
(Our report on his Union shows it was sound)
And our Social Psychology workers found
That he was popular with his mates and liked a drink.
The Press are convinced that he bought a paper every day
And that his reactions to advertisements were normal in every way.
Policies taken out in his name prove that he was fully insured,
And his Health-card shows he was once in a hospital but left it cured.
Both Producers Research and High-Grade Living declare
He was fully sensible to the advantages of the Installment Plan
And had everything necessary to the Modern Man
A phonograph, a radio, a car and a Frigidaire
Our researchers into Public Opinion are content
That he held the proper opinions for the time of year;
When there was peace, he was for peace: when there was war, he went
He was married and added five children to the population,
Which our Eugenist says was the right number for a parent of his generation
And our teachers report that he never interfered with their education

Was he free? Was he happy? The question is absurd:
Had anything been wrong, we should certainly have heard.

SUMMARY OF THE POEM

In the poem *The Unknown Citizen* Auden has portrayed the picture of a modern man living in the urban areas. He has lost his identity and his name. In the official records he is not known by his name but by a number. His records may be preserved with the Bureau of Statistics but the touch of emotional attachment is missing.

He worked in a factory where records about this unknown citizen may be found. Records are kept as a matter of routine.

The unknown citizen's name has not been mentioned. His number is IS/07/M378. Records show that there was no official complaint against him. All reports agree that in the modern sense of an old fashioned word he was a saint. It means that he was a perfect citizen who upheld the values of the society. Records also show that he served the society or the nation well. He worked in a factory and was never dismissed from service. It shows that he was not a mean or worthless fellow. His Union reports that he paid his dues regularly. The Social Psychology Workers found that he was popular with his mates and liked a drink. He bought a newspaper everyday and his reactions to advertisements were normal in every way. He was a fully insured man. His health cards show that he was quite healthy. Both "Producers Research" and "High Grade Living" declare that he was regular in the payment of installment plans.

From the material point of view the unknown citizen was a prosperous man. He had a phonograph, a radio, a car and a refrigerator. He acted according to the requirements of the situation. When there was peace he was for peace. When there was war he supported it.

He was married and had five children. Records show that he had all the modern amenities but there is no mention

of emotive issues. The poem ends with the question "Was he happy?" The poet thinks that this question is not pertinent. This is so because had there been any wrong it would have been heard. It should be presumed that he was happy.

GLOSSARY (WORD MEANINGS)

Word	Meaning
Bureau	: an office or organization that supplies information on a particular subject
Statistics	: a collection of information shown in numbers
Conduct	: a person's behavior in a particular place or in a particular situation.
Community	: all the people who live in a particular area as a group.
Got fired	: dismissed from service.
Fridge Motor Inc	: name of an imaginary company
Scab	: a mean, worthless fellow
Odd	: eccentric, whimsical
Dues	: charges, for example, dues to be paid as membership fee.
Social	: connected with society (like social issues)
Psychology	: scientific study of the mind and how it influences behaviour
Social Psychology	: the name of an organization
Mates	: co-workers, persons with whom you share accommodation or activity
Reactions	: What you say or do as a result of something
Cure	: to make a person healthy again after illness.
Producers Research	: name of an imaginary organization
High Grade Living	: name of an imaginary organization
Sensible	: be aware of something
Installment	: one of the number of payments that are made regularly

Phonograph	: Record Player
Frigidaire	: Refrigerator
Content	: happy and satisfied with what you have done
Eugenist	: scientists who study the problems of population control
Generation	: all the people who were born about the same time
Interfere	: to get involved in and try to influence a situation
Absurd	: not logical or sensible, ridiculous

VERY SHORT QUESTIONS

Q.1. What did the Bureau of Statistics find about the unknown citizen?
Ans. The Bureau of Statistics found that there was no official complaint against him.

Q.2. What did all the reports about the conduct of the unknown citizen agree?
Ans. All the reports agree that in the modern sense of the word he was a saint.

Q.3. Why was he considered a saint?
Ans. He was considered a saint because he served the Greater Community.

Q.4. Was he ever fired?
Ans. No he was never fired during his service period.

Q.5 Why was he not considered a scab or odd?
Ans. He was not considered a scab or odd because his Union reports said that he paid his dues regularly.

Q.6. What did Social Psychology workers find?
Ans. Social Psychology workers found that the unknown

citizen was popular with his mates and he liked a drink.

Q.7. How were his reactions to the advertisements?
Ans. His reactions to the advertisements were normal in every way.

Q.8. What did his health card show?
Ans. His health card showed that he was once in a hospital and left it cured.

Q.9. What did Producers Research Living declare?
Ans. They declared that the unknown citizen was fully sensible to the advantages of the Instalment Plan.

Q. 10. What things did the unknown citizen possess?
Ans. The unknown citizen had a phonograph, a radio, a car and a refrigerator.

Q.11. How did he have the proper opinion for the time of war?
Ans. When there was peace, he was for peace. When there was war he went to it.

Q.12. How many children had the unknown citizen?
Ans. He had five children.

Q.13. What did Eugenist say about his children?
Ans. The Eugenist said that it was the right number for a parent of his generation.

SHORT QUESTIONS

1. Explain with reference to the context the following lines:
   (a) "He was found by the Bureau of Statistics to be One against whom there was no official complaint."

These lines have been taken from the poem *The Unknown Citizen* by W.H. Auden, one of the greatest poets of the twentieth century. In this poem the poet has presented an ironical picture of the modern man. Modern man has lost his identity and his name. He is referred to by a number in the records of Bureau of statistics. According to the records of Bureau of statistics he was a man against whom there was no official complaint. He had no criminal record. The poet has painted the picture of a modern man in a direct, straightforward manner in colloquial diction.

(b) Yet he wasn't a scab or odd in his views
For his Union reports that he paid his dues.

In these lines W.H. Auden has presented the picture of the unknown citizen in an ironical manner. All information about him is available in reports yet he is an unknown citizen. It is so because he has lost his name and identity. He is known only by his number.

In these lines the poet says that this unknown citizen was not a mean or worthless fellow. He was not a whimsical person. It is evident from the fact that the Union reports that he paid his dues.

The language in these lines is bold and diction is colloquial. The manner of narration is direct and straightforward.

ESSAY TYPE QUESTIONS

1. Attempt a critical appreciation of the poem *The Unknown Citizen* by W.H. Auden.
2. In *The Unknown Citizen* Auden protests against a society which manipulates man by the laws of mass organization, commercial exploitation and a social research and spying system: Comment.

Answer:

"The Unknown Citizen" is a light satirical poem. It portrays an ironical picture of a modern man in a modern industrial society. In this poem Auden protests against a society which exploits man by the laws of mass organization and commercial exploitation. Man is the victim of a social research and spying system.

The poem is a compilation of the details about an average man. This compilation contains the details of his work at Fridge Motors factory, his union membership and the newspaper he bought. All the investigating agencies like the Bureau of Statistics, Producers Research and High Grade Living are satisfied that he is average and normal. At the end of the poem the poet poses the question "Was he happy?" and the answer given is "Had anything been wrong, we should certainly have heard.

The poem may appear light but it attacks the concept of a human being made to conform to a standard pattern of life. In this conformity man loses his own identity, individuality and even his name. He is a subject of investigation for the various spying and reporting agencies. They are more interested in finding what newspaper he read and whether he paid his dues regularly or not. They want to judge his happiness from his possession of things like monogram, radio and refrigerator. A modern man has all these amenities yet we cannot say definitely whether he is happy or not. In fact modern man is emotionally starved, bored and lonely in a crowd.

Auden has reflected the spirit of his age and in this sense his poetry makes a valuable contribution.

The thoughts have been presented in a flat, matter of fact tone. The language is colloquial. Allusions to Frigidaire's, radios installment plans and trade unions make us at home with this poem. The poem presents a realistic picture of a common citizen living in urban areas and thus makes criticism of life.

16

The Character of A Happy Life

Sir Henry Wotton

Sir Henry Wotton was a great author, a successful politician and an able diplomat. He was born in 1568 and died in 1625. He was educated at New College, Oxford and graduated from Queens' College.

He had a number of diplomatic assignments and travelled a lot. He gave the famous definition of an ambassador as an honest man sent to lie abroad for the good of his country.

Sir Wotton suffered from serious financial problems. He was elected M.P. of Sandwich in 1627. He received a pension of 200 pounds which was later raised to 500 pounds.

Wotton was not an industrious writer. His literary output is scant. He published about fifteen poems of which two have obtained a place among the best known poems. These are:

(i) *On his Mistris, the Queen of Bohemia*;

(ii) *The Character of a Happy Life*

* * * * *

HOW happy is he born and taught
That serveth not another's will;
Whose armour is his honest thought,
And simple truth his utmost skill!

Whose passions not his masters are;
Whose soul is still prepared for death,

Untied unto the world by care
Of public fame or private breath;

Who envies none that chance doth raise,
Nor vice; who never understood
How deepest wounds are given by praise;
Nor rules of state, but rules of good;

Who hath his life from rumours freed;
Whose conscience is his strong retreat;
Whose state can neither flatterers feed,
Nor ruin make oppressors great;

Who God doth late and early pray
More of His grace than gifts to lend;
And entertains the harmless day
With a religious book or friend;

—This man is freed from servile bands
Of hope to rise or fear to fall:
Lord of himself, though not of lands,
And having nothing, yet hath all.

SUMMARY OF THE POEM

In the poem *The Character of A Happy Man* Sir Henry Wotton has discussed the features of the character of a happy man. He has discussed the traiut's of the man who is born happy and is taught to live happy.

The man who does not serve another's will is born happy and lives happy. He is the master of himself. He serves his own will. If a man's defence is his honest thought, he is happy. His ultimate skill is truth. Such a man is born happy and he is taught to live a happy life.

The man who is the master of his passions is a happy man. His passions are under his control. He does not allow his passions to become his master. The man who is not afraid of death and who is prepared for death is a happy man. He

is not bothered by the cares of his world. He is immune to the attractions of public fame.

The man who does not envy the person who advances in life through sheer chance is a happy man. Such a man leads a happy life. He even does not envy the man who advances in life through vice. He has not understood how deepest wounds are given by praise. He is not affected by praise. If a man gives no significance to the rules of the state but cares only for the rules of good and follows them, he lives a happy life.

How can man lead a happy life? The man who does not believe in rumours lives a happy life. He follows the dictates of his own conscience. Whenever he is in doubt he goes back to his own conscience for guidance. This man's condition is not fed by flatteries. He is not affected by ruin.

The happy man always prays God. He prays not for His gifts. He pryas for God's graces. He welcomes the harmless day with a religious book or a friend.

The man who lives such a life is safe from the great servile bands of Hope and Fear. He is not the lord of land but he is the lord of himself.

Such a man may seem to have nothing but in reality he has everything.

GLOSSARY (WORD MEANINGS)

Serveth	: serve, to work under someone
Will	: A feeling of strong determination to do something
Armour	: metal cover for protection (here - defence)
Utmost	: greatest, extreme
Skill	: the ability to do something well
Passion	: strong feelings of love, hartred, jealousy etc.
Untied	: not tied, not attached, not fixed
Fame	: state of being known and talked about
Envy	: the feeling of wanting something that others have

Vice	:	evil or immoral behaviour
Rumour	:	a piece of information people talk about but it may not be true
Conscience	:	the part of the mind that tells you whether your actions are right or wrong
Retreat	:	to move away from a place
Flatterer	:	one who praises somebody excessively and insincerely
Ruin	:	lose all value, pleasure or other things
Oppressor	:	One who treats others cruelly, unkindly
Grace	:	the kindness that God shows to human race
Entertain	:	Welcome, invite guests
Religious	:	Connected with religion
Servile	:	Wanting too much to serve and please, attitude of slavery
Band	:	a group of people
Lord (here it means)	:	master

VERY SHORT QUESTIONS/ANSWERS

Q.1. What kind of thought has a happy man, What is his armour?

Ans. A happy man has honest thoughts. These are his armour.

Q.2. What kind of skill has a happy man?

Ans. Simple truth is the utmost skill of a happy man.

Q.3. Who is the master of the passions of a happy man?

Ans. A happy man is the master of his own passions.

Q.4. What is the attitude of a happy man towards death?

Ans. A happy man is not afraid of death. His soul is ready to meet death.

Q.5. For whom has a happy man no envy?

Ans. A happy man has no envy for the man who rises in life by chance or through vice.

Q.6. By what are the deepest wounds given?

Ans. The deepest wounds are given by praise.

Q.7. Whose rules does a happy man follow?

Ans. A happy man does not follow the rules of the state. He follows the rules of good.

Q.8. For what does a happy man pray God?

Ans. He prays not for the grant of God's gifts. He prays for His grace.

Q.9. Whom does a happy man entertain and how does he do it?

Ans. A happy man entertains the harmless day. He entertains it with a religious book or a friend.

Q.10. Who are the servile bands?

Ans. Hope to rise and Fear to fail are servile bands.

SHORT QUESTIONS

Q.(1) Explain the following lines:

"He hath his life from rumours freed whose conscience is his strong retreat.

Ans. In these lines the poet has described the virtues of a happy man. He has freed himself from rumours. He does not believe in rumours. He trusts his own conscience. Whenever he has any doubts he goes back to his conscience for guidance.

Q. (2) Explain the following lines:

"Lord of himself though not of lands,
And having nothing, het hath all.

Ans. What does a happy man possess and what does a happy man not possess?

He is not the master of lands. He has no material possessions. But he is the master of himself, the master of his will. He has no material possessions. Yet he has the grace of God, the moral values which is everything.

ESSAY TYPE QUESTION

1. Attempt a critical appreciation of Sir Henry Wotton's poem *The Character of a Happy Man*.

2. What, according to Sir Henry Wotton, is the character of a happy man?
3. "A great poem delights as well as it instructs". Discuss Sir Henry Wotton's poem: *The Character of a Happy Man* in the light of the above statement.

Answer:
Sir Henry Wotton is one the greatest poets of the Elizabethan age. He wrote some beautiful poems which are remarkable both for the delight they give and moral guidance they provide. His poems give moral instruction and show the way how to lead a purposeful life.

"The Character of a Happy man" is a charming poem. It depicts the character of a happy man. It discusses the essential features of the conduct of a happy man. It answers the question as to who is born happy and lives a happy life. Such a man is free from all vices and he has virtues.

The man who is born happy and lives happy is the master of his own will. He is not the slave of another man's will. He has honest thoughts. They are his armour. He always follows the path of simple truth. This is his art of life.

The most important trait of the character of a happy man is that he is not the slave of his passions. He is the master of his passions. He is not afraid of death. Rather he is prepared for death. He is not worried about the cares of the world. He is not worried about public fame or about his private life.

A happy man is free from envy. He does not envy the person who gets advancement by chance or through vice. He is not affected by praise. He does snot care about the rules of the state. He cares for and follows the rules of good.

A happy man always prays God. He prays not for the grant of God's gifts but prays for God's grace. He welcomes the harmless day with a religious book or with a friend.

There are two servile bands of Hope to rise and Fear to fail. A happy man is free from these two bands. He is not the lord of lands but he is the lord of himself. The poet ends the poem with a paradoxical statement that he has nothing but he has all.

The poem is remarkable both for the contents as well as for its versification.

The poem is divided into stanzas of four lines each rhyming a b, a b with regular meter.

The poem has charming rhythm. The diction is simple and lucid. The poet has used all the sound devices like alliteration, assonance etc. The alliteration on the following lines is noteworthy:

1. How happy.
2. His honest.....
3. ....simple .....skill

There is also abundant use of soft sounds especially, *l*, m and p as in the following line –

"Whose passions not his masters are".

17

No Men Are Foreign

James Kirkup

James Krikup was a prolific poet, translator and travel writer. He was born in 1918 and died in the year 2009. He was educated at South Shields Secondary School and Durham University. He wrote about 30 books including novels and plays. He became a fellow of the Royal Society of Literature in 1962.

The publication of his poem *The Love That Dares to Speak its Name* in the newspaper Gay News in 1977 brought him public attention.

Kirkup's published work encompasses collections of poetry, six volumes of autobiography, over a hundred monographs and translations.

Kirkup held the Atlantic Award for Literature from the Rockfeller Foundations in 1950. He won the Japan P.E.N. club prize for Poetry in 1965. He was awarded the Scott Monocrieff Prize for Translation in 1992. He was presented the Japan Festival Foundation Award in 1997.

* * * * *

Remember, no men are strange, no countries foreign
Beneath all uniforms, a single body breathes
Like ours: the land our brothers walk upon
Is earth like this, in which we all shall lie.

They, too, aware of sun and air and water,
Are fed by peaceful harvests, by war's long winter starv'd.
Their hands are ours, and in their lines we read
A labour not different from our own.
Remember they have eyes like ours that wake
Or sleep, and strength that can be won
By love. In every land is common life
That all can recognise and understand.
Let us remember, whenever we are told
To hate our brothers, it is ourselves
That we shall dispossess, betray, condemn.
Remember, we who take arms against each other.
It is the human earth that we defile.
Our hells of fire and dust outrage the innocence
Of air that is everywhere our own,
Remember, no men are foreign, and no countries strange.

SUMMARY OF THE POEM

In the poem *No Men Are Foreign* James Krirup emphasizes the essential basic unity of mankind. There are many ways of thinking that men are different from each other. Men may look different from others. They may have different nationalities. They may have different castes or religions. But they are basically one living on the earth like the earth we live on.

The poet asks the people to remember that no men are strange and no countries are foreign. He argues that beneath all the uniforms a body breathes which is like our bodies. All of us walk on the same earth and we shall lie in the same earth. In this lies the basic one-ness of all humanity.

The poet emphasizes the point that all the people of the world enjoy the blessings of the same sun. All of us breathe the same air and use the same water. All men are fed by harvests during peace time. They are starved by the destructive war. All of us have similar hands. All of us have lines on our hands in which we can read our fates and the hours of labour. This is a common feature of all humanity which makes us one. Then how one can say that some men are strange and they belong to a foreign country.

Emphasizing the basic similarities of all human beings the poet says that all men have eyes like ours that wake or sleep in the same manner. All the people have strength. This strength can be won by love. There may be different lands but life in every land is the same. This fact can be recognized and understood by all.

Sometimes we are told to hate our brothers. Whenever we are told to hate we ourselves are the losers. We dispossess ourselves of all the moral values. We betray ourselves and condemn ourselves.

When people take up arms against each other they defile the earth. By this action they let loose the hells of fire. We let loose the dust. These outrages spoil the innocence of the air which is our own. Through these logical arguments the poet has proved his point that no men are strange and no countries are foreign.

GLOSSARY (WORD MEANINGS)

Strange	: not familiar because you have not met earlier.
Foreign	: from a country that is not your own.
Beneath	: under, in a lower position than something.
Uniforms	: not varying, the same in all parts of the world
Breathe	: to take air into your lungs.
Fed	: (past tense of feed) to give food to a person or animals

Peaceful : times without war, violence or argument
Winter : coldest season of the year (here it means unfriendly, hard, difficult)
Starve : suffer or die because you have no food
Labour : work especially physical work.
Recognize : to know who somebody is or what something is.
Dispossess : lose possession of, deprive
Betray : to deceive somebody who trusts you
Condemn : to express strong disapproval of somebody
Defile : make dirty, impure, pollute
Outrage : act in a very cruel or wrong way
Innocence : without guilt, without sin, simple, honest, in natural and pure from.

QUESTIONS REQUIRING VERY SHORT ANSWERS

Q. 1. By what are men fed?
Ans. Men are fed by peaceful harvests.

Q.2. How are men starved?
Ans. Men are starved by war's long winter.

Q.3. What is the meaning of winter in this poem?
Ans. In this poem "Winter" is the symbol of death and destruction.

Q.4. What do we read in the lines of hands of men?
Ans. In the lines on the hands of men we read the hours of labour which is the common fate of all men.

Q. 5. How can strength be won?
Ans. Strength can be won by love.

Q.6. What can all recognize and understand?
Ans. All can recognize and understand that life is common in every land.

Q.7. What happens when we are told to hate our brothers?
Ans. When we are told to hate our brothers we dispossess ourselves of all virtues. We lose all our virtues and we betray and condemn ourselves.

Q.8. What happens when we take arms against each other?
Ans. When we take arms against each other we defile the human earth.

Q.9. What outrages the innocence of the earth?
Ans. Our hells of fire and dust outrage the innocence of the earth.

QUESTIONS REQUIRING SHORT ANSWERS

1. Explain the following lines with reference to the context:
"Remember, no men are strange, no countries foreign
Beneath all uniforms, a single body breathes Like ours"

Ans. These lines have been taken from the poem *No Men Are Foreign* by James Krikup. In this poem the poet has stressed the one-ness of all human-beings.

In these lines the poet has logically argued that there is basic unity of all human beings. He reminds us that no person living on this earth is a stranger. No country is foreign to us. Men living on various lands breathe like everyone else and this proves the one-ness of all human beings and no one is a stranger and no country is foreign.

2. "Let us remember, whenever we are told
To hate our brothers, it is ourselves
That we shall dispossess, betray, condemn

Ans. These lines have been extracted from James Kirkup's famous poem.

No Men Are Foreign the poet has emphasized the essential unity of all mankind.

In these lines the poet has told us what happens when we are told to hate our brothers. Whenever we are told to hate our brothers we dispossess ourselves. We dispossess ourselves of all virtues of a human being. We lose all moral values and we betray ourselves and stand condemned.

ESSAY TYPE QUESTIONS

1. How does James Kirkup emphasize the one-ness of all humanity in his poem *No Men Are Foreign*?
2. How far are the views expressed in the poem *No Men Are Foreign* relevant to the present age?
3. Attempt a critical appreciation of James Kirkup's poem *No Men Are Foreign*.

The poem *No Men Are Foreign* by James Kirkup is remarkable both for its contents and for the art of versification. James Kirkup wrote to delight but also to instruct. His poems convey some great messages to humanity. His poems give messages which are relevant to all ages.

The poem *No Men Are Foreign* has a very useful message to give. It emphasizes the one-ness of all human-beings. This message is most relevant today when the world is torn by narrow selfish interests. The lesson of the poem is very significant when the society is torn by narrow parochial interests. The message of one-ness of all humanity is very important when the world is on the brink of destruction because of conflicts of nationalities, castes, and colour. In the prevailing circumstances approach to life advocated by the poet can save the world from sure destruction.

The important question is whether some people are strange or are other countries foreign. We have many ways of thinking of other people as different from us. We may think that they belong to different countries or they speak different languages. However, in this poem the poet reminds

us of the many ways in which all of us are the same because we are all human beings.

The poet has established the one-ness of all human beings by logical reasoning. He argues that beneath all uniforms a single body breathes. It means that all human beings breathing in the world have similar bodies. They have bodies like ours. We inhabit the same earth which our brothers inhabit and all of us shall lie in it. This shows that no men are strange and no country is foreign.

The same sun shines over all of us. All of us breathe the same air and drink the same water. All the people of the world are fed by peaceful harvests. All of us are starved by war's destructive power. All of us have similar hands. All the hands have similar lines wherein we can read our fates. This makes us one.

The people all over the world have eyes like ours that wake or sleep. All of us have strength that can be won by love. Life is common in every land. This simple fact can be recognized and understood by all. Then how is one man stranger to the other and how can one be foreign to the citizens of other country.

The poet says that sometimes we are told to hate our brothers. If we do so we ourselves are the losers. We lose our virtues. We betray and condemn ourselves. If we take arms against each other, we defile our earth, we make it impure, the earth that gives everything to us. The poet reminds us that our hells of fire and dust outrage the innocence, the purity of air - the air which is our own. This establishes the fact that no men are strange and no country is foreign.

The poem *No Men Are Foreign* is remarkable both for its content and for the art of versification. Poetry has two functions to perform, to delight and instruct. This poem fulfils both these functions.

The poem's message is significant and relevant to all ages. It has been expressed in a simple, straightforward manner.

The poem is unrhymed with irregular meter. The greatest strength of the poem is the simplicity of the language. The diction is simple and the expression is spontaneous. It has charming rhythm. The poet has used all the sound devices like assonance, alliteration and soft sounds. The use of alliteration in the following lines is noteworthy:

1. Some people..... strange
2. Like ours the land.....
3. Like this....., we shall all lie.

If neither foes nor loving friends can hurt you,
If all men count with you, but none too much;
If you can fill the unforgiving minute
With sixty seconds' worth of distance run,
Yours is the Earth and everything that's in it,
And – which is more – you'll be a Man, my son!

SUMMARY OF THE POEM

IF is one of the most popular poems by Rudyard Kipling. Kipling is a great poet and story teller. He was born in India and this Indian connection is quite evident in his stories.

In the poem *IF* Kipling has defined Man. Obviously a creature possessing two legs and two arms cannot be called a man unless he possesses virtues worthy of a Man. Only a person who has all the virtues of a man is entitled to be called a Man. In this wonderful poem Kipling has described all the virtues that a man should possess.

The poem *IF* is spoken by a father, may be the poet himself, and is addressed to his son. He tells his son that he will regard him a Man if he can keep his head when all about him are losing their heads and blame it on him. In this poem 'head' means patience and control over oneself and this is a great virtue. He will consider his son a Man if he trusts himself when all men have doubts about him and even he gives consideration of their doubts. He will be a Man if he can wait and not be tired by waiting, if people lie about him and he does not respond by lying, or if being hated, he does not hate.

He tells his son that if he dreams but does not make dreams his master, if he can think but does not make his thoughts his aim, he will be a Man. There are two impostors in our life. They are Triumph and Disaster. His son should be able to treat these two impostors in the same manner,

treat them with equal disregard, and then he will be regarded as a Man. He should be able to bear to hear the twisting of the truth spoken by him by dishonest persons to trap fools. If he can watch the things broken, the things he had given his whole life to make, he will be a Man. If he can bend and use his worn out tools to make things again, he will be a Man.

Man can make one heap of all his winnings and risk it on chance and fate. He may start again at his beginning and never complain about his loss. If he can use all his mental and physical strength to achieve this purpose when all others have gone to rest, he will be a Man. If he can hold on even when he has no strength except the Will, he will be a Man.

The speaker tells his son that he will be a Man if he can preserve virtue even when he is living with crowds or walking with the kings. Even in such circumstances he does not lose the common touch. What makes a person a Man? If he cannot be hurt either by enemies or loving friends, if all men have regard for him but not too much, if he can make use of every minute and lead a meaningful life, he can be regarded as a Man. If he has all the above mentioned virtues he is the master of the earth and of everything that is in it. What is more important than being a master of the earth and of everything in it is that he will be a Man.

GLOSSARY (WORD MEANINGS)

Blame	: to say that somebody is responsible for something bad
Allowance	: to give consideration to something, to some point
Dream	: a wish to have or be something especially one that seems difficult to achieve
Triumph	: a great success, achievement or victory
Disaster	: a very bad accident or event
Impostor	: a person who pretends to be somebody else. Not real. Not existing in reality

Twisted : to deliberately change the meaning of something
Knave : a dishonest man
Trap : a clever plan to trick somebody
Stoop : to bends your body forward and downwards
Worn-cut : badly damaged or no longer useful
Heap : a lot of something, collect all the things together
Winnings : all the achievements or successes of life
Pitch and toss : throwing of coins in a game, lose or win in a game
Nerve and Sinew : physical and mental strength
Hold on : to continue to hold something, not to leave
Will : strong determination to do something
Foes : enemies
Count : to trust somebody to do something or to be sure that something will happen
Unforgiving : unpleasant and causing difficulties for people
Distance : amount of space between two places

VERY SHORT QUESTIONS

Q.1. What is the theme of the poem *IF*?
Ans. In this poem the poet has described the virtues of a Man.

Q.2. What is the meaning of "Keep Your Head"?
Ans. "Keeping Your Head" means to have self control and keep balance of mind

Q.3. What should a Man do when people lie about him?
Ans. He should not deal in lies.

Q.4. What should Man do when he is being hated upon?
Ans. He should not give way to hatred.

Q.5. What should a Man not do about dreams?
Ans. He should not make dreams his master.

Q.6. What should he not do about thinking?
Ans. He should not make his thoughts his aims,

Q.7. What are the two impostors referred to in the poem?
Ans. The two impostors are Triumph and Disaster.

Q.8. How should a Man treat Triumph and Disaster?
Ans. He should treat these two impostors with equal disregard.

Q.9. By whom is the truth twisted and why?
Ans. Truth is twisted by knaves to make a trap for fools.

Q.10. Who says to Man "Hold on"?
Ans. Will says to Man to hold on.

Q.11. What one should do when walking with the crowds?
Ans. When walking with the crowds one should keep one's virtues.

Q. 12. What should a man do when he walks with the King?
Ans. He should not lose his common touch.

Q.13. What should be the attitude of a Man towards time?
Ans. A Man should make the best use of every moment of his life.

Q. 14. What will happen if a man has all the virtues described in the poem?
Ans. He will be the master of this earth and of everything that is in it. Moreover he will have the right to be regarded as a Man.

SHORT QUESTIONS

Q.1. Explain the following with reference to the context. "If you meet with Triumph and Disaster and treat those impostors just the same".

Ans. These lines have been taken from the poem *IF* by Rudyard Kipling, the renowned poet and scholar. In this poem the poet has described all those qualities which make one a Man.

There are two impostors in our life. The impostors are Triumph and Disaster. We are also often the victim of these impostors. If someone can treat these two impostors with equal unconcern he is a Man.

Q. 2. "If you can fill the unforgiving minute with sixty seconds worth of distance run?"

Ans. In his great poem *IF* Rudyard Kipling has described all those virtues that entitle someone to be regarded as a Man.

The Poet says that if someone can make the best use of every second of a minute, if he can do something meaningful then he can be regarded as a Man.

Time is unforgiving. If we do not use this time properly it will not forgive us. Life is a journey. We must run the distance creatively. Time has been personified and given a living entity.

ESSAY TYPE QUESTIONS

1. What are the virtues which entitle someone to be regarded as a Man?
2. List all the virtues mentioned by Rudyard Kipling in his great poem *IF*.
3. Attempt a critical appreciation of the poem *IF* by Rudyard Kipling.
4. *IF* is more a sermon than a poem. Discuss.

Answer:

IF is one of the very well-known poems by the great poet Rudyard Kipling. Kipling is not only a poet but also a great story-teller and thinker. He was born in India and lived in this country for a long time. His Indian connection is quite evident in his fiction.

The poem *IF* illustrates all those virtues which entitle someone to be regarded as a Man. It is because of this that some critics regard this creative effort of Kipling more as a sermon than a poem.

Obviously any creature with two legs and two arms cannot be regarded as a Man unless he has virtues worthy of a Man. To be regarded as a man, one must have virtues worthy of a Man. In this sense this poem teaches moral values.

The poem is in the form of an address. It is spoken by a father, may be the poet himself, and addressed to his son.

The speaker tells his son that one must possess certain virtues to be regarded as a Man.

Virtues which entitle someone to be regarded as a Man.

A man should be able to keep his head when others about him are lying and blaming on him. He should be able to trust himself when all men doubt him. He can wait and not be tired by waiting. He does not deal in lying when he is lied about. If he is hated he does not give way to hating.

A Man can dream but does not make dreams his master. He can think but does not make his thoughts his aim. There are two impostors in our life. He treats these two impostors Triumph and Disaster, with equal unconcern. He is a Man if he can bear to hear his truth twisted by dishonest persons to make a trap for fools. He can watch the things being broken, the things he gave his life to make, and build them again. If a Man can risk all his successes and achievements on a chance and can start again, he is indeed a Man. He has a strong Will which says to him "Hold On".

If he is not affected by crowds or the company of kings, if he makes the best use of his time, living meaningfully every second of his life, he is indeed a Man.

The poem's content bears the stamp of universal truth relevant to all the people of all ages. Some scholars and poets believe that poets are teachers and they teach moral values of life. The great poet William Wordsworth said that he would like to be known more as a teacher than as a poet. The primary function of the poet is to delight and instruct. This poem fulfils this concept of poetry.

The poem has charming rhythm. The poet has used sound devices like assonance, alliteration and soft sounds to enhance the lyrical quality of the poem.

The most important feature of this poem is the simplicity of the language. The diction is simple lucid and colloquial. The expression is spontaneous.